FOREIGN TRADE, INVESTMENT AND THE LAW IN THE PEOPLE'S REPUBLIC OF CHINA

EDITOR
Michael J. Moser

CONTRIBUTORS

Jesse T. H. Chang Franklin D. Chu Jerome Alan Cohen
Charles J. Conroy Timothy A. Gelatt Jamie P. Horsley
Stanley B. Lubman Michael J. Moser Richard D. Pomp
Clark T. Randt, Jr. Preston M. Torbert

OXFORD NEW YORK HONG KONG
OXFORD UNIVERSITY PRESS
1984

Oxford University Press

Oxford London New York Toronto
Kuala Lumpur Singapore Hong Kong Tokyo
Delhi Bombay Calcutta Madras Karachi
Nairobi Dar es Salaam Cape Town
Melbourne Auckland

and associated companies in
Beirut Berlin Ibadan Mexico City Nicosia

First published in 1984

ISBN 0 19 581539 4

Printed in Hong Kong by Nordica Printing Co.
Published by Oxford University Press, Warwick House, Hong Kong

Foreword

DURING the past several years, China has made great efforts to implement a more open economic policy. The hallmarks of this policy are an acceptance of foreign capital and a recognition of the importance of importing advanced technology and equipment, with the aim of speeding up the pace of our nation's socialist construction.

In order to implement this economic policy effectively, China has promulgated a number of laws and regulations dealing with taxation, investment, customs and many other matters. This book provides a valuable introduction to many of these laws. In my opinion, it will prove extremely useful not only to businessmen, lawyers and accountants but also to scholars and other persons who have an interest in the development of China's legal system. In no less manner, it will enlighten Chinese readers on what is needed to help China's legislation cope with the development of her economic relations with other countries. It is my hope and belief that this book will help to foster greater understanding and co-operation between China and her foreign friends.

Beijing, China.
April 1984

GU XIANCHENG,
Adviser, China International Trust
and Investment Corporation;
Vice-President, China International
Economic Consultants, Inc.

Acknowledgements

A VOLUME of collected essays by different authors is by its very nature not the work of one person. Nonetheless, it is the task of the editor to forge at least a semblance of unity of theme, style and focus from disparate perspectives and personalities. In endeavouring to accomplish this task, my path has been made easier by the goodwill which has prevailed among the contributors throughout the project. I am grateful to each of them for agreeing initially to contribute to the volume and for their understanding and co-operation in dealing with the demands which a work of this kind requires.

In addition to the contributors, I should like to thank Mr Gu Xiancheng for kindly agreeing to write the Foreword; Mrs Christine Bonnar who skilfully typed a substantial part of the book in manuscript form; Steven Pikus and Zhang Langlang for assistance in compiling the table of legislation and index; my wife, Yvonne Wei, for supplying the calligraphy which graces the cover; and my employer, Baker & McKenzie, for generously providing logistical and other support to the project. I am especially grateful to my editor, Mrs Gail Pirkis of Oxford University Press, who guided the project from its inception with both a firm and (when deadlines were not met) an iron hand. Were it not for her patience, good humour and determination in dealing simultaneously with such a large group of lawyers the volume would never have reached its present form.

Finally, I should also like to acknowledge the very special contribution of my late father, Joseph G. Moser, who first suggested the idea of this book.

Friendship Hotel,
Beijing, China.
April 1984

MICHAEL J. MOSER

Contents

Foreword *v*
Acknowledgements *vi*

Introduction
MICHAEL J. MOSER 1
1. The Regulation of China's Foreign Trade
JAMIE P. HORSLEY 6
2. China's Tax System: An Overview and Transactional Analysis
TIMOTHY A. GELATT AND RICHARD D. POMP 36
3. Technology Transfer to China: Policies, Law and Practice
STANLEY B. LUBMAN 84
4. Foreign Investment in China: The Legal Framework
MICHAEL J. MOSER 106
5. Law and Investment in the Guangdong Special Economic Zones
MICHAEL J. MOSER 143
6. Offshore Oil Exploration and Development in China: The Current Regulatory Regime
MICHAEL J. MOSER 179
7. Contract Law in the People's Republic of China
PRESTON M. TORBERT 214
8. Banking and Finance in the China Trade
FRANKLIN D. CHU 229
9. Trade-mark Law in the People's Republic of China
JESSE T.H. CHANG AND CHARLES J. CONROY 267
10. Representative Offices in China: Legal Aspects of Registration and Control
CLARK T. RANDT, JR. 281
11. The Role of Arbitration in Economic Co-operation with China
JEROME ALAN COHEN 296
12. China's New Patent Law
MICHAEL J. MOSER 319

Appendix: Table of Legislation 331
Contributors 336
Index 338

Introduction

MICHAEL J. MOSER

IN the not so distant past, foreign businessmen in China operated within the context of what was to all intents and purposes a legal vacuum.[1] Apart from the standard provisions contained in the purchase and sales contracts negotiated between parties, law rarely impinged on the business relationship between the seasoned China trader and his Mao-suited counterpart. Today, however, the character and dimensions of this relationship have changed dramatically. Since the inauguration of China's 'open-door' economic policy in 1978, the foreign trade of the People's Republic has increased dramatically. In addition, the permissible forms of business transactions have expanded and become more complex, encompassing not only commodity sales and purchases but also technology licensing, compensation trade, co-operative production arrangements and direct equity investments in Chinese-foreign joint ventures. Following the débâcle of China's decade-long 'Cultural Revolution' (1966–76), these changes have been accompanied by a revival of interest in law and legality. With the aim of regulating the scope and content of China's increasing economic contacts with the outside world, literally hundreds of laws and regulations have been promulgated or reinstituted since 1979 and scores of others are now being drafted.

One consequence of these developments is that for the businessman of today a knowledge and understanding of Chinese law has become a vital necessity. Regardless of the nature of its business, every foreign company must now confront and deal with a wide variety of legislation, including tax laws, registration rules and other regulations which will affect its operations in China. Unfortunately, however, much of this legislation is not well known in the West. As a result, business transactions are often hampered by a lack of experience and understanding on the foreign side of the rules governing foreign economic activity in China and their implementation.

This volume provides an introduction to the legal framework established by the People's Republic of China to regulate foreign commercial transactions and investment activity. Each chapter treats separately a specific topic relating to trade, investment and other commercial activities in China, and examines the relevant Chinese legislation in the field as at the end of March 1984 and the problems such laws have posed in practice. For the most part, the contributors are foreign lawyers actively engaged in advising clients with commercial dealings in China. Their intention has not been to formulate a 'handbook' of China trade or a compilation of recipes for business success.

Nor is the volume designed exclusively for the foreign businessman. Rather, the aim has been to provide persons having an interest in Chinese affairs with an overview of the current status of China's efforts to establish a legislative framework for the conduct of business affairs and to shed light on how China's economic laws are being implemented in practice.

Before turning to a preview of the contents of the volume, it will be useful to consider briefly the types of rules used by China to regulate foreign business activities and their sources. In general, these fall into two different categories: published legislation and internal (*neibu*), or restricted regulations.

Published legislation is issued in a variety of forms by Chinese legislative bodies and administrative agencies. Under China's Constitution,[2] the power to enact and amend basic statutes (*falü*) in the civil area is granted to the National People's Congress (NPC). The NPC's Standing Committee may enact statutes in certain areas not specifically reserved to the NPC itself and may issue decrees (*faling*), decisions (*jueyi*), orders (*mingling*), and instructions (*zhishi*) based on existing laws when the NPC is not in session. In addition, China's State Council, designated by the Constitution as 'the highest organ of state administration',[3] as well as administrative organs directly responsible to the State Council, are authorized to issue administrative regulations (*guiding*) and measures (*banfa*) to implement existing legislation. Finally, local organs of state power such as local people's congresses and their standing committees at the provincial, municipal and autonomous region levels are empowered to enact local laws and administrative regulations subject to the approval of the central government.

Access to published Chinese legislation has often proved to be a problem for foreigners. The only officially published compilation of Chinese laws and regulations has not been kept up-to-date for some years.[4] As a result, the student of Chinese law has had to rely on newspapers, magazines and other publications which often print the texts of newly enacted laws and regulations.[5] These sources have not always proved to be entirely satisfactory, however. In many cases, legislation has not been made public until well after the date of promulgation even though the law has already been put into effect. Moreover, although 'unofficial' translations are sometimes circulated, all published laws are officially promulgated in Chinese. To meet the demands of foreigners for access to published rules and regulations, a number of commercial compilations of China's economic laws have recently begun to appear in English. However, the accuracy of the translations has varied and none of the compilations is entirely complete.[6] Moreover, there is a lack of uniformity among the various translations not only with respect to the substantive content of the statutes but also as regards the names of the laws. To relieve the reader of the burden of familiarizing himself with the various forms of citation for the same law, I have asked the contributors to this volume to conform to a uniform system of citation at least as regards the formal name of the law, leaving the abbreviated citation form to each author's preference. The complete citation form for the most important and most commonly cited laws is set forth in the Appendix, together with the original title in Chinese characters.

Published rules and regulations, even when they are accessible to foreigners, form only a part of the legal framework governing business transactions in China. In addition, Chinese units and officials are guided in their dealings with foreigners by internal rules, the content of which in most cases may not be directly revealed. Most of these internal rules consist of directives which must be followed by Chinese negotiators in interpreting and implementing statutory law. Some herald the introduction of new policies which may in time find their way into published law. Others are simply a formalization of practices which have developed as a product of experience gained in similar or related transactions. Whatever their source, internal rules complicate the elucidation and definition of China's legal system and as such pose constant pitfalls in the way of attempts to understand the nature and operation of the rules regulating commercial transactions.

Chapter 1 begins the volume with an examination of China's current system for the regulation of foreign trade. As Jamie Horsley notes at the outset of her chapter, this system is now in 'a state of flux'. Since the late 1970s China has begun to move away from the highly centralized system for the control of foreign trade that was established in the 1950s. In this process, efforts have been made to streamline China's traditionally bureaucratic control apparatus and to stimulate local initiative by granting a higher degree of economic decision-making and responsibility over foreign trade to local authorities and enterprises. At the same time, the Chinese authorities have initiated a number of substantive changes in the administrative procedures used to regulate foreign trade. As Ms Horsley describes in detail, indirect administrative tools — such as quotas, standards, import and export licensing, inspection requirements, and customs duties and procedures — now play a major role in the regulation of China's foreign trade.

Hand in hand with the growth of trade and investment activity in China has been the development of a tax system applicable to foreign business transactions. As Timothy Gelatt and Richard Pomp note in Chapter 2, this system has been built virtually from scratch since 1978. The chapter provides an overview of the structure of China's tax system as it relates to foreign economic activity and analyses how the laws are implemented and interpreted in the context of selected transactions. As the authors show, China's law-making in the field of taxation stands as a remarkable achievement and has produced a system which is at once both sophisticated and conventional.

In Chapter 3 Stanley Lubman looks at some of the legal and practical problems encountered by foreign businessmen in technology transfer transactions. In his view, the Chinese regulatory framework governing licensing and other means of transferring technology presently lacks definition and as a result poses special problems for foreign licensors. Among the most important are problems related to third parties, such as patent infringement, confidentiality clauses and restrictions on the use of technology by the Chinese licensee. Although some of these issues will be resolved when China's Patent Law comes into effect, others will remain. As Mr Lubman notes, until far more extensive legislation is put into place foreign parties to technology transfer agreements in China will have little choice but to rely primarily on contractual provisions to protect their rights and interests.

Commodity trade and technology transfer transactions have long been a feature of China's economic contacts with the West. Since the late 1970s, however, the scope of foreign economic activity has broadened significantly to include direct investments by foreign companies. The next three chapters describe the legal framework that has been developed to govern various forms of investment in China. Chapter 4 examines current Chinese rules and regulations pertaining to compensation trade, co-operative business arrangements, equity joint ventures and wholly-owned foreign enterprises in China. Chapter 5 follows with a discussion of the special provisions established for the Guangdong Special Economic Zones. Finally, Chapter 6 examines the regulatory regime that has emerged to deal with the exploration and development of China's offshore oil reserves in co-operation with foreign companies.

The next six chapters in the volume address various specific topics of particular importance to foreign businessmen in China. In Chapter 7, Preston Torbert looks at the current state of Chinese law and practice regarding economic contracts, focusing in particular on such matters as governing law, dispute settlement and the standard-form purchase and sales contracts developed for use by Chinese trade corporations. In the following chapter, Franklin Chu looks at the structure of China's banking system and the role of foreign banks in financing China trade, as well as such topics as Chinese payment practices in commercial transactions and the structure of China's system for the regulation of foreign exchange. In Chapter 9, Jesse Chang and Charles Conroy examine the protection afforded under Chinese law to foreign trade marks. Clark Randt's chapter focuses on Chinese laws regulating the registration and activities of representative offices of foreign companies, at present the only form of permanent commercial establishment permitted in China. In Chapter 11, Jerome Cohen examines in depth Chinese practices relating to dispute settlement and arbitration, looking at the issues from both a historian's and a lawyer's perspective. Finally, Chapter 12 provides an overview of the main provisions of China's Patent Law which is due to come into effect on 1 April 1985.

The legal framework established by China for the conduct of business transactions is still in its infancy. As a result, it is hardly surprising that significant problems — such as lack of uniformity in the implementation of existing laws, inconsistency of interpretation and legislative lacunae — remain to be resolved. In this regard, it is important to remind ourselves that China's current law-making efforts cannot be viewed as an isolated phenomenon, but are only one aspect of a much more complex and infinitely more difficult task aimed at the transformation of an economically backward but culturally rich society. Seen from this perspective, the essays in this volume should be viewed as portraying the beginning rather than the end, and only a part rather than the whole, of a dynamic and evolutionary process.

Notes

1. See S. Lubman, 'Emerging Functions of Formal Legal Institutions in China's Modernization', *China Under the Four Modernizations, Part 2: Selected Papers Submitted to the Joint Economic Committee, Congress of the United States* (Washington, DC, United States Government Printing Office, 1982), p. 285.

2. Promulgated on 4 December 1982.

3. Constitution of the People's Republic of China, Art. 85.

4. The Collected Laws and Regulations of the People's Republic of China (*Zhonghua Renmin Gongheguo Fagui Huibian*). The Collected Laws were issued in a number of volumes over many years, beginning in 1949. Publication ceased during the Cultural Revolution.

5. Among the most important of these are the *State Council Gazette (Guowuyuan Gongbao)*, published in Chinese by China's State Council.

6. Among the most widely circulated compilations are *China's Foreign Economic Legislation* (Beijing, Foreign Languages Press, 1982); P. Chan, *China: Modernization and its Economic Laws* (Hong Kong, The Economic Newspaper, 1982); *Laws and Regulations of the People's Republic of China, Vol. I* (Hong Kong, Kingsway International Publications, Inc., 1982); and F. Chu, M. Moser and O. Nee (eds.), *Commercial, Business and Trade Laws: People's Republic of China* (Dobbs Ferry, Oceana Publications, Inc.,1982).

1. The Regulation of China's Foreign Trade

JAMIE P. HORSLEY

I. Introduction

CHINA'S system for regulating foreign trade, traditionally highly centralized in view of the importance of controlling exports and imports in a planned economy, is in a state of flux. As part of its current drive towards rapid modernization, the Chinese government has abandoned its insistence on self-reliance and has called for an unprecedented expansion of foreign trade, to obtain from abroad necessary raw materials, commodities, equipment and technology, and to help pay for these foreign imports with increased export earnings. In order to realize this goal, China is seeking to stimulate and streamline foreign trade activity, in part by dispersing some direct trading authority to local governments and individual enterprises, rather than leaving it all in the hands of the national foreign trade corporations. This decentralization of direct foreign trade control is being accompanied by a legislative effort to establish commercial laws and administrative rules to regulate the newly sanctioned foreign trade activity more indirectly, through such means as licensing and inspection requirements and the imposition of, or exemption from, tariffs and taxes. China's administrative goal in this area is to develop a system that efficiently balances increased local trading autonomy with overall central direction and control, under the slogan of 'unified planning and policy and co-ordinated action'.

Since the adoption in late 1978 of an 'open-door policy' with respect to foreign economic relations, China's foreign trade has grown rapidly,[1] and, to date, the People's Republic of China has established trade relations with over 180 countries and regions and has signed trade agreements or protocols with over 80 countries.[2] Moreover, in addition to becoming increasingly active in international trade matters under the auspices of United Nations bodies, China established relations with the General Agreement on Tariffs and Trade (GATT) in 1980, began to send official observers to GATT meetings in 1982 and joined the GATT arrangement regarding international textile trade in late 1983.

China's open-door foreign trade policy is closely interrelated with widespread political and economic reform that is intended to spur local enterprise and individual initiative, and increase and improve production through the easing of central administrative controls and greater reliance on 'market forces'. Just as economic decision-making and profit accountability in certain sectors are devolving to lower administrative and enterprise levels, so in the area of foreign trade the authority to negotiate, sign and implement contracts is becoming more diversified.

The actual process of decentralizing the foreign trade system began in 1979,[3] when authorities at the provincial, municipal and autonomous regional level were authorized to take over gradually control of the export of locally produced commodities and the import of locally required goods. At the same time, these local authorities are held accountable for their own foreign trade profits and losses, and are permitted to retain a portion of their foreign exchange trade earnings, rather than turn them all over to the central government as was previously required. Since 1979, certain provinces, especially Guangdong and Fujian, and the special municipalities of Beijing, Tianjin and Shanghai, as well as other large coastal cities and the inland city of Chongqing (Sichuan Province), have been granted broad trade and economic autonomy, and the Chinese ministries have been encouraged to set up their own specialized trading corporations to export the products under their respective jurisdictions and to import the commodities and technology that they need. Moreover, selected individual enterprises have been permitted to engage directly in import and export trade within a specified scope.

The decentralization of trading authority has been accompanied by the adoption of new 'flexible' forms of trade, such as processing and assembly of imported materials and parts and compensation trade, the seeking of foreign trade financing, the expansion of overseas channels for trade and the export of Chinese labour and engineering for construction projects abroad.

The revitalization of foreign trade as a significant factor in the development of China's planned economy has been neither smooth nor a straightforward process. The lack of an efficient foreign trade infrastructure and a comprehensive set of regulations or guidelines for trading activity, combined with local inexperience with respect to foreign trade matters, gave rise initially to unforeseen consequences. In the words of one Chinese official:

> [Following the structural reform of China's foreign trade] more departments and enterprises began to engage in foreign trade. This in turn stimulated the central departments, local authorities and enterprises to create additional channels to do business abroad. However, some problems cropped up, such as [the] indiscriminate importation of consumer goods, which had an adverse impact on the domestic market and production. Left unchecked, this would have impaired the development of China's industry and inflicted losses on the national economy. Expansion of some exports which were in short supply domestically also upset the state plan, and at that point enterprises even began to compete with each other to sell goods at lower prices on the world market. This was detrimental to the normal development of China's export trade, affected economic results and had a negative impact on normal profits earned by foreign firms handling Chinese goods regularly.[4]

The year 1980 witnessed the ascension of Premier Zhao Ziyang and a general movement to tighten central management of the economy, including foreign trade. This harnessing of the decentralization process does not appear to represent a policy reversal, since an increasing number of provinces, municipalities, departments and enterprises continue to be given expanded foreign trade autonomy. Rather, it signals a realization that decentralization should evolve in a more planned and co-ordinated manner.

In the area of foreign trade, new export and import licensing regulations have been issued to improve control over the types, quantity and prices of commodities being traded, as well as to insure that only authorized Chinese units engage directly in foreign trade business. The watchdog Customs Administration has recently been separated from the foreign trade ministry and made directly subordinate to the State Council, presumably to make it a more independent check on foreign trade activity, and the commodity inspection apparatus has been reorganized and strengthened to increase quality control over both exports and imports. In an exercise of more indirect control, import duties on over 100 commodities were adjusted upward or downward in late 1982 and export duties were imposed on more than 30 goods to inhibit trading in certain strategic items. As of early 1984, the licensing system is in the process of being streamlined and the customs laws updated.

The most recent institutional development in China's search for a foreign trade system under which the necessary control and co-ordination can be exercised without unduly dampening local trading initiative is the establishment of special trade commissioner offices directly under the Ministry of Foreign Economic Relations and Trade (MOFERT). In February 1983 MOFERT announced that chief trade commissioners and deputy trade commissioners had been dispatched to the four major port cities of Shanghai, Tianjin, Dalian and Guangzhou.[5]

Although it is not yet clear what concrete role these special trade offices will play, the chief trade commissioners reportedly have the equivalent of vice-ministerial status and are to be responsible for (1) supervising and co-ordinating foreign trade activities around the port cities where they are located, under a unified policy and plan determined by the central authorities; (2) strengthening administrative control over the export and import licensing system and issuing some export and import licences within a scope to be approved by MOFERT; (3) assisting the head offices of the national import and export corporations gradually to reach unified management over major export commodities; (4) convening trade-related joint conferences between economic and trade departments in the ports and inland areas; (5) setting up joint enterprises around the ports, specializing in different lines of trade; and (6) generally advising MOFERT on trade policy and reform of the foreign economic and trade structure.[6] Although the State Council reportedly has approved relevant provisional regulations governing these commissioners and their offices, no such regulations have yet been published.[7]

The establishment of the special trade commissioner offices appears to be a move to reconcentrate below the centre some of the administrative authority that had been exercised by the local foreign trade bureaux in the wake of decentralization. Each trade office has been assigned the task of strengthening 'traditional economic relations' between the port cities and China's hinterland by co-ordinating trade activities within designated parts of China. Shanghai is to supervise the East and South-west, including trade in Fujian Province and its Special Economic Zone at Xiamen; Tianjin, the North and North-west; Dalian, the North-east; and Guangzhou, the Central-south region, including Guangdong Province and the three Special Economic Zones there.[8] Whether the special trade offices will actually replace the foreign trade bureaux in the areas under their administrative jurisdictions remains to be seen. It is also unclear what their role will be with respect to areas such as Fujian and Guangdong Provinces and their Special Economic Zones, which have been given a great deal of independence in connection with economic and trade matters.

II. China's Foreign Trade Apparatus

China's foreign trade management structure has recently been undergoing virtually continual readjustment. The basic decentralization of trading authority is being accompanied by a simultaneous drive to recentralize a certain amount of administrative control and to define more clearly the division of authority and work between the central and local trade units within the general framework of a unified plan and policy.

The major institutions involved in China's foreign trade system are MOFERT, the national foreign trade corporations directly under MOFERT and their local branches, other commodity-specialized import and export corporations established by ministries other than MOFERT, and the local foreign trade bureaux and corporations administered by the provinces, special municipalities, other large cities and autonomous regions, as well as official Chinese commercial offices located abroad.[9] Apart from the institutional participants, an increasing number of individual enterprises are being granted the authority to engage directly in export and import trade.

A. MOFERT

China's foreign trade apparatus is headed by MOFERT, which was established in March 1982 as an amalgamation of two former ministries and two commissions: the Ministry of Foreign Trade, the Ministry of Foreign Economic Relations, the Foreign Investment Commission and the State Import-Export Commission. The Ministry is responsible for helping to formulate the national foreign trade plans in consultation with the State Planning Commission, managing the foreign trade system, approving import and export licences, handling technology transfers, negotiating international trade agreements and participating in relevant international trade organizations. In addition, MOFERT supervises the local foreign trade bureaux in each province, major city and autonomous region, and some 16 specialized national foreign trade corporations that are primarily responsible for conducting foreign trade on behalf of China. MOFERT also controls several trade-related service companies, including the China Resources Company, the Foreign Trade Consultancy and Technical Services Corporation (CONSULTECH), and the Foreign Trade Science and Technology Service Corporation. The Customs Administration and the commodity inspection apparatus work closely in conjunction with MOFERT, but they are now specialized agencies directly under the leadership of the State Council.

MOFERT is organized into 7 administrative and 13 functional or regional departments, including departments for general planning, foreign trade administration, treaties and law, import-export administration and technology transfers.[10]

B. The National Foreign Trade Corporations

Despite the movement toward the decentralization of trade management and contracting authority, the national foreign trade corporations (FTCs) under MOFERT, headquartered in Beijing, and their local branches remain responsible for negotiating and conducting a major portion of China's foreign trade.

The FTCs are constituted as independent legal entities, like subsidiaries of MOFERT. Each FTC handles a separate category of trade commodities or services, such as chemicals, metals and minerals, textiles, arts and crafts, cereals, oil and foodstuffs, light industrial products, native produce and animal by-products, packing materials, the purchase of whole plants and the licensing of technology.[11] The FTCs have local branches in various cities that are supervised by the local authorities, with respect to administrative matters, as well as by the head office in Beijing.[12] Some head offices do not directly handle import and export business but rather delegate that responsibility to the branches. Some branches are further specialized in terms of exclusively handling certain commodities or handling export commodities that are locally produced.

The FTCs normally implement China's bilateral trade agreements by negotiating and signing the individual contracts under those agreements, or else by arranging for some other entity to conclude the contracts under their supervision.

Traditionally, the FTCs have also acted as trading middlemen for ultimate Chinese end-users or manufacturers. Although such Chinese entities may participate in trade negotiations, the final contract is generally signed by, and commercial aspects such as price and delivery terms are concluded by, the relevant FTC.

Due to the proliferation of new local and ministerial trading corporations and individual enterprises with trading authority that compete with the FTCs, this traditional middleman function is being somewhat circumscribed. The director of MOFERT's Foreign Trade Administration Bureau, Shen Jueren, estimates that, as of the end of 1982, nearly 1,000 enterprises had the authority to engage in foreign trade.[13] However, the FTCs continue to be responsible for handling foreign trade on behalf of entities not authorized to trade directly and with respect to commodities beyond the scope of the authorized trading scope of various entities, and for the export and import of major and staple commodities,[14] as well as other state-monopolized commodities such as cigarettes and alcoholic beverages.[15]

Moreover, unless otherwise directed by the State Council, the FTCs are responsible for negotiating and contracting with foreign firms in respect of commission sales, imports for sales at exhibitions, maintenance services in China and imports for various state departments as designated by the State Council.[16] The FTCs also handle jointly with the unit concerned the importation of commodities that are highly monopolized in the international markets.[17]

In addition to trading, the FTCs conduct foreign market research on the production and sales of various commodities,[18] and often act as distribution agents in China for foreign sellers.[19]

C. The Foreign Trade Bureaux and Local Foreign Trading Corporations

On the local level, the foreign trade bureaux, located in each province, special municipality and autonomous region, are subject to the dual leadership of MOFERT and the local government.[20] These administrative bureaux are charged with the task of supervising local foreign trade enterprises and implementing their respective plans, conducting relevant market research and developing local sources for import and export commodity trade, and issuing some import and export licences for their localities.

Certain political subdivisions have been authorized to establish their own foreign trading corporations, which are responsible for exercising unified control over import and export trade (including a measure of authority over the local branches of the national FTCs), transportation, ship chartering, export commodity packaging and advertising, as well as other foreign trade matters relating to their locality.[21]

D. Independent Enterprises

To complicate further the trade management structure outlined above, designated state enterprises may also be given the authority to deal directly with foreign traders and conclude foreign trade contracts, at least up to a specified value or within the scope of an approved plan. In particular, large industrial enterprises located in coastal and other major cities may be authorized to export their own products directly, bypassing the FTCs and provincial import-export corporations.[22]

Given the recent reorganization of the central foreign trade structure and the many units now involved in foreign trade, the lines of trading authority are often unclear. Jurisdiction to make or approve a given foreign trade contract may depend upon the Chinese entity, the commodity or the value of the contract involved, or a combination of these three factors. Foreign partners will generally have to rely upon the assurances of their Chinese counterparts or advice of the Treaty and Law Department of MOFERT, the Legal Department of the China Council for the Promotion of International Trade (CCPIT), or some other qualified Chinese organization that their contracts have been properly approved, are signed by the appropriate legal entity and will be enforceable as written. The Legal Counsel Office of the CCPIT's Legal Department and China International Economic Consultants, Inc., a subsidiary of the China International Trust and Investment Corporation (CITIC) located in Beijing, can issue legal opinions to this effect. Notarization of foreign trade contracts pursuant to the 1982 Provisional Regulations of the People's Republic of China on Notarization should also provide assurance that the trade contract is legal and binding on the parties.

E. Specialized Agencies

Apart from the primary trading organizations, many specialized agencies render trade-related services. Some of these agencies, such as the China National Foreign Trade Transportation Corporation, which organizes the transport of China's imports and exports, are directly under the supervision of MOFERT. Others are independent entities. For example, the Bank of China handles trade financing and, together with the State Administration for Exchange Control, controls the use and disposal of foreign exchange; the People's Insurance Company of China provides relevant insurance coverage; and the China Ocean Shipping Company, the China Ocean Shipping Agency and the China Ocean Shipping Tally Company are responsible for maritime matters. The Customs Administration and commodity inspection apparatus are discussed below.

No description of China's foreign trade structure would be complete without mention of the role of the CCPIT. Established in 1952 as a non-governmental 'people-to-people' organization, the CCPIT promotes economic and trade relations between China and foreign countries, organizes trade exhibitions in China and abroad, arranges technical exchanges, oversees the Foreign Economic and Trade Arbitration Commission and the Maritime Arbitration Commission, issues and certifies trade and marine transport documentation upon request, and offers legal counselling services in connection with trade negotiations, problems, or disputes.[23]

The CCPIT, headquartered in Beijing, is an autonomous body under the general sponsorship of MOFERT and other trade and economic organizations, which provide a portion of its finances. The CCPIT's board of directors is comprised of some 20 officials from MOFERT, the Bank of China, the People's Insurance Company of China and other economic and trade departments.[24]

F. Methods of Foreign Trade

China's foreign trade is generally conducted either pursuant to bilateral exchange agreements with foreign governments and trade associations or in accordance with individual trade contracts, comprising what the Chinese refer to as 'payment' trade.

The great majority of trade agreements are inter-governmental and provide binding or non-binding exchange quotas of listed commodities.[25] Such trade is essentially barter trade in nature and does not usually involve actual foreign exchange payments. These trade agreements are normally supplemented by payments' agreements specifying the currency that will serve as the unit of account and settlement, as well as payment should a trade deficit occur under the agreement. The relevant FTCs, on behalf of the Chinese government, negotiate and sign the individual contracts implementing these trade agreements that contain the basic terms such as price and delivery.

Non-agreement or 'payment' trade accounts for the lion's share of China's import and export activity. As described above, the Chinese trading partner may be an FTC or local branch thereof, a local foreign trading corporation, a ministerial import or export corporation, or an enterprise authorized to conduct foreign trade business directly. Business is conducted by correspondence, or by direct negotiations in China or abroad, at the semi-annual Guangzhou Export Commodities Fair, or at various mini-fairs and exhibitions for specific commodities sponsored by Chinese or foreign organizations.

The Guangzhou fair has been held nearly every spring and autumn since 1957, with foreign attendance by invitation only. The fair has been scaled down somewhat and has become a less important way of meeting potential Chinese partners and doing business in the wake of the decentralization of foreign trade authority. However, it continues to provide a useful channel for making trade contacts in China.

In addition to pure import and export activities, foreign firms may contract for the processing of raw or semi-finished materials supplied by them, or for the assembly of supplied parts and components in China, or they may enter into compensation trade deals, providing for payment in commodities rather than in cash.[26] Some sales may also be made through exhibitions held in China with the assistance of the CCPIT.

III. Import and Export Controls

China's foreign trade is an integral part of the planned economy, and MOFERT develops the national foreign trade plans, which must be approved ultimately by the National People's Congress as part of the overall national economic plan, in close co-ordination with other economic sectors. China exports basically in order to be able to earn the foreign exchange with which to purchase imported goods, technology and services necessary for realizing its targeted socialist modernization.

China, like most countries, restricts imports and exports in a variety of ways, ranging from absolute bans on trading in certain commodities[27] to more limited restrictions achieved by means of quotas and 'standards' requirements. China's import and export licensing system, resurrected in 1980 and currently under revision, helps directly to implement national import and export plans, current trade policies and quota restrictions,[28] while the commodity inspection apparatus enforces the requirement that imports and exports meet applicable domestic or international standards. China also indirectly influences the nature and volume of two-way trade through the selective imposition of, or exemption from, customs duties.

A. Export Licensing

In 1980, the Chinese government provisionally put into effect a revised export licensing system, to be administered by MOFERT.[29] The Interim Procedures Concerning the System of Export Licensing (hereafter cited as the Export Licensing Procedures), effective from 3 June 1980 but never officially published, characterize export licensing as a necessary measure to strengthen control over export commodities and to co-ordinate the export trade activities of the various localities and departments concerned.[30] In general, the FTCs and their branches, and other corporations approved by the state to engage in export business, are deemed to have obtained permission to export the commodities within the approved scope of their business and need not apply specifically for export licences.[31] These 'general' licences will not, however, apply in the case of (1) goods subject to a quota placed by the country of import; (2) export commodities that MOFERT has restricted in order to prevent flooding of the international market; (3) commodities subject to a minimum export price imposed by MOFERT; (4) export commodities restricted or banned by the State Council; and (5) commodities subject to export controls imposed by MOFERT in order to meet conditions in the world market or due to foreign policy constraints. The latter condition, for example, would apply to the ban on all trade with South Korea, South Africa and Israel, including re-exports of Chinese goods via Hong Kong or third countries.[32]

As of 15 April 1983, over 90 commodities reportedly had been placed under the special export licensing system, applicable to all Chinese exporters.[33] Before February 1982, the list of controlled commodities covered some 32 miscellaneous goods, including herbal medicines such as ginseng, pilous antler and Chinese caterpillar fungus, red dates, freshwater pearls, leather work gloves intended for West Germany and Hong Kong, hempsole shoes destined for France, peppermint oil, Arab robes, resin and reed matting. As of 2 February 1982, 48 additional commodities organized into 11 categories were also made subject to special export licensing. These additional commodities include crude and heavy oil and refined oil products; coal; rolled steel; pig iron, coke, ferro-alloys and chromite ore; plate glass; cement; timber and timber products; non-ferrous metals; natural rubber; soda ash, caustic soda, polyethylene, polyprophylene phosphorus, sulphurous iron ore, sulphur, benzoic anhydride and liquid hydrocarbons; and agricultural products such as rice, corn, soybeans, sugar, cotton, resin, tung oil and tobacco.[34] As of 1 August 1982, drawn-work goods, including embroidered and hand-worked goods, were made subject to the export licensing system;[35] and as of 15 April 1983, silk garments, hand tools, 1-cystine, ascorbic acid, tetracycline, sodium sulphate and inner combustion engines and units also require a special export licence.[36]

Many of these controlled commodities, such as crude oil, steel and steel products, non-ferrous metals, rubber, cereals and sugar, are in short supply on the Chinese domestic market, reportedly at least in part due to excessive exports.[37] Some reports indicate that other of these commodities, such as ascorbic acid, embroidered curtains and nails, are being placed under licensing control in order to prevent Chinese exporters from violating exclusive distribution agreements with foreign customers.[38]

In addition to the special licences required of all Chinese exporting units for controlled commodities, special export licences are also necessary for (1) goods being exported by entities and individuals not authorized to engage in export business; (2) goods exported for foreign exhibition and sales; (3) goods exported directly, rather than through an FTC, by factories and enterprises that produce the goods under a processing or compensation trade contract with a foreign party; (4) goods being shipped out of China by diplomatic missions, representatives of foreign enterprises, foreign nationals and tourists; and (5) goods exceeding a reasonable amount for personal use taken out of China by foreign nationals and tourists.[39]

The Export Licensing Procedures provide that MOFERT may at any time reduce, suspend or terminate exports of any commodity to any country or region when the export (1) does not conform to Chinese policies with respect to the place of destination; (2) does not conform to the content and spirit of any relevant bilateral trade or payments' agreement, such as the textile agreements that China has signed with the European Economic Community, the United States and Canada; (3) must be postponed or curtailed due to an imbalance in China's foreign exchange situation; or (4) does not meet the standards set by the state or in the relevant export contract, as determined by the commodity inspection authorities.[40]

Export licence applications must be filed with the Foreign Trade Administrative Department of MOFERT in the case of (1) controlled commodities that MOFERT subjects to the special export licensing system; (2) exports of commodities that must be handled jointly with the specialized FTCs; (3) exports by ministries other than MOFERT and the departments and enterprises directly under them, if not otherwise authorized by MOFERT; and (4) cargo shipped out of China by foreign embassies in China.[41] The local foreign trade bureaux have been authorized by MOFERT to handle licence applications with respect to (1) commodities handled by the local export corporations and not co-ordinated by the FTCs or by other specialized corporations; (2) cargo shipped out of China by foreign consulates in China; and (3) goods exported by local departments and enterprises.[42] As mentioned above, the recently established special trade commissioner offices will also be responsible for issuing some export licences, although the scope of their authority in this respect has not yet been made clear.

In addition, the Shanghai Municipal Government has announced that it is now authorized to issue import and export licences to its foreign trade departments and enterprises.[43] Again, it is not yet known how and to what extent Shanghai is to co-ordinate with MOFERT in this respect.

The term of each licence, which may not exceed six months, is determined on a case-by-case basis, except for general export licences, which reportedly are good for six-month periods.[44] Special licences will be granted separately on the basis of applications that describe the commodity and its specifications, destination, quantity, unit price, total price, delivery date and method of payment.[45] The applicant retains one copy of the licence and presents two copies to the Customs authorities for inspection at the time of export. The Customs in turn forward one copy, stamped by Customs, to the local branch of the Bank of China for verification that the foreign exchange proceeds are properly collected.[46]

B. Import Licensing

The Chinese import licensing system, also administered by MOFERT, is designed to help implement the state import plans and control the goods that the provincial and ministerial import corporations and authorized enterprises may buy and the foreign exchange expenditures therefor. In 1980, the Chinese implemented, but never made officially public, a provisional import licence system and rules concerning imports by localities.[47] These rules were replaced on 10 January 1984 by the Interim Regulations on the System of Import Licensing of the People's Republic of China (hereafter cited as the Import Licensing Regulations).[48]

The Chinese government periodically issues import guidelines for domestic units in accordance with its foreign exchange reserves situation and development needs. China now stresses the import of advanced technology and equipment in order to renovate existing enterprises, in a shift away from the import of complete plants and sets of equipment.[49] China generally adheres to the following import guidelines: (1) China will not import goods that are harmful to the people's health; (2) if China-made products fall short of demand in terms of quantity, quality or variety, a limited amount of such goods may be imported; (3) imports of important raw materials and semi-finished materials that China cannot produce are encouraged; (4) priority is given to sophisticated technology and equipment that can advance China's modernization effort; and (5) China will permit imports of materials that are to be processed or assembled for export.[50]

Through the licensing system, China has severely curtailed imports of consumer or luxury goods in order to protect domestic industry and conserve valuable foreign exchange for more pressing needs.[51] From October 1982, special import licences were required for commodities such as vehicles (including bicycles), certain electronic equipment and household appliances, some business equipment, consumer goods and chemical fibres and fabrics.[52]

Pursuant to the Import Licensing Regulations, the FTCs and authorized import corporations under the ministries and provincial governments are deemed to have a general licence with respect to commodities that they are authorized to handle,[53] excepting only designated controlled imports and imports of prohibited goods. In addition, uncontrolled goods imported within the scope of approved contracts with foreigners for processing, assembly, compensation trade and construction projects do not require an import licence, except for any such materials and spare parts and the finished products thereof under processing and assembly projects that are actually sold on the domestic Chinese market, rather than exported as originally planned.[54]

Other imports of uncontrolled goods that are exempt from the import licensing requirements include: (1) samples imported by or given to Chinese entities authorized to engage in import business in the course of their normal import and export activities; (2) urgently needed work-related articles purchased abroad at a price of US$5,000 or less by scientific research, cultural, athletic, medical and health departments with government approval; (3) urgently needed parts and accessories for machines, meters and instruments purchased abroad at a price of US$5,000 or less by factories and mines with government approval; and (4) commodities imported with special MOFERT approval.[55]

Chinese-foreign equity joint ventures do not need to apply for an import licence for any uncontrolled machinery, equipment, spare parts, raw or other materials contributed as part of the foreign party's investment or, when such items cannot be purchased in China, otherwise needed for the venture's production within the scope of the approved joint venture contract.[56] Controlled commodities and imports beyond the approved business scope of a joint venture, however, will require a special import licence.

In sum, special import licences will be required for all imports not falling within the categories listed above, that is, for all controlled goods regardless of the importing unit and for uncontrolled goods imported by entities not authorized to engage in the import business or by FTCs and other authorized entities beyond the approved scope or monetary limit of their import authority.

Import licences shall be denied or may be revoked when: (1) the state decides to suspend or cease the import of certain goods; (2) the import of goods would violate China's foreign policy; (3) the import would violate bilateral trade or payments' agreements; (4) the import goods do not meet the state's hygienic or quarantine standards; (5) the import would be harmful to the state's interests; or (6) the import goods are procured by illegal means.[57]

Imports from South Korea, South Africa and Israel are banned,[58] and imports from Taiwan, entitled for a time to special exemptions from licensing and payment of customs duties, have been made subject to the import licensing system and 'adjustment taxes', rather than duties, reportedly in order to discourage the excessive import of consumer goods from the island.[59]

MOFERT, the provincial foreign trade bureaux and, as recently authorized, the four special trade commissioner offices may issue required import licences. The division of responsibility in this respect has not been made clear, but is to be prescribed by MOFERT.[60]

Licence applications must state the kind of commodities, quantity, specifications, price, usage, country of export, source of foreign currency and the name of the foreign exporter.[61] Licences are to be valid for one year from the date of issue and may be extended upon application.[62] In the case of special applications, licences may be obtained in as little as two to three days.[63]

Although foreign traders are often told that the licensing system is an internal matter and the sole concern of the Chinese side, foreigners have a substantial interest in knowing that the licensing procedures have been duly complied with. In at least one reported case, the responsible Chinese ministry refused to approve a licence application for a provincial export contract ready to be signed, unless the negotiated price was raised by 15 per cent.[64] Thus, foreigners are advised to request proof or assurances that any necessary licences have been obtained or are forthcoming before expending time and money in negotiating a trade contract.[65] Even in the case of goods and Chinese units covered by a long-term general licence, one should ascertain that the particular order conforms to any price, quantity and delivery terms applicable to the general licence.

C. Commodity Inspection

The Chinese commodity inspection network is designed to ensure that import and export goods meet national standards and any specifications contained in relevant contracts or trade agreements. Certain import and export commodities are required by Chinese law to go through inspection and will not be cleared by Customs without certification that they have passed inspection.

The Chinese Import and Export Commodity Inspection Bureau was established under the former Ministry of Foreign Trade pursuant to regulations approved in 1953,[66] which charged the Bureau with the task of controlling the quality of import and export commodities through inspection, survey, technical appraisal and certification. The Bureau was reorganized into the General Administration of Import and Export Commodity Inspection and placed under the direct supervision of the State Council in February 1980, and its name was changed to the State Administration of Import and Export Commodity Inspection (SACI) in 1982.[67] Despite these changes, its duties remain basically the same. Local commodity inspection bureaux under the direct supervision of the head office have been established in all of the provinces (except Taiwan), autonomous regions and special municipalities.

The SACI is responsible for certifying all major commodities designated in a list prepared by MOFERT (the Legal Inspection List), other commodities requiring inspection pursuant to export or import contracts, animals and plants and products thereof subject to quarantine, and foodstuffs subject to sanitary inspection.[68] In addition, the SACI is authorized to conduct 'interventional' inspection of commodities not included on the Legal Inspection List, such as any goods suspected of being contaminated. The SACI may also investigate cases of alleged import or export fraud.[69]

In addition to the SACI, a number of other agencies have been charged with specialized quality assurance responsibilities. These include: (1) the Animal and Plant Quarantine Centre, responsible for the quarantine of plant imports and exports and for the quarantine of imported and exported animals and animal products other than wild animal products and animal by-products, which are under the jurisdiction of the SACI; (2) the Ship Inspection Bureau, responsible for the inspection of imported ships and major ship equipment; (3) the Medical and Sanitary Quarantine Centres under the Ministry of Public Health, responsible for the inspection of imported foodstuffs and drugs;[70] and (4) the National Bureau of Weights and Measures, responsible for inspecting imported weighing and measuring equipment.

As of the end of 1983, over 200 export commodities and 15 import commodities were designated as legally requiring inspection. These commodities generally include those imported or exported in large volume in terms of quantity or value, traditional exports, exports of high revenue-earning potential, and commodities of fluctuating quality that may affect the health of humans or animals.[71] In addition, commodities not legally or contractually required to undergo inspection are still subject to possible inspection by the SACI or other authorized departments to make certain that they comply generally with state laws, standards and policies.[72]

Commodities are inspected for quality, conformance to relevant specifications and packaging. Inspection is carried out in accordance with any applicable contractual provisions or else pursuant to standards set by the state or the departments concerned.[73] Inspection certificates must be presented to obtain customs clearance and are often used as settlement documents in the case of a dispute. China's standard export and import contracts previously provided that certificates issued by the SACI were to be used as conclusive evidence in the event of any dispute over quality, quantity or other product specification. However, the Chinese recently have permitted foreign buyers to use the results of their own reinspection as a basis for bringing claims.[74]

The China National Import-Export Commodities Inspection Corporation (CCIC) was set up in 1980, under the leadership of the SACI, specifically to deal with inspection work entrusted by foreign traders or Chinese units with respect to commodities not on the Legal Inspection List. The CCIC is authorized to issue certificates that are also legally effective for the purposes of customs clearance, calculating customs duties and settling claims.[75] The CCIC will conduct inspection in accordance with any requirements set forth in the relevant contract or letter of credit. If inspection standards are not clearly defined by the contract, the CCIC will apply, in the case of imports, the prevailing standards of the country of origin or those that are internationally recognized and, in the case of exports, relevant Chinese standards.[76]

The CCIC has branches in Shanghai, Guangzhou, Tianjin, Dalian, Qingdao, Wuhan and Nanjing.[77] In the summer of 1982, the CCIC established a Hong Kong subsidiary, China Inspection Company Limited (CICL), to act as the CCIC's inspection agent in Hong Kong and to provide inspection services to Hong Kong enterprises. Certificates issued by the CICL for goods imported by China via Hong Kong are recognized by the SACI for the purposes of accepting the goods and settling accounts.[78]

IV. Customs Regulation

The General Administration of Customs of the People's Republic of China, reorganized and placed directly under the State Council in February 1980 to replace the Customs Bureau of the former Ministry of Foreign Trade, is responsible for overall management of customs work throughout China. The major responsibilities of the Customs Administration are to enforce China's foreign trade regulations through the supervision and control of goods, currency, means of conveyance, passenger baggage and postal articles that enter or leave Chinese territory, the collection of customs duties and other taxes and fees that are to be collected by Customs, and the prevention of smuggling.[79] The Customs Administration has established some 40 offices and 27 sub-offices at ports, railway stations, airports and international parcel post and mail exchange bureaux that are open for foreign trade, as well as at border areas open for passenger, parcel and conveyance traffic. In addition, a branch office of the Customs Administration was set up in Guangzhou in 1980 to supervise the especially heavy customs traffic in Guangdong Province.[80]

China announced in August 1983 that it had joined the 95-member Customs Co-operation Council (CCC), a Brussels-based international governmental customs organization. The CCC was formed to promote co-operation between the customs administrations of member states, to improve customs regulations and techniques, to exchange data about customs procedures and to co-operate with other international organizations.[81] This move would seem to reflect China's concern with updating its customs system and further integrating itself into the international commercial community. Indeed, on the domestic front, MOFERT reports that the 1951 Customs Law is undergoing extensive revision to update its provisions and make the system more efficient. However, the exact content of the proposed new customs law, and its expected date of enactment, are not yet known.

A. Customs Formalities

All cargo and international means of conveyance must pass through Customs upon entry into or exit from Chinese territory. Cargo is released after verification of any required import or export licence or other official document of approval, as well as of inspection certificates in the case of goods subject to commodity inspection, animal or plant quarantine, medical tests or other state restrictions.

All imports and exports, except those specially exempted, must be cleared through Customs by the cargo owner or his agent. Customs officials are responsible for checking that shipping marks, the number of packages, weight specifications, and country of origin or destination correspond with the terms of the relevant licence or trade document, and that the shipment does not violate any foreign trade regulations. In addition, Customs must ascertain whether there has been any damage to or loss of cargo and whether the quality and packaging satisfy relevant requirements.[82] After examination and approval, cargo will be released with the relevant shipping documents signed and verified by the Customs authorities.

As a rule, cargo is examined at the wharf warehouse or open yard at the place of entry into or exit from Chinese territory, but examination may take place elsewhere upon prior written request,[83] as in the case of goods packed in containers for import or export.[84] In addition, certain bulk cargo and dangerous or perishable goods may be cleared during loading or unloading so as to expedite their transport, prevent loss and minimize operating costs.

Transit cargo from abroad destined for another foreign country is subject to customs supervision and control while it is in China. In general, such goods may be inspected without unpacking or may be exempted from examination when the cargo is legal and appears to be above suspicion.[85] Trans-shipment of weapons and ammunition requires special licences.[86]

Commodities imported for exhibition in China are subject to special procedures promulgated in 1975.[87] The Chinese organization hosting the exhibition must submit approval documents to the Customs office at the place of the exhibition prior to importation, and the exhibitor or his agent must also submit to that Customs office a list of exhibition goods and their specifications and value. Exhibition goods that are re-exported from China within three months from the end of the exhibition are exempt from import duties. However, products and exhibits sold or disposed of in China will be handled retroactively in accordance with normal licensing and duty regulations.

Gifts and commodity samples without commercial value that are accepted by Chinese government entities or Chinese enterprises may be cleared duty-free and without a licence, upon declaration to the Customs authorities by the recipient.[88]

Special rules[89] covering bonded goods, such as stored commodities needed to service international aircraft, and the warehouses in which they are kept, were issued in 1981. They exempt bonded goods from customs duty and normal licensing procedures and may apply, by analogy, to customs treatment of imports for processing, assembly and compensation trade transactions.[90]

All inward- and outward-bound vessels, trains, civil aircraft and motor vehicles, as well as their cargo, are also subject to customs supervision and must be covered by a declaration form and undergo inspection upon entering or leaving China.[91] Only after inspection and approval of the means of conveyance can unloading of the cargo, under customs supervision, take place.

Incoming and outgoing personal baggage and goods brought into China through the mail (except by diplomatic personnel) are all subject to customs supervision. Baggage and goods accompanying tourists and foreign residents in China are limited to reasonable amounts necessary for personal use. On entering or leaving China, non-diplomatic passengers must fill out baggage declaration forms. Specified items, such as foreign currency, wristwatches, cameras and jewellery, must be declared upon entering China and taken out again, or else the passenger will be subject to a potentially stiff fine. The import of arms, ammunition or explosives of any kind, radio transmitter-receivers and parts, unauthorized renminbi, material detrimental to Chinese political, economic, cultural and moral interests, illegal drugs, infected plant and animal matter, unsanitary foodstuffs and other articles proscribed by regulations is forbidden.[92]

The export of arms, ammunition and explosives, radio transmitters and parts, renminbi and renminbi-denominated securities, unauthorized foreign currency and securities, materials containing state secrets or otherwise prohibited for export, rare animal and plant matter, precious metals and jewellery made therefrom in excess of permitted amounts,[93] and valuable cultural relics and rare books relating to China's revolution, history and culture is also prohibited.[94] Cultural relics permitted for export, jewellery, precious stones and metals, and jade and ivory articles will be cleared by Customs only against verification of the relevant sales receipts issued by state-run friendship stores or cultural relic shops, plus a foreign exchange memorandum issued by the Bank of China showing that the purchase price thereof was paid with renminbi obtained by exchanging foreign currency.[95]

Most personal goods can be brought in duty-free, but the import of wristwatches, bicycles, cameras, radios, sewing machines, foodstuffs, smoking materials and liquor are restricted, and duty must be paid on amounts in excess of prescribed limits.[96] As in the case of unaccompanied imports, trade samples, gifts, advertising material and the like brought into China by passengers for business purposes must be declared and will be cleared only after the receiving unit submits proper certification.[97]

B. Customs Duty

China pursues a protective tariff policy in order to safeguard its domestic economy from disruptive or undesirable imports and exports. Conversely, through duty exemptions or low rates of duty, China seeks to encourage the import of strategic commodities and materials to be processed or assembled for export, and the export of all commodities that are not in short supply domestically. In order to strengthen control in this respect, the Customs Administration announced in late 1981 that henceforth Chinese entities could no longer sign trade contracts that contained provisions purporting to exempt without authorization the contract commodity from duty.[98]

Regulations issued in 1951 on the imposition of import and export duties[99] divide import and export commodities into 17 general categories containing some 89 groups and 936 specific classifications based on the natural properties, composition and use of the commodities. To encourage exports, the Chinese government does not levy customs duties on most export commodities. However, as of 1 June 1982, 34 commodities are subject to duties ranging from 10 per cent to 60 per cent. Except for coal, which is charged at the rate of 40 renminbi per metric ton, export duties are levied on the basis of the F.O.B. (free on board) value as determined by the Customs authorities, less export duty.[100] Dutiable export commodities include crude oil and oil products, iron alloys, steel products, pig iron, timber and wood products, cement, rubber, liquified gas, several non-ferrous metals, pearls, rice, soybeans, sugar, tung oil, raw lacquer, some freshwater and seafood products, and traditional medicinal goods. Most of these dutiable export goods also require a special export licence. The motive behind imposition of the duties appears to be to restrain local trade units from exporting scarce strategic commodities that may be sold abroad at prices higher than those paid by the Chinese government or determined by the state price-control authorities.[101]

On the import side, the most extensive duty adjustment since the tariff system was instituted in 1951 became effective in January 1982, when the import duties on 149 commodities were adjusted upward or downward.[102] Commodities subject to reduced rates, so as to encourage imports, fall into three general categories: natural raw materials for industry and primary products such as rubber, timber, leather and paper, which are in chronic short supply in China; commodities temporarily in short domestic supply, such as crude oil, fuel oil, coal, cement, some chemicals, raw materials and certain equipment for light and textile industries; and components and spare parts for machines and instruments.[103] At the same time, import duties on most power, farming, mining, metallurgical, petroleum-exploiting and universal machinery, machine tools, electric motors, automobiles, ships, and civil electrical appliances were raised to protect domestic manufacture.[104]

The customs duty rate schedule prescribes an ordinary rate and a 'minimum' preferential rate applicable to imports from countries that have signed trade agreements or treaties with China providing for lower rate treatment. The ordinary rates are from 20 to 100 per cent higher than the preferential rates.

Rates are set and adjusted based on China's need for the commodities and the gap between their production costs in China and prices abroad.[105] Top priority imports such as rice, wheat and other grains, cooking oil, agricultural and animal goods, some special medicines, most printed matter, metal ores, gold, silver and platinum, crude oil, and astronomical and nautical instruments are exempt from import duty, while low duty rates of 5 to 20 per cent are imposed on other needed commodities such as chemical fertilizers, pesticides, rubber, timber, paper pulp, certain rolled steel, industrial and farm machines, aircraft, rolling stock and trucks. Less crucial commodities and imports that can be produced in China are charged at higher rates, while the highest rates of all, currently 250 per cent ordinary and 150 per cent preferential, are applied to luxury items such as liquor, cosmetics, tobacco products and edible delicacies.

In general, import duties are assessed on the basis of C.I.F. (cost, insurance and freight) value. The Chinese Customs authorities calculate this amount based on the wholesale price at the place the commodity was purchased, foreign export duties and all packing, transport, insurance and service expenses.[106] If the foreign purchase price cannot be determined, the Customs office at the place of import applies a formula using the local price (less import charges and business expenses) or otherwise determines the dutiable value.[107]

Import duties are also levied at the preferential rates on certain personal articles brought into China by passengers or through the mail. Rules issued in 1978[108] exempt printed matter and educational visual materials, contraceptives, gold and silver, and tax 12 categories of foodstuffs, clothing, pharmaceuticals, electronic equipment, fabrics and other daily use items at rates ranging from 20 to 200 per cent. Most personal imports are also taxed on their C.I.F. value. In September 1981, however, the Customs Administration announced that television sets, radio-recorders and electronic computers brought in by individuals for private use will be taxed on the basis of the higher Chinese domestic retail prices in order to protect domestic production.[109]

Export duties are imposed on articles in excess of prescribed reasonable amounts taken out of China by overseas Chinese, foreigners residing in China and Chinese nationals going abroad to visit relatives.[110]

China also levies tonnage dues on foreign vessels, Chinese vessels under foreign charter, and vessels owned or chartered by Chinese-foreign enterprises that call at Chinese ports.[111] Vessels under the flag of a country that has signed an agreement with China calling for most-favoured-nation treatment are subject to preferential rates. Tonnage dues, levied from the date of application for entry, may be paid for a period of three months or 30 days, at the option of the applicant. Those electing to pay on a monthly basis are charged at half the prescribed rates. Vessels used by diplomatic missions, vessels entering Chinese waters for 24 hours or less solely for purposes of repair or shelter and not unloading any cargo or passengers, and vessels requisitioned by, or under charter to, the central or local people's governments are exempt from tonnage dues.

C. Exemptions: Special Procedures, Assembly and Compensation Trade

The 1951 Customs Law exempts or reduces otherwise payable import duties on the amount of goods lost or damaged during transport or during storage prior to Customs clearance, and on goods to be re-exported from China within six months.[112]

Advertising matter and trade samples without commercial value to be presented to Chinese units as gifts are also exempt from duty,[113] as well as from licensing requirements.

In addition, the Customs Administration has ruled that raw materials, spare parts and necessary equipment imported by foreigners for processing, assembly and small or medium-sized compensation trade transactions,[114] as well as machinery and equipment, spare parts and raw materials brought in by foreigners as part of their investment in Chinese-foreign equity joint ventures or purchased with invested funds in accordance with their relevant contracts, may be exempted from import duty and the Consolidated Commercial and Industrial Tax (hereafter cited as the Consolidated Tax), imposed on imports together with the customs duty.[115] Moreover, a Chinese-foreign joint venture may apply to the Ministry of Finance and the Customs Administration for exemption from the import duty and Consolidated Tax applicable to raw and other materials, spare parts, components, accessories and packaging materials imported specifically to produce export commodities.[116] However, if any portion of such joint-venture products made for export is for any reason instead sold on the domestic Chinese market, it will be subject retroactively to import duty (and Consolidated Tax) on the raw materials, parts and other items originally exempted.[117] Export commodities produced in connection with processing, assembly and compensation trade and by Chinese-foreign joint ventures may also be exempted from any otherwise applicable export duty.[118]

In 1979 the Chinese government issued special procedures which apparently have only been implemented on a trial basis, if at all, for handling goods imported and exported in connection with processing and assembly for foreign customers.[119] These have been superseded in part by similar Customs rules concerning factories engaged in processing only, effective on 1 January 1984.[120] Pursuant to the more detailed 1979 procedures, the Chinese unit or FTC concerned should file the appropriate certificate of approval of the transaction, a copy of the contract and any required licence with the local Customs office within five days of signing the contract.[121] The Chinese party should then fill out a schedule of the commodities to be imported and the finished goods to be exported, and the Customs office will issue a registration booklet reflecting that information. This registration booklet, together with the normal customs declaration forms and other documentation, such as invoices or bills of lading, will be used as the basis for clearing the items without duty upon import and export. After full performance of the contract, the booklet must be handed in for cancellation. Under both sets of provisions all finished goods, as well as leftover materials and parts, must in principle be exported. Except in special circumstances, they may not be sold domestically or turned over to the foreign customer in China. The 1984 processing rules also require registration of the materials imported and cancellation once the finished goods are exported. If they are in fact disposed of domestically, the normal import duty and licensing requirements will apply retroactively.[122]

Article 118 of the Customs Law generally permits applications for exemption from customs duty in circumstances other than those specified above. For example, imports of advanced technology and machinery samples approved by the state and of equipment, tools and materials for developing China's Special Economic Zones may be exempted from the Consolidated Tax.[123] Since the import duty is generally collected by the Customs authorities together with the Consolidated Tax on imports at the point of entry of the goods, it is reasonable to assume that the above commodities may also be exempted, upon application, from the import duty.

D. Special Customs Provisions with Respect to the Co-operative Chinese-Foreign Exploitation of Offshore Oil in China

The Customs Administration and the Ministry of Finance have jointly issued special rules exempting from customs duties most imports of machinery, equipment, spare parts, components and materials for direct use in the exploration for and co-operative Chinese-foreign development and exploitation of offshore oil, as well as machinery and other engineering equipment temporarily imported for exploration and guaranteed by the foreign contractors to be re-exported.[124] Crude oil received and exported by the foreign contractors is exempted from export duty, although crude oil is subject to payment of a 5 per cent Consolidated Tax and to export licensing procedures.

The Customs Administration has also exempted from customs duties the personal luggage and all household articles brought into China in one shipment by foreign personnel hired by foreign oil companies to work in China for more than one year.[125] Each employee is permitted to bring in one private car, subject to customs duty, and postal articles and personal baggage taken in or out of China during his residence in China will be handled in accordance with normal customs regulations, described above. The baggage and articles brought in by foreign employees working in China for less than one year are also to be handled in accordance with customs procedures regarding passengers coming to China for a short visit.

V. Conclusion

At this stage in the reform and decentralization of China's foreign trade system, much confusion and uncertainty is evident. Some of the present rules for regulating foreign trade activity are unpublished; others are incomplete and outdated, or are in the process of being revised; and many are not always implemented in a consistent manner.

The confusion exists for both Chinese and foreign parties. On the Chinese side, the rapid growth of foreign trade and dispersal of trading authority have brought many inexperienced Chinese personnel on to the scene, and some uncertainty on the part of all Chinese participants concerning the proper procedures and lines of authority seems inevitable during this period of structural and legislative reform. On the foreign side, the decentralization of foreign trade activity seems to afford greater opportunities for finding a variety of Chinese trade partners and bypassing the traditionally centralized and slow negotiation and approval process for concluding trade contracts. On the other hand, the increasing number of potential partners may make it more difficult or time-consuming to locate appropriate Chinese parties, and the inexperience of the Chinese personnel involved may lead to some initial delays or errors due to lack of understanding of the complex trade procedures and restrictions.

The Chinese government is well aware of the present confusion and is striving to streamline the cumbersome system, train sufficient numbers of competent personnel, formulate or revise the necessary legislation, and strike the right balance between central direction and local initiative. The Chinese are in the initial stages of drafting a comprehensive foreign trade law but have not yet determined precisely what its scope and content will be.

In the reform process, China must also seek to balance domestic protectionism against its desire for free access to foreign markets. All nations, to one extent or another, employ some restrictive trade devices, such as tariff barriers, import quotas, licensing procedures, product standards and testing requirements, complex customs procedures, and direct or indirect subsidies to protect and control their domestic economies. As China's foreign trade activity has increased, China itself has encountered some difficulties in dealing with trade barriers imposed by other nations and has demonstrated its willingness to work toward mutual limitation of disruptive trade practices through entering into bilateral trade agreements and participating in various international trade forums, including its recent entry into the GATT textile arrangement and participation in the Multinational Customs Co-operation Council.

China's current quest to achieve a dynamic but manageable foreign trade system is not unusual in international experience. All nations continually reorganize their trade institutions and their operative policies and rules to adapt to the ever-changing domestic and international economic situation. What may distinguish China in this regard is that it has only recently abandoned its commitment to self-reliance and truly 'opened the door' to foreign trade and investment. With China's decision to make expanded foreign trade a cornerstone of its economic development plan, the foreign trade system established in the 1950s to handle a relatively small amount of import and export activity needs a basic renovation. This process is certain to require several years and the acquisition of considerable practical experience.

Notes

1. Total exports and imports in 1983 amounted to some US$40.14 billion, up nearly 90 per cent over two-way trade in 1978. *Xinhua News Bulletin* (Beijing), 25 January 1984, p. 28. During the period of the Sixth Five-Year Plan (1981–5), total foreign trade is targeted to reach US$57.4 billion, and China's Minister of Foreign Economic Relations and Trade, Chen Muhua, has announced China's ambitious goal to quadruple its import and export volume by the year 2000, to reach some US$160 billion. *Xinhua News Bulletin* (Beijing), 20 September 1982, p. 22.

2. *China's Foreign Trade*, No. 4, 1982, p. 12.

3. See A. Lee, 'Foreign Trade Decentralization: Its Origin and Future', *China Trader*, Vol. 4, June 1981, p. 66.

4. J.R. Shen, 'China's Import and Export Licensing System', *China's Foreign Trade*, No. 4, 1983, p. 6.

5. *Renmin Ribao (People's Daily)* (Beijing), 23 February 1983, p. 1.

6. *China's Foreign Trade*, No. 1, 1983, p. 11; and *China Market*, No. 4, April 1983, p. 11.

7. *Ta Kung Pao* (Hong Kong), 3 August 1982, p. 2.

8. *Shijie Jingji Daobao* (*World Economic Herald*) (Shanghai), 21 February 1983, p. 1 (hereafter cited as the *World Economic Herald*); and *Ta Kung Pao* (Hong Kong), 2 August 1982, p. 4.

9. The establishment of local import and export commissions directly responsible to the province, special municipality or autonomous region that set them up to oversee all trade activity within their respective jurisdictions was first reported during 1980. Although they apparently still exist, the official literature on China's trade system does not mention them and they do not engage in actual trade transactions themselves. See, for example, T.A. Gelatt, 'Delegation Report from Chengdu', *Amcham* (Journal of the American Chamber of Commerce in Hong Kong), Vol. 19, October 1982, p. 14.

10. Ludlow, 'China's New Foreign Trade Structure', *China Business Review*, May–June 1982, p. 31.

11. A complete list of the national foreign trade corporations as constituted early in 1982 can be found in China Council for the Promotion of International Trade, *China's Foreign Trade Corporations and Organizations* (Beijing, 1982).

12. National Council for US–China Trade, *China Business Manual* (1981), p.73 (hereafter cited as the *China Business Manual*). A highly-placed foreign trade official privately informed the author that the head offices and branches of the FTCs must register to obtain business licences with the State Administration for Industry and Commerce and may also have to register with the local tax authorities, although at present they appear to be exempt from taxation. *Xinhua News Bulletin*, 27 April 1983, p. 58.

13. *World Economic Herald*, 13 December 1982, pp. 1–2, note 8 above. Another Chinese newspaper puts the figure at more than 740 enterprises and departments, including some 480 engaged in export trade. *Guoji Jingji Xiaoxi* (*International Economic News*) (Beijing), 6 January 1983, p. 1.

14. Speech by Jia Shi, a Vice-Minister of the Ministry of Foreign Economic Relations and Trade, portions of which are reproduced in Ta Kung Pao, *China Handbook* (1982 edition), p. 539 (hereafter cited as the *China Handbook*).

15. Provisional Procedures for the Control of Imports by Localities in Foreign Trade, described in *China Economic News*, 13 October 1980, p. 2.

16. Provisional Procedures for the Control of Imports in Foreign Trade (hereafter cited as the Import Procedures), described in *China Economic News*, 13 October 1980, p. 2; and in Xinhua Publishing House, *The China Directory of Industry and Commerce and Economic Annual* (1982–3), p. EA-25 (hereafter cited as the *China Directory*).

17. Import Procedures, note 16 above.

18. China's Foreign Trade, Editorial Department, *China Trade Guide* (1980), p.14 (hereafter cited as the *China Trade Guide*).

19. L. Edinger, 'Who Needs an FTC?', *Amcham*, Vol. 19, June 1982, p. 34.

20. *China Trade Guide,* p. 15, note 18 above.

21. *China Trade Guide*, p. 15, note 18 above.

22. V.K. Fung, 'China's Decentralization of Foreign Trade', *Asian Wall Street Journal*, 24 November 1982, p. 6; and *Wen Hui Bao* (Hong Kong), 7 November 1982, p. 1. According to some reports, eliminating the need to go through the national foreign trade corporations may nearly halve the time required to fulfill an export contract. See, for example, *People's Daily*, 18 April 1983, p. 2 (article on the Beijing Silk Flower Factory).

23. *China Trade Guide*, p. 87, note 18 above.

24. *China Business Manual*, p. 68, note 12 above.

25. For more details, see *China Trade Guide*, p. 93, note 18 above; and C.J. Liu and L.S. Wang, *China's Foreign Trade: Its Policy and Practice* (1980), pp. 29–32.

26. Liu and Wang, pp. 37–9, note 25 above; and *China Handbook*, pp. 556–8, note 14 above.

27. A list of prohibited imports and exports may be found in 'Customs Guide for Passengers Entering and Leaving the People's Republic of China', *China Trade Guide*, p. 137, note 18 above.

28. Some 9,000 export licences and 4,000 import licences were issued between early 1981 and mid-1982, *China Economic News*, 11 October 1982, p. 1.

29. Interim Procedures of the State Import-Export Commission and the Ministry of Foreign Trade of the People's Republic of China Concerning the System of Export

Licensing (hereafter cited as the Export Licensing Procedures), promulgated on 3 June 1980, and translated in Foreign Languages Press, *China's Foreign Economic Legislation* (1982), Vol. I, p. 182. These procedures reportedly are currently under revision to make the licensing process simpler and more efficient.

Provisional Regulations for the Control of Foreign Trade, promulgated soon after Liberation on 8 December 1950, had required all organizations and individuals engaged in foreign trade to obtain import and export licences for designated goods. The 1950 Provisional Regulations and interim implementing rules on licensing were replaced in 1957 with the Procedures for Issuing Licences for Import and Export Goods, in Falu Chubanshe (Legal Publishing House), *Zhonghua Renmin Gongheguo Fagui Huibian (Compilation of Legislation of the People's Republic of China)* (January–June 1957), Vol. 5, p. 168 (1980 edition). These procedures also required that the specialized foreign trade corporations, then established under the Ministry of Foreign Trade, and all other Chinese units, private merchants and foreign businessmen obtain export and import licences for listed commodities. However, with the consolidation of the foreign trade apparatus in 1956, under which the foreign trade corporations achieved a virtual monopoly on foreign trade, the foreign trade corporations were deemed to have obtained required licences, and the licensing system apparently fell into disuse until it was revived in 1980 in order to regulate the activities of the growing number of other authorized trading units.

30. Art. 1.

31. Art. 3. These entities file their business licences, which specify their authorized scope of business activity with the Customs Administration, which enforces the licensing system.

32. *Asian Wall Street Journal*, 1 September 1982, p. 3.

33. *World Economic Herald*, 13 December 1982, p. 1, note 8 above; *China Market*, No. 8, August 1982, p. 74; *Xinhua News Bulletin*, 15 April 1983; and *Wen Hui Bao* (Hong Kong), 22 April 1983, p. 7. The latter article further reports that licensing requirements for seven herbal medicinal ingredients and turpentine, which had been imposed during the previous two years, were lifted at the beginning of 1983 due to improved market and operating conditions. See also *China Market Intelligence* (Newsletter of the National Council for US–China Trade, Washington, DC), June 1983, p. 3.

34. Lists with translations of these 48 commodities were carried in several publications. See, for example, *China Business Report*, April 1982, p. 9; and *China Market*, No. 8, August 1982, p. 74.

35. *Zhongguo Caimaobao* (*China's Finance and Trade Journal*), 3 August 1982, p. 1.

36. *Xinhua News Bulletin*, 15 April 1983, pp. 18–19.

37. *Hong Kong Business Standard*, 19 June 1982, p. 1.

38. *China Market Intelligence*, June 1983, p. 3.

39. Export Licensing Procedures, Art. 4, note 29 above.

40. Export Licensing Procedures, Art. 5, note 29 above.

41. *China Economic News*, 11 October 1982, p. 2.

42. *China Economic News*, 11 October 1982, p. 2.

43. 'Shanghai Promotes Foreign Economic Co-operation', *Xinhua News Bulletin*, 3 August 1983, p. 33.

44. *Ta Kung Pao* (Hong Kong), 28 February 1982, p. 3.

45. Export Licensing Procedures, Art. 6, note 29 above.

46. Export Licensing Procedures, Art. 7, note 29 above.

47. *China Directory*, p. EA-24, note 16 above. See, for example, *Waimao Zhishi Shouce* (*Foreign Trade Handbook*) (Tianjin Science and Technology Publishing House, second edition, 1981), p. 515–16 (hereafter cited as the *Foreign Trade Handbook*), which states that the Import Procedures were issued on 26 August 1980, together with the procedures governing imports by localities. See note 15.

48. *Wen Hui Bao* (Hong Kong), 27 January 1984, p. 3.

49. *Xinhua News Bulletin*, 11 October 1982, p. 33.

50. Interview with Sun Chun, *China Economic News*, 12 October 1981, p. 2.

51. *China Daily* (Beijing), 12 October 1982, p. 2; and *World Economic Herald*, 13 December 1982, p. 2, note 8 above.

52. *Foreign Trade Handbook*, p. 516, note 47 above. The commodities requiring a special import licence include: cars, tourist buses, tool trucks, jeeps, small tonnage passenger-cargo vehicles, motorcycles and bicycles; television sets, television-picture tubes, radio sets, recorders, complete sets of video-recording equipment and video recorders; household refrigerators, sewing machines and washing machines; cameras, photographs and electric fans; copying machines, electronic computers and calculators, recording and video tape duplication equipment; and chemical fibres and fabrics. *China Economic News*, 11 October 1982, p. 2.

53. Import Licensing Regulations, Art. 4, note 48 above.

54. Import Licensing Regulations, Art. 5, note 48 above.

55. Import Licensing Regulations, Art. 7, note 48 above.

56. Import Licensing Regulations, Art. 9, note 48 above; and the Implementing Act for the Law of the People's Republic of China on Joint Ventures Using Chinese and Foreign Investment (hereafter cited as the JV Regulations), Art. 63, *China Economic News,* Supplement No. 4, 3 October 1983.

57. Import Licensing Regulations, Art. 10, note 48 above.

58. *China Economic News*, 12 October 1981, p. 2; and V.K. Fung, 'China Reasserts Its Ban on Trade with 3 Nations', *Asian Wall Street Journal*, 1 September 1982, p. 3.

59. 'Statement by Spokesman of the Customs Administration Concerning Customs Procedures and Taxation of Commerce Between the Mainland and Taiwan', *Zhonghua Renmin Gongheguo Guowuyuan Gongbao* (*State Council Gazette*), 28 May 1980, p. 120 (hereafter cited as the *State Council Gazette)*; V.K. Fung, 'China Curbs Imports of Taiwan Products', *Asian Wall Street Journal*, 24 February 1982, p. 1; and V.K. Fung, 'China Begins Imposing Tax on All Imports from Taiwan', *Asian Wall Street Journal*, 30 March 1983, p. 1.

60. Import Licensing Regulations, Art. 3, note 48 above.

61. Import Licensing Regulations, Art. 11, note 48 above.

62. Import Licensing Regulations, Art. 12, note 48 above.

63. Interview with Shen Jueren, *World Economic Herald*, 13 December 1982, p. 2, note 8 above.

64. *China Business Report*, April 1982, p. 9.

65. J.R. Shen, 'China's Import and Export Licensing System', *China's Foreign Trade,* No. 4, 1983, p. 7. Mr Shen, who is the Director of the Foreign Trade Administration Department of MOFERT, also points out: 'If a Chinese enterprise fails to obtain a licence for unjustifiable reasons, it will be held responsible for all consequences arising therefrom'.

66. Provisional Regulations on the Inspection and Testing of Import and Export

Commodities, effective from 3 January 1954 (hereafter cited as the Inspection Regulations), in *China Trade Guide*, p. 101, note 18 above.

67. General Administration of Import and Export Commodity Inspection, *Import and Export Commodity Inspection in China* (1981), pp. 1–2; and Notice of the State Administration for Import and Export Commodities of the People's Republic of China, 28 January 1983 (on file with the author).

68. See, for example, Regulations of the People's Republic of China on the Quarantine of Animal and Plant Imports and Exports, promulgated by the State Council on 4 June 1982, in *State Council Gazette*, 25 July 1982, p. 503, note 59 above.

69. Inspection Regulations, Art. 3, note 66 above.

70. See also, Food Hygiene Law of the People's Republic of China (For Trial Implementation), approved on 19 November 1982, Art. 28 (concerning inspection of imported food, additives, containers, packaging materials and tools and equipment used for food handling), in *East Asian Executive Report*, Vol. 5, January 1983, Section A.

71. The most recently published list can be found in *China Market*, No. 2, February 1983, pp. 67–9.

72. *Foreign Trade Handbook*, p. 517, note 47 above.

73. See, for further details, *China Trade Guide*, pp. 101–3, note 18 above; and Liu and Wang, pp. 108–12, note 25 above.

74. Liu and Wang, p. 112, note 25 above.

75. *China Market*, No. 8, August 1982, p. 37.

76. *China Market*, No. 8, August 1982, p. 37.

77. For the addresses of these offices, see *China Trade Guide*, pp. 114–16, note 18 above.

78. *China Market*, No. 8, August 1982, p. 39.

79. Provisional Customs Law of the People's Republic of China, promulgated on 18 April 1951, Art. 2 (hereafter cited as the Customs Law).

80. Zhonghua Renmin Gongheguo Haiguan Zongshu (General Administration of Customs of the People's Republic of China), *Zhongguo Haiguan Fagui Shouce* (*Handbook of China's Customs Regulations*) (1982), pp. 13–14 (chart), (hereafter cited as the *Customs Handbook*).

81. 'China Joins Customs Co-operation Council', *Xinhua News Bulletin*, 3 August 1983, p. 8.

82. *China Trade Guide*, p. 119, note 18 above; and Liu and Wang, p. 132, note 25 above.

83. *China Trade Guide*, p. 120, note 18 above; and Liu and Wang, p. 133, note 25 above.

84. Provisional Procedures for the Supervision and Control of Import and Export Containers and Their Contents, issued by the Customs Administration on 29 June 1981, effective from 1 August 1981, in *Zhonghua Renmin Gongheguo Haiguan Fagui Xuanbien (Compilation of the Customs Legislation of the People's Republic of China)* (General Administration of Customs, 1982 edition), p. 64 (hereafter cited as the *Customs Laws*).

85. Liu and Wang, p. 134, note 25 above.

86. Liu and Wang, p. 134, note 25 above.

87. Procedures for the Supervision and Control by Customs of Goods Imported for Exhibition, promulgated by the Ministry of Foreign Trade, and effective from 3

November 1975, an English translation of which can be found in *China Trade Guide*, p. 129, note 18 above.

88. Liu and Wang, p. 133, note 25 above; and *China Trade Guide*, p. 120, note 18 above.

89. Provisional Procedures of the Customs of the People's Republic of China for the Supervision and Control of Bonded Cargo and Bonded Warehouses, issued by the General Administration of Customs on 10 February 1981, and effective from 1 March 1981, the Chinese text of which is in *Customs Laws*, p. 67, note 84 above.

90. See the description of the 1979 Procedures for Developing Processing, Assembly and Small and Medium-Scale Compensation Trade with Foreign Interests, in *Wen Hui Bao* (Hong Kong), 8 October 1982, p. 4.

91. See the following rules of the Chinese Customs, issued by the former Ministry of Foreign Trade, the Chinese texts of which appear in *Customs Laws*, note 84 above: (1) Procedures for the Supervision and Control of Vessels Engaged in International Navigation and Cargo Carried Thereon (31 December 1958); (2) Procedures for the Supervision and Control of Trains Leaving and Entering Chinese Territory and the Cargo, Passenger Baggage and Parcels Carried Thereon (5 November 1958), co-issued with the Ministry of Railways; (3) Provisional Procedures for the Supervision and Control of Motor Vehicles Entering and Leaving Chinese Territory and Cargo Carried Thereon (29 August 1963); (4) Procedures for the Supervision and Control of International Civil Aircraft (1 October 1974), the English translation of which is contained in *China Trade Guide,* p. 125, note 18 above; and (5) Procedures for the Supervision and Control of Small-Scale Vessels Coming From or Going to Hong Kong and Macao (10 July 1958).

92. Customs Guide for Passengers Entering and Leaving the People's Republic of China, in *China Trade Guide*, pp. 137–9, note 18 above.

93. *China Trade Guide*, p. 138, note 18 above.

94. *China Trade Guide*, p. 138, note 18 above.

95. *China Trade Guide,* p. 139, note 18 above.

96. Procedures of the People's Republic of China Concerning the Levy of Import Duty on Articles in Passengers' Baggage and Personal Postal Articles, approved by the State Council on 16 June 1978, and put into force by the Ministry of Foreign Trade on 1 August 1978, in *China Trade Guide*, pp. 132–3, note 18 above.

97. *China Trade Guide*, p. 120, note 18 above; and Liu and Wang, p. 135, note 25 above.

98. *China Daily* (Beijing), 1 January 1982, p. 1.

99. Import and Export Duty Rates of the Customs of the People's Republic of China, effective from 16 May 1951 to 31 December 1981, in *Customs Handbook,* pp. 49–129, note 80 above; and revised schedule in English in Business International, Inc., *China Hand* (March 1982), p. VIII-47 (hereafter cited as the Duty Rate Schedule); see also, Provisional Implementing Regulations of the Customs of the People's Republic of China Concerning Import and Export Duties, approved on 4 May 1951, English text in China International Economic Consultants, Inc. and Economic Information & Consultancy Co., (eds.), *Guide to Investment in China* (1982), pp. 152–6 (hereafter cited as the Provisional Duty Regulations).

100. *Zhongguo Caimaobao* (*China Trade and Finance Journal*), 29 May 1982, p. 1; Customs Law, Art. 116, note 79 above; and Provisional Duty Regulations, Art. 8, note 99 above.

101. *Business China,* 16 June 1982, p. 86.

102. *China Daily* (Beijing), 1 January 1982, p. 1.
103. Z. Li, 'Adjustment of China's Policy on the Customs', *China's Foreign Trade*, No. 6, 1982, p. 5; adjusted rates are set forth in the Duty Rate Schedule, note 99 above.
104. Li, p. 5, note 103 above.
105. H. Xue, 'Inside China's Tariff System', *China Business Review*, September–October 1981, p.52.
106. Customs Law, Art. 115, note 79 above; and Provisional Duty Regulations, Art. 5, note 99 above.
107. Provisional Duty Regulations, Art. 6, note 99 above. Article 6 provides the following formula for determining dutiable value when domestic wholesale prices are used:

$$\frac{\text{Domestic wholesale price} \times 100}{100 + \text{minimum import duty rate}} = \text{Dutiable value}$$

108. Procedures of the People's Republic of China Concerning the Levy of Import Duties on Articles in Passengers' Baggage and Personal Postal Articles, effective from 1 August 1978, in *China Trade Guide*, pp. 132–3, note 18 above.
109. *Xinhua News Bulletin*, 26 September 1981, p. 22.
110. Provisional Rules of the Customs of the People's Republic of China for the Supervision and Control of Articles in Baggage of Incoming and Outgoing Overseas Chinese and Other Passengers, effective from 5 April 1978, in *China Trade Guide*, pp. 134–6, note 18 above.
111. Provisional Procedures of the Customs of the People's Republic of China for Levying Tonnage Dues on Vessels, effective from 19 September 1952, in *China Trade Guide*, pp. 122–4, note 18 above.
112. Customs Law, Arts. 120–3, note 79 above.
113. Customs Law, Art. 121, note 79 above.
114. *Customs Handbook*, p. 149, note 80 above; see also, The Administrative Regulations of Customs Concerning Bonded Factories that Process Imported Materials (hereafter cited as the 1984 Processing Provisions), effective on 1 January 1984, *Wen Hui Bao* (Hong Kong), 27 November 1983, p. 5.
115. JV Regulations, Art. 71, note 56 above.
116. JV Regulations, Art. 71, note 56 above.
117. JV Regulations, Art. 71, note 56 above; see also, *Customs Handbook*, p. 149, note 55 above; and Procedures for the Development of Processing, Assembly and Medium and Small-Scale Compensation Trade, issued by the State Council on 3 September 1979 and reportedly being implemented in Shenzhen, Guangzhou and Dongbei, described in *Wen Hui Bao* (Hong Kong), 8 October 1982, p. 4 (hereafter cited as the 1979 Processing Procedures); and (Trial) Customs Rules Relating to the Supervision and Control of and Levy and Exemption from Customs Duty and Tax on Imports and Exports for Processing, Assembly and Medium and Small-Scale Compensation Trade (undated) (hereafter cited as the Customs Processing Rules), in Zhao Chengbi (ed.), *Waimao Shiwu Shouce (Handbook of Practical Foreign Trade Work)* (Liaoning People's Publishing House, 1982), pp. 553–5.
118. JV Regulations, Art. 72, note 56 above; 1979 Processing Procedures, para. 3, note 117 above; and Customs Processing Rules, Art. 3, note 117 above.
119. See note 117 above.

120. 1984 Processing Provisions, note 114 above.

121. 1979 Processing Procedures, para. 2, note 117 above; and *Customs Handbook*, p. 149, note 80 above. Except for those import and export commodities that MOFERT has designated as requiring a special licence and export commodities subject to a quota in the country of destination, materials, parts and equipment brought in for processing, assembly or compensation trade, and the finished export products or compensation commodities, do not require a licence. *Customs Handbook*, p. 147, note 80 above; and the 1979 Processing Procedures, para. 3, note 117 above.

122. 1979 Processing Procedures, para. 5, note 117 above; 1984 Processing Provisions, Art. 3, note 114 above; and Customs Processing Rules, Art. 6, note 117 above.

123. Provisions of the Ministry of Finance Concerning the Levy of and Exemption from Industrial and Commercial Tax for Import and Export Commodities approved by the State Council on 30 December 1980, effective from 1 January 1981, *State Council Gazette*, 1 March 1981, p. 15, note 59 above.

124. Rules for the Levy and Exemption of Customs Duties and the Consolidated Industrial and Commercial Tax on Imports and Exports in Connection with the Chinese-Foreign Co-operative Exploitation of Offshore Petroleum, approved by the State Council and promulgated on 1 April 1982 (copy on file with the author).

125. Customs Notice Concerning the Import of Personal Baggage and Articles by Staff of Foreign Oil Companies in Connection with the Chinese-Foreign Co-operative Exploitation of Offshore Petroleum, issued on 1 April 1982 (copy on file with the author).

2. China's Tax System: An Overview and Transactional Analysis

TIMOTHY A. GELATT AND RICHARD D. POMP

I. Introduction

As recently as 1979, the People's Republic of China had no systematic way of taxing foreign business. During the summer of that year, the Chinese invited several American tax professors to help initiate a group of China's tax officials into the arcane world of source rules, foreign tax credits, and tax treaties. Because the Chinese had, for so many years, been largely divorced from the Western legal, financial, and accounting professions, much of that summer was spent in bridging this gap. Today, however, Chinese officials converse fluently with foreigners about the merits of per-country limits versus overall limits on the foreign tax credit, the differences between the United Nations and the OECD model tax treaties, the attribution of income and expenses of foreign companies, and other complex tax issues. The sophistication with which foreign tax concepts are being absorbed and put to use in developing China's tax system represents a significant achievement by China's Ministry of Finance and provides a record of accomplishment for other Chinese organizations to emulate as they work to create a legal infrastructure for foreign business.

Since 1979, China, which has an extensive and complex domestic tax structure,[1] has adopted three major taxes affecting foreign business activity: the Individual Income Tax,[2] the Joint Venture Income Tax,[3] and the Foreign Enterprise Income Tax.[4] In addition, tax regimes have begun to be designed to cover investment in the Special Economic Zones (SEZs). The major pieces of the Chinese tax system are now in place. The resulting structure comports well with generally accepted international practice and concepts, reflecting what Ministry of Finance officials had often told foreigners — that wherever possible, China would opt for membership in the mainstream of the international tax community.

A foreigner doing business in China now faces a situation similar to that encountered elsewhere: a variety of available business and investment vehicles, each with different tax consequences, creating opportunities for tax planning. The tax consequences of various activities, however, are not always obvious from a reading of the statutes or regulations. Initially, when China's new tax laws for foreign business had just been issued, foreigners had no choice but to speculate on the tax treatment of specific transactions with only the general and imprecise language of the statutes as a guide. Foreigners quickly learned that the Chinese would not necessarily interpret their tax laws in the same manner as a Western-trained lawyer. Rigorous statutory construction, no matter how logically impeccable or internally consistent, was not always persuasive in dealings with tax officials, nor was it necessarily probative in predicting a transaction's treatment.

More recently, this state of uncertainty has given way to a body of accumulated experience, as the tax authorities' administrative posture on key issues has slowly emerged. Unfortunately, this administrative posture is still often set forth in documents not available publicly and must be gleaned from discussions with ranking officials and the collective experience of foreigners. Nonetheless, while some fundamental questions remain unanswered, the tax consequences of common transactions can now be described with a degree of accuracy not previously possible.

Tax planning for doing business in China is not only feasible but also essential. Foreigners, however, should not necessarily pursue the opportunities that exist to minimize or eliminate their Chinese taxes. Whenever the Chinese tax is fully creditable against its home country tax, a foreign company should consider such potential benefits as the goodwill and increased business opportunities that might accrue from contributing to the Chinese fisc. As the experience of certain multinationals in other countries demonstrates, a history of paying little or no tax, even if completely legal, can stigmatize a company and ultimately prove detrimental to its interests.

This chapter presents an overview of the tax structure generally applicable to foreign business. Part II analyses the individual income tax, the industrial and commercial tax, the joint venture income tax, and the foreign enterprise income tax. Part III traces the effect of the major taxes discussed in Part II on common forms of doing business in China, distilling the interpretations and administrative practices of the tax authorities in the context of common types of transactions, including representative offices, compensation trade, co-operative ventures, and equity joint ventures. Part III thus applies on a transactional basis the analysis presented in Part II.

II. An Overview of the Tax Structure for Foreign Business

A. The Individual Income Tax Law

i. Taxpayers

China's Individual Income Tax Law (IITL), passed on 10 September 1980,[5] follows the pattern used throughout the world by providing different tax treatment for non-residents and residents. Further, the treatment of a resident varies depending on the length of his residency.

a. Residents for Less than One Year

An individual not residing in China or an individual residing in China for less than one year is subject to taxation on income gained within China.[6] The regulations provide a favourable exception to this rule for an individual who is resident for not more than ninety *consecutive* days[7] during the taxable year. Such a person is exempt from taxation on any compensation paid by an employer outside China for services performed within China.[8]

A Notice issued in June 1981 by the Ministry of Finance[9] interpreting the ninety-day exemption rule clarified what foreign taxpayers had already discovered in their dealings with local tax bureaux — that the word 'consecutive' is not to be interpreted literally and that 'residency' is interpreted as the right to remain in China, as evidenced by a taxpayer's visa. More specifically, the Notice provides that a foreigner entering China with a visa valid for more than ninety days is presumptively a resident for more than ninety days and is therefore subject to tax on all income gained within China starting from the date on which he entered the country. Absences from China are disregarded for purposes of the ninety-day exemption provided the taxpayer returns at any time during the effective period of his visa.[10] Consequently, a businessman who repeatedly visits China on a multiple-entry visa valid for more than ninety days will find himself ineligible for the ninety-day exemption even if he is in China for less than a total of ninety days. A Chinese tax official has indicated, however, that a foreigner who spends ninety days or less in China and who leaves without intending to return during the effective period of his visa may have his presumptive 'resident' status revoked and qualify for the ninety-day exemption.[11]

Although not found in either the Notice or in any other document, a special interpretation of the ninety-day exemption is applied to foreigners entering China on short-term visas, typically valid for between thirty and sixty days. Foreigners who obtain a succession of short-term visas will have their periods of stay in China aggregated for purposes of determining their eligibility for the ninety-day exemption, even if these periods straddle more than one tax year.[12] Absences from China of over thirty days, however, trigger an entirely fresh count. For example, a businessman who: (1) obtains a short-term visa and remains in China for thirty days; (2) leaves China for less than thirty days and then returns on a new visa and remains for another thirty days; (3) leaves China for more than thirty days; and (4) returns to China under a new visa and stays for thirty-one days, remains eligible for the ninety-day exemption. His absence from China for more than thirty days erases, for purposes of the exemption, the sixty days that were already spent in China. By comparison, if the same businessman had, after his second visit, left for less than thirty days and had then returned again for thirty-one days, he would have become taxable on his income gained within China starting from his initial date of entry.

A foreigner whose visa is valid for 'less than ninety days'[13] need not register with the tax authorities. If it could be 'determined in advance', however, that his visa would be extended beyond ninety days, he must register from the beginning of his stay. If the extension could not have been determined in advance, the foreigner may wait until the end of the ninety days and then register.[14] At this time, he must pay taxes owed for the prior three months.[15] Chinese tax authorities have been unclear as to how they will determine whether an extension could have been 'determined in advance'. Also uncertain is whether a foreigner whose extension could have been 'determined in advance' but who does not pay tax from the outset of his stay in China will be subject to the IITL's penalty provisions.[16]

b. Residents for One Year or More

Under the IITL, an individual residing in China for a full 365 days within a taxable year — defined as a calendar year[17] — is taxable on income 'gained within or outside' China.[18] The regulations provide an exception to this rule in the case of an individual who resides in China for one year or more but not for more than five years. While this individual is taxable on his income gained within China, he is taxable on income gained outside China only if it is remitted to China.[19] An individual residing in China for more than five years is, under the regulations, taxable on his worldwide income regardless of whether income gained outside China is remitted to China.[20] However, in a 1983 document, the Ministry of Finance reversed its policy on non-China-source income. Under this document, such income will *not* be taxable regardless of whether it is remitted to China. This exemption applies whether the residency is for one year or more, or for more than five years, provided that the foreigner's presence is attributable to his employment by a joint venture, co-operative venture or foreign enterprise in China and not to a general intention to take up long-term residency in China.[21]

The regulations state that 'temporary absences' from China during the tax year are not counted for purposes of the one-year or more residency provision.[22] Consistent with this regulation, the 1981 Notice clearly indicates that foreigners with one-year residence permits or visas who leave China and return during the effective period of their permits or visas (including extensions approved after entry) are considered residents of China for one full year regardless of the amount of time actually spent abroad.[23]

ii. Source Rules

Under the regulations, the following items of income are considered as gained or sourced within China:[24] income from work and compensation for services performed within China; dividends and bonuses gained within China; remuneration for staff members sent to work abroad by any Chinese governmental office; fees for the use of proprietary rights within China; rent for the lease of property within China; and interest from within China. These items of income are considered as gained within China regardless of where the income is actually paid.[25]

Notwithstanding these regulations, Chinese tax officials have adopted a rather startling view regarding the source of wage and salary income of foreigners, deeming all wage and salary income earned by an over-ninety-day resident of China (as defined in the MOF Notice)[26] during his period of residency as gained or sourced in China and thus taxable. No distinction is made, in other words, between the concept of *residency*, which subjects a foreigner to tax, and that of *source*, which determines the income upon which he is taxed. The holder of a six-month visa who, for example, spends four of those months working in China and two months working in the United States is taxable in China on all of the wage and salary income earned during the entire six months, despite the regulation indicating that only compensation for services performed 'within China' is Chinese source income. The extent and manner in which the tax authorities will implement and enforce this approach, which requires that a taxpayer submit information on income earned while abroad, remain to be clarified.

iii. Tax Base

The individual income tax is levied on wages and salaries,[27] compensation for personal services,[28] fees for the use of proprietary rights,[29] interest,[30] dividends,[31] bonuses,[32] and rental income.[33] The Ministry of Finance may classify other items of income as taxable.[34]

Per diem or fixed periodic allowances paid by foreign companies to their employees in China are taxable as wages or salaries. Not taxable, however, are advances or reimbursements by foreign companies to their employees for specific 'company expenses' — including lodging, transportation, postage, telephone and telegraph, office expenses, advertisement and business-related entertainment expenses, provided the employer submits 'proof' that is verified by the local tax authorities. This 'proof' must establish that the payments were for 'company expenses' and not for food, laundry or other personal expenses of the employee, and were not part of the employee's salary.[35] Reimbursement or payment of an employee's Chinese income tax by a foreign company gives rise to taxable income for the employee, though the Chinese tax authorities seem unclear as yet about how to implement this approach.[36]

In calculating taxable income, certain statutory allowances are provided against specific categories of income. In the case of wages and salaries, for instance, a monthly deduction of RMB 800 is allowed.[37] These statutory deductions are automatically allowed regardless of whether actual expenses are greater than or less than the stipulated amount. No other deductions are allowed.[38]

iv. Rates

Wages and salaries are taxed monthly under a seven-bracket progressive rate schedule. The standard RMB 800 deduction is built into the rate schedule through a zero bracket for monthly income under RMB 800. Monthly income between RMB 801 and RMB 1,500 is taxed at 5 per cent; monthly income between RMB 1,501 and RMB 3,000 is taxed at 10 per cent. After RMB 3,000, the marginal tax rate increases by ten percentage points until it reaches 40 per cent on income between RMB 9,001 and RMB 12,000. Income above RMB 12,000 is taxed at 45 per cent.[39] Compensation for personal services, royalties, interest, dividends, bonuses, rents and 'all other kinds of income' are taxed at a flat rate of 20 per cent.[40]

B. The Industrial and Commercial Tax

The industrial and commercial tax,[41] which generates a substantial portion of China's tax revenue,[42] can be generally described as a broad-based turnover tax or as a combination of cascading sales and excise taxes. Unlike the sales taxes that are used in the United States, which generally apply only at the retail level, the industrial and commercial tax is imposed at each stage of production when taxable goods or services are transferred from entity to entity. The tax is also levied at the retail level when the goods or services are sold to the ultimate consumer.[43] Unlike a value-added tax, no credit is provided for any tax previously paid. The Chinese recognize the detrimental economic effects of the industrial and commercial tax's pyramiding structure and are experimenting with converting it into a value-added tax.[44]

The Consolidated Industrial and Commercial Tax Act (CICTA) and its regulations,[45] both adopted in 1958, form the basic structure of the industrial and commercial tax system. Until 1972, the CICTA was applied to all enterprises in China, both domestic and foreign. In 1972, a draft Industrial and Commercial Tax Act[46] was promulgated, simplifying the language of the CICTA and adjusting the taxable items and rates but not otherwise altering the basic structure of the industrial and commercial tax as set out in the CICTA.[47] The 1972 Act applies to domestic enterprises, while the CICTA continues to apply to foreign enterprises in China.[48] Recently, the Chinese have announced that they intend to apply the 1972 Act to equity joint ventures between Chinese and foreign enterprises, treating these ventures as domestic Chinese entities.[49] To the extent specific considerations apply under the 1972 Act to equity joint ventures, they will be covered in Part III F; the following discussion focuses on the structure of the CICTA.

i. Taxpayers and Taxable Activities

The CICTA applies to enterprises in China engaged in the production of industrial products, the importation of foreign goods, commercial retailing, communications, transportation, or the rendering of services.[50] The tax is paid only with respect to business conducted by establishments within China.[51]

The tax is usually imposed on the gross amount of proceeds received from the sale of goods and services. Taxpayers engaged in the purchase of agricultural products or the importation of foreign goods, however, pay the tax on the amount of their purchases.[52] In the case of imported industrial goods, the tax is computed on the basis of the sum of the cost-insurance-freight (C.I.F.) price of the goods and the customs duty divided by 1 minus the industrial and commercial tax rate.[53] In the case of imported agricultural products, the tax is computed only on the basis of the C.I.F. price.[54]

ii. Taxable Items and Rates

Over 100 categories of taxable industrial and agricultural products are listed in the CICTA's tables, some of which are divided further into sub-categories. Rates range from 1.5 per cent (for cotton grey cloth) to 69 per cent (for Grade A cigarettes), with over forty different rates within this range.[55] A 5 per cent catchall rate applies to any industrial product that is not listed specifically in the categories of taxable items; no similar catchall rate applies to unlisted agricultural products. Taxable items under the categories of services and commercial retailing are subject to tax rates ranging from 3 per cent to 7 per cent.[56] A surtax of 1 per cent is levied by local governments.[57]

In general, the industrial and commercial tax rates are set low on those goods and services which the state is seeking to encourage. Industrial goods tend to be taxed at lower rates than are consumer goods. Among consumer goods, necessities tend to be taxed lower than luxuries. Possibly as a way of reducing the pyramiding problem, the rates seem generally to be set low on goods that are likely to be inputs into the chain of production and distribution rather than final products.

The industrial and commercial tax, like any turnover tax, provides an advantage for a firm that is vertically integrated. In order to reduce this advantage, the industrial and commercial tax is applied to certain items produced by an enterprise and used by the same enterprise in further production, to certain products manufactured by an industrial enterprise and used by the enterprise in capital construction, and to products that are transferred from the production to the retail department of an enterprise that retails its own products.[58]

C. The Joint Venture Income Tax Law

i. Taxpayers

Under the Joint Venture Law of July 1979, an equity joint venture with Chinese and foreign investment must be organized as a limited liability company incorporated in China.[59] This Chinese joint venture corporation and its branches within or without China are taxable under the JVITL.[60]

The JVITL applies to all joint ventures for which contracts were approved on or after 10 September 1980.[61] Joint venture contracts approved before 10 September 1980 which contain tax rates or incentives different from those in the JVITL are subject to special transitional rules. These joint ventures are allowed to enjoy the benefits of any tax rates and incentives that were agreed upon for the initial period of the venture.[62] Subsequent extensions of these joint ventures, however, are subject to the JVITL's rates and other provisions.[63]

ii. Tax Base

The income tax is imposed on a joint venture's worldwide income derived from 'production, business, and other sources'.[64] 'Income from other sources' includes dividends, bonuses, interest, royalties, rental income, 'and other income'.[65] The law contains no capital gains concept; income or loss from the sale of fixed assets enters into the year's accounts at its full amount.[66]

Taxable income is defined as 'net income' after deduction of costs, expenses and losses, and is computed on a calendar-year basis under accrual accounting.[67] Losses may be carried forward for five years.[68]

Detailed rules are provided for the depreciation of fixed assets and for the amortization of intangible assets.[69] These rules follow generally accepted practices. Assets worth less than RMB 500 that have a 'short' useful life may be expensed rather than depreciated.[70] In general, fixed assets are depreciated on the basis of their 'original price' (cost) less residual value using the straight-line method of depreciation.[71]

A minimum useful life is prescribed for three broad classes of fixed assets: twenty years for houses and buildings, ten years for trains, ships, machines, equipment and other facilities used for production, and five years for electronic equipment and transportation equipment other than trains and ships.[72] The regulations do not specify what useful life is to apply for assets not covered by these three classes.

The regulations provide for the amortization of intangible assets, which include know-how, patents, trade marks, the right to use a site, and copyrights.[73] Goodwill is not mentioned. Intangible assets are amortized over the term provided for their use, or, if no term is provided, over a ten-year period.[74] Expenses incurred in starting up a joint venture are amortized once the venture begins operating. The amount of amortization cannot exceed 20 per cent per year.[75]

A detailed list of allowable costs, expenses or losses is not set forth in either the law or the regulations. However, the regulations do list various items that are not allowable in computing taxable income.[76] This list includes the JVITL tax and surtax (other taxes, such as the industrial and commercial tax, are deductible),[77] fines and penalties, and expenditures that must be capitalized. Business-related entertainment expenses are limited to 0.3 per cent of total sales income or 1 per cent of total operational income.[78] In addition, a deduction for 'interest on capital' is denied.[79]

The regulations provide a set of rules for computing the taxable income of a service joint venture, a commercial joint venture and an industrial joint venture.[80] Although these rules are complicated, the calculation of taxable income appears to be consistent with Western practices and concepts.

Under the regulations, inventory is computed at cost.[81] The regulations specifically list three computational methods — first-in, first-out (FIFO), shifting average and weighted average — but leave open the possibility of using other methods.[82]

The Joint Venture Law provides that the net profit of a joint venture can be distributed after the joint venture income tax is paid and after payments are made into the venture's reserve funds, bonus and welfare funds, and expansion funds.[83] Chinese sources have confirmed that payments made *into* these funds are not currently deductible,[84] a position that is consistent with the practice of the United States and other countries. Less understandable is the position of the Ministry of Finance that payments subsequently made *out of* these funds are also not deductible for tax purposes, notwithstanding that expenditures for the same purposes, for instance worker bonuses, made out of general joint venture funds, *are* deductible.[85]

iii. Rates

The JVITL provides for a basic 30 per cent tax rate.[86] In addition, a local surtax of 10 per cent of the tax paid is levied for use by the local treasuries, bringing the total tax rate, assuming no reductions, to 33 per cent.[87] 'On account of special circumstances', the surtax can be eliminated or reduced by the government of the province, municipality or autonomous region in which the joint venture is located.[88]

A tax of 10 per cent is levied on a foreign participant that remits its share of profits out of China.[89] Presumably, China intends to follow the practice of many countries, including the United States,[90] of levying a tax on the payment of dividends to foreign shareholders. One significant distinction, however, is that the Chinese 10 per cent tax applies only to profits remitted out of China. Accordingly, a dividend that is reinvested within China without first being remitted outside China will be free of the 10 per cent tax.[91]

The JVITL provides for a number of possible rate reductions or exemptions. Implementing an incentive referred to in the Joint Venture Law,[92] the JVITL allows a newly established joint venture that is scheduled to operate for a period of ten years or more to apply for a full exemption from tax in its first profit-making year and a 50 per cent reduction in the following two years.[93] These periods have subsequently been extended to two years of exemption and three subsequent years of 50 per cent reduction.[94] The first profit-making year is defined as the year in which a joint venture begins to make a profit after taking into account any loss carry-overs.[95] Under the Joint Venture Law, these exemptions and reductions are limited to a joint venture 'equipped with up-to-date technology by world standards'.[96] This requirement is not found in the JVITL, but it is unclear whether its absence signals any change in policy. In any event, most if not all of the joint ventures operating in China today appear to be enjoying this tax exemption and reduction scheme.

The JVITL implements another tax incentive referred to in the Joint Venture Law[97] by allowing a participant that reinvests in China[98] for at least five consecutive years its share of profits from a joint venture to obtain, upon approval by the tax authorities, a refund of 40 per cent of the income tax paid on the reinvested funds.[99] The refund is apparently granted upon the taxpayer's stated intent to reinvest for the five-year period; if the funds are withdrawn before the end of the period the taxpayer must pay back the refunded tax.[100] The tax refund, which is paid to the reinvesting participant and not to the joint venture, does not include the local surtax.[101]

As the final step in the calculation of its tax liability, a joint venture may take a credit for income taxes paid abroad on income earned outside China. The credit cannot exceed the Chinese tax payable on the income earned abroad.[102]

D. The Foreign Enterprise Income Tax Law

The Foreign Enterprise Income Tax Law (FEITL), effective as of 1 January 1982,[103] fills a major gap in the Chinese tax structure. Before the FEITL's adoption, the only tax law of apparent applicability to foreign investment was the 1980 JVITL. The JVITL, however, covers only equity joint ventures, which constitute a relatively small part of business activity in China. A much greater proportion of foreign investment activity takes the form of non-equity or 'contractual' joint ventures, sometimes known as co-operative production ventures. The JVITL does not apply to this mode of investment, which is not conducted through a joint venture corporation.[104] Until the FEITL was adopted, the tax consequences of non-equity joint ventures had been unclear.

The FEITL divides taxpayers into two basic categories: foreign companies, enterprises, and other economic organizations that have 'establishments'[105] in China, and those which do not. Taxpayers that have establishments are generally taxed on their net income at progressive rates. Taxpayers that do not have establishments are taxed on certain categories of Chinese source income — for example, interest, rent, and fees for the use of proprietary rights[106] — at a flat rate of 20 per cent which is levied on the gross amount of the income and is withheld by the payor.[107] In broad outline, this approach is similar to that adopted by many other countries.

i. Definition of Establishment

The significant difference in tax treatment between a progressive tax on net income and a 20 per cent flat tax on gross income makes it critical for a foreign company to determine whether it has an 'establishment'. The FEITL and its regulations provide that 'establishments' refer to organizations, sites, or business agents engaging in production or business operations either independently or in co-operative production or joint business operations with Chinese enterprises. 'Organizations' include management organizations, branches, and representative offices. 'Sites' include factories, sites where natural resources are being exploited and sites where construction, installation, assembly, exploration, and other projects are undertaken.[108]

The tax administration's current administrative posture suggests that 'establishment' will not be interpreted as broadly as the statute and regulations might seem to allow, but rather will be interpreted in a manner akin to the concept of a 'permanent establishment' commonly embodied in tax treaties. In other words, the Chinese will require a high order of presence or activity in China before concluding that an 'establishment' exists. For example, representative offices that are characterized as engaged in information-gathering or liaison activities,[109] or independent agents[110] are unlikely to be regarded as 'establishments', a position in accord with that of many tax treaties.

ii. Tax Base

Taxpayers with establishments in China are taxed on their income from 'production, business operations, and other sources'.[111] The definitions of these types of income basically parallel those in the JVITL.[112]

Although the law and regulations clearly intend to reach a broad range of income, they fail to answer a critical question: will foreign companies with establishments be taxable on their worldwide income or just on their Chinese-source income? Chinese tax officials have indicated that only Chinese-source income is taxable under the FEITL,[113] a position that in principle is consistent with international practice. The FEITL is silent, however, on the source rules applicable to significant categories of income. While source rules are included for dividends, interest, rentals, and technology fees earned by companies without establishments in China,[114] no rules are provided for such major categories as sales or manufacturing income of companies with Chinese establishments.[115]

Provisions in the FEITL governing the definition and calculation of taxable income generally follow the JVITL. The list of non-deductible expenditures[116] substantially overlaps that in the JVITL.[117] Particularly noteworthy is the FEITL's incorporation of the JVITL's denial of a deduction for 'interest on capital'.[118] The FEITL Regulations provide at least some limitation on the interpretation of this highly controversial provision by allowing the deduction of 'reasonable' interest on loans deemed by the local tax authorities to be 'normal loans'.[119] While no definitive interpretations of 'reasonable' and 'normal' yet exist, the regulations suggest, at the least, that 'interest on capital' will not be read to deny a deduction for all interest paid.[120]

The FEITL prohibits a deduction of fees paid by a foreign company to its head office for the use of proprietary rights.[121] This prohibition is presumably intended to prevent foreign companies from avoiding tax in China by reducing their income through transactions that may lack economic substance. The effect of this provision is tempered, however, by the allowance of deductions for payments to the head office for overhead and administrative expenses attributable to the Chinese establishment and for payments for services performed by the head office for the establishment provided these payments are properly documented and approved by the local tax authorities.[122] Little experience exists to determine the degree of vigilance the Chinese will exert in monitoring these fees, which in many cases could be substituted for the above-mentioned prohibited payments as a means of reducing taxable income in China.

The depreciation and amortization provisions of the FEITL are generally similar to those of the JVITL.[123] Special rules are provided for companies in offshore petroleum and coal projects — most notably, a provision that fixed assets involved in the development and subsequent stages of these projects may be depreciated in a 'composite' manner over at least six years.[124]

A provision in the FEITL not found in the JVITL involves taxpayers who cannot provide acceptable documentation of their costs and expenses. In these situations, the local tax authorities may assess taxes by imputing a 'normal' rate of profit based on that of other similar businesses. For companies engaged in trade, the imputed profit rate is applied to net sales; for other companies, it is applied to gross business income.[125] At present, it is unclear how the Chinese will determine which businesses are similar enough to the taxpayer's to serve as a norm.[126]

iii. Rates

The tax rates for foreign companies with establishments in China range from 20 per cent on the portion of annual income up to RMB 250,000 to 40 per cent on income over RMB 1 million.[127] In addition, the localities levy a tax of 10 per cent, not on the amount of the national income tax paid, as under the JVITL, but rather on the amount of taxable income.[128] Consequently, the total tax rates range from 30 per cent to 50 per cent, though a reduction in or exemption from the local tax may be available for certain enterprises.[129]

The FEITL's provisions on tax exemptions and reductions are generally more restrictive than those of the JVITL. Under the JVITL, equity joint ventures are entitled to apply for exemptions and reductions provided only that they are scheduled to operate for at least ten years. By comparison, the FEITL not only incorporates the ten-year rule, but also requires that a foreign company seeking an exemption for the first profit-making year and a reduction for the following two years[130] be engaged in certain types of 'low-profit' operations.[131] Whereas most equity joint ventures have received tax holidays and rate reductions, few foreign companies are likely to engage in the types of 'low-profit' operations that qualify for tax preferences under the FEITL.[132]

In addition, because non-equity projects are often of a shorter duration than equity joint ventures, many taxpayers will not satisfy the FEITL's ten-year requirement.

iv. Taxpayers without Establishments

Foreign companies without establishments in China are taxable only on their Chinese-source dividends, interest, rentals, fees for the use of proprietary rights, and 'other' income as determined by the Ministry of Finance.[133] These categories of income are taxed under the FEITL at a flat 20 per cent rate and no deductions or credits are allowed for any expenses incurred in the generation of the income.[134]

a. Dividends

Dividends are from Chinese sources if they are obtained from or represent profits shared with enterprises in China.[135] Although this definition could be read to cover dividends paid by joint venture corporations and perhaps dividends paid by non-Chinese corporations with Chinese-source income, Chinese officials have indicated that neither of these situations are subject to the FEITL.[136] In the first case, dividends paid by joint venture corporations are not subject to the FEITL, presumably because their taxation is governed exclusively by the JVITL.[137] In the second case, involving, for example, a dividend paid by a United States corporation with a Chinese establishment, administrative considerations weigh heavily toward exclusion of the income from the FEITL.[138] Because these cases describe most, if not all, of the likely situations in which Chinese-source dividends are paid to foreign companies, the 20 per cent tax on dividends will at present affect few foreign companies.

b. Interest

Of more immediate relevance is the withholding tax on interest 'gained from China' from deposits, loans and securities as well as other interest 'such as that from payments made for others and deferred payments'.[139] Exemption from this tax is available to foreign banks lending to China's various state banks and to certain of China's 'trust and investment corporations'[140] at a 'preferential rate'.[141] Although the term 'preferential rate' is defined in the FEITL Regulations only to mean a rate at least 10 per cent below the prevailing international financial market rate,[142] subsequent Ministry of Finance regulations[143] have provided for a number of other situations in which foreign banks may, upon the approval of the local tax organs, be exempted from the withholding tax. These include loans made to China's state banks or trust and investment companies at the 'international interbank rate for call funds', a term that includes the LIBOR rate or similar interbank rate. An exemption, however, may also be available for loans at up to 0.5 per cent above the interbank rate.[144] Loans to the China National Offshore Oil Corporation, the body responsible for the co-operative offshore oil exploration and development projects with foreign oil companies, may also, under certain circumstances, be exempted from the withholding tax.[145]

In response to the impact that the FEITL's 20 per cent withholding tax was apparently having on lending to China, the rate was reduced to 10 per cent for loan contracts signed between 1983 and 1985.[146] Contracts signed and approved before 1 January 1983, the effective date of the regulation reducing the rate, remain subject to the then effective tax provisions for the life of the contract.[147]

c. Rentals

Also subject to the FEITL withholding tax is income derived from the rental of property for use in China.[148] Chinese entities are becoming increasingly interested in leasing foreign capital equipment, which among other advantages may enable them to avoid some of the foreign exchange and import licence regulations that hamper their outright purchase of this type of equipment.[149] While rental payments are generally taxable to the foreign lessor at 20 per cent under the FEITL withholding tax,[150] special tax treatment applies to 'lease-sale' or 'hire-purchase' transactions. In these transactions, a leasing company rents a piece of equipment to the Chinese with ownership ultimately passing to the Chinese. Hence, in contrast to an actual 'rental' transaction, the payments made by the Chinese in a 'lease-sale' arrangement contain a portion attributable to the 'principal', or purchase price, of the equipment. These payments also include a component that may be characterized by the parties as a 'lease' fee but is actually interest, usually imposed at a rate that represents the leasing company's cost of funds it borrowed to obtain the equipment in question. Finally, payments made to the leasing company also include a service charge or spread imposed by the leasing company over its own cost of funds, that is over the interest component mentioned above.

Under a 1983 tax regulation, the portion of the payments attributable to the purchase price is exempt from tax.[151] In addition, the regulation reduces the tax on the interest component in these lease-sale transactions to 10 per cent for transactions made between 1983 and 1985, and provides for total exemption of tax for interest in lease-sales under certain circumstances.[152] The service charge or spread imposed by the leasing company is taxable, but at a reduced rate of 10 per cent.[153]

d. Fees for the Use of Proprietary Rights

Perhaps the most significant targets of the FEITL withholding tax are what the Chinese term 'fees for the use in China of proprietary rights', a concept encompassing royalties or licence fees for the use in China of patented or other proprietary technology, trade marks and copyrights.[154] In addition, fees for technical training,[155] technical services and technical documentation provided by a foreign company to an entity in China are considered to fall within this category of income.[156] Income from computer software — whether 'sold' or 'licensed' — may also be taxed under this rubric.[157]

Fees received by foreign companies for such services as consultation with Chinese enterprises on management methods and assistance in performing feasibility studies, fees for technical seminars, and fees for the design of construction sites and equipment are not taxable to the extent that they do not involve the transfer of the right to the use of proprietary technology.[158]

Partly in response to significant foreign pressure, especially from companies whose home countries allow no foreign tax credit, the Ministry of Finance has provided for the possibility, with the approval of the tax authorities,[159] of a reduction in the withholding tax to 10 per cent for certain technology-related fees, and total exemption from the tax if the technology is 'advanced' and offered on 'preferential' terms.[160] The categories eligible for this special tax treatment include nuclear technology, certain types of computer technology, and technology used in agriculture, energy exploration and conservation.[161]

III. The Tax Consequences of Various Forms of Business Activity

A foreign company contemplating business with China can choose from a variety of approaches not dissimilar from those existing in other countries. At one end of the spectrum, a foreign company can simply export its goods or technology to China, either through an outright sale, or through a licensing or leasing arrangement. In conjunction with these activities, some technical training or ancillary support services might be provided to the Chinese customer. At the other end of the spectrum, a company seeking a more substantial involvement can enter into a compensation trade agreement, a co-operative venture, or an equity joint venture.

A company may decide that in order to explore and pursue business opportunities in China, it needs a permanent presence in the country. Having made this decision, a company can choose several approaches — retaining one of the many trading or consulting firms with offices in Beijing and other major Chinese cities to represent its interests, appointing an exclusive agent, or establishing a representative office in China.

Numerous factors will influence how a foreign company will structure its business activities in China. Many of these factors will involve internal company policy with respect to doing business abroad and the degree of commitment and involvement the company seeks with China. In addition, China's expanding system of laws and regulations governing foreign business must be considered, with taxation becoming an increasingly prominent factor.

As China's tax structure for foreign business becomes more complex, the tax ramifications of different forms of business become more significant. For instance, under the current Chinese approach, mere intermittent sales to China will not subject a foreign company's income to taxation. If, however, the foreign company also provides installation, training, or other services at the end-user's site over a period of time, the company may be creating an 'establishment', subjecting its service income to the progressive foreign enterprise income tax.[162] If its activities are not sufficient to create an establishment, the withholding tax may instead apply on some of the technical service income.[163] The various forms of joint Chinese-foreign business associations also result in different treatment under China's income and other tax laws.

The following sections explore on a transactional basis the tax consequences of several common forms of business activity in China. Specifically discussed are representative offices and business agents, consignment sales and service centres, compensation trade, co-operative ventures, contracted projects, and equity joint ventures.

A. Representative Offices and Business Agents

The most common form of foreign business presence in China currently is the 'representative office' (*daibiao jigou*), established and registered under a 1980 regulation.[164] With the exception of a few bank branches established before 1949, most foreign companies with permanent presences in China have 'representative offices'.

Under the FEITL, a representative office can be an 'establishment' for tax purposes only if it engages in 'production or business operations'.[165] Chinese tax officials have repeatedly stated that they do not view the representative offices of foreign industrial or manufacturing companies as 'operating' establishments, but rather see them as liaison centres, engaging in market development, exploration of business opportunities, and the forging of contacts in China on behalf of their home offices. The fact that many of these offices engage in actual business negotiations and even sign contracts in the name of their home companies does not, at least under current Chinese thinking,[166] appear to change the tax analysis, despite the contrary impression that certain tax and trade officials have given to some foreign businessmen.[167] Consequently, industrial or manufacturing companies having only a representative office in China have been treated as companies without Chinese establishments and are taxed under the FEITL's withholding tax rather than being taxed on a net basis at progressive rates.[168]

Chinese tax officials have indicated, however, that they regard differently the offices of foreign service companies — consultants, accountants, trading companies, and the like. Although these offices are all registered as 'representative offices' under the same regulations as industrial companies, in addition to performing general liaison and information services for their own companies, they provide professional services for outside clients on a compensated basis. Although the fees for these services are usually paid to the foreign firm outside China and not to the representative office itself, Chinese tax officials have stated that these fees should in principle be treated as those of an operating establishment and taxed accordingly under the FEITL progressive tax.[169] The extent to which this interpretation is being implemented is unclear.

This interpretation would presumably require that these offices also pay the industrial and commercial tax on their service income.[170] In any event, whether or not a representative office is treated as an FEITL establishment, it pays the industrial and commercial tax, as well as import duties, on the importation of goods such as office equipment.[171]

Also treated as a separate category for tax purposes are foreign banks with representative offices in China. As a general matter, such offices are not considered as operating business establishments, and until recently, foreign banks were subject exclusively to the FEITL's gross withholding tax. Recently, however, in an attempt to respond to the request of banks that they be allowed to account for at least some of their business expenses in China rather than paying tax on a gross basis, the Ministry of Finance has adopted a special regulation. Under this regulation, if a loan agreement is signed 'directly' with a Chinese entity by the representative office of a foreign bank, the Chinese will use an imputed profit rate, provisionally fixed at 15 per cent of the interest income under the agreement, to determine the taxable income, which income will be subject to the FEITL progressive rates.[172] The regulation providing for this treatment appears to anticipate the adjustment of this imputed rate if necessary to reflect more accurately a bank's costs and expenses. Actual branches of foreign banks in China, as opposed to representative offices, are considered fully-fledged 'operating establishments' and are taxed on their net income at the progressive rates. They are also subject to the CICTA.[173]

Some companies do business in China not through their own representative offices but through one of the many foreign trading companies or consulting firms that have set up representative offices in China's major cities. As indicated above, these trading or consulting firms are taxable on the commissions and other fees generated by their representative offices. More uncertainty exists regarding the clients of these firms. Under a possible interpretation of the FEITL, any foreign company transacting business through another firm operating in China could be deemed to have 'set up a business agent in China',[174] thereby having an establishment that is taxable on its Chinese-source income. Chinese tax officials, however, have expressed their intention to incorporate into the FEITL the common distinction between independent and dependent agents.[175] If this distinction is adopted, a foreign company's use of a trading or other firm that also acts for other companies will not create an establishment for the purposes of the FEITL. The appointment, on the other hand, of an agent that acts exclusively for the foreign company may create an establishment and subject the foreign company to taxation on its Chinese net income. This issue awaits more practical experience before any conclusions can be drawn.

B. Consignment Sales and Service Centres

Foreign companies that sign agreements with Chinese corporations under which the latter sell the foreign company's products on a consignment or agency basis, or under which the Chinese set up a service centre to service and sell parts for the foreign company's machinery in China, may be subject to tax under the FEITL, the CICTA, or under both. A recent Ministry of Finance tax notice[176] provides that in cases where an independent place of business is established by a Chinese entity with its sole or primary function being the sale of a foreign company's products, or the maintenance or sale of parts for a foreign company's machinery, the foreign company will be subject to the FEITL establishment tax on any 'profit' it earns from the service centre[177] and subject to the CICTA on its 'business income'.[178]

If, on the other hand, no place of business is specially established but a Chinese corporation simply sells a foreign company's goods on a consignment or agency basis, the latter will not be subject to the FEITL. Depending on the nature of the consignment or agency arrangement, the foreign company may be subject to the CICTA. If the Chinese do not actually purchase the goods but simply take delivery and sell them at a price set by the foreign company, or at a mutually agreed price — the parties sharing the sales proceeds according to an agreed ratio — the foreign company will be subject to the CICTA on its share of the sales proceeds.[179] If, on the other hand, the Chinese first import the goods from the foreign company and resell them at their own price, the foreign company will be exempt from the CICTA.[180]

C. Compensation Trade

In a typical compensation trade, or counter-trade, project, a foreign company provides machinery, equipment or technology to a Chinese entity and receives payment in kind. The in-kind payment can consist of goods produced with the transferred assets, other goods, or some combination of the two. The foreign company usually resells these goods on the international market or in its home market.

Compensation trade can be broadly characterized in two ways. The Chinese sometimes describe compensation trade as a loan transaction: the foreign company 'lends' the machinery or equipment to the Chinese unit and the loan is repaid in kind. Under this interpretation, the repayments of goods consist of both principal and interest. Alternatively, compensation trade can be viewed as an instalment sale of the machinery or equipment, or what the Chinese term a 'deferred payment' arrangement.[181] Under this interpretation, each in-kind payment represents a partial payment of the purchase price and an interest component.[182] The foreign company may also provide some training or technical services together with equipment. In this case, a portion of the in-kind payment would be payment for these services. Also, the portion of the product payment attributable to any technology transferred may be viewed as a licence fee, or, in the Chinese terminology, a 'fee for the use of proprietary rights'.[183]

The tax consequences of compensation trade depend upon which interpretation is adopted, upon whether the foreign company is deemed to have an establishment in China, and upon the applicable source rules. For example, if the instalment sale characterization were adopted, and if the foreign company were deemed to have an establishment in China, then at the least, the interest component inherent in the in-kind payment would presumably be taxable on a net basis at progressive rates, as would any technology fees. Moreover, if the sale of the machinery and equipment generated Chinese-source income — an unknown question at present because the relevant source rules have not been formulated — any gain on the sale would also be taxable.[184] If the foreign company were not deemed to have an establishment, only the interest component and any technology or service fees would be taxable on a withholding basis. The gain on the sale, even if it were Chinese-source income, would not be taxable under the FEITL's withholding tax because it would not be one of the categories of income subject to that tax.[185]

If the loan characterization were adopted, and if the foreigner were deemed to have an establishment in China, the interest component inherent in the in-kind payment would again be taxable on a net basis at progressive rates, as would any technology fees. If the foreigner were actually to receive back the equipment or machinery at the end of the loan, no further tax consequences would result. Usually, however, the foreign company does not receive back the actual assets that were lent; instead, it receives back the value of such assets in kind. If the lent assets themselves are not returned, the putative loan is similar to an instalment sale. The loan of an asset that is repaid in kind would appear to constitute a realization under generally accepted principles of taxation. If the gain realized were treated as Chinese-source income, it could be taxed on a net basis at the FEITL's progressive rates. If the loan characterization were adopted but the foreigner were not deemed to have an establishment in China, the interest component and technology or service fees would be taxable on a gross withholding basis.

A critical element in the tax treatment of compensation trade is whether the foreign company is deemed to have an establishment. Although the FEITL does not refer explicitly to compensation trade arrangements, these projects could fall within the 'site' category of the definition of 'establishment'.[186] The Chinese, however, have stated that they do not view compensation trade arrangements as creating an establishment.[187] Therefore, until recently, foreign companies were taxed on the part of the in-kind payments that represented payments of interest, technology, or service fees under the 20 per cent gross withholding tax. The amount of this tax was withheld in kind.[188]

Subsequently, however, both for administrative reasons and to encourage this type of business, the Chinese have decided to allow a provisional exemption from the FEITL withholding tax, with the approval of the tax authorities, for both interest and leasing fees paid in kind.[189] However, this exemption only applies if both the principal and interest in a compensation trade arrangement are paid in kind. If the interest is paid in kind but the principal is paid with foreign exchange, the interest remains subject to the withholding tax.[190] This latter situation is not common in compensation trade transactions.

No explicit exemption has been provided from the FEITL withholding tax for technology service fees paid in kind, although the 1983 regulations reducing or eliminating the taxation of technology and related service fees in certain circumstances will benefit many companies engaged in compensation trade.[191] Thus, at least for the present, foreign companies engaging in compensation trade and related projects will in most cases be exempt from Chinese income taxation.

The Chinese party in compensation trade is subject to the industrial and commercial tax, both on the importation of the equipment and on the sale of any of the finished goods that are not part of the payback to the foreigner.[192] The products received by the foreign party in a compensation trade transaction or the income from their resale could conceivably be subject to the CICTA. However, the CICTA has not been applied to these cases. The tax authorities apparently consider that compensation trade is not, as regards the foreign participant, 'business conducted by an establishment within China'.[193]

D. Co-operative Ventures

In co-operative ventures, also known as non-equity or 'contractual' joint ventures or co-production projects, the Chinese and foreign parties contribute resources or technology and share profits according to a contractual formula. In some cases, the profits are paid in kind with the goods produced by the venture. The Chinese and foreign parties calculate and pay tax separately,[194] the Chinese under relevant domestic tax legislation,[195] the foreign party under the FEITL and other relevant tax laws.

Foreign companies engaging in co-operative ventures have an establishment in China and are taxable under the FEITL on their Chinese-source net income at progressive rates.[196] Foreign companies receiving their profits in kind calculate their gross income 'based on the sales price to a third party or by reference to the prevailing market price of the goods in question'.[197] The 'market price' refers to the current sales price in China of the goods, but this price will be used only if no actual third-party sale takes place.[198]

The foreign participant in a co-operative venture that imports items in connection with its participation is generally subject to the CICTA. Special provisions have been made allowing exemption for certain items imported by foreign companies participating in co-operative petroleum projects, for 'advanced' equipment unobtainable in China imported for co-operative ventures in a wide range of fields including energy, transport, agriculture and scientific research, and for materials and parts imported for the purpose of processing for export.[199] Reduction or exemption may also be available for various imports in connection with co-operative hotel construction projects.[200]

The CICTA is imposed on the sale of products produced by co-operative ventures under the normal rules. If the foreign party receives its profits from the venture in kind, the consolidated tax is applied to the sales proceeds if the products are sold from or within China. If the foreign company takes its in-kind share out of China for later resale in its home market or on the international market, it is unclear whether the Chinese will assess the consolidated tax in kind or use a 'prevailing market price' theory such as that used for the purposes of the FEITL and collect the tax in cash.[201]

The Chinese provide for reductions in or exemptions from the industrial and commercial tax for export products of co-operative ventures, upon application to the tax authorities, if paying the tax would cause 'difficulties'.[202] It is unclear whether this favourable treatment would be available only to the Chinese participant on its share of export proceeds or also to the foreign participant. Foreign companies paying the industrial and commercial tax on sales or service income may in any event deduct the tax paid in computing their taxable income for the purposes of the FEITL.[203]

E. Contracted Projects

A foreign company whose business activity consists of what the Chinese call a 'contracted project' such as a construction, installation, assembly or other service project is deemed to have an 'establishment' in China by virtue of the project 'site', and is therefore taxable under the FEITL on its Chinese-source net income at progressive rates.[204]

The definition of an installation or site could encompass three situations that are common in China. The first includes the case of a foreign company that sells equipment to a Chinese entity and then sends employees to the customer's site for a period of time to provide ancillary installation, construction, training, or related services. The second situation involves a foreign company that contracts with a Chinese entity for a construction project, seismic survey, or other service project, with perhaps the incidental sale of some machinery or equipment. This situation includes the foreign companies hired to perform exploration and other work for China's offshore oil development projects. The third situation covers a foreign company that provides on-site installation, training, or other technical services in conjunction with a transfer of technology.

The first situation has been explicitly exempted from establishment tax treatment until 1990.[205] In this situation, even if establishment treatment were applied after 1990, only the service income and not the sales income would be taxable, since income from the sale of goods or equipment to China by a foreign company is not regarded as China-source income.[206] Also exempted from establishment tax treatment until 1990 is the on-site provision of technical instruction, consultation and other technical services to Chinese enterprises for the reform of their existing technology.[207] In the case of a foreign company's on-site installation and the provision of technical services in connection with a transfer of new technology, the third situation described above, the Chinese seem thus far also to be leaning against establishment treatment.[208]

The only situation described above to which establishment tax treatment has thus far been applied is the second one — that of foreign companies contracting for a service project in China. Companies in this situation may pay tax on the basis of their actual net income, calculated in accordance with the normal FEITL rules.[209] However, for companies engaging in contracted projects that are unable adequately to substantiate their costs and expenses, the Chinese have made available a system of taxation under which the FEITL rates are applied to a deemed profit of 10 per cent of total receipts from a project.[210]

The Chinese have not set a minimum period within which a contracted project can be completed without creating an establishment for tax purposes. The FEITL Regulations provide only that foreign enterprises that have operated in China for less than one year are taxable on the income earned during the actual period of operation.[211] In addition, the deemed profit tax system mentioned above is particularly intended to meet the needs of companies involved in 'relatively short' projects,[212] suggesting that no minimum period is contemplated for tax purposes. Chinese tax officials, however, have stated that they intend to set a minimum period within which a project can be completed without creating an establishment, an approach used by some other countries and often incorporated into tax treaties.[213]

Service income earned by foreign companies from contracted projects in China is subject to the CICTA. The Chinese have provided the same exemptions under the CICTA, valid until 1990, as those granted under the FEITL for service income earned in connection with equipment sales and in connection with technology reform projects for Chinese enterprises.[214] Companies such as the petroleum service subcontractors, taxable on the establishment basis under the FEITL, pay the CICTA and may deduct the latter tax in calculating taxable income under the FEITL.[215] Although the CICTA is normally imposed on gross receipts,[216] a recent regulation allows the deduction of certain expenses by companies engaged in contracted projects, for CICTA as well as FEITL purposes.[217] These include payments to a Chinese or foreign business to which part of the project work is subcontracted,[218] amounts for the purchase of equipment outside China for purposes of the project, and amounts for data analysis and processing done outside China.[219]

F. Equity Joint Ventures

As discussed in Part II, equity joint ventures are taxed on their income under the JVITL. Until recently they had been subject to the CICTA. The Chinese have now apparently decided to apply the domestic 1972 Industrial and Commercial Tax Act to equity joint ventures,[220] at least where its rates are lower than those of the CICTA.[221] Where the CICTA rates are lower than those of the 1972 Act, equity joint ventures will be able to enjoy the CICTA rates.[222]

Various exemptions from the industrial and commercial tax as applied to imports are available to equity joint ventures. Machinery, equipment, parts and other materials imported under a joint venture contract as part of the foreign party's capital contribution to the venture are exempt from the industrial and commercial tax, as well as from customs duties.[223] A joint venture that imports equipment or machinery, parts or other materials with funds within the total amount of investment of a joint venture is exempt from the industrial and commercial tax and customs duties,[224] as is a venture that, with the authorization of the same authorities that approved the joint venture, imports with additional capital machinery, equipment, parts and other materials whose production and supply cannot be guaranteed in China.[225] Also free from the industrial and commercial tax and customs duties are raw materials, auxiliary materials, components, parts and packaging materials imported by a joint venture for the production of export products.[226] To the extent any items imported tax free are diverted for sale in China or incorporated into products for sale in China, taxes will be imposed as appropriate.[227]

Export sales are treated like any other 'sale' for purposes of the industrial and commercial tax.[228] Consequently, a joint venture that exports its products is in principle subject to the tax. However, joint ventures may be exempted from the tax on exports, with the approval of the Ministry of Finance.[229] In addition, joint ventures that 'have difficulty' at the beginning of their operations paying tax on products produced for domestic sale may apply for a reduction in or exemption from the industrial and commercial tax for a fixed period.[230]

Equity joint ventures are subject to the Provisional Urban Real Estate Tax Act (PURETA),[231] which is imposed on the beneficial owners of land and buildings located in cities. Only the buildings tax of the PURETA is applied to joint ventures; the land tax does not apply.[232] If the Chinese participant in a joint venture contributes its right to the use of a building as part of its capital contribution to the venture, the joint venture is the taxpayer under the PURETA.[233] If, on the other hand, the joint venture rents buildings from the local government, the lessor will remain the taxpayer.[234]

IV. Conclusion

Now that the major elements of the tax structure for foreign business are in place, Chinese officials can turn their attention to resolving ambiguities, filling lacunae, and responding to the myriad of situations and complexities unanticipated when the statutory framework was being constructed — tasks faced by tax administrators everywhere. These further developments will occur against a backdrop of the highly significant changes unfolding on China's domestic tax front. These changes include the imposition of a corporate income tax on state enterprises that had previously turned all their profits over to the state,[235] and the trial use of a value-added tax to correct defects in the industrial and commercial tax.[236]

These domestic experiments seem designed to further a major goal — the use of taxation as an 'economic lever' that will assure the state treasury an appropriate share of an enterprise's income while encouraging both initiative and productivity. To a large extent, the evolution of the tax system for foreign business reflects this same philosophy. The Chinese have attempted to balance their right as a sovereign nation to participate in the gains accruing to foreign companies with the need to encourage foreigners to provide capital and technology. The result thus far is a generally conventional tax system.

Foreign businessmen are of course heartened by these developments, but Third World countries might be disappointed. Unlike many other developing countries, China is in a position to innovate and formulate alternative approaches to the traditional patterns of international taxation — patterns that have evolved in the context of the developed countries and should not be imported indiscriminately by a developing country.[237]

But neither the international business community nor the Third World should pass final judgment on China's tax structure. The adoption of a generally orthodox approach probably results more from inexperience than from a decision not to innovate. As tax officials gain more experience and confidence, they are likely to develop techniques and approaches that deviate from the mainstream and fulfill the expectations of many Third World leaders that China will emerge as an intellectual leader in tax issues. In every area of its contemporary legal development, China stresses the importance of 'walking on two legs' and 'letting foreign things serve China'. Taxation should prove to be no exception.

Notes

1. For detailed descriptions of the Chinese tax system, see R. Pomp, T. Gelatt and S. Surrey, 'The Evolving Tax System of the People's Republic of China', *Texas International Law Journal,* Vol. 16, No. 11 (1981), pp. 12–40, and sources cited therein, in note 7, p. 13.

2. The Individual Income Tax Law of the People's Republic of China, passed by the Third Session of the Fifth National People's Congress on 10 September 1980 (hereafter cited as the IITL); and Detailed Rules and Regulations for the Implementation of the Individual Income Tax Law of the People's Republic of China, approved by the State Council on 10 December 1980 and promulgated by the Ministry of Finance on 14 December 1980 (hereafter cited as the IITL Regulations).

3. The Income Tax Law of the People's Republic of China Concerning Joint Ventures Using Chinese and Foreign Investment, passed by the Third Session of the Fifth National People's Congress on 10 September 1980 (hereafter cited as the JVITL); and Detailed Rules and Regulations for the Implementation of the Income

Tax Law of the People's Republic of China Concerning Joint Ventures Using Chinese and Foreign Investment, approved by the State Council on 10 December 1980 and promulgated by the Ministry of Finance on 14 December 1980 (hereafter cited as the JVITL Regulations).

4. The Income Tax Law of the People's Republic of China Concerning Foreign Enterprises, passed by the Fourth Session of the Fifth National People's Congress on 13 December 1981 (hereafter cited as the FEITL); and Detailed Rules and Regulations for the Implementation of the Income Tax Law of the People's Republic of China Concerning Foreign Enterprises, approved by the State Council on 17 February 1982 and promulgated by the Ministry of Finance on 21 February 1982 (hereafter cited as the FEITL Regulations).

5. A Notice issued by the State Council provides that in the case of contractual provisions, signed and approved by the 'state organs in charge' before the promulgation of the IITL, 'granting preferential treatment as regards the tax burden on income of individuals, the matter is to be carried out in accordance with the originally fixed provisions of the contract.' This treatment will only be valid for the initial term of the contract in question; subsequent extensions of the contract will be subject to the IITL without exception. Notice of the State Council Regarding Questions of the Levy of Taxation on Chinese-Foreign Joint Venture and Co-operative Projects, 21 September 1982, Art. 3 (hereafter cited as the State Council Notice), in *Zhonghua Renmin Gongheguo Guowuyuan Gongbao* (*People's Republic of China State Council Gazette*) (1982), pp. 695 and 696 (hereafter cited as the *State Council Gazette*). See also [Document] Regarding the Question of Levy and Exemption of Taxation on Wages and Salaries of Technical Personnel Sent to China to Work by Foreign Businesses in Order to Perform Contracts Signed Before the Promulgation of the [Individual Income] Tax Law, 20 November 1980 (hereafter cited as the Wage and Salary Document), in Zhonghua Renmin Gongheguo Caizheng Bu Shuiwu Zongju (People's Republic of China Ministry of Finance General Bureau of Taxation), *Zhongguo Duiwai Shuiwu Shouce (Handbook of China's Foreign Taxation)*, Vol. I (1983), pp. 70–2 (hereafter cited as the *Handbook*). All documents in the *Handbook* are official documents of the Ministry of Finance. Under this Document and the State Council Notice, contractual provisions stipulating that the Chinese party agrees to pay any Chinese taxes, including individual income taxes, imposed on the foreign party as a result of the contract, remain valid for the initial term of the contract.

6. IITL, Art. 1, para. 2, note 2 above.

7. IITL Regulations, Art. 5(1), note 2 above. Our italics.

8. IITL Regulations, Art. 5(1), note 2 above. The term 'employer outside of China' refers to an entity that is not taxed in China on its net income and therefore cannot deduct the wages in question from its gross income. T. Gelatt, discussion with Ministry of Finance tax official, 23 February 1983. The term includes foreign companies that have only a representative office in China. See text, pp. 51–2.

9. Notice of the Ministry of Finance Regarding Several Questions of Individual Income Tax, 2 June 1981, in *Zhongguo Jingji Nianjian* (*Almanac of China's Economy*) (1982), p. III–57 (hereafter cited as the *Almanac*). This Notice (hereafter cited as the MOF Notice) formed the basis for a Notice of 30 June 1981 issued to foreign taxpayers by the Beijing Municipal Tax Bureau Foreign Tax Collection Office (FTCO).

10. MOF Notice, Art. 6, note 9 above. The MOF Notice states that the localities may 'leniently' interpret this principle under 'exceptional circumstances'.

11. T. Gelatt, discussion with the FTCO, 8 October 1981.

12. See MOF Notice, Art. 6, note 9 above.

13. MOF Notice, Art. 6, note 9 above. It is unclear why the Notice uses the formulation 'less than ninety days' rather than 'ninety days or less'. See IITL Regulations, Art. 5(1), note 2 above; and text accompanying note 7 above.

14. MOF Notice, Art. 6, note 9 above.

15. T. Gelatt, discussion with the FTCO, 8 October 1981.

16. See IITL, Arts. 11 and 12, note 2 above; and IITL Regulations, Arts. 21 and 22, note 2 above.

17. IITL Regulations, Art. 2, para. 2, note 2 above.

18. IITL, Art. 1, para. 1, note 2 above; and IITL Regulations, Art. 2, para. 1, note 2 above. It is unclear how literally this rule will be interpreted if the 365 days straddle two taxable years. For example, if a foreigner enters China on 2 January of year 1, when will he be considered as having resided for a full 365 days within a taxable year — on 2 January of year 2, or on 1 January of year 3, the latter being the result under a literal interpretation of the rule?

19. IITL Regulations, Art. 3, note 2 above.

20. IITL Regulations, Art. 3, note 2 above.

21. Notice [of the Ministry of Finance] Regarding the Exemption From Tax Reporting and Payment of Individual Income Tax For Income Gained Outside China by Personnel of Foreign Nationality Working in China, 7 March 1983. In effect, the benefit to foreigners of this liberalization will primarily result in the areas of non-wage and salary income, because of the PRC's peculiar interpretation of China-source wages and salaries. See text following note 25 below. Foreigners residing in China and working for Chinese organizations apparently will not benefit from this liberalization on foreign-source income.

22. IITL Regulations, Art. 2, para. 1, note 2 above.

23. MOF Notice, Art. 7, note 9 above. The emphasis of these rules is understandably on when a foreigner obtains or severs his residency; eventually, rules will have to be developed regarding the circumstances under which a Chinese citizen can sever his residency for tax purposes.

24. IITL Regulations, Art. 5, note 2 above.

25. IITL Regulations, Art. 5, note 2 above.

26. See text accompanying notes 7–11 above.

27. IITL, Art. 2(1), note 2 above. Wages and salaries include incentive bonuses (*jiangjin*) and 'year-end extras'. IITL Regulations, Art. 4(1), note 2 above. Because wages and salaries are taxed monthly under a progressive rate schedule, the MOF Notice provides a special 'income-averaging rule' for taxpayers receiving several months' incentive bonuses in one month. If the bonus income results in the recipient's being taxed at a higher marginal tax rate than otherwise, a special calculation is provided. First, the bonus income attributable to services performed in the month in question (rather than the total amount of bonuses received that month) is added to that month's wages and salaries. The marginal tax rate applicable to the resulting amount serves as a ceiling on the marginal rate applicable to all of the bonus income received that month, plus that month's wages and salaries. In other words, while all of the bonus income and wages is taxed in the month received, the marginal tax rate is determined as if only that month's bonus had been received. MOF Notice, Art. 2, note 9 above.

The Chinese regard that portion of technical service fees paid by the Chinese party in technology transfer or equipment sale contracts which represents wages and salaries paid by the foreign party to its personnel performing services in China in connection with the contract as wage and salary income taxable under the IITL to the personnel in question, assuming the personnel do not fall within the ninety-day exemption, see text accompanying notes 7–11 above. Wage and Salary Document, note 5 above; and [Document] On the Question of Levy of Taxation on the Income of Foreign Personnel Sent to China by Foreign Companies to Provide Services, *Handbook*, pp. 73–4, note 5 above. In cases where the foreign company is taxed on its gross income, that portion of the technical service fee which is taxable as wage and salary income to the foreign individuals may also be taxable to the foreign company under the FEITL because there will be no offsetting deduction. See text accompanying notes 156 and 158–161 below.

28. IITL, Art. 2(2), note 2 above. Compensation for personal services includes earnings from such personal services as designing, installation, drafting, medical treatment, law practice, and accounting. IITL Regulations, Art. 4(2), note 2 above. A glossary of IITL terminology specifies that compensation for personal services is limited to fees for the above services paid on a case-by-case basis and does not cover, for instance, the income of lawyers or accountants who are paid on a salary basis. 'Explanation of Terms in the Two Income Tax Laws', *Renmin Ribao (People's Daily)*, 4 September 1980, p. 4. Presumably, the differentiation is similar to that drawn under United States law between independent contractors and employees.

29. IITL, Art. 2(3), note 2 above. These fees include income from the provision and transfer of patent rights, copyrights, proprietary technology and 'other rights'. IITL Regulations, Art. 4(3), note 2 above.

30. IITL, Art. 2(4), note 2 above. Interest includes interest received from deposits, loans and securities. IITL Regulations, Art. 4(4), note 2 above. Some types of interest, such as that on savings deposits in China's state banks, are exempt from taxation. IITL, Art. 4(2), note 2 above.

31. IITL, Art. 2(4), note 2 above. 'Dividends' refers to dividends 'from investment'. IITL Regulations, Art. 4(4), note 2 above.

32. IITL, Art. 2(4), note 2 above. 'Bonuses' (*hongli*) refers to bonuses 'from investment', IITL Regulations, Art. 4(4), note 2 above, and seems to cover a distribution to investors that is not based on shares of stock, such as a distribution to members of a collective.

33. IITL, Art. 2(5), note 2 above. Rental income includes income from the rental of houses, warehouses, machinery and equipment, motor vehicles and boats, and other kinds of property. IITL Regulations, Art. 4(5), note 2 above.

34. IITL Regulations, Art. 4(6), note 2 above. Income from the sale of property is not mentioned in either the IITL or the IITL Regulations and it is unclear whether the Ministry of Finance will classify this income as taxable should it become significant in the future.

35. MOF Notice, Art. 1, note 9 above; see also Notice of the Ministry of Finance Regarding Questions of Individual Income Tax Payment of Foreign Work Personnel in China, 24 October 1980, Art. 5, in *Almanac*, p. III–50, note 9 above; see also Ministry of Finance Supplementary Explanation 2, 7 July 1981, *Handbook*, p. 77, note 5 above. Subsidies received by foreign personnel resident in China during brief trips out of China are considered China-source income and are taxable with that

month's wages and salary. [Document] Regarding the Question of Levy of Taxation on Subsidies Earned by Foreign Taxpayers on Short Trips Out of China, 7 July 1981, in *Handbook*, p. 74, note 5 above. See text accompanying and following note 26 above. Presumably, such subsidies that represent 'company expenses' will not be taxable if adequate proof is available. See accompanying text.

Various other exemptions from taxation are provided, for instance, for prizes and awards for scientific, technological or cultural achievements, and the Ministry of Finance has the power to exempt income other than that specifically listed in the IITL and IITL Regulations. See IITL, Art. 4, note 2 above; and IITL Regulations, Arts. 8–10, note 2 above.

36. The IITL and its Regulations do not specifically cover this issue. The oil tax section of the Ministry of Finance General Bureau of Taxation issued an internal document in early 1983 that apparently leaves to the local tax authorities decisions on implementation and precise formulae for 'grossing up' the employee's income by the tax paid. According to an official of the Ministry of Finance, the basic factor guiding these local decisions will be whether a foreign company has an operating business 'establishment' in China and is paying tax on its net income — for example, oil companies engaged in co-operative exploration and oil subcontractors, see pp. 56–7 below — or whether a foreign company is taxable on its gross income, or is not taxable at all. The principle is apparently that a foreign company that is taxable on its net income will deduct as a business expense taxes paid for employees; therefore, the employees should have to offset this deduction by paying tax on the payment. On the other hand, companies taxable on their gross rather than net income or not taxable at all, for example, those with only representative offices, cannot deduct these payments and thus their employees should not be taxed on them. This approach would explain the implementation of the gross-up system in the offshore oil base of Zhanjiang, where oil companies and other net income taxpayers are involved, but not in Beijing, where mainly representative offices are present. T. Gelatt, discussions with Ministry of Finance tax official and foreign oil company representatives, March 1983. Whether this distinction and approach will be clarified in a public regulation remains to be seen.

37. IITL, Art. 5(1)1, note 2 above. As of 30 January 1984, US$1 equals RMB 2.06.

38. Despite this general position under the IITL, in at least one published case the Ministry of Finance has allowed a resident foreign businessman to deduct alimony payments from his taxable income in China, in addition to his standard RMB 800 deduction. The reasoning behind this decision was that the RMB 800 deduction was intended to cover 'normal living expenses' and not extraordinary expenses such as alimony payments. [Document] Regarding the Question of Whether the American [. . .] May Deduct from his Income Alimony Payments to his Former Wife, *Handbook*, p. 83, note 5 above. The Ministry should expect that it will be called upon to refine its reasoning as taxpayers attempt in the future to deduct a whole range of expenses they claim to be 'extraordinary'.

39. IITL, Art. 3(1), note 2 above, and Schedule of Individual Income Tax Rates.

40. IITL, Art. 3(2), note 2 above. For a discussion of the administrative and enforcement procedures under the IITL, see Pomp, Gelatt and Surrey, pp. 49–51, note 1 above.

41. Consistent with Chinese practice, the term 'industrial and commercial tax' is

used in this chapter to refer generically to the turnover tax applied under both the Consolidated Industrial and Commercial Tax Act (CICTA), see note 45 below and accompanying text, and the Draft Industrial and Commerical Tax Act (1972 Act), see note 46 below and accompanying text. Unless otherwise indicated, the discussion in the text applies to both the CICTA and the 1972 Act.

42. See Guojia Shuishou Jiaocai Bianxie Zu (National Taxation Teaching Materials Editorial Group), *Guojia Shuishou (The National Taxation)* (1983), pp. 31–2 (hereafter cited as the *National Taxation).*

43. The tax has not in the past been imposed on wholesalers. See *National Taxation*, p. 40, note 42 above. Recently, the scope of the tax has been expanded to include wholesalers. Regulations of the Ministry of Finance Regarding the Levy of the Industrial and Commercial Tax on Wholesale Business Income from Goods, undated, *State Council Gazette* (1983), p. 1051, note 5 above; and Report of the Ministry of Finance Regarding the Levy of the Industrial and Commercial Tax on Wholesale Business Income from Goods, 16 October 1983, *State Council Gazette* (1983), p. 1049, note 5 above.

44. These experiments are being conducted in several different parts of China and several different forms of value-added taxes are being employed. See Wu Ruqing and Sun Yunsu, 'Discussion of a Few Questions in the Current Reform of the Industrial and Commercial Tax', *Caimao Jingji (Finance and Trade Economy)*, No. 10 (1982), p. 37; and 'The Ministry of Finance Promulgates Temporary Measures for the Value-Added Tax for Products such as Farm Implements', *Caizheng (Finance)*, No. 10 (1982), p. 25.

45. Consolidated Industrial and Commercial Tax Act of the People's Republic of China (Draft) (cited elsewhere in this volume as the Consolidated Industrial and Commercial Tax Regulations of the People's Republic of China), passed in principle by the One Hundred and First Meeting of the Standing Committee of the National People's Congress on 11 September 1958 and promulgated for trial implementation by the State Council on 13 September 1958 (hereafter cited as the CICTA); Detailed Rules and Regulations for the Implementation of the Consolidated Industrial and Commercial Tax Act of the People's Republic of China (Draft), promulgated for trial implementation by the Ministry of Finance on 13 September 1958 (hereafter cited as the CICTA Regulations).

46. Industrial and Commercial Tax Act of the People's Republic of China (Draft), approved and transmitted by the State Council on 30 March 1972 (hereafter cited as the 1972 Act). For the text of the 1972 Act, see Guowuyuan Jingji Fagui Yanjiu Zhongxin Bangongshi, Zhongguo Shehui Kexue Yuan Faxue Yanjiu Suo Minfa, Jingjifa Yanjiushi (State Council Economic Law Research Centre Office and Chinese Academy of Social Sciences Civil Law and Economic Law Research Sections), *Chengzhen Feinongye Geti Jingji Fagui Xuanbian (Compendium of Laws and Regulations on the Non-agricultural Individual Economy in Cities and Towns)* (1982), pp. 32–41.

47. The 1972 Act contains only 12 brief articles, a number of which consist of political statements reflecting the tenor of the time. Article 2, for instance, states that the industrial and commercial tax must 'take Mao Zedong Thought as its leader [and] uphold the mass line'. The 1972 Act basically repeats the essential structure of the CICTA, though it omits many of the CICTA's detailed rules on the calculation of taxable income, constructive sales, and tax administration. Although the 1972 Act purports to replace the CICTA and 'related stipulations', 1972 Act, Art. 12, note

46 above, official Chinese sources indicate that the various detailed CICTA provisions referred to above continue to apply in essentially the same form even to those enterprises to which the 1972 Act applies. T. Gelatt, discussions with Chinese tax officials; and *National Taxation*, pp. 26–8 and 31–55, note 42 above.

48. See 'Severely Handle the Question of Tax Evasion by the Beijing Watch Factory', *Zhongguo Fazhi Bao (China Law Weekly)*, 28 January 1983, p. 1; T. Gelatt, conversation with Ministry of Finance tax official, 22 November 1982; see Zhou Weiping, 'Taxation in the Special Economic Zones', *Gangao Jingji (Economy of Hong Kong and Macao)*, No. 1 (1983), p. 47.

49. *China Daily*, 9 April 1983, p. 1. See notes 220–222 below and accompanying text.

50. CICTA, Art. 2, note 45 above.

51. CICTA Regulations, Art. 2, note 45 above.

52. CICTA, Arts. 5 and 6, note 45 above.

53. CICTA, Art. 6, note 45 above; and CICTA Regulations, Art. 11, note 45 above. See *National Taxation*, p. 45, note 42 above. As an example, if the C.I.F. price = RMB 12,000, the customs duty = RMB 2,400 and the industrial and commercial tax rate is 10 per cent, the basis for calculation of the industrial and commercial tax is (12,000 + 2,400) ÷ (1 − 10 per cent), or RMB 16,000. Despite this provision of the CICTA Regulations, at least one foreign company has been told that the F.O.B. price, not the C.I.F. price, is the relevant price for purposes of the CICTA. Experience of T. Gelatt in foreign trade negotiation in China, 1981.

54. CICTA Regulations, Art. 11, note 45 above. For a discussion of the collection and enforcement procedures for the industrial and commercial tax, see Pomp, Gelatt and Surrey, pp. 26–8, note 1 above.

55. CICTA, note 45 above, and Schedule of Taxable Items and Rates. The 1972 Act, note 46 above, adjusted the CICTA Schedule of Taxable Items and Rates to some extent. Under the 1972 Act, rates range from 3 per cent for cotton grey cloth to 66 per cent for Grade A cigarettes. 1972 Act, note 46 above, Schedule of Taxable Items and Rates. The 1972 Act contains fewer and less detailed product categories than does the CICTA. Various adjustments of the industrial and commercial tax rates have taken place since 1972, including an adjustment of a number of rates in July 1982. Notice of the Ministry of Finance Regarding the Adjustment of the Industrial and Commercial Tax Rates on Certain Products and the Expansion of Taxable Items (hereafter cited as the Industrial and Commercial Tax Notice). *State Council Gazette* (1982), p. 552, note 5 above.

56. CICTA, note 45 above, Schedule of Taxable Items and Rates. Under the 1972 Act, the 5 per cent catchall rate remains; rates for services and commercial retailing range from 3 per cent to 5 per cent. 1972 Act, note 46 above, Schedule of Taxable Items and Rates.

57. The surtax is levied under an internal Ministry of Finance Notice of 1961. The authors know of the existence of this Notice but have not seen the actual text. It is unclear whether the surtax applies to enterprises subject to the 1972 Act.

58. CICTA, Art. 4, note 45 above; and CICTA Regulations, Arts. 6 and 12, note 45 above. See also Regulations of The Ministry of Finance Regarding Industrial and Commercial Tax Levy and the Handling of Profits for the Products of Industrial Enterprises Sold by Themselves, 1 August 1981, *State Council Gazette* (1981), p. 553, note 5 above. For further discussion of these aspects of the industrial and commercial tax, see Pomp, Gelatt and Surrey, pp. 24–6, note 1 above.

59. The Law of the People's Republic of China Concerning Joint Ventures Using Chinese and Foreign Investment, passed by the Second Session of the Fifth National People's Congress on 1 July 1979 (hereafter cited as the Joint Venture Law), Art. 1 and Art. 4, para. 1; and Implementing Act for the Law of the People's Republic of China Concerning Joint Ventures Using Chinese and Foreign Investment, promulgated by the State Council on 20 September 1983 (hereafter cited as the Joint Venture Implementing Act), Art. 19.

60. See JVITL, Art. 1, note 3 above. Any tax due on a branch's income is paid by the head office in China. JVITL, Art. 1, para. 2, note 3 above. The legal definition of the term translated as 'branch' is unclear. The Chinese term, *fenzhi jigou*, might also include subsidiaries, so that income earned by a subsidiary of a Chinese joint venture would be subject to the JVITL.

61. Notice of the Ministry of Finance, *Ta Kung Pao*, 10 November 1980, p. 1 (hereafter cited as the Notice of the Ministry of Finance). For explanations in English, see *China Economic News*, 17 November 1980, p. 3; and *Business China*, 25 November 1980, p. 175.

62. Notice of the Ministry of Finance, note 61 above. See also State Council Notice, Art. 1, note 5 above.

63. Notice of the Ministry of Finance, note 61 above; and State Council Notice, note 5 above.

64. JVITL, Art. 1, para. 1, note 3 above. A non-exclusive list of examples of 'production and business income' is provided in JVITL Regulations, Art. 2, para. 1, note 3 above.

65. JVITL Regulations, Art. 2, para. 2, note 3 above.

66. JVITL Regulations, Art. 15, note 3 above.

67. JVITL, Art. 2, note 3 above; and JVITL Regulations, Arts. 7 and 23, note 3 above.

68. JVITL, Art. 7, note 3 above. There is no provision for the carry-back of losses.

69. JVITL Regulations, Arts. 10, 13, 16 and 17, note 3 above.

70. JVITL Regulations, Art. 10, note 3 above. 'Short' is to be interpreted as less than one year. Explanation Regarding the Scope of Fixed Assets, 1 December 1981, *Handbook*, p. 13, note 5 above.

71. JVITL Regulations, Art. 12, note 3 above. Under 'special circumstances' a joint venture may be granted permission by the tax authorities to use accelerated depreciation. JVITL Regulations, Art. 13, para. 2, note 3 above. For the rules on determination of original price and residual value in various circumstances, see JVITL Regulations, Art. 12, note 3 above.

72. JVITL Regulations, Art. 13, para. 1, note 3 above. A Notice of the Ministry of Finance provides for certain situations in which shorter lives than the minimum lives prescribed in the regulations may possibly be used:

(1) where a joint venture's term is shorter than the minimum useful life prescribed in the regulations and the Chinese are to own the asset after the term of the joint venture;
(2) equipment of an acidic or alkaline nature prone to excessive corrosiveness, or factories and buildings subject to continuous vibration; and
(3) machines or equipment that are perennially operated on a continuous basis to increase their productivity.

Notice of the Ministry of Finance Regarding Several Questions on the Joint Venture

Income Tax, 8 June 1981, Art. 6 (hereafter cited as the Joint Venture Tax Notice), in *Almanac*, p. III–60, note 9 above.

73. JVITL Regulations, Art. 16, para. 1, note 3 above.

74. JVITL Regulations, Art. 16, para. 2, note 3 above.

75. JVITL Regulations, Art. 17, note 3 above.

76. See JVITL Regulations, Art. 9, note 3 above.

77. See JVITL Regulations, Art. 8, note 3 above.

78. JVITL Regulations, Art. 9(9), note 3 above. Presumably, joint ventures that do not engage in sales use the 1 per cent test. In no event can a joint venture deduct entertainment expenses that are not 'relevant to production and operations'. JVITL Regulations, Art. 9(9), note 3 above.

79. JVITL Regulations, Art. 9(3), note 3 above. This provision is intended to deny a deduction by the joint venture of interest on loans incurred by either joint venture partner to obtain its capital contribution to the joint venture. However, interest on loans later taken by the joint venture company to finance expansion, and so on, is deductible. T. Gelatt, discussion with Ministry of Finance tax official, 23 February 1983. Apparently, the provision is also intended to prohibit the deduction of what are actually dividends or distributions of profits. See Wang Xuanhui, 'Clarify the Procedures for Computation of Losses and Gains, Reasonably Stipulate the Scope of Deduction of Expenditures', *Caizheng (Finance)*, No. 8 (1982), p. 35.

80. See JVITL Regulations, Art. 8, note 3 above. For an analysis of these rules in the context of standard Western accounting rules, see Pomp, Gelatt and Surrey, pp. 56–8, note 1 above.

81. JVITL Regulations, Art. 18, note 3 above.

82. JVITL Regulations, Art. 18, note 3 above. Chinese officials have apparently stated that the last-in first-out (LIFO) method is also acceptable. D. Foster and J. Horsley, 'Business Operations in the People's Republic of China', *Tax Management Portfolio*, No. 443 (1983), p. A–20. The permission of the local tax authority must be obtained to change accounting methods. JVITL Regulations, Art. 18, note 3 above.

83. Joint Venture Law, Art. 7, para. 1, note 59 above.

84. Yu Dongzhou, 'A Critique of the Law on Joint Ventures Using Chinese and Foreign Investment From the Viewpoint of Legislative Technique', *Shehui Kexue Zhanxian (Social Science Battlefront)*, No. 2 (1980), p. 123; T. Gelatt, discussion with Ministry of Finance tax official, 22 November 1982.

85. Gelatt, discussion, note 84 above.

86. JVITL, Art. 3, note 3 above.

87. JVITL, Art. 3, para. 1, note 3 above; and JVITL Regulations, Art. 3, para. 1, note 3 above. The local tax is collected together with the national tax and later distributed to the local authorities.

88. JVITL Regulations, Art. 3, para. 2, note 3 above.

89. JVITL, Art. 4, note 3 above; and JVITL Regulations, Art. 4, note 3 above.

90. See United States Internal Revenue Code (hereafter cited as the I.R.C.) §§ 871 (a)(1)(A), 881(a)(1).

91. See JVITL Regulations, Art. 4, note 3 above; and Wang Xuanhui, 'A Discussion of the Income Tax Burden on Chinese-Foreign Joint Ventures', *Caizheng (Finance)*, No. 6 (1982), p. 21. It is unclear how the Chinese will treat a situation in which the dividend is initially deposited in a bank account within China and subsequently

remitted outside China. Presumably, the 10 per cent tax applies when the dividend is withdrawn and remitted abroad, but rules will have to be developed to identify what part of the withdrawal from the deposit represents the dividend, and what part represents interest or principal.

To implement the 10 per cent tax, the Chinese will also need to develop rules defining the term 'profits'. The term cannot be synonymous with taxable income because certain outlays, such as the payment of the joint venture tax, reduce the amount of profits available for distribution even if they are not deductible for the purposes of calculating taxable income. Unless the calculation of profits takes into account such outlays, the 10 per cent tax might be levied on a distribution that actually constitutes a return of a shareholder's capital, rather than a distribution of profits. For the United States rules on what constitutes a distribution of profits, see I.R.C. §§ 301, 312, 316, note 90 above.

92. Joint Venture Law, Art. 7, para. 2, note 59 above.

93. JVITL, Art. 5, para. 1, note 3 above. As the Chinese text of the relevant provision makes clear, the following two years refer to the two years immediately subsequent to the first profit-making year and not, as has been understood by some foreigners, to the second and third profit-making years.

If a joint venture starts in mid-tax year, and makes a profit that tax year, that tax year is generally to be considered the first profit-making year for purposes of the above provision of the JVITL. However, this rule may be modified in 'special circumstances' upon application to and consideration by the local tax authorities. [Document] Regarding the Question of the Periods of Tax Reduction and Exemption for Newly Opened Joint Ventures, 8 June 1981, *Handbook*, p. 12, note 5 above.

Certain types of enterprises are entitled to further tax reductions. Joint ventures in 'low-profit' operations such as farming or forestry, or ventures located in remote, undeveloped outlying areas may apply for a 15–30 per cent reduction in income tax for an additional ten-year period. JVITL, Art. 5, para. 2, note 3 above. The local tax authorities are empowered to approve the first three years of exemption and reduction, but the Ministry of Finance must approve the additional ten-year reduction. JVITL, Art. 5, note 3 above. Enterprises involving Hong Kong and Macao or overseas Chinese investors engaging in the above operations enjoy even more benefits under a recently announced policy. They may be granted a 20–40 per cent reduction in tax for 10–15 years after the original exemption and reduction period, which for enterprises with Hong Kong, Macao or overseas Chinese investors has recently been increased to six years. 'What Tax Reduction and Exemption Regulations Does China Have in Utilizing Foreign Investment?', *Caizheng (Finance)*, No. 6 (1983), p. 46 (hereafter cited as Tax Reduction and Exemption). See note 94 below.

94. Decision Regarding Amendment of the Joint Venture Income Tax Law of the People's Republic of China, passed by the Second Session of the Standing Committee of the Sixth National People's Congress, 2 September 1983 (hereafter cited as the JVITL Amendment Decision), Art. 1. It is unclear from the JVITL Amendment Decision itself whether these extended holidays and reductions apply to pre-existing joint ventures. A subsequent Ministry of Finance Notice provides that the extended holidays and reductions will apply to pre-existing ventures which have not yet earned profits or whose tax exemption and/or reduction periods have not expired. Notice of the Ministry of Finance Regarding the Earnest Implementation of the Decision of the Standing Committee of the National People's Congress Regarding Amendment of

the Joint Venture Income Tax Law of the People's Republic of China, 12 October 1983 (hereafter cited as the Joint Venture Implementation Notice), Art. 1.

In Shanghai, even more liberal treatment is potentially available. According to one report, the initial exemption may be for one to three years, starting from the first profit-making year, with a further two to four years of half-rate taxation. Further 'appropriate' reductions may be granted to joint ventures which have 'difficulties' paying income tax after the expiration of the originally granted exemption and reduction periods. 'A Few Financial Questions Regarding Chinese-Foreign Economic Co-operation in Shanghai', *Wen Hui Bao*, 29 March 1983, p. 7 (hereafter cited as Shanghai Economic Co-operation).

Joint ventures in China with Hong Kong and Macao and overseas Chinese investment will reportedly be granted one year of tax exemption for the first profit-making year and five further years of fifty per cent reduction. Tax Reduction and Exemption, p. 46, note 93 above.

A question not specifically covered by the JVITL is whether the tax holidays and reductions include the local surtax. However, Ministry of Finance officials have said that the local surtax is included in the holidays and reductions. Speech by Liu Zhicheng, Director of the General Bureau of Taxation, Ministry of Finance, in Los Angeles on 8 June 1981. Because the local surtax is based on a percentage of the national tax *paid*, see text accompanying note 87 above, the Ministry's position avoids the administrative complication of requiring a taxpayer entitled to a national tax holiday or reduction to calculate its national tax that would otherwise have been paid for the sole purpose of calculating the local surtax.

95. JVITL Regulations, Art. 5, note 3 above. This approach favours investors since it means that an initial period of start-up losses will not count against the joint venture's period of eligibility for tax exemption or reduction.

96. Joint Venture Law, Art. 7, para. 2, note 59 above.

97. Joint Venture Law, Art. 7, para. 3, note 59 above.

98. The JVITL Regulations specify that the profits must be reinvested in the same or another Chinese joint venture. JVITL Regulations, Art. 6, note 3 above. See also Joint Venture Tax Notice, Art. 1(1), note 72 above, stating that to qualify for the refund of tax the profits may be invested in the same joint venture or another existing joint venture in China, or used to form a new joint venture with a Chinese entity.

99. JVITL, Art. 6, note 3 above; and JVITL Regulations, Art. 6, note 3 above. Although these articles could be read as requiring that all of a participant's after-tax profit must be reinvested to obtain a refund, China's Finance Minister, Wang Bingqian, in discussions in September 1980 with American lawyers in Washington, DC, indicated that any part of the profit reinvested would entitle the investor to a proportional refund.

100. JVITL, Art. 6, note 3 above. It is unclear whether during the five-year period reinvested funds can be withdrawn from one joint venture in China and reinvested in another joint venture in China without triggering the payback requirement. It is also unclear what approach, for example FIFO or LIFO, will be used in determining the 'age' of any withdrawn funds for purposes of the five-year rule.

101. Joint Venture Tax Notice, Art. 1(4), note 72 above. A foreign participant which repatriates its tax refund is not subject to the 10 per cent tax on remitted profits. See notes 89–91 above and accompanying text. Joint Venture Tax Notice, Art. 1(5), note 72 above. Presumably, the Chinese felt that the tax incentive to

reinvest would be undercut if the refund were subject to the 10 per cent tax on remitted profits.

102. JVITL, Art. 16, para. 1, note 3 above; and JVITL Regulations, Art. 32, note 3 above. A per-country limitation is used for the joint venture tax credit. Joint Venture Tax Notice, Art. 4, note 72 above.

For a full discussion of the JVITL's administrative and enforcement provisions, see Pomp, Gelatt and Surrey, pp. 61–3, note 1 above.

103. FEITL, note 4 above; and FEITL Regulations, note 4 above. Under the State Council Notice, Art. 1, note 5 above, 'preferential provisions' regarding enterprise income tax burdens in contracts signed and approved before the FEITL remain valid for the life of the contract, but will not apply to any extensions. The preferential provisions referred to include provisions, common in investment, technology transfer and other contracts signed before the FEITL, under which the Chinese party is to pay all taxes arising in China under the contract. These provisions are prohibited in contracts signed after the FEITL. See [Document] Regarding Questions Relating to Taxation of Such Contracts as Introduction of Technology Contracts, Loan Contracts and Leasing Contracts Approved Before the Promulgation of the Tax Law, 29 March 1982, *Handbook*, p. 37, note 5 above.

104. See pp. 55–6 of the text. The Chinese have indicated that a venture designated as a 'contractual' or 'co-operative' venture in the contract but having the characteristics of an equity joint venture, for instance, a board of directors, may be taxed under the JVITL, not the FEITL. T. Gelatt, discussion with Ministry of Finance tax official, 23 February 1983.

105. The Chinese term is *jigou*.

106. FEITL, Art. 11, para. 1, note 4 above. The Chinese term, *texuquan shiyongfei,* is translated as 'royalties' in the Chinese unofficial translation of the FEITL, see *China Daily*, 17 December 1982, p. 2. The term 'royalties' is too narrow and fails to capture the intended scope of *texuquan shiyongfei*. See pp. 49–50 of the text. The precise Chinese term for 'royalties' in the Western sense is *ticheng fei*.

107. This approach is widely known as a 'withholding tax'. Technically, withholding is a means of collecting a tax and should not be used to refer to the imposition of a tax. Nonetheless, because the term withholding tax is so commonly adopted throughout the world, it is used throughout this chapter.

108. FEITL, Art. 1, para. 2, note 4 above; and FEITL Regulations, Art. 2, note 4 above. It is unclear whether 'establishment' will be interpreted as encompassing a Chinese subsidiary that is wholly owned by a foreign company. This issue has not, up to now, needed resolution because outside of the Special Economic Zones, where a special tax regime applies, there are no corporations wholly owned by foreigners. Should such wholly-owned corporations be allowed to operate elsewhere, as is apparently now under active consideration, the Chinese will have to decide whether the FEITL is applicable, or whether some other tax regime, such as the JVITL, or China's domestic income tax system, should apply. A recent Chinese treatise states without elaboration that the FEITL applies to wholly-owned ventures. Chu Baotai, *Zhongwai Hezi Jingying Qiye Fa Shishi Jingyan Wenda (Questions and Answers on the Implementing Experience of the Law on Joint Ventures Using Chinese and Foreign Investment)* (1983), p. 42.

109. See p. 51 of the text.

110. See p. 52 of the text.

111. FEITL, Art. 1, para. 1, note 4 above.
112. See FEITL Regulations, Art. 4, note 4 above.
113. The language of the FEITL, Art. 1, para. 1, note 4 above, stating that 'in the *People's Republic of China*, the income of foreign enterprises [with establishments in China] from production, business operations and other sources will all be taxed according to the provisions of this law' (our italics), is ambiguous, but could be read to mean that only income from China is taxable. See also Wang Xuanhui, 'Reasonably Explain the Source of Taxable Income, Encourage Low Interest Loans and Deposits', *Caizheng (Finance)*, No. 10 (1982), p. 43.
114. FEITL, Art. 11, para. 1, note 4 above; and FEITL Regulations, Art. 27, note 4 above. See pp. 48–50 of the text.
115. Should it be decided to tax Chinese subsidiaries of foreign companies under the FEITL, see note 108 above, the Chinese would presumably want to tax their worldwide income, as in the case of joint ventures, see text accompanying note 64 above, to avoid the use of China as a tax haven for shell companies having no China income.
116. FEITL Regulations, Art. 10, note 4 above.
117. The FEITL Regulations provide a more complex scheme regarding business entertainment expenditures than the JVITL. See FEITL Regulations, Art. 13, note 4 above. The FEITL Regulations also prohibit deductions for all 'other expenditures not related to production or operations', FEITL Regulations, Art. 10(10), note 4 above, a prohibition presumably intended to be implicit in the JVITL. Examples of such expenditures given by an official commentary are moving expenses, staff retirement funds, educational expenses for staff children, and extraordinary losses from natural disasters. 'Explanation of Terms in the [FEITL Regulations]', *Handbook*, p. 133, note 5 above.
118. FEITL Regulations, Art. 10(3), note 4 above.
119. FEITL Regulations, Art. 12(3), note 4 above.
120. Interest on a bank loan incurred by a participant in a co-operative venture for its contribution to the venture may be deducted by that participant, provided it meets the 'reasonable' and 'normal' tests, a more liberal interpretation than that applied to joint ventures. See note 79 above. T. Gelatt, discussion with Ministry of Finance tax official, 23 February 1983. However, a Ministry of Finance document provides that interest on a loan taken out for investment in a project in China may only be deducted as an expense after the project enters the production or operating phase. Until that time, the interest must be capitalized and depreciated or amortized as part of the cost of the property that the loan was used to acquire. [Document] Regarding the Question of Listing Interest on Loans of a Foreign Enterprise as an Expense, 7 May 1982 (hereafter cited as the Interest Document), in *Handbook*, pp. 41–2, note 5 above. Similarly, interest on loans taken out after a project begins operating to acquire new capital equipment may only be expensed after the equipment goes into use; before that time, it must be capitalized. Interest Document, pp. 41–2.

A Chinese official has said that 'reasonable' interest means interest 'not above the general interest rate on commercial loans'. Wang Xuanhui, p. 36, note 79 above. See also Interest Document, above, p. 41; and 'Explanation of Terms in the [FEITL Regulations]', *Handbook*, p. 134, note 5 above, stating that a 'normal loan' is one incurred by an enterprise that actually needs funds because its production or operating capital is insufficient or the enterprise's own capital cannot satisfy the investment requirements of a particular project, or incurred for expansion of the scale of production or operations. 'Any [such] loan on which the interest rate is not higher than the commercial lending rate at the location where the loan is obtained, and for which a loan contract has been signed, may be considered a "normal loan" '.

An intercorporate loan, for instance, from a parent to its subsidiary corporation, might be subject to greater scrutiny and be viewed as 'free capital' (*ziyou ziben*), resulting in the denial of a deduction. T. Gelatt, discussion with Ministry of Finance tax official, 23 February 1983. A foreign enterprise might, however, have the opportunity to prove that such an intercorporate loan meets the 'reasonable' and 'normal' tests, in which case a deduction would be allowed for the interest. See Foreign Taxation Section, General Bureau of Taxation, Ministry of Finance, 'Questions and Answers on Foreign Taxation (2)', *Caizheng (Finance)*, No. 7 (1982), p. 39.

121. FEITL Regulations, Art. 10(9), note 4 above. See note 106 above.

122. FEITL Regulations, Art. 11, para. 1, note 4 above.

123. See FEITL Regulations, Arts. 14, 15, 16, 17, 18, 19, 21 and 22, note 4 above.

124. FEITL Regulations, Art. 18, para. 3, note 4 above. See Wang Xuanhui, 'Distinguish Capital Expenditures and Expenses, Establish the System of Depreciation and Amortization of Property', *Caizheng (Finance)*, No. 9 (1982), p. 40. A detailed discussion of offshore oil tax issues may be found in Chapter 6.

125. FEITL Regulations, Art. 24, para. 1, note 4 above.

126. Apparently the Chinese will look to domestic businesses or other foreign businesses in China. An official commentary has warned of the need to be sensitive to differences among enterprises, such as differing scales of operations, which may invalidate their comparison for tax purposes. Wang Xuanhui, 'Adopt Reasonable Substitutional Methods to Calculate the Amount of Taxable Income', *Caizheng (Finance)*, No. 12 (1982), p. 36. Taxpayers subject to this imputed profit system must still report their accounting records, vouchers, and so on to the tax authorities. Wang Xuanhui, p. 36, above.

127. FEITL, Art. 3, note 4 above.

128. FEITL, Art. 4, para. 1, note 4 above. See FEITL Regulations, Art. 5, note 4 above.

129. Enterprises with an annual profit of RMB 1 million or less qualify for a potential reduction or exemption upon approval of the provincial-level people's governments. FEITL, Art. 4, para. 2, note 4 above; and FEITL Regulations, Art. 6, note 4 above. Fujian Province has reportedly granted a complete exemption from the local tax for these enterprises and Guangdong has granted a 70 per cent reduction. Tax Reduction and Exemption, p. 46, note 93 above.

For the administrative rules governing foreign companies with establishments, see Provisional Regulations of the General Bureau of Taxation of the Ministry of Finance of the People's Republic of China Regarding Tax Registration of Foreign Enterprises for the Commencement and Termination of Operations, promulgated by the General Bureau of Taxation of the Ministry of Finance of the People's Republic of China on 15 April 1982; FEITL, Arts. 7, 8, 10, 14, 15 and 16, note 4 above; and FEITL Regulations, Arts. 33, 35 and 43–47, note 4 above.

130. See note 93 above. The JVITL definition of the first profit-making year as the first profit-making year after exhausting the five-year loss carry-over, see note 95 above and accompanying text, is not repeated in the FEITL, which contains the same

loss carry-over as the JVITL. See FEITL, Art. 6, note 4 above. The same definition will apparently be applied in practice. National Council for United States-China Trade meeting with the Beijing Municipal Tax Bureau FTCO, 19 March 1982.

The FEITL does not state whether the possible holidays or reductions apply to the local 10 per cent tax. Administratively, there is no reason why these holidays or reductions should necessarily apply, since unlike in the case of the JVITL, see text accompanying note 87 above, the FEITL's local tax is not a function of the national tax. See note 94 above. However, a Chinese tax official has indicated that the local tax is included in the holidays and reductions under the FEITL. 'Interview with Liu Zhicheng, Director, General Bureau of Taxation, Ministry of Finance', *Zhongguo Caimao Bao (China Finance and Trade Journal*), 17 December 1981, p. 1.

131. FEITL, Art. 5, note 4 above; and FEITL Regulations, Art. 7, note 4 above. Examples of low-profit operations mentioned in the FEITL and its regulations are farming, forestry, animal husbandry and those low-profit enterprises engaged in exploiting coal resources in deep wells. Under the JVITL, the low-profit requirement has to be satisfied only in order to qualify for the ten-year, 15–30 per cent rate reduction (after the initial exemption and reduction). See note 93 above. Neither the JVITL nor the FEITL defines 'low profit' in this context.

132. See note 131 above.

133. FEITL, Art. 11, para. 1, note 4 above; and FEITL Regulations, Art. 27, note 4 above. Under the State Council Notice, Art. 2, note 5 above, preferential tax treatment of foreign or Hong Kong businesses receiving fees for the use of proprietary rights provided in contracts signed and approved before the promulgation of the FEITL continues to be valid for the initial life of the contract.

134. FEITL Regulations, Art. 28, note 4 above. This article indicates that 'separate stipulations' may alter this gross withholding treatment. An example of such a separate stipulation is that allowing certain foreign banks to be taxed on interest income on a progressive basis. See p. 52 of the text.

135. FEITL Regulations, Art. 27, para. 2, note 4 above.

136. See 'Questions and Answers on Foreign Taxation (2)', note 120 above; and T. Gelatt, discussion with Ministry of Finance tax official, 22 November 1982.

137. See text accompanying notes 89–91 above.

138. A withholding tax on distributions by foreign corporations with China-source income to their foreign shareholders *was* included in a 1981 draft of the FEITL circulated for comment but was later dropped. Comment of Carl Nordberg at Practising Law Institute Conference, Legal Aspects of Doing Business with China, New York, 27 January 1983.

139. FEITL Regulations, Art. 27, para. 3, note 4 above. Included within the scope of this provision is interest paid by foreign companies with establishments in China such as co-operative ventures, see text accompanying note 196 below, on loans related to that establishment. A Ministry of Finance document suggests, however, that only interest that is allowed to be currently deducted as an expense by such companies is subject to the withholding tax. Interest Document, p. 42, note 120 above. See note 120 above. Implementation of the withholding tax in these situations may be difficult since the interest will usually be paid by the foreign company outside China.

140. Chinese corporations that have reportedly been granted approval to grant tax exemptions under this provision include the China International Trust and Investment Corporation, the Shanghai International Trust and Investment Corporation, and the

Tianjin International Trust and Investment Corporation. These corporations, in addition to acting as intermediaries between foreign investors and potential Chinese partners, may under their charters accept loans from abroad for investment projects.

141. FEITL, Art. 11, para. 3, note 4 above; and FEITL Regulations, Art. 30, note 4 above.

142. FEITL Regulations, Art. 29, para. 2, note 4 above.

143. Provisional Regulations of the Ministry of Finance of the People's Republic of China Regarding the Reduction and Exemption of Income Tax Relating to Interest Earned by Foreign Businesses from China, 7 January 1983 (hereafter cited as the Interest Regulations).

144. Interest Regulations, Art. 2 (1), note 143 above; and T. Gelatt, discussion with Ministry of Finance tax official, 9 March 1983. Another official has specified that a margin of 0.5 per cent above LIBOR is acceptable only for loans of three or more years. For loans of one and two years, only spreads of 0.25 per cent and 0.375 per cent, respectively, are acceptable for purposes of the withholding tax exemptions. Comment of Luo Youde of the Offshore Oil Tax Bureau, Ministry of Finance, in Washington, DC, 7 April 1983.

Interest that a foreign seller who has received a seller's credit from its state bank passes on to the Chinese buyer at a rate no higher than that the Chinese side would be paying for a buyer's credit is also eligible for tax exemption. Interest Regulations, Art. 2 (3), note 143 above.

145. Interest Regulations, Art. 2 (2), note 143 above. Under this provision, the interest rate must be no higher than the interbank interest rate for call funds. See note 144 above, and accompanying text.

146. Interest Regulations, Art. 1, note 143 above.

147. Interest Regulations, Art. 6, note 143 above.

148. FEITL, Art. 11, para. 1, note 4 above; and FEITL Regulations, Art. 27, para. 4, note 4 above.

149. See F. Ching, 'China Executives Seek Advantages through Leasing', *Asian Wall Street Journal*, 4 January 1983, p. 1.

150. FEITL, Art. 11, para. 1, note 4 above.

151. Interest Regulations, Art. 3, para. 1, note 143 above.

152. Interest Regulations, Art. 3, paras. 1 and 2, note 143 above. To be exempt from taxation, interest in a lease-sale transaction must meet the criteria of the Interest Regulations regarding interest in the seller's credit situation. Interest Regulations, Art. 3, para. 2, note 143 above; and see note 144 above.

153. Interest Regulations, Art. 3, para. 2, note 143 above. This spread is referred to in the cited provision as the 'amount remaining after deduction of the interest'. T. Gelatt, discussion with Ministry of Finance tax official, 9 March 1983.

154. FEITL Regulations, Art. 27, para. 5, note 4 above. See note 106 above.

155. Fees for training conducted in China or abroad are taxable provided they relate to technology to be used in China. T. Gelatt, discussion with Ministry of Finance tax official, 9 March 1983.

156. See Provisional Regulations of the Ministry of Finance of the People's Republic of China Regarding the Reduction and Exemption of Income Tax on Fees for the Use of Proprietary Technology, 13 December 1982 (hereafter cited as the Technology Regulations), Art. 1.

157. The current position of the Ministry of Finance on computer software apparently

distinguishes between two situations. In the first, a foreign company merely sells computer programmes to the Chinese, with or without computer equipment, and the Chinese use the programmes as desired. The technology that would enable the Chinese to write and develop programmes of their own is not transferred. This situation is regarded as the simple sale of a good, and the resulting income is not taxable. In the second, technology for creating computer programmes is transferred to the Chinese, and the resulting income is treated as fees for the use of proprietary technology, taxable under the FEITL withholding tax if the company has no establishment in China. T. Gelatt, discussion with Ministry of Finance tax official, 9 March 1983.

158. Technology Regulations, Art. 2, note 156 above.

159. See Technology Regulations, Art. 3, note 156 above. This provision makes it clear that without consideration and approval of the tax authorities, the units introducing technology may not of their own accord grant tax reductions or tax exemptions.

160. Technology Regulations, Art. 1, note 156 above. In determining whether technology is 'advanced' for purposes of the Technology Regulations' tax exemption, the importing Chinese entity must evaluate which of the available technologies will be most effective, and transmit its findings to the tax authorities for a decision. T. Gelatt, discussion with Ministry of Finance tax officials, 9 March 1983. In addition to being 'advanced', technology must, under the cited provision of the Technology Regulations, be offered on 'preferential terms' to qualify for exemption. The tax authorities will consider such factors as whether the cost is low relative to comparable technology, whether free training is included, whether payment may be made in kind rather than in cash (see text accompanying note 191 below) and whether the Chinese transferee may continue to use the technology free of charge after the termination of the contract. T. Gelatt, discussion with Ministry of Finance tax official, 9 March 1983.

161. Technology Regulations, Art. 1, note 156 above.

162. See pp. 56–7 of the text.

163. See pp. 49–50 of the text.

164. See Provisional Regulations of the State Council of the People's Republic of China Concerning the Control of Resident Representative Offices of Foreign Enterprises, promulgated by the State Council on 30 October 1980 (hereafter cited as the Office Regulations); and Measures of the State Administration of Industry and Commerce of the People's Republic of China Regarding the Control of Registration of Resident Representative Offices of Foreign Enterprises, approved by the State Council on 5 March 1983, and promulgated by the State Administration of Industry and Commerce and effective on 15 March 1983 (hereafter cited as the Office Registration Measures).

165. FEITL, Art. 1, para. 2, note 4 above; and FEITL Regulations, Art. 2, para. 1, note 4 above.

166. T. Gelatt, discussion with Ministry of Finance tax official, 23 February 1983.

167. See, for example, 'Ministry of Finance Clarifies Provision of Enterprise Tax Law', *China Market Intelligence*, January 1983, p. 2.

168. The rationale of Chinese tax officials for this approach is that under Chinese law representative offices cannot be engaged in actual business activity. See Office Registration Measures, Art. 3, note 164 above, providing that 'representative offices of foreign enterprises shall be representative offices that engage in activities that are not direct business operations'. The Chinese interpretation of 'direct business operations' is unclear. For instance, it is uncertain whether the term encompasses the signing of

sales or other contracts by a representative office. See note 172 below and accompanying text regarding representative offices of foreign banks.

169. T. Gelatt, discussion with Ministry of Finance tax official, 22 November 1982.

170. See text accompanying notes 50–51 above. Chinese legal officials have confirmed that the CICTA will be applied to these offices. Communication of China Council for the Promotion of International Trade Legal Advisory Office to a colleague of T. Gelatt, March 1983.

171. See text accompanying note 52 above; and see Office Regulations, Art. 10, para. 1, note 164 above.

172. Interest Regulations, Art. 4, note 143 above. This provision raises a serious question in light of a separate regulation prohibiting the representative office of a foreign bank from engaging in 'any direct profit-making business activities'. Provisional Regulations for the Establishment of Representative Offices in China by Overseas Chinese and Foreign Financial Institutions, promulgated by the People's Bank of China on 1 February 1983, Art. 8, para. 1 (hereafter cited as the Financial Institutions Measures). The term 'direct profit-making business activities', *zhijie yingli de yewu huodong,* is somewhat narrower than 'direct business operations', *zhijie jingying huodong,* in the Office Registration Measures, note 164 above, see note 168 above, but it is still unclear what the former is intended to cover. The signing of a loan agreement by a representative office of a foreign bank so as to take advantage of the tax treatment mentioned in the text might violate the cited provision of the Financial Institutions Measures. The tax authorities, however, apparently view the signing of a loan agreement by the representative office of a foreign bank as merely an administrative act performed on behalf of the head bank, which is considered to have performed all the actual business in connection with the transaction. T. Gelatt, discussion with Ministry of Finance tax official, 23 February 1983; see 'Finance Ministry Spokesman on Income Tax Reduction and Exemption for Foreign Companies', *China Economic News*, 21 March 1983, p. 4. On the other hand, the Bank of China has stated that it is the position of the People's Bank of China that the signing of a loan agreement by the representative office of a foreign bank in China would constitute a 'direct profit-making business activity' in violation of the Financial Institutions Measures. As a matter of policy, Bank of China officials have stated that the People's Bank, which has the power of enforcement of the Financial Institutions Measures, has decided to punish violators of this provision by revoking their registration certificates.

173. The rate applicable to foreign bank branches is not specified in the CICTA. See CICTA, Schedule of Taxable Items and Rates, note 45 above.

174. See FEITL Regulations, Art. 2, para. 1, note 4 above.

175. Comments of PRC tax officials at Hong Kong Seminar on PRC Taxation and Accounting Practices, 15 June 1982.

176. Notice of the General Tax Bureau of the Ministry of Finance Regarding Questions of the Levy of Tax on the Agency or Consignment Sale of Goods or the Establishment of Maintenance Service Centres and the Agency Sale of Spare Parts and Fittings by Chinese Corporations and Enterprises Entrusted by Foreign Businesses, 6 October 1983 (hereafter cited as the Consignment Notice).

177. Consignment Notice, Art. 1, note 176 above. The term 'profit' presumably corresponds to the concept of net income under the FEITL.

178. Consignment Notice, Art. 1, note 176 above.

179. Consignment Notice, Art. 2, note 176 above. An exception exists for chemical

products and instruments and equipment for use by Chinese and foreign ocean-going freighters sold by Chinese enterprises on behalf of foreign businesses. These may be exempted from the CICTA regardless of how the prices are determined, on the assumption that they will be provided directly from bonded warehouses to the freighters. Consignment Notice, Art. 4, note 176 above.

180. Consignment Notice, Art. 3, note 176 above. Under a possible reading of the Consignment Notice, a foreign company would be exempt from the FEITL, as well as the CICTA, even if an independent place of business existed for sale of its products, so long as the pricing were handled as described in the text. See Consignment Notice, Arts. 1 and 3, note 176 above.

181. See text accompanying note 139 above.

182. Related to this characterization is a lease-sale or hire-purchase, where each payment in kind includes a 'lease fee' consisting of interest and a contribution toward the purchase price of the equipment. See p. 49 of the text.

183. See note 106 above and accompanying text.

184. Although no written source rules exist, such a sale is currently *not* considered as generating China-source income. See text accompanying note 206 below.

185. See text accompanying note 133 above; and T. Gelatt, discussion with Ministry of Finance tax official, 23 February 1983.

186. See text accompanying note 108 above.

187. T. Gelatt, discussion with Ministry of Finance tax official, 9 March 1983.

188. FEITL Regulations, Art. 32, note 4 above, appears to contemplate such an application of the withholding tax, stating that income on which the withholding tax is to be applied may include payments made in kind. The Chinese payor in this type of situation apparently withheld products equal in value to 20 per cent of the total payback and converted these into cash for payment to the tax authorities.

189. Interest Regulations, Arts. 2(5) and 3, para. 3, note 143 above. On the lease-sale aspect of compensation trade, see note 182 above. The regulations also cover arrangements, akin to compensation trade, whereby the foreigner provides equipment or technology with which a Chinese unit processes or assembles materials or parts into finished goods for the foreigner. Like compensation trade, these projects can be characterized as loans or instalment sales. The Chinese entity in these cases often discounts the processing or assembly fees payable to the Chinese entity by the foreigner. The discount is in lieu of the payment by the Chinese of principal and interest for the equipment. Under the regulations, this discount will not result in withholding tax. Interest Regulations, Art. 2(5), note 143 above.

190. Reply of the Ministry of Finance Regarding the Question of Exemption from Income Tax in Cases of the Use of Products to Repay the Price and Interest for Equipment and Fees for the Use of Proprietary Technology, 9 March 1983, in *Caizheng (Finance)*, No. 5 (1983), p. 45 (hereafter cited as the Interest Reply).

191. See note 160 above and accompanying text. Because in-kind payments save foreign exchange for China their use will be a positive factor in determining whether technology is being offered on 'preferential terms'. If the 'advanced' test is also satisfied, the technology may be eligible for the withholding tax exemption under the Technology Regulations, note 156 above.

The title of the Interest Reply, note 190 above, makes reference to 'fees for the use of proprietary technology'. However, neither the Technology Regulations, note 156 above, nor the Interest Regulations, note 143 above, provide any blanket exemption for technology fees paid in kind, so the import of the above reference is unclear.

192. The Chinese party is subject to the 1972 Act, note 46 above. See text accompanying notes 50–52 above. Exemptions from the industrial and commercial tax on importation may in many cases be available to the Chinese party. See Regulations of the Ministry of Finance Regarding the Levy and Exemption of the Industrial and Commercial Tax on Imported and Exported Goods, approved by the State Council on 30 December 1980, Art. 2 (hereafter cited as the Import/Export Regulations) in *State Council Gazette* (1981), p. 16, note 5 above. See also *Wen Hui Bao,* 13 May 1983, p. 8; and *Ta Kung Pao*, 18 May 1983, p. 1. The Chinese are also considering revisions of the industrial and commercial tax to exempt exports by Chinese entities of compensation trade products. T. Gelatt, discussion with Ministry of Finance tax official, 9 March 1983.

193. See text accompanying note 51 above. This analysis parallels the Chinese view that compensation trade does not create an 'establishment' for purposes of the FEITL. See text accompanying note 187 above. Compare the situation with regard to co-operative ventures. See pp. 55–6 of the text.

194. FEITL Regulations, Art. 3, note 4 above. A Chinese tax official analogizes co-operative ventures to partnerships in the Western sense for tax purposes. Wang Xuanhui, 'Concretely Explain the Scope of Taxpayers, Give Lenient Consideration to the Tax Burden of Medium and Small Enterprises', *Caizheng (Finance)*, No. 7 (1982), p. 42. This separate tax payment for participants in co-operative ventures is applicable in the absence of special stipulations. FEITL Regulations, Art. 3, note 4 above. A tax official has suggested that in the case of small-scale co-operative projects where it is not 'convenient' to calculate and pay tax separately, such special stipulations may be made. Wang Xuanhui, p. 42, above.

The Chinese sometimes refer to a 'Type A' contractual joint venture that, despite the name, is treated for most purposes like an equity joint venture and taxed under the JVITL. See *Zhongguo Touzi Zhinan (Guide to Investment in China)* (1982), a book sponsored by the Ministry of Foreign Economic Relations and Trade (MOFERT) (hereafter cited as the MOFERT Guide), pp. 46–7 (all page references cited refer to the Chinese text).

195. Wang Xuanhui, p. 42, note 194 above.

196. FEITL, Arts. 1–3, note 4 above; and FEITL Regulations, Arts. 2 and 4, note 4 above. In some cases a deemed profit system may be applicable to foreign companies in contractual joint ventures. See note 210 below and accompanying text.

197. FEITL Regulations, Art. 26, para. 1, note 4 above.

198. See FEITL Regulations, Art. 26, para. 1, note 4 above; and Wang Xuanhui, 'Determine Prices, Reasonably Calculate the Amount of Income from Division of Products', *Caizheng (Finance)*, No. 1 (1983), p. 35. Wang suggests that since the CICTA will also be levied on the foreigner's share of products, see text accompanying note 200 below, 'leniency' should be applied in determining the relevant price for application of the FEITL Regulations, Art. 26, para. 1, note 4 above. Wang suggests that in the case of agricultural and related products, the price may be determined by reference to the commercial purchase price for state enterprises; for industrial products, the ex-factory price may be used or if there is no ex-factory price, the commercial wholesale price for state enterprises may be used as a reference. Wang Xuanhui, p. 36, above.

199. See Regulations Concerning the Levy and Exemption of Customs Duties and

Consolidated Industrial and Commercial Tax on Imports and Exports of Goods for Chinese-Foreign Co-operative Exploitation of Offshore Petroleum, approved by the State Council on 28 February 1982 and promulgated by the General Administration of Customs and the Ministry of Finance on 1 April 1982; and Regulations Concerning the Supervision and Control of and the Levy and Exemption of Tax on Goods Imported and Exported by Chinese-Foreign Co-operative Ventures, promulgated on 31 January 1984 by the General Administration of Customs, the Ministry of Finance and the Ministry of Foreign Economic Relations and Trade (hereafter cited as the Co-operative Venture Tax Regulations), Arts. 4(1), (2), and 6.

200. Co-operative Venture Tax Regulations, Art. 4(3), note 199 above.

201. Wang Xuanhui, p. 36, note 198 above, suggests that the latter may be the Chinese intention. In at least one case, however, that of co-operative offshore petroleum projects, the Chinese have provided for the consolidated tax to be levied in kind. Regulations Regarding the Use of Crude Oil for the Payment of the Industrial and Commercial Consolidated Tax and the Mining Area Use Fee in the Chinese-Foreign Co-operative Development of Oil, 3 April 1982.

202. Tax Reduction and Exemption, p. 47, note 93 above. The Co-operative Venture Tax Regulations, note 199 above, make no reference to the industrial and commercial tax on exports, providing only that customs duties must be paid on co-operative venture products to which export duties apply. Co-operative Venture Tax Regulations, Art. 8, note 199 above.

203. FEITL Regulations, Art. 9, note 4 above.

204. FEITL, Arts. 1–3, note 4 above; and FEITL Regulations, Arts. 2 and 4, note 4 above.

205. Provisional Regulations of the Ministry of Finance Regarding the Levy of Industrial and Commercial Consolidated Tax and Enterprise Income Tax on Foreign Businesses Contracting for Project Work and Providing Labour Services, 5 July 1983 (hereafter cited as the Project and Labour Regulations), Art. 2(1).

206. T. Gelatt, discussion with Ministry of Finance tax official, 9 March 1983.

207. Project and Labour Regulations, Art. 2(2), note 205 above.

208. T. Gelatt, discussion with Ministry of Finance tax official, 9 March 1983. To the extent service or related income received under any of the situations discussed in the text accompanying notes 205–208 is deemed to involve fees for the use of proprietary technology, it will be taxable under the FEITL withholding tax. See Project and Labour Regulations, Art. 2, note 205 above; and see text accompanying notes 154-158 above.

209. The rules for calculation of net income for a service company under the FEITL correspond to those under the JVITL. See note 80 above.

210. This system was initially available only to subcontractors in the petroleum development projects. FEITL Regulations, Art. 24, para. 2, note 4 above; and [Document] Regarding the Question of Calculation of the Income of Enterprises Contracting for the Exploration and Development of Offshore Petroleum Resources, 6 April 1982, in *Handbook*, p. 40, note 5 above. Although the wording of the regulations could be interpreted to mean that the deemed rate is mandatory for petroleum subcontractors, and one commentator, Wang Xuanhui, p. 36, note 126 above, has so stated, an official has said that while subcontractors are likely in most cases to prefer the deemed profit system, they may also elect to substantiate their actual costs and expenses and calculate their taxable income according to the FEITL's usual rules. T. Gelatt, discussion with Ministry of Finance tax official, 22 November

1982. Indeed, subcontractors operating in South China are apparently being given the choice between the two approaches. T. Gelatt, discussion with foreign oil company representative, 23 March 1983.

The Chinese have extended the 10 per cent deemed profit system to all foreign businesses contracting for projects and providing labour services in China. Project and Labour Regulations, Art. 3, note 205 above. Under this article, a foreign company may, with the confirmation of the local tax office, use the deemed profit system in a case where the period of work or provision of services is relatively short and accurate evidence of costs and expenses cannot be provided.

Neither the FEITL Regulations nor the Project and Labour Regulations would appear to limit the use of the deemed profit system to foreign companies contracting independently for projects in China. Thus, this system would appear to be applicable to a foreign company participating in a contractual joint venture (see pp. 55–6 of the text) for the performance of a construction project, exploration services, and so on.

The Chinese are, as of early 1984, re-evaluating the deemed profit system for contractors and are apparently considering raising the deemed profit rate and restricting the availability of the system to very short-term projects.

211. FEITL Regulations, Art. 34, note 4 above. A commentary points out that the intent of this provision is to tax foreign enterprises operating for less than one year at the FEITL rate applicable to the actual income earned, rather than basing the tax rate on the annualized amount of income. Wang Xuanhui, 'Facilitate Tax Payment Procedures on the Basis of a Strict and Impartial Tax System', *Caizheng (Finance)*, No. 2 (1983), p. 32.

212. Project and Labour Regulations, Art. 3, note 205 above.

213. The period of six months has been used by the Chinese in various tax treaty negotiations but the period to be fixed for general purposes under the FEITL has not yet been decided. T. Gelatt, discussion with Ministry of Finance tax official, 23 February 1983. The Project and Labour Regulations, Art. 6, note 205 above, make clear that where tax treaties exist they will prevail over the Regulations.

214. Project and Labour Regulations, Art. 2, note 205 above. See text accompanying notes 205-207 above.

215. FEITL Regulations, Art. 9, note 4 above.

216. See text following note 51 above.

217. Project and Labour Regulations, Art. 1, note 205 above.

218. Project and Labour Regulations, Art. 1(1), note 205 above. A foreign company engaged in project work in China which subcontracts part of the project to another foreign company is responsible for withholding the CICTA from its payments to the latter. If the deemed profit rate has been adopted for the latter, the first foreign company must also withhold the FEITL. Project and Labour Regulations, Art. 4, note 205 above.

219. Project and Labour Regulations, Arts. 1(2) and (3), note 205 above. Like the deemed profit system, the tax treatment described in notes 217–219 and accompanying text would appear to apply to the foreign company in a co-operative venture as well as a foreign company performing a contracted project independently in China. See note 210 above.

220. See note 49 above and accompanying text.

221. *Ta Kung Pao*, 28 September 1983, p. 3; and Ma Meili, 'China's New Policy

on the Utilization of Foreign Funds', in Policy Research Department and Foreign Investment Administration, Ministry of Foreign Economic Relations and Trade, China (ed.), *Guide to China's Foreign Economic Relations and Trade Investment Special* (1983), p. 169.

222. Ma Meili, p. 169, note 221 above. See 1972 Act, Schedule of Taxable Items and Rates, note 46 above, which includes a useful column listing the CICTA items and rates for comparative purposes. In addition to lowering some of the CICTA rates, the 1972 Act omits a number of items from the schedule of taxable items.

223. Joint Venture Implementing Act, Art. 71(1), note 59 above. 'Other materials' are defined for purposes of this provision and those cited in notes 224–225 below as referring to materials required for a joint venture's construction of the factory or site and for installation and reinforcement of machinery. Joint Venture Implementing Act, Art. 7(1), note 59 above. See also Regulations [of the State Economic Commission] For the Control of and Levy and Exemption of Tax on Items Imported by Chinese-Foreign Joint Ventures (no date), 1983 (hereafter cited as the SEC Joint Venture Tax Regulations), Art. 3(1).

224. Joint Venture Implementing Act, Art. 71(2), note 59 above. The 'total amount of investment' of a joint venture is defined as the total of the basic construction funds and the production circulating funds (working capital) needed to be invested in accordance with the scale of production stipulated in the joint venture contract and charter. Joint Venture Implementing Act, Art. 20, note 59 above. The SEC Joint Venture Tax Regulations, Art. 3(2), note 223 above, exempt 'equipment and other necessary materials purchased abroad with registered capital and imported for the start-up of the joint venture'. The use of the term 'registered capital' as opposed to 'total amount of investment' in the above-cited provision of the Joint Venture Implementing Act is unclear. 'Registered capital' appears to be a narrower concept than 'total amount of investment' and would not, for instance, include loans taken out by the joint venture for start-up funds. See Joint Venture Implementing Act, Arts. 20 and 21, note 59 above.

225. Joint Venture Implementing Act, Art. 71(3), note 59 above. See also SEC Joint Venture Tax Regulations, Art. 3(3), note 223 above.

226. Joint Venture Implementing Act, Art. 71(4), note 59 above. Although the language of the cited provision of the Joint Venture Implementing Act indicates that all such items imported with the stated intention of using them to produce export goods are exempt from the industrial and commercial tax, a document published in the official organ of the Ministry of Finance states that only 85 to 95 per cent of any given batch of goods so imported will be exempt from tax. Tax Reduction and Exemption, p. 47, note 93 above. The rationale for this provision is apparently to catch at the outset at least some of the spillover to the domestic market that the Chinese find generally occurs with goods imported for export production, rather than relying solely on taxation of such spillover as it occurs (see text accompanying note 227 below). T. Gelatt, discussion with PRC legal official, 30 June 1983. The extent to which this Ministry of Finance policy is being applied, in light of the language of the Joint Venture Implementing Act, is unclear.

In any event, joint ventures importing materials which they are to process into finished products for export may benefit from a bonded warehouse system recently initiated under which such materials are exempted from industrial and commercial tax and duties. See Control Regulations of the Customs for Bonded Warehouses for

Imported Materials to be Processed, for trial implementation from 1 January 1984.
227. Joint Venture Implementing Act, Art. 71, para. 2, note 59 above. See also SEC Joint Venture Tax Regulations, Art. 5, note 223 above.
228. T. Gelatt, discussion with Ministry of Finance tax official, 22 November 1982; and see Import/Export Regulations, Art. 1, note 192 above.
229. Joint Venture Implementing Act, Art. 72, para. 1, note 59 above. The exemption does not apply to items whose export is restricted by the state.
230. Joint Venture Implementing Act, Art. 72, para. 2, note 59 above. Any industrial and commercial tax paid on sales income is deductible in computing taxable income under the JVITL. JVITL Regulations, Art. 8, note 3 above.
231. Provisional Urban Real Estate Tax Act, promulgated by the Government Administration Council of the Central People's Government on 8 August 1981 (hereafter cited as the PURETA). For a brief summary of the PURETA's structure and rates, see Pomp, Gelatt and Surrey, p. 14, note 9, note 1 above.
232. Tax Reduction and Exemption, p. 47, note 93 above. Joint ventures were apparently exempted from the PURETA's land tax by a 1980 Ministry of Finance document. T. Gelatt, discussion with PRC legal official, 30 June 1983.
233. See Joint Venture Law, Art. 5, para. 3, note 59 above; and PURETA, Art. 3, note 231 above.
234. See Joint Venture Law, Art. 5, para. 3, note 59 above; and PURETA, Art. 3, note 231 above.

The PURETA has been factored into the rates of the 1972 Act, note 46 above. *National Taxation,* pp. 25 and 143–4, note 42 above. The PURETA will presumably cease to apply separately to joint ventures taxed under those rates. See note 222 above and accompanying text.
235. Under these experiments, state enterprises will pay a fixed income tax rate of 55 per cent with the balance of their profits to be divided between the government and the enterprise itself. Gradually, all straight profit turnovers to the state will be phased out and taxation used exclusively. Small-scale state enterprises are already using an eight-rate progressive income tax system with no further turnover of profits to the state. In addition to the income tax on state enterprises, various other taxes, such as a fixed assets tax, or 'fee', and an 'adjustment tax' used to compensate for income differentials among enterprises attributable to exogenous factors are being employed on an experimental basis. See A. Bennett, 'China Slowly Levies New Taxes Designed to Spur Development', *Asian Wall Street Journal*, 18 March 1983, p. 1; 'Changing From Profits Turnover to Taxation is the Direction', *Jingji Ribao (Economic Daily)*, 1 March 1983, p. 1; 'Why Are the Eight-Scale Progressive Tax Rates Applied to Small-Scale Enterprises?', *Jingji Ribao (Economic Daily)*, 1 March 1983, p. 2; Wu Ruqing and Sun Yunsu, note 44 above; Chai Wen, 'The Direction of Changing from Profits Turnover to Turnover of Taxes Should be Confirmed', *Caizheng (Finance)*, No. 2 (1983), p. 23; 'Actively Support Enterprises' Carrying Out the Change from Profits Turnover to Turnover of Taxes', *Renmin Ribao (People's Daily)*, 30 March 1983, p. 1; Provisional Measures [of the Ministry of Finance] for Changing from Profits Turnover to Taxation for State Enterprises, effective 1 January 1983, published in *Renmin Ribao (People's Daily)*, 3 May 1983, p. 2; and Wang Chuanlun, 'Some Notes on Tax Reform in China', *The China Quarterly*, March 1984, p. 53.
236. See note 44 above and accompanying text.

237. The need to re-examine these traditional patterns is graphically illustrated by the United Nations' work on a model tax treaty for use between the developed and developing countries. The United Nations' involvement was in response to the OECD's model tax treaty, which has been widely accepted by the developed countries in their bilateral agreements, but is considered by many developing countries as unresponsive to their special circumstances and needs.

3. Technology Transfer to China: Policies, Law and Practice

STANLEY B. LUBMAN

I. Introduction

THIS chapter emphasizes practical problems in negotiating technology transfer to the People's Republic of China (PRC). Such transfers are possible in a variety of contexts other than the pure licence, such as agreements on countertrade and on equity joint ventures. Although this chapter does not discuss such other transactions in detail, by reason of its subject matter it addresses a variety of problems that lie at the heart of many transactions other than licences.

A necessary preliminary to the survey which follows, as it must be to any exploration by foreign companies of likely transactions, is an understanding of some of the influences resulting from changing Chinese policies on technology transfer. The parts of this chapter which follow immediately below discuss such policy influences.

II. Changing Chinese Policies towards Technology Transfer

A. The Movement away from Whole-plant Imports

Chinese imports of technology since 1949 have been characterized by four peaks.[1] During the first, throughout the 1950s, technology transfer was effected largely through the importation by China of large, complete sets of equipment, mostly from the Soviet Union and Eastern Europe. Speaking of the period 1952–60, one expert observer has said:

> It was largely that experience which shaped Chinese attitudes toward technology. In that 7-year period, China was the recipient of what was undoubtedly the most comprehensive technology transfer in modern industrial history . . . The Soviet contribution encompassed much more than their production technology. It ran the gamut from scientific and technical education to project design, and from production

engineering to creating a modern industrial organization, complete with planning, budgeting, and management systems.[2]

This major infusion of technology under Soviet tutelage was to cause technology transfer to be conceptually linked to large projects; and in the eyes of some Chinese leaders the Soviet experience also tied technology transfer to dependence on imports. After the Sino-Soviet break in 1960, China engaged in a long and costly experiment with 'self-reliance' throughout the 1960s and well into the following decade, which hampered the modernization of her industry.

A second wave of importation of complete plants took place from 1973 to 1977. Also, for the first time since the PRC was established in 1949, the imports included contracts with American firms, notably Pullman-Kellogg, from whom the Chinese purchased 8 large ammonia plants worth US$215 million in 1972. As one Chinese commentator later stated, the transactions of this period emphasized 'large sets, large series, high speed, high efficiency, automatic control and the highly integrated use of thermal energy.'[3] Once again, as in the 1950s, technology was principally imported embodied in large plants.

Some of the problems which Chinese commentators have perceived in projects associated with this stage have influenced current Chinese thinking on technology imports. Of particular interest is the view that because the technology that was imported was incorporated into large plants, it has been difficult to absorb it and learn from it. Difficulties have included construction delays in many projects; in others, the plants have operated under capacity because of shortages of raw materials and energy. Chinese critics have stated that the returns on the investment in some of these projects have been low. The chemical fertilizer plants, in particular, encountered considerable shortages of raw materials, oil and gas, and the rise in the price of oil affected the profitability of a number of other plants.

One of the projects that has encountered considerable difficulties is at Wuhan, where iron and steel manufacturing facilities were imported from Germany and Japan. There, not only did power shortages greatly impede testing, but also facilities were constructed and made ready at differing and uneven rates of speed. It turned out that the entire province in which the plant is located lacks the power needed for the new plant. In addition, integrating old and new sections of the plant proved difficult. Moreover, some of the imported technology and equipment was found to be too advanced for Chinese needs, so that the plant now produces steel sheets that are too thin to be used in old Chinese casting equipment, and some types of steel for which there is little demand from Chinese end-users.[4]

The third wave of buying, a short-lived spree in 1978–9, again included large projects such as the Baoshan iron and steel plant in Shanghai, which was allocated approximately one-third of the total amount of funds committed during this brief period.[5] Most of the 22 projects contracted for were metallurgical and petrochemical projects which consumed a high amount of energy and caused other extensive economic dislocations. For example, raw materials such as iron ore and other materials such as refractory materials and chemicals have had to be imported for them. These imports caused other distortions such as shipping and storage problems. Moreover, the planning for these projects was poorly done, and some projects were authorized without prior feasibility studies and were carried out without strict adherence to orderly construction procedures. A thorough assessment of needs, and of the relationships between the imported projects and the rest of the Chinese economy was also lacking.

'Readjustment', the reaction to the errors summarized above, began in 1979 and caused the suspension or cancellation of some of the largest projects and a reappraisal of import policies. In the last few years, a noticeable new orientation towards technology transfer has developed, a delayed but probably desirable response to the perceived errors of the three previous waves of imports. Now, in a fourth wave, fewer whole plants are likely to be contracted for, and greater conservatism has been shown in making commitments for large expenditures of foreign exchange. Emphasis has been placed on rehabilitating and improving existing factories. Of particular interest has been a shift away from importing technology that is incorporated into equipment and towards the importation of technology and know-how, a shift which Chinese commentators have variously characterized as a move from 'hardware' to 'software', or from 'eggs' to 'hens'.

The lessons of the great buying spree of 1978 have also caused commentators to urge better planning and feasibility studies, with a view to planning for the integration of domestically manufactured equipment with that purchased from abroad. A warning has been repeated that it is not necessary to purchase the most advanced, 'state of the art' technology, but rather that it is preferable instead to consider the appropriateness of the technology and the Chinese capacity to absorb it. Other criteria which have been emphasized include reducing energy consumption, promoting import substitution, and, at the same time, increasing the Chinese capacity to export and thereby earn foreign exchange to repay the foreign technology transferor. Some of these aims may be mutually inconsistent. At any rate, their articulation reflects the outcome of considerable reflection on, and criticism of, blind adherence to the earlier Soviet model.

B. The Transfer of Technology within China

Greater emphasis on absorbing technology has also resulted in an increased interest in the more efficient use of Chinese domestic resources for developing and transmitting technology. In recent years, Chinese leaders have become acutely aware of the weaknesses in their science and technology and research and development systems.[6] These shortcomings are particularly evident in four crucial areas: (1) difficulty in incorporating scientific research results into large-scale production; (2) limited management capabilities, especially in such areas as operations research and systems management; (3) the backwardness of key technical prerequisites, particularly with regard to precision instruments; and (4) a shortage of qualified scientific and technical personnel.

Chinese leaders have attacked these problems in earnest since the late 1970s. Such policies as sending thousands of students and scholars abroad, developing domestic post-graduate education, and improving living and working conditions for intellectuals generally, are all essential prerequisites for overcoming, or at least partially alleviating, these bottlenecks. Nonetheless, it should be noted that many of the constraints mentioned above can only be eased gradually, and that remedial measures will take time. Consequently, a solution to these problems will only come about in the long term.

Potential licensors need to be aware of these important influences on the Chinese capacity to absorb technology. Yet Chinese resources should not be underestimated. These include the 'capacity to mobilize large amounts of technical, financial and personnel resources to accomplish a particular task',[7] experience in handling 'engineering-related problem-solving tasks',[8] and strong encouragement from official policy which favours technology borrowing. At the same time, however, the Chinese suffer from severe technical constraints. They have a history of 'poor performance in translating research results into the serial production process',[9] which stems in part from a lack of adequate testing and measurement instrumentation, a lack of numerically controlled machine tools, and an excessive vertical integration which reduces technical specialization. As a result, standardization in quality-control instrumentation and precision-testing equipment is low. Perhaps even greater constraints on the capacity to absorb foreign technology are imposed by poor management and inadequate planning. Chinese 'bureaucratism', the primacy of economic output quotas, and the verticality and cellularity of the Chinese industrial and research and development systems impede innovation and the flow of information.

C. The Reorganization of the Chinese Foreign Trade Apparatus

Another influence on the Chinese importation of technology has been the repeated reorganization of the Chinese foreign trade bureaucracy. In 1978–9 a decision was made to reduce the rigidities in the highly centralized, Soviet-style foreign trade apparatus which had existed in China since 1949. This led to the introduction of massive decentralization.[10] A direct consequence for technology transfer of this decentralization was that whilst formerly only a few agencies had the authority to enter into contracts with foreign companies for the importation of technology, notably the China National Technical

Import Corporation (Techimport), now new organizations appeared on the scene ready to contract for technology imports.

The problems ensuing from decentralization — namely, considerable lack of co-ordination and planning, resulting duplication and confusion, and the signing of contracts which departed from economic plans — prompted the Chinese leadership to move towards partial recentralization.[11] Attempts have been made to co-ordinate and monitor the activities of entities which are permitted to engage in trade transactions in addition to the traditional foreign trade corporations. However, the proliferation of organizations which can engage in foreign trade transactions has meant that technology transfer is no longer the province of a very small number of organizations. Nor is it limited to Beijing: for the Special Economic Zones (SEZs) and a number of cities (such as Shanghai, Tianjin and Beijing) and provinces are now able to enter into trade transactions.

Organizational flux and the resulting confusion have created problems, some of whose practical implications are discussed below. Although many of these problems may be transitional, foreign businessmen and their advisors must be prepared to encounter considerable overlapping of jurisdiction, bureaucratic rivalries, and delays in their dealings with Chinese partners in transactions involving the transfer of technology.

The Chinese leadership is well aware of the difficulties caused by the organizational changes, which have been further aggravated by the absence of promulgated laws and regulations. The difficulties are being addressed both by continued experimentation with the organization of the foreign trade apparatus and by promulgation of new legislation.

The latest in a series of reorganizations is a further partial recentralization of foreign trade that was announced in March 1984. The first legislation specifically devoted to rules applicable to non-tax aspects of technology transfer has also appeared, the Provisional Regulations of the Shenzhen Special Economic Zone on the Introduction of Technology, promulgated by the Guangdong Provincial People's Congress in February 1984 (hereafter cited as the Shenzhen Provisional Technology Regulations). In addition, Regulations of the Shenzhen Special Economic Zone on Foreign Economic Contracts were also promulgated in February 1984. These contain rules applicable to all contracts involving foreign and Chinese enterprises in the Shenzhen Special Economic Zone (hereafter cited as the Shenzhen Foreign Economic Contracts Regulations). Since the Shenzhen SEZ is a pioneer and model zone widely discussed in the Chinese press, and since it is likely that the new regulations were first reviewed in Beijing, their significance may extend beyond the Shenzhen SEZ.

The two new pieces of legislation mentioned above will henceforth greatly influence trade and investment transactions of all types in the Shenzhen SEZ. By stating the subjects which must be covered in contracts and prescribing procedures for obtaining contract approvals, they will serve to promote standard contract documentation. The new regulations are not discussed at length here, but certain important clauses are discussed below.[12]

III. Approaches to Negotiating Technology Licences in China

The discussion that follows reviews terms and practice in agreements to license technology, followed by some brief concluding observations. It is based principally on experience in negotiations with Techimport and, in recent years, with other Chinese organizations. Although reference is made frequently to 'licences', as noted earlier the discussion is equally applicable to the transfer of technology, not so denominated, in other types of transactions such as contracts for equity joint ventures.

A. Coverage of the Licence

The licensor (whom Chinese organizations insist on calling the 'Seller') can expect the Chinese side (the 'Buyer') to attempt to define as broadly as possible the scope of the contract and the technical documentation which the licensor is expected to deliver. For example, a standard Techimport clause provides for the Seller to grant the Buyer the right to design and manufacture the product in China, and to provide 'all relevant technical documentation including design, calculations and research reports, quality control, product drawings, manufacturing technology, inspection, installation, operation and maintenance' of the product, as defined in an appendix. The terminology employed in contracts with other organizations may not be so detailed, and often the short cut employed obligates the Seller to transfer documentation 'identical' with that which it uses. References to 'assembly drawings', 'process instructions', 'equipment operation instructions', 'tool drawings', and 'parts and material specifications' are also common.

Problems have sometimes been encountered in the past in obtaining agreement on a satisfactory formulation of the technical documentation. Chinese end-users may be particularly demanding. They and the organization handling the commercial negotiations may want to list types of documents which a licensor does not ordinarily supply to licensees, such as engineers' notebooks. Perhaps influenced by the rigid and highly bureaucratic, Soviet-style system that they adopted in the past, Chinese engineers seem to assume that foreign companies are more orderly in keeping track of their research than they may be in practice. In some negotiations, Buyers have agreed to accept clauses which require Sellers to supply only the material that is readily available. In this regard, too, care must be taken to define what is included by references to 'design'.

Similar problems may also arise in defining the extent of the improvements to which the Chinese side should be entitled under the agreement. As in many developing countries, both end-users and commercial negotiators are concerned about licensors selling technology for products which may soon be replaced. Given the suspiciousness of potential Chinese licensors, and their need to justify the transactions to their superiors and to other organizations which must approve the transactions, licensors are well advised to be sensitive to this problem. Licensors may find that if they are unwilling to agree to include improvements throughout the term of the licence without charging any additional technology fee, the Chinese licensee may insist that the royalty rate decline after the expiry of the period during which improvements will be transferred. On the other hand, problems have sometimes been encountered in dealing with improvements by the *Chinese* licensee; the Chinese side will want to own them, and may expect a fee for the use of them from the licensor after the licence has expired.

B. Price, Payment and Valuation Conditions

A standard Techimport form provides for payment of a lump-sum contract price in instalments. The first instalment is payable after the signing of the contract and receipt of an export licence, the second instalment within 30 days after receipt of the technical documentation has been certified, and the third within 30 days after successful completion of the acceptance test has been certified. The percentages are left blank in the contract form, and are obviously negotiable.

An alternative method of payment has been acceptable to Techimport, that is, a 'small' down-payment and a royalty computed either according to an agreed number of planned units or according to the number actually produced. A lump-sum royalty is also possible. Techimport has required detailed information from the Seller on how it has calculated a proposed rate, after which it may provide its own calculation of a per-unit royalty, which the Seller can expect to be low.

Licensors can expect considerable differences of opinion on the valuation of their technology. The Chinese inevitably and understandably prefer low fees and low royalty rates. They express considerable antipathy towards even considering the cost of the licensor's research and development efforts. Reflecting Chinese concern about the overevaluation of technology, the Shenzhen Provisional Technology Regulations provide that when technology is capitalized as part of the establishment of a joint venture, the value of the technology may not exceed 20 per cent of the registered capital of the enterprise, and the foreign side must also supply an equivalent amount of 'cash or materials as investment capital' (Art. 23).

After the parties have agreed on the value of the technology, other difficulties with respect to pricing can be anticipated. If royalties are expected by the licensor, he may find that the Chinese side ordinarily prefers to key them to its net profits or to actual sales, while the licensor may be more interested in establishing a minimum regardless of Chinese production or sales.

C. Buying Back and Export

Also related to price is a common Chinese attempt to require the licensor to buy back from the Chinese licensee some units or quantity of the licensed product. The differences between the parties on this matter may be fundamental: the licensor may not want the product at all, but even if he wishes to accept some shipments he may be doubtful of the Chinese capacity to sell to him competitively. The parties may also find it difficult to agree on the price of buying back products, especially since the Chinese may prefer a fixed price while the licensor will normally want a provision for adjustments to be made to reflect changes in world market prices.

Merely to mention these issues is to suggest the difficulty they pose and the additional time and trouble they may add to a negotiation. It has been possible for parties to compromise by agreeing on the buying back of some parts and components, although any licensor who contemplates obtaining such parts and components from a Chinese enterprise other than the one where the licensed technology will be used is likely to be disappointed; the current organization of the Chinese economic system prevents such flexibility.

Chinese licensees commonly insist on obtaining rights to export products manufactured with the licensed technology. This reflects policy emphases on the need for the transaction to earn foreign exchange and the desire to enlarge China's export capacity. Indeed, the Shenzhen regulations provide that,

> Products using the manufactured technology should have lawful and reasonable international markets. If the sale of the products is affected due to reasons caused by the supplier [of the technology], the supplier must pay for the loss [Art. 12].

Apparently, internal regulations make it mandatory or nearly mandatory for Chinese licensees to exact *some* export rights, and it is not uncommon for the parties to agree to exports to markets with which the licensor may not be greatly concerned, but often only after considerable negotiation on the subject.

D. Duration

Negotiations on this clause have been marked by the reluctance of Chinese licensees to sign agreements that obligate them to make payments over long periods of time, or to be dependent on licensors for components or raw materials. A period of five years has been common, in this author's experience, although longer periods are possible. The Shenzhen regulations provide that 'the term of the contract must, in general, not exceed five years, except in a case where technology is regarded as investment capital [although the term may be extended with the approval of the Shenzhen government]' (Art. 19).

E. Training and Technical Assistance

The foreign licensor will find the Chinese side eager to receive training and technical assistance, but reluctant to pay more than a limited per diem fee for such assistance. It is rare for this fee to exceed several hundred dollars per day. Chinese licensees commonly request that such charges be included in the technology fee and that they should not be separately identified in the contract. Standard Chinese documentation on training requires insertion of the details of the person/days to be spent in either country by the personnel of the other side. Responsibility for international travel and for living expenses is negotiable, although it is both common and reasonable to adjust the scale of living of foreign personnel in China to local levels.

Quite apart from the inclusion of appropriate language on financial responsibility for such costs, it is essential to include language on the living and working conditions of foreign personnel in China. This is especially important because the precise conditions under which foreign personnel (and, in some cases, their dependents) will live are often not studied carefully by the Chinese side or discussed in detail by the two sides at the time the contract is negotiated.

F. Acceptance Tests

Some of the most potentially vexing problems in negotiating licensing transactions arise from the clause on acceptance tests. One aspect of Chinese Buyers' attitudes toward these transactions is to treat the transaction like the sale of a bundle of documents intended to ensure that the Buyer, after using the instructions contained in the documents, will produce a product which meets the contract specifications. The standard contract clause does not contain language which requires Buyers to follow the licensor's instructions strictly, although Buyers will agree to insert such a requirement if Sellers insist.

Another aspect of Chinese Buyers' attitudes that colours these transactions is the assumption that the two parties are contracting to enter into a relationship in which the Seller will have a long-standing and continuous duty to assist the Buyer. So paramount is this relationship, and the obligations to assist the Buyer, that the Buyer's failure to follow correctly the licensor's technical specifications may be regarded as almost irrelevant. The Chinese side will first of all assume that the procedure for establishing fault, if the product fails to pass the acceptance test, should be strictly bilateral, that is by consultation between the parties. In addition, it will want the contract to reflect agreement that, by nature of the relationship between the parties, the two will together work out and resolve any difficulties that may arise, without looking to any third-party dispute settlement.

Clauses on acceptance tests, whether in Techimport standard-form contracts or in others which are known to this author, are similar in their organization and language. Such clauses commonly provide that the tests shall be conducted in China in the presence of the Seller's technicians, with test methods and other technical aspects to be provided in detail in an appendix. If the acceptance test demonstrates that the product conforms to the specifications agreed on in advance, then the parties are required to sign an acceptance certificate.

If, however, the product fails to pass the acceptance test, the clause requires both parties to consult together, analyse the causes, conduct another acceptance test, and, as one Techimport clause has it, 'clarify the responsibility'. The clause may also require that in such an event, the period for which the Seller is required to keep his technicians in China may be extended for an agreed number of weeks.

If responsibility for the failure is determined by the parties to lie with the Buyer, then the parties shall sign a certificate of acceptance test 'termination', but standard Techimport language requires the Seller to 'assist the Buyer in taking means to eliminate the defects'. If responsibility lies with the Seller, Techimport contracts require the Seller to 'correct his mistakes as soon as possible', supply the Buyer with the correct documentation, and assist the Buyer in taking measures to eliminate the defects. If the defect cannot be remedied within an extended time period agreed by the parties, then the Seller must pay a penalty under the penalty clause in the contract, to which the clause on acceptance tests cross-refers, and which is normally expressed in terms of a percentage of the contract price. Since the penalty clause is in its terms directly addressed to the problems of incompleteness, incorrectness and unreliability of the documentation, the cross-reference is very awkward.

This awkward Techimport language has remained unchanged for years, probably because it is used only very rarely. In the Chinese view, the parties have entered into a complex relationship which does not amount merely to the sale of a commodity, and they are expected to work out their problems in the context of that relationship. The outlook may be caused by cultural attitudes, as well as by the dependence of the Buyers on knowledgeable and expert licensors. Whatever the reason, licensors should expect the Chinese to think in terms of a continuing relationship that extends beyond the end of the licensor's formal obligations under the agreement.

Both parties must agree at the outset on a precise definition of the test methods that will be used, and on the standards that will be used to measure conformity of the tested sample or prototype to contract specifications. If the end-user representatives are technically competent, it should not be too difficult to reach agreement with them on these matters, which are normally the subject of a detailed appendix.

G. The Guarantee and the Penalty

The lengthy guarantee clause in the standard Techimport contract requires the Seller to guarantee that the documentation 'shall be the latest technical achievement possessed by the Seller' at the effective date or while the contract is in effect. The documentation must also be 'complete, correct, reliable, legible and dispatched in time'. Definitions of these terms are then supplied, of which the most notable is that of 'correct', which requires that the documentation shall be 'without mistake' and that the 'parts and components to be manufactured by skilled and experienced people strictly in accordance with the documentation shall be [products that are deemed to meet contract standards].' This makes performance of the product a function of the 'correctness' of the documentation.

If the Buyer discovers that the documentation does not comply with the foregoing stipulations, the Seller must dispatch the missing documentation. A penalty is provided for delay, in terms of a percentage of the contract price which increases with the length of the delay. The same penalties are theoretically applicable to 'incorrect' or 'unreliable' documentation.

The standard contract provides for a ceiling on all the above-mentioned penalties of 5 per cent of the contract price. Since the penalties stated are cross-referred to in the clause on acceptance tests, this ceiling presumably applies when the Chinese-manufactured sample product does not pass the acceptance test, and when this clause would theoretically also apply, as discussed above.

Licensors are understandably concerned about the extent of their guarantees of performance after equipment prototypes or manufacturing facilities, as the case may be, are completed and tested. The quality of materials and equipment used by the Chinese side, the technical level of the personnel on both sides, and the test methods may influence the performance of the tested product. Chinese negotiators emphasize the desire of both sides to assure a satisfactory outcome, that is that the test results must conform exactly to the specifications in the appendices. Co-operation seems to be the keynote. Both sides must test the equipment together after agreeing on the tests and the specifications.

In practice, Techimport appears to be most reluctant to invoke penalty clauses, preferring first to investigate and decide on the nature of the defect and the method of its elimination, and then to concentrate on bringing the quality of the product up to contract specifications. Negotiations suggest that this view of the transaction is so strong that it may be possible to bargain hard to limit the penalty or even to eliminate a penalty clause, although much less flexibility exists with regard to the guarantee of quality.

H. The Licence Agreement and Third Parties: Patent Infringement, Restrictions on Use, Confidentiality, and Approval of the Transaction

i. Patent Infringement

With regard to third parties, Chinese contract language is often skeletal if, indeed, it is there at all. The standard Techimport clause on patent infringement is very general, requiring the Seller to bear full 'relevant legal and economic responsibilities' arising out of alleged patent infringement. Lately, Techimport has insisted on more specific language requiring the licensor to assist the licensee and defend at its expense any claim against the licensee for patent infringement. The Shenzhen Provisional Technology Regulations state that,

> if the patent rights are invalidated halfway through the process or if the applications for patent rights are refused, the recipient will have the right to revise or terminate the contract [Art. 12].

Licensees have been known to insist on contract clauses that would give them the same rights.

ii. Confidentiality and Unauthorized Use

The problem of protecting proprietary information in China is a legitimate concern for any company considering a transaction involving technology transfer.

A confidentiality clause frequently used by Techimport provides that 'within the validity time of the contract, the Buyer shall not disclose or publish in any form to any third party *outside* China the contents of the know-how supplied by the Seller to the Buyer.' Getting Techimport to accept non-disclosure to entities *inside* China may be rather more difficult.

Curiously, when foreign negotiators have tried to limit disclosure within China to the end-user with whom negotiations have been carried out, some Techimport negotiators have been willing to state (in private) that any Chinese organization other than Techimport or the end-user would constitute a 'third party' to whom disclosure would be unauthorized. Yet some of these same Techimport negotiators have also been unwilling to express this interpretation in the contract. In one recent negotiation, the Techimport representative agreed to add language preventing disclosure by the Buyer 'to any person without connection with the present contract', which is still not completely satisfactory. Fortunately, other importing organizations and end-users in China seem to be increasingly willing to limit disclosure or use of the licensed know-how to a named manufacturing facility, an encouraging sign that the need for more explicit protection is gaining wider recognition in the PRC.

Yet, despite the likelihood that protection against improper disclosure may be possible, a company must nonetheless ask what it can do if it suspects or discovers that its technology has been improperly disclosed. What remedies are available?

China's new Patent Law, discussed below, provides for damages for infringement. Even though it has been promulgated, it is still important to pay attention to the contract, which Chinese legal specialists consistently assure foreigners will always be honoured. Foreign companies should obtain clear contractual expression of the obligations of the Chinese partner not to disclose or duplicate licensed technology or other proprietary information without the licensor's consent. It is also necessary to insist that licensees agree to require key employees to sign agreements obligating them not to disclose or transfer the protected technology. In licensing and other trade or investment agreements a satisfactory clause on dispute settlement should be included as well.

The need for stronger guarantees has led some to ask whether Chinese courts can enforce contractual stipulations prohibiting technology transfer. In practice, although the role of courts in Chinese society has expanded recently, and although they are intended to function with regard to disputes with foreigners,[13] foreigners would be well advised to look initially at extrajudicial remedies. They should first contact the Chinese party to the contract whom they suspect is breaching the confidentiality of the technology concerned. Restrained, tactful, but nevertheless unambiguous expressions of concern that duplication of the company's technology would violate a prior agreement (perhaps, in the case of technical seminars, also reinforced by an offer to enter into discussions about additional licence agreements) should carry the company's message convincingly. If such discussions do not succeed, the company should bring the violation to the attention of a high-level agency, such as a ministry, whose authority runs *vertically* downward to the organization that has violated the contract or is duplicating the technology. Another course would be to seek out other organizations with equal or greater political clout that can approach the bureaucratic hierarchy involved *horizontally*. These choices are not mutually exclusive. For example, if a licensor believes that a provincial chemical enterprise is wrongfully duplicating its technology, not only should the licensor complain to the enterprise's superiors, such as the provincial chemical industry bureau and the ministry itself, but also to the local government (the horizontal route), and to the Ministry of Foreign Economic Relations and Trade.

Regardless of how much progress is made toward regularizing Chinese law, the settlement of disputes involving foreigners is more likely to be through negotiation than any form of third-party adjudication. Foreigners who encounter problems arising out of alleged contract violations should take the system as it is — highly incomplete — and try to gain access to, and seek the assistance of, non-judicial Chinese agencies that have a large stake in China's commercial credibility abroad.

iii. Other Third-party Problems

The problems discussed thus far in this part have in common the fact that they involve third parties to the contract. Other potentially serious third-party problems deserve attention, namely identifying a potential partner, ascertaining the authority of a particular prospective partner, and establishing the identity of agencies which must approve a proposed transaction. It is at this point that some practical problems intersect with the effects of recent policy changes noted at the beginning of this chapter. The lines of jurisdiction between organizations are often unclear, and a stable equilibrium between centralization and decentralization has yet to be found. As noted above, the number of Chinese agencies authorized to negotiate technology transfer agreements has increased dramatically in the last five years.

Given the blurred lines of authority that exist, a foreign firm may have to discount assurances of Chinese organizations that claim to possess the authority not only to enter into technology transfer agreements, but also to protect the foreign firm in certain necessary ways. Consider, for example, a promise to a US firm by a provincial bureau of the chemical industry that factories in other provinces will not export to the United States. Does the provincial bureau really have the means to prevent its parent body, the Ministry of Chemical Industry, from transferring the necessary know-how to subordinate plants in other provinces or to prevent their provincial bureaux from negotiating with competing licensors? The US company would do well to be sceptical. Suppose, too, that the bureau cautions the foreigner not to go elsewhere, such as Beijing, for assurances. If the foreign company is confronted with a choice between accepting a local organization's assurances at face value, or seeming to be impolite or mistrustful, it seems desirable to try to obtain fuller assurances and support at the central level, and to tell the local Chinese organization that such action is being taken. It behoves the foreigner to risk embarrassment in order to avoid future problems.

I. Arbitration

It has been standard for some years for Techimport to agree to third-country arbitration, reflecting a compromise between foreigners' unwillingness to agree to arbitration by the Foreign Economic and Trade Arbitration Commission of the Chinese Council for the Promotion of International Trade (CCPIT), and unwillingness on the part of the Chinese to litigate in a foreign court. The standard Techimport arbitration clause calls for arbitration in Stockholm. The rules of the Stockholm Chamber of Commerce, or of the United Nations Commission on International Trade Law (UNCITRAL) are usually stated as applicable. It is expected that a Chinese party would abide by an agreement to arbitrate, although the Chinese Code of Civil Procedure, adopted in 1982, seems on its face to permit Chinese courts to take jurisdiction of a foreign trade dispute where the parties have not agreed to submit to arbitration by a *Chinese* arbitration organization.

A major problem in dispute settlement clauses, likely to become more difficult to resolve in a manner satisfactory to foreign licensors, is that of agreeing on the applicable law, to which standard Chinese clauses conspicuously omit reference. General trends, not limited to transactions involving technology transfer, are relevant here. In a relatively small number of transactions, particularly loan transactions involving the Bank of China, Chinese parties have agreed to the applicability of foreign law. More often, though, in the relatively few cases in which they are willing to agree to reference to foreign law, Chinese parties to transactions would prefer to allow the arbitrators to choose that law, a solution that injects uncertainty into the proceedings. Recently, in a variety of transactions, reflecting both an earlier and lingering distaste for submission to foreign law and the more recent development of Chinese laws and regulations applicable to foreign trade transactions, Chinese negotiators have insisted that Chinese law be applicable.

Insistence on the applicability of Chinese law may increase. The Shenzhen Foreign Economic Contract Regulations provide that in arbitration arising out of contracts performed in the Guangdong SEZs, co-operative activities, contracts relating to natural resources, and other contracts which have a 'close relationship to Chinese sovereignty', Chinese law must be applied (Art. 35). The same article provides that arbitration of disputes arising out of the enumerated types of contracts shall be arbitrated by the arbitration organs in the SEZs, but that the parties 'may choose other arbitral organs'. There is no reference to any right of the parties to choose to apply a law other than Chinese law, which suggests an intent to require that disputes arising out of all contracts in the SEZs with foreigners, for technology transfer and otherwise, must be decided under Chinese law.

Limitations of space make it impossible to discuss at length the implications of the conclusions reached here. Suffice it to say that insistence that Chinese law apply to disputes involving investment in China, because China is the host country, is consistent with the view of many other developing nations. At the same time, the newness and irregularity of application of Chinese laws on foreign trade and investment detract very much from the uniformity and certainty of the promulgated Chinese rules as they are carried out in practice. The problem of ascertaining Chinese law will not be solved merely by their publication; here, too, as in technology transfer, the infrastructure does not yet match Chinese expectations. At the same time, Chinese legal officials seem likely to continue to advocate compromise and conciliation as the most desirable methods of settling disputes.[14]

J. Taxes

Since the new Foreign Enterprise Income Tax Law was enacted,[15] income earned in China by foreign companies is subject either to taxation at a progressive rate up to 40 per cent if they have an 'establishment' in China, or at a 20 per cent withholding rate on interest, royalties and other passive income if they do not have an 'establishment'. As a result, these foreign companies stand to be taxed at one or the other rate on royalties paid under licence agreements. A variety of methods have been employed, or have become available, to enable a licensor without an 'establishment' to escape the withholding tax on royalties.

In some transactions, especially just after the new tax law was promulgated, foreign licensors and Chinese licensees have agreed that the Chinese side would pay the tax. This practice has been disapproved of by the Ministry of Finance. A variant of this arrangement is for the Chinese side to agree to reimburse the foreign side after the withholding tax is withheld from royalty payments.

In discussions, Ministry of Finance officials have stated that, although it is not illegal, this practice violates Ministry policy.

The Ministry positions described above are understandable affirmations of the policy expressed in the Foreign Enterprise Income Tax Law of reaching China-source income of foreign companies. A contractual arrangement which would permit the Ministry to collect all taxes due under the law, while yet protecting the foreign licensor, would be simply an agreement to guarantee the licensor's income after Chinese taxes. The result of this, of course, would be to raise the cost of the licence, although it would seem to violate no tax policy.

In order to promote the importation of advanced technology, the Ministry of Finance adopted regulations in January 1983 which provided that the withholding tax rate would be halved to 10 per cent, and certain transactions made wholly exempt, 'where the technology is advanced and the terms preferential', in certain cases.[16] These are fees for the use of 'proprietary technology' in 'agriculture, forestry, fishing and animal husbandry' activities; where 'proprietary technology' is provided 'in the conducting of scientific research or scientific experiments' for certain named types of institutions; in 'China's key construction projects in exploiting energy and developing communications and transport, areas of energy conservation and prevention and cause of environmental pollution'; and in eight named 'important technical spheres'. The regulations state that the fees which may fall under the exception include fees for technical documentation, technical services and training. Also exempt are fees for consulting services for Chinese 'engineering, construction or enterprises'; 'technology instruction fees' arising out of instruction or seminars on 'enterprise management and application of production technology'; 'technical assistance fees' related to assistance for 'present equipment or products of Chinese enterprises'; and technical services and design or documentation fees for construction sites or equipment.

Under the new regulations, the agencies charged with approving the transactions must submit relevant documents to the local tax authorities. Tax *reductions* will be decided locally, but complete tax *exemptions* will be decided by the Ministry of Finance on application from local tax bureaux. If recent experience is any guide, concrete guidance on tax exemptions is likely only to become available to prospective foreign licensors slowly in the near future, and they will have to rely on informal interpretations and suggestions from local tax bureaux and the Ministry of Finance. It is also likely that the time between the signing of a contract and completion of all formal approvals may be lengthened, because of the need to submit applications for tax reduction to local tax bureaux, and applications for exemptions to both local bureaux and the Ministry of Finance in Beijing.

It should be noted that the problems of the applicability of the Foreign Enterprise Income Tax Law and of regulations on exemptions from the tax in that law may be legally avoided if payments by a Chinese party to a foreign one are not denominated as 'royalties' and are not otherwise classified as a type of passive income to which the withholding tax applies. The Ministry of Finance has confirmed, for instance, that where the foreign side is repaid for its know-how in products, such payments are not taxable under the Foreign Enterprise Income Tax Law.[17] Thus, a considerable tax incentive exists to fold technology transfer into co-production or countertrade transactions, rather than to enter into pure technology licensing agreements.

K. Chinese Patent Law

China's new Patent Law now extends legal protection of industrial property rights beyond the protection afforded by contract, which previously was all that was available to a foreign party. Changes in the strictly domestic sphere have preceded consideration of protection of foreign patents. New regulations on the reward and certification of inventions were issued in late 1978. A State Patent Bureau was established in late 1979, and interest in international patent protection has grown. In February 1980, China sent a delegation to the World Intellectual Property Organization (WIPO) meeting in Geneva to discuss revision of the Paris Convention, and the PRC has been a member of WIPO since then. Finally, after many years, marked first by neglect of patent matters and then by slow and patient study of foreign patent legislation and administration, the Patent Law of the People's Republic of China was passed, on 12 March 1984, by the Standing Committee of the National People's Congress. For a discussion of the salient features of the new law, the reader is referred to Chapter 12 of this volume.

IV. Conclusion

The foregoing discussion has only touched on some of the problems that may arise in the course of the parties' negotiations and other relations with each other. Other forces may shape transactions or their outcomes. For example, the influence of US export controls on technology transfer to the PRC has not been considered here. During the summer of 1983 the Reagan Administration decided to loosen the controls on sales of strategic goods to China, but only time and continued scrutiny will tell whether the United States Department of Defence will become less of an obstacle than it has been in the past.

This chapter began with a survey of changing Chinese policies, which will no doubt continue to show variations that will affect transactions of the type discussed here. At the same time, though, if any current Chinese policy is likely to be a long-term one it is the commitment to import technology. It would be difficult for China's leaders to contemplate carrying out a genuine effort to modernize Chinese industry without continuing such a commitment. If this perception is accurate, China will continue to import considerable quantities of technology in the foreseeable future, and the legal framework for transactions giving expression to the policy should therefore continue to develop and increase in definition.

Yet even if policy remains consistent and new laws add greater certainty to the expectations of parties to technology transfer transactions, some problems in the relations between foreign transferors and Chinese transferees of technology are likely to continue to exist, and are discussed briefly in final observations which follow below.

It has been common for Chinese negotiators to want broader, less precise expressions of licensors' obligations in contracts, and to disdain detailed documentation, especially if it is legalistic. In this regard, foreign licensors would be well-advised to render some of their favourite legalisms into plain English; at the same time, they should insist on documentation that adequately covers the contingencies which most concern them.

The foregoing advice seems especially appropriate in light of the fact that the Chinese side, viewing the contract as a document that creates a strong relationship between the parties, may view that relationship as the basis for requesting favours or other actions by the licensor which the licensor views as additional impositions, and sometimes costly burdens, on him. If the contract is sufficiently detailed, unwelcome elasticity in interpreting the agreement may be more easily resisted. Also, as elementary as it may seem, unwritten commitments by either side should be avoided as much as possible. This is particularly true in view of the fact that the Chinese side may have difficulties in performing obligations which involve the participation of another Chinese organization which was not consulted when the contract was drafted.

Perhaps the greatest source of problems between licensors and licensees in China is the frequent gap between high Chinese expectations and the inability of the Chinese infrastructure to aid realization of such expectations. This is reflected in many aspects of transactions involving transfers of technology, ranging from Chinese hopes about the speed and effectiveness with which the technology can be transferred, learned and applied, to such mundane but important details as the availability and adequacy of Chinese goods and services and living quarters for expatriate employees.

At the same time, responsibility for misunderstandings which may arise because of the gap between Chinese hopes and the limited resources of the Chinese economy and Chinese society cannot be laid exclusively on the Chinese side. Foreign businessmen are frequently inexcusably ignorant about the realities of the Chinese economy simply because they have not taken the trouble to inform themselves adequately. Perhaps because China is so distant and is assumed to be unknowable, Western businessmen often take less trouble to inform themselves about China than they would if they were going to another Western nation to discuss a similar transaction. Given the amount of literature now available, not only in English but also in other Western languages,[18] failure to learn about recent developments in China has become even more unwarranted that it was before.

This chapter has focused on three disparate elements of the business environment in which the foreigner finds himself in China. Policy has been changeable, the legal framework is new and uncertain, and practice is difficult to follow closely. However, new regularities have begun to appear, albeit slowly, to bring about an increase in the expectations of the parties to the transactions discussed here. In the foreseeable future, each side will have to continue its efforts to understand the other. Foreigners should not demand Chinese adherence to exaggerated ideals. At the same time, it is hoped that Chinese agencies will sustain their efforts to fashion fair, uniform and ascertainable rules and practice.

Notes

1. The discussion in this section is based on Chen Weiqin, 'The direction of introducing technology should be changed', *Jingji Guanli (Economic Management)*, No. 4, April 1981, pp. 22–5, translated in 'Joint Publications Research Service China Report' (hereafter cited as the JPRS), 29 June 1981, *Economic Affairs*, No. 146, pp. 27–32; Lin Senmu, 'Lessons Drawn from the Importation of 22 Complete Sets of Equipment', *Jingji Guanli*, No. 6, June 1981, in JPRS, No. 78743, 13 August 1981, *Economic Affairs*, No. 160, pp. 13–18; Rao Bin, 'Provide Technical Equipment for Different Departments of the National Economy to Raise Economic Results', *Jingji Guanli*, No. 4, April 1982, in JPRS, No. 81087, 21 June 1982, *Economic Affairs*, No. 240, pp. 25–33; Zhu Yuening, 'Give Weight to the Importation of Technology and Machinery', *Renmin Ribao (People's Daily)*, 9 August 1982, in *Foreign Broadcast Information Service, Daily Report, China* (hereafter cited as the FBIS), 13 August 1983, pp. K12–K15; Xinhua News Agency, 'Technology Import Official on Trade Policies', in FBIS, 25 October 1982, pp. K17–K18; Huang Bingwen, 'Technological Transformation is a Strategic Measure in Revitalizing Industry', *Fujian Ribao (Fujian Daily)*, 26 November 1982, in JPRS, No. 82986, 2 March 1983, *Economic Affairs*, No. 317, pp. 22–5; Commentator, 'Boldly Import Technology in Transforming Small and Medium-sized Enterprises', *Renmin Ribao*, 14 January 1983, in FBIS, 18 January 1983, pp. K1–K2; Chen Lianzhen, 'A Breakthrough is Necessary in Importing Advanced Technology', *Fujian Ribao*, 23 January 1983, in JPRS, No. 83440, 10 May 1983, *Economic Affairs*, No. 337, pp. 76–9; Wang Dekuan, 'Knowledge is Strength and Wealth', *Nanfang Ribao* (*Southern Daily*), 31 January 1983, in JPRS, No. 93367, 29 April 1983, *Economic Affairs*, No. 333, pp. 43–4; Zi Yu and Gao Xiaoxiao, 'Through Importing Advanced Equipment from Foreign Countries and Supporting Improvement in Industrial Technology, the Shanghai Foreign Trade Department Vigorously Promotes Production of Export Commodities and has Improved Industrial Technology in 323 Items, Resulting in an Annual Increased Output of 11.4 Billion Yuan', *Jiefang Ribao*, 19 February 1983, in JPRS, No. 83440, 10 May 1983, *Economic Affairs*, No. 337, pp. 74–5; Commentator, 'Do a Good Job in Digesting Imported Technology', *Renmin Ribao*, 27 March 1983, in FBIS, 14 April 1983, pp. K6–K8; and Denis Fred Simon, 'China's Capacity to Assimilate Foreign Technology: An Assessment', in *China Under the Four Modernizations — Selected Papers Submitted to the Joint*

Economic Committee, U.S. Congress (Washington, Government Printing Office, 1982), pp. 514–52. For recently published discussions of note see Liu Jing-tong, *On Introducing Technology to China* (New York, China-International Business Series, East Asian Institute, School of International and Business Affairs, Graduate School of Business, Columbia University, 1983); and R. Conroy, 'Technological Innovation in China's Recent Industrialization', *China Quarterly*, No. 97, March 1984, pp. 1–23.

2. Hans Heymann, Jr., 'Acquisition and Diffusion of Technology in China', in *China, A Reassessment of the Economy, Compendium of Papers Submitted to the Joint Economic Committee, Congress of the United States* (Washington, Government Printing Office, 1975), p. 686.

3. Chen, p. 28, note 1 above.

4. Simon, pp. 543–4, note 1 above.

5. On the vicissitudes of the Baoshan iron and steel complex, see Martin Weil, 'The Baoshan Steel Mill: A Symbol of Change in China's Industrial Development Strategy', in *China Under the Four Modernizations — Selected Papers Submitted to the Joint Economic Committee, U.S. Congress* (Washington, Government Printing Office, 1982), Vol. I, p. 365.

6. This paragraph and the two following are based on Simon, pp. 514–52, note 1 above.

7. Simon, p. 537, note 1 above.

8. Simon, p. 538, note 1 above.

9. Simon, p. 540, note 1 above.

10. A Chinese planner has explained the reasoning behind such a shift: 'Since liberation, the system of foreign trade has basically been the one China learned from the Soviet Union in the 1950s. It has emphasized monopoly, control and high concentration. Consequently, all import and export trading is centralized and dealt with by the state-run foreign trade corporations. Lacking authority to decide for themselves in operational and financial matters, these corporations have grown accustomed to acting in accordance with administrative orders and requesting instruction from high levels, thus introducing red tape into their operations.

'In managing and supervising business, they care little about loss, wastage and the turnover and application of funds, nor do they pay any attention to economic accounting and efficiency. Since the head office is far away in Beijing, how can it completely understand the situation in other parts of the country? As a result, what should have been interfered with has been left alone and what should have been left alone has been interfered with. The fact is that the head office is incapable of supervising the branch office . . .

'In reforming the foreign trade system, we should encourage local initiative. . .' Zhang Chongwen, 'The System of Foreign Trade Must Be Reformed', *Jingji Guanli*, No. 12, December 1979, in JPRS, No. 75345, *Economic Affairs*, No. 49, 21 March 1980, pp. 60–1.

The decentralization was described as follows: 'The head offices of a number of national import and export corporations under the Ministry of Foreign Trade now deal with only a few, important commodities. Most of the national import and export business is done by coastal or local trading corporations, or by newly-established corporations under other ministries and departments. The new corporations set up by ministries and the Chinese Academy of Sciences will also engage in joint ventures, co-publication, compensatory trade, processing and assembly work.

'Foreign trade corporations have been set up in the municipalities of Beijing, Tianjin and Shanghai, the provinces of Guangdong, Fujian, Liaoning and Hebei, and the Guangxi Zhuang Autonomous Region. These corporations handle their own import-export business as well as foreign trade transportation, chartering, warehousing, packaging and advertising.' 'Reform of Foreign Trade Structure Described', FBIS, 31 December 1980, pp. L41–L42.

11. See, for example, Stanley B. Lubman, 'Trade Contracts & Technology Licensing' in J.A. Cohen (ed.), *Legal Aspects of Doing Business in China 1983* (New York, Practising Law Institute, 1983), pp. 12–27.

12. 'The latest recentralization was described by a spokesman for the Ministry of Foreign Economic Relations and Trade [earlier formed by the consolidation of the former Ministry of Trade and the former Ministry for Economic Relations with Foreign Countries] on March 15, 1984, who said that "the [Ministry] would exercise overall administrative power over foreign trade and reinstitute the system of unified leadership and management. All major export and import goods will be put under the unified management of national foreign trade corporations. . ." ', 'Centralized Control of Foreign Trade Announced', FBIS, 15 March 1984, pp. K3–K4. See also 'Trade Ministry Official interviewed on Protection of Rights of Foreign Licensers', *China Economic News*, 23 January 1984, p. 3: 'After the expansion of the departmental and local authority, the organ to examine and approve technology transfer controls and to supervise the fulfillment of the contract obligations by the technology licensed enterprise is still the Ministry of Foreign Economic Relations and Trade, or some other organ authorized. . . in the light of actual needs.'

The Shenzhen Provisional Technology Regulations and the Shenzhen Foreign Economic Contracts Regulations were approved by the Standing Committee of the Guangdong Provincial People's Congress on 11 January 1984, and promulgated by the Guangdong Provincial People's Congress on 7 February 1984. They were published in *Nanfang Ribao* (*Southern Daily*, Guangzhou), 8 February 1984.

13. Recent legislation has made Chinese courts appropriate forums in labour and tax disputes involving foreigners. See, for example, Regulations on Labour Management in Joint Ventures Using Chinese and Foreign Investment; The Income Tax Law of the People's Republic of China Concerning Joint Ventures Using Chinese and Foreign Investment; and Individual Income Tax Law of the People's Republic of China, in F. Chu, M. Moser and O. Nee (eds.), *Commercial, Business and Trade Laws: People's Republic of China* (Dobbs Ferry, Oceana Publications, Inc., 1982), Pt. 13.

14. A recent expression of current Chinese views on this subject is Shao Xunyi, 'Conciliation Is a Good Method for Settling International Economic and Trade Disputes — An Introduction to China's Practice of Conciliation', paper presented to the Seventh International Arbitration Congress, Hamburg, West Germany, 7–11 June 1982.

15. The Income Tax Law of the People's Republic of China Concerning Foreign Enterprises, promulgated on 13 December 1981. An English translation of the law appears in F. Chu, M. Moser and O. Nee (eds.), *Commercial, Business and Trade Laws: People's Republic of China* (Dobbs Ferry, Oceana Publications, Inc., 1982), Pt. 13, p. 41. For a detailed discussion of the law, see Chapter 2 in this volume.

16. See the Provisional Regulations of the Ministry of Finance of the People's Republic of China Regarding the Reduction and Exemption of Income Tax on Fees for the Use of Proprietary Technology, issued on 13 December 1982.

17. 'Finance Ministry Spokesman on Income Tax Reduction & Exemption for Foreign Companies', *China Economic News*, No. 11, 21 March 1983, pp. 3 and 4.

18. See, for example, *Schweiz-China*, published quarterly by the Swiss-China Chamber of Commerce in Zurich; *Economie et Commerce*, published by Comité France-Chine in Paris; and *Chinas Recht*, translations of Chinese laws circulated by Franz Münzel of the Max Planck Institut für Internationales Privatrecht in Hamburg.

4. Foreign Investment in China: The Legal Framework

MICHAEL J. MOSER

FOREIGN investment in the People's Republic of China is a phenomenon that has emerged only very recently. For nearly thirty years following the Communist liberation in 1949, China eschewed direct participation by foreign capitalist entities in the nation's economy. As a result, when China embarked on its 'open-door' policy in the late 1970s the nation's planners and economic managers lacked experience in how to absorb and regulate foreign investment, and the country had no body of law capable of providing a viable framework for foreign investment activity. Viewed against this background, China's success in recent years in attracting foreign investment and in developing a legal infrastructure for the regulation of foreign economic activity has been remarkable. According to Chinese sources, direct foreign investment in China during the period 1979–82 amounted to US$1,769 million.[1] During the same period China promulgated more than twenty laws relating specifically to foreign investment; and more than three times as many laws and regulations touching on matters dealing with investments by foreigners have been put into effect.

This chapter will provide a summary description of the legal framework governing foreign investment in China today. The main focus of the chapter will be on legal practices and problems relating to four different forms of foreign investment in China, namely (1) compensation trade; (2) 'co-operative' business arrangements; (3) equity joint ventures; and (4) wholly-owned foreign enterprises. Before turning to these subjects, however, I will first discuss current Chinese rules and practices relating to the approval of foreign investment projects.

I. The Approval of Foreign Investment Projects

Despite China's current policies encouraging foreign investment, the People's Republic remains committed to the basic principles of a planned socialist economy. As a result, the approval of foreign investment projects is closely linked to China's state planning mechanism.

State planning is mandated by the Chinese Constitution, which vests in the State Council the authority to draw up and implement the national economic plan with the aim of ensuring 'the proportionate and co-ordinated growth of the national economy'.[2] Precisely how such plans are formulated is not well understood. What is known, however, is that in general all proposed projects utilizing foreign capital or technology which are to be undertaken directly by Chinese ministries and bureaux at the state level or by administrations and bureaux at the provincial or municipal levels, as well as such projects as are undertaken indirectly through subordinate corporations or other business units of such entities, must first be submitted to the relevant state or provincial economic planning commission for examination. Upon approval, the projects will then be included in the annual plans of the commissions which are sent to the State Council for ratification.[3]

Viewed within the context of China's economic planning system, the foreign investment approval process is principally a policing mechanism instituted for the purpose of ensuring that only those projects that are 'in the plan' are allowed to be implemented. As a matter of law, a project must first have been approved and included in the annual plan before the Chinese corporation, factory or other business unit is authorized to conduct negotiations with a foreign party.[4] To prevent the implementation of unauthorized investment projects, and to confirm that authorized projects will be carried out within the scope originally set by the state plan, all projects must be approved by the relevant government authorities before the contracts and agreements entered into between the foreign investor and its Chinese counterpart may be considered legally binding. As a matter of practice, this approval process often begins during the initial stages of discussion between the parties with the preparation of feasibility studies and the signing of non-binding letters of intent which are submitted by the Chinese side to its higher authorities for review. The final step in this process is the issue of formal approval of the signed contract by the Ministry of Foreign Economic Relations and Trade (MOFERT) or the provincial import-export commission or other local authority where the project is to be undertaken.

Precisely what level of approval is required for different types of projects has been the subject of continued and often confusing debate. The only existing Chinese legislation that addresses the issue squarely is the Joint Venture Law which requires that equity joint ventures be approved by the Foreign Investment Commission, now a part of MOFERT functioning under the new name of Foreign Investment Bureau.[5] However, this provision has since been amended, in effect, by the Joint Venture Law's Implementing Act, promulgated in 1983, which provides that MOFERT may in certain circumstances entrust its approval powers to other authorities.[6]

In the absence of clear statutory guidance regarding the appropriate approvals required for different types of investment projects, foreign investors and their legal counsel have had to rely on evidence gleaned from Chinese practice, the advice of their Chinese counterparts and public statements of various Chinese officials familiar with the current status of Chinese policy and thinking regarding foreign investment approvals. Based on these sources, it is generally believed that the following rules were being applied at the end of 1983.

The basic criteria that are considered in determining the identity of the appropriate approval authority are the total amount of Chinese and foreign investment involved in the project and its location. As a general rule, any project with a total investment of US$3 million or less need only be approved by the ministry under whose authority the project is being undertaken or by the government of the province where the project is located. All projects with a total investment in excess of this ceiling which are undertaken by the ministries or any of their subordinate units or are located in any of China's provinces or autonomous regions must be approved directly by MOFERT. Exceptions to this general rule exist in certain special cases. For example, the Beijing municipal authorities and the government of Liaoning Province may approve projects with a total investment of up to US$5 million, and the Shanghai municipal government has been authorized to approve investment projects up to a ceiling of US$10 million. According to one Chinese source, the Tianjin authorities have been permitted for some time to exercise the same approval authority as Beijing but may be placed in the same category as Shanghai in the near future.[7]

In addition to the general rules described above, special regulations exist with respect to the approval of foreign investment projects located in Guangdong and Fujian Provinces and in the Special Economic Zones established there. Although the rules applied in these areas remain somewhat hazy,[8] it is generally thought that provincial and special zone authorities may independently approve projects within their jurisdiction even though total investment is in excess of US$10 million. The only proviso to this far-reaching grant of authority is that all raw materials and energy required for such projects must be supplied locally. Although local approvals granted in such cases do not require further review by MOFERT, the investment contracts must be reported to MOFERT 'for the record' *(bei an)*.

As a final remark it should be noted that the criteria mentioned above for determining the proper approval authority for an investment project are not in all cases determinative. For example, a project involving a total investment below a specific ceiling may be deemed to be of particular national importance, with the result that central rather than local government approval will be required. Similarly, an investment project which may be negotiated and entered into by a ministry or one of its subordinate business units may only be coincidentally located in a Special Economic Zone. In such cases, the investment amount and location of the project are given less weight in determining the proper approval authority. Rather, the decisive factors appear to be the nature of the project and the relative importance of the Chinese unit that sponsors or participates directly in its implementation.[9]

II. Compensation Trade

Compensation trade *(buchang maoyi)* is perhaps the simplest form of foreign investment in China. Broadly defined as any transaction involving the purchase by a Chinese entity of foreign capital equipment and technology with repayment made in kind from the production of such equipment and technology, compensation trade has been aptly described as essentially 'an intermediary step between traditional foreign trade and conventional capital investment'.[10]

Compensation trade first began to develop in the mid-1970s but was largely restricted in the initial stage to arrangements between Hong Kong firms and Chinese enterprises in Guangdong and Fujian Provinces. Since then, however, this form of investment has extended throughout China. According to official Chinese statistics, 872 compensation trade transactions were consummated between 1979 and 1982 involving actual foreign investments of US$413 million.[11]

Compensation trade in its pure form is essentially a loan transaction.[12] The loan principal, which consists of the agreed purchase price of the equipment, is repaid in fixed instalments of products, produced directly with the equipment purchased; in addition there is an interest factor which is usually built in and which is also paid in kind. Variations on this pure form of compensation trade also exist. One such variation is a kind of combined processing and compensation trade arrangement. Under this arrangement, the Chinese party processes materials supplied by the foreign side on consignment using equipment provided by the foreign side. The Chinese party earns a fee for its processing services, from which is deducted instalment payments attributable to the purchase of the processing equipment. A similar type of hybrid arrangement exists with respect to assembly operations combined with equipment purchase by Chinese enterprises. Other variations on the pure compensation trade model also exist. For example, in some cases repayment for technology and equipment provided by the foreign party may be made with products other than those manufactured using such equipment and technology.

At present, there exists no published Chinese law or regulation that deals specifically with compensation trade. Nonetheless, a number of laws do affect the conduct of compensation trade transactions. For example, the Foreign Exchange Control Regulations and the Detailed Rules issued thereunder govern the handling of foreign exchange earned by the Chinese party in hybrid arrangements involving processing and assembly operations.[13] In addition, China's normal commodity inspection rules relating to the export of goods[14] and Chinese customs and tax laws also apply to compensation trade transactions. With respect to customs and tax treatment, however, specific provisions exist providing special benefits to both Chinese and foreign parties in a compensation trade arrangement. An exemption from the Consolidated Industrial and Commercial Tax, normally levied on importers of capital equipment,[15] may be granted. Moreover, foreign parties may be exempted from Chinese income tax with respect to payments received by them pursuant to compensation trade arrangements.[16]

Compensation trade arrangements have not been without their problems.[17] The most important of the problems encountered by foreign investors has been lack of adequate quality control resulting in frequent disputes over claims for defective goods. For many investors, however, the risk that such problems will occur is outweighed by the numerous advantages of the compensation trade format over other forms of investment in China. Among these advantages are, firstly, the fact that the risks involved are relatively low. The term of most compensation trade agreements is three to five years and investments are typically less than US$1 million. In addition, many investors have been able to arrange guarantees from the Bank of China to secure product payment. Secondly, as noted above, income earned by foreign parties pursuant to compensation trade arrangements generally has not, to date at least, been subject to Chinese taxation. Finally, compensation trade arrangements are particularly flexible and do not require joint management or any similar organization for their execution. As a result the foreign party need not become directly involved in the day-to-day operations of the Chinese partner.

III. Co-operative Investment Arrangements

The term 'co-operative investment' refers to a wide variety of arrangements whereby Chinese and foreign entities agree to co-operate for a specified period of time for the purpose of jointly producing certain items or rendering certain services or for any other specified task. Co-operative investment arrangements, because of their broad scope and flexibility, have proved to be the most popular form of foreign investment in China. Between 1979 and 1982, 792 co-operative investment projects were set up in China with a total foreign investment of US$530 million.[18]

Co-operative investment arrangements may in general be divided into two major categories: joint development arrangements and contractual joint ventures. The main characteristics of these forms are described below.

A. Joint Development

Joint development (*hezuo kaicai*) arrangements have to date been limited to Chinese-foreign activities with respect to the exploration and development of offshore oil and gas reserves. Under this type of arrangement, foreign investors agree to conduct exploration programmes at their own financial risk. Once petroleum is discovered, both parties make investments to develop the finds jointly. Income from commercial production is distributed to the parties in accordance with a fixed formula that takes into account exploration costs, development expenses and allocable profits.

Since 1981, when China began its offshore oil development programme in earnest, the Chinese government has made strenuous efforts to put into place a regulatory regime governing joint petroleum development activities. These efforts have included the promulgation of the national Petroleum Regulations, the formulation of a Model Petroleum Contract, and the enactment of special customs and tax rules, registration regulations and other rules. These laws and other legal aspects of joint petroleum development are discussed in detail in Chapter 6 of this volume.

B. Contractual Joint Ventures

Contractual joint ventures — sometimes also referred to as 'co-operative' joint ventures — are the most common form of co-operative investment arrangement. While considerably different from true equity joint ventures, contractual joint ventures are formed for many of the same purposes. For example, contractual joint ventures have been established for the joint construction and management of hotels, to provide services in the offshore oil industry and for the production of manufactured goods. In addition, this investment format has been used as a vehicle for joint Chinese-foreign tenders in World Bank-supported development projects and, more recently, for the joint development of coal and other mineral resources. Many contractual joint ventures are formed as short-term 'trial co-operation agreements' which contemplate the formation of full equity joint ventures at a later stage. Others, however, are established on a long-term basis in the belief that the advantages of the contractual format outweigh those provided by the statutory equity joint venture.

Unlike joint development activities and equity joint ventures, contractual joint ventures are not governed by any specific set of regulations. According to Chinese sources, rules governing contractual joint ventures are currently being drafted but it is expected that it will be some time before they are formally promulgated. In the interim, certain 'internal' (*neibu*) rules — not generally available to foreigners — are being applied by Chinese negotiators. However, these rules for the most part only consist of broad guidelines for the formation of contractual joint ventures. As a result, at present the establishment and operations of contractual joint ventures are based principally on the provisions contained in the contract, which are largely a matter for negotiation in each individual case.

i. Forms

Contractual joint ventures may take one of two different forms.[19] In the first instance no company or other legal entity separate and distinct from the contracting parties is established. In the absence of a separate corporate body, each party is responsible for making its own contributions to the venture, paying its own taxes on profits distributed to it and bearing its own liability for risks and losses. In true contractual joint ventures of this type, there exists a clear separation of the liabilities, rights and obligations of the parties, all of which must be specified in the underlying contract.

The second type of contractual joint venture is actually a hybrid form of investment vehicle which takes on some of the characteristics of both true contractual joint ventures and pure equity joint ventures. In this format, a 'business entity' which has the status of a legal person is established, but the attributes of this entity bear a closer resemblance to the Western concept of a partnership than to the corporate form prescribed for equity joint ventures by the Joint Venture Law. Under this type of arrangement, the business entity itself is not a limited liability company; rather, the partners remain liable for their own debts in accordance with the ratio specified in the contract. Like true contractual joint ventures, the contract provides the basic framework for the organization and operation of the venture. As we will see, however, for some purposes this hybrid form of contractual joint venture is treated as an equity joint venture with the result that the statutory rules governing equity joint ventures are in some instances applied to it by analogy.

ii. Capital Contributions and Profit Distribution

Capital contributions by the parties in both types of contractual joint venture may take any of the forms specified in the Joint Venture Law. These include industrial property rights and know-how, buildings, plant and equipment, land-use rights, trade marks and cash.[20] In addition, the parties to a contractual joint venture may also contribute natural resource rights, labour and utilities, all of which are not permitted under the equity joint venture format. In any event, the treatment of capital contributions in the case of contractual joint ventures is considerably different from equity joint ventures. In contractual joint ventures such contributions are not treated as part of 'equity' or 'registered capital' as these concepts are not employed in contractual joint ventures. Rather, they are viewed as separate contributions by the parties to the project or undertaking as such. As a result, the parties to contractual joint ventures are able to avoid many of the protracted debates regarding the valuation of in-kind contributions to the registered capital of the company which often plague equity joint venture negotiations.

The distribution of profits in contractual joint ventures is another area where there are significant differences from the practices employed by equity joint ventures. Under the contractual format, the ratio agreed by the parties for the sharing of profits of the venture may be different from the ratio of the parties' capital contributions. The method employed by equity joint ventures, as prescribed by the Joint Venture Law, takes a different approach. Under this system, the joint venture partners are required to share profits in accordance with the ratio of their capital contributions. Consequently, contractual joint ventures are considerably more flexible than equity joint ventures, permitting various schemes whereby the profit share owing to the parties is not tied to the value of their contributions but may increase or decrease over the life of the contract.

With respect to profit distribution, it should be noted that different rules are applied to true contractual joint ventures and the hybrid type of venture described above. Under the hybrid format, the joint business entity is a separate accounting unit that functions in much the same manner as an equity joint venture company. Joint operating expenses are paid by the business entity from gross revenues, and taxes are levied on the net profit. Prior to making any distribution to the parties, the business entity is normally required to deduct certain amounts as contributions to the venture's reserve fund, the bonus and welfare funds established for the project's workers and the venture's expansion fund. In true contractual joint ventures, the parties may provide for the distribution of joint reserves in cash or in kind after allocating a fixed amount of the total revenues to a common fund to cover joint operating expenses. Each party then makes its own expense calculations and pays its own taxes on the income received.

iii. Management and Operation

In equity joint ventures, the foreign party is generally able to exercise a certain degree of control over the management and operations of the venture. In accordance with the Joint Venture Law's Implementing Act, the Board of Directors is the 'highest organ of authority' of the venture and seats on the board are allocated to the parties based on their respective equity holdings.[21] Although by law the chairman of the board must be appointed by the Chinese side,[22] in practice the general manager is usually appointed by the foreign party, a fact which generally ensures that the foreign investor has a voice in the day-to-day operation of the joint venture.

Hybrid contractual joint ventures typically adopt a management system that closely resembles that of equity joint ventures. In the case of true contractual joint ventures, however, the management structure is a good deal more flexible. Most ventures of this type are governed by a joint management committee or similar organization consisting of representatives of each of the parties. Because no independent corporate entity exists, there is usually no executive officer as such. Moreover, the separation of the rights and responsibilities of the Chinese and foreign parties in contractual joint ventures tends to encourage unilateral, rather than joint, decision-making. Consequently, control over everyday operational activities is often diffused, rather than concentrated in a single management structure, with the result that the Chinese party is often able to exercise a greater degree of influence than is the case in equity joint ventures.

A major practical problem confronted by the parties to a true contractual joint venture relates to the absence of a legal entity capable of contracting on behalf of both parties jointly. Under China's domestic Economic Contracts Law, only Chinese legal persons have the capacity to enter into binding contracts with other Chinese entities for the lease of land, the procurement of supplies and other purposes.[23] As a result of these strictures, the Chinese partner is usually named as the contracting party in such cases, although powers of attorney are often granted by the foreign side authorizing the Chinese partner to act on its behalf in the interests of both parties pursuant to the joint venture contract.

iv. Taxes and Customs Duties

As mentioned previously, the income tax treatment of contractual joint ventures differs depending on whether the venture is of the hybrid or true contractual joint venture type. Hybrid joint ventures are taxed in precisely the same way as equity joint ventures under the provisions of the Joint Venture Income Tax Law and the Detailed Rules issued thereunder.[24] By contrast, in true contractual joint ventures each party pays its own taxes on the income distributed to it. For the foreign party this means that net income is taxed under the Foreign Enterprise Income Tax Law at progressive rates ranging from 30 per cent to 50 per cent, including a local surtax.[25] Unlike hybrid joint ventures where profits remitted to the foreign party are subject to an additional withholding tax of 10 per cent, no withholding tax is imposed on the remittance of profits by foreign investors in true contractual joint ventures.[26]

In addition to the enterprise income tax, parties to contractual joint ventures are also subject to China's other tax laws. For example, individual income tax is imposed on the income of personnel stationed in China in connection with the joint venture.[27] In addition, the Consolidated Industrial and Commercial Tax is also levied on the import of items and on the sale of products of the contractual joint venture.[28] Finally, customs duties also apply to the importation of certain items and the export of products. It should be noted that in early 1984 new regulations were issued liberalizing the tax treatment of contractual joint ventures, providing exemptions from the Consolidated Industrial and Commercial Tax and customs duties in certain cases.[29]

Finally, a brief word should be said about the tax treatment of contractual joint ventures in China's Special Economic Zones. Based on regulations in force in the Guangdong zones, the income of both hybrid contractual joint ventures and the foreign party in true contractual joint ventures is taxed at the preferential rate of 15 per cent, with no local surtax. In addition, a number of exemptions from taxes and customs duties and other tax incentives are available to both types of contractual joint ventures. For a detailed discussion of taxation in the Special Economic Zones, see Chapter 5 of this volume.

v. Foreign Exchange Controls

In general, contractual joint ventures are subject to the same foreign exchange rules that apply to equity joint ventures, whether they be of the hybrid or true contractual joint venture type.[30]

vi. Registration

Upon approval by the relevant foreign investment authorities, contractual joint ventures are required to register with the local bureau of the State

Administration for Industry and Commerce before commencing business operations. In the case of hybrid ventures, it is the business entity itself that is registered and issued a business licence. By contrast, true contractual joint ventures register as a 'project' in the names of both parties. The registration regulation, which was formulated to govern equity joint ventures but which is applied by analogy to contractual joint ventures, provides for the payment of fees upon registration in accordance with the amount of registered capital of the joint venture.[31] As contractual joint ventures do not have equity capital, registration authorities generally look to the amount of total investment in the project as the basis for the computation of fees. In most instances, the value of such interests is difficult to compute with the result that as a practical matter registration fees for contractual joint ventures are frequently levied at the maximum statutory rate of RMB 30,000.

IV. Equity Joint Ventures

Of the various forms of investment in China, equity joint ventures have attracted the most attention from both foreign investors and the Chinese authorities. The possibility that foreign companies would be permitted to engage in direct equity investments in Chinese companies was first rumoured in the Western press in 1978. These rumours, which were greeted with a good deal of excitement by foreign investors, became a reality in 1979 when China enacted the Joint Venture Law. Since then, literally thousands of foreign firms have come to China to discuss the establishment of equity joint ventures. Their initial enthusiasm was shared and encouraged by the Chinese government, which saw in the equity joint venture format a means by which Chinese companies could absorb advanced technology and Western managerial skills and become major foreign exchange earners in the world's leading markets.

Despite these high expectations, equity joint ventures have proved to be something of a disappointment. As of September 1983, only 112 equity joint ventures had been formally established in China, involving a total foreign investment of approximately US$260 million.[32] Most of these investments have been in small- and medium-scale projects, largely concentrated in the tourist and service industries and in the production of consumer goods. As a result, foreign investments on a project basis have tended to be comparatively small, averaging US$2–3 million.[33]

The reasons why equity joint ventures have failed to live up to early Chinese and foreign expectations are numerous. First, the general downturn in the world economy in the early part of the 1980s led to a reduction in foreign investment generally. Moreover, this downturn coincided with the introduction of economic 'readjustment' policies by the Chinese government during 1980–1, as a consequence of which a number of proposed projects were shelved.

Secondly, many foreign investors have been sceptical of the benefits of direct equity investments in China, particularly when compared with the more generous terms granted to foreign investors by neighbouring Asian states.[34] Finally, extraordinary difficulties have been encountered by foreign investors in attempting to establish joint ventures in China. Negotiations have often proved to be lengthy and complicated, burdened by the bureaucratic style of Chinese decision-making. In addition, due to China's lack of experience in establishing and operating equity joint ventures, many fundamental issues have had to be hammered out and resolved on a case-by-case basis. As a result of these difficulties, many foreign investors who were initially enthusiastic about the establishment of equity joint ventures in China abandoned their original investment plans in favour of more flexible business arrangements such as compensation trade and contractual joint ventures.

In an effort to recapture some of the initial excitement generated by equity joint ventures, the Chinese government began in 1983 to institute a number of reforms aimed at making the equity joint venture format more attractive to foreign investors. Partly as a consequence of these reforms, investment in joint ventures has recently begun to accelerate. During the first nine months of 1983 alone 29 equity joint ventures were established.[35] Foreign investment in these projects totals some US$120 million, an amount nearly equal to the total amount of foreign investment in equity joint ventures during the three-year period of 1980–2.[36] This increase in investment volume has been accompanied by a change in the character of joint venture investments. Many of the ventures established in 1983, such as the American Motors Corporation venture for the production of American-style Jeep vehicles, constitute major industrial projects. A number of others involve the transfer of sophisticated technology to Chinese enterprises in the fields of offshore oil exploration and manufacturing. Hence, equity joint ventures began to experience something of a revival in 1983, a trend which many observers believe is likely to continue in the years ahead.

Compared to the other forms of investment in China, only the equity joint venture is governed by a substantial body of published law. However, the statutory framework governing equity joint ventures has not been built up in one stroke but has tended to evolve in a piecemeal fashion. The Joint Venture Law of 1 July 1979, while in many ways a path-breaking piece of legislation, consists of a mere 15 articles and states little more than the general principles to be adhered to in establishing and operating equity joint ventures. This law has been followed by a number of detailed regulations addressing specific issues such as the registration of joint ventures, labour management, taxation, customs treatment, foreign exchange, and borrowing by joint ventures from the Bank of China. Finally, on 20 September 1983, China issued long-awaited detailed rules under the Joint Venture Law in the form of an Implementing Act. This law consists of 118 articles that attempt to pull together a number of earlier statutory threads and spell out the main features of equity joint ventures in relative detail.

At present, therefore, the various laws and regulations applicable to equity joint ventures, when viewed as a whole, provide for a fairly systematic regulatory regime. Nonetheless, a number of gaps remain in this system which continue to pose problems for foreign investors. The sections that follow provide an outline of the main provisions of this statutory framework and discuss a number of the problem areas encountered by investors in establishing and operating equity joint ventures.

A. Nature and Legal Status

Both the Joint Venture Law and the Implementing Act provide that equity joint ventures shall take the form of a 'limited liability company' (*youxian zeren gongsi*) incorporated and registered in the People's Republic of China.[37] In addition, the Implementing Act states that equity joint ventures are 'Chinese legal persons' (*zhongguo faren*).[38] As such, the Act provides that equity joint ventures are 'subject to the jurisdiction and receive the protection of Chinese law'.[39] Each of these statements raises significant legal questions for foreign investors which existing Chinese law can only answer in part.

The first question relates to the definition of 'limited liability company'. At present China has no Company Law. According to Chinese officials, matters relating to the organization, powers and responsibilities of joint venture companies will be dealt with in the Chinese Civil Code which is now being drafted, but this law is not expected to be formally promulgated for some time. In the interim, investors must rely on the provisions set forth in existing joint venture legislation to provide guidance as to the legal dimensions of the prescribed limited liability company form. In this regard, the Joint Venture Law and the Implementing Act themselves provide the basic outline of a general company law, with provisions relating to capital contributions, registered capital, transfer of interests, management structure and dissolution of the company. With respect to the issue of 'limited liability', however, the legislation goes no further than to state that the liability of the parties shall be 'limited to the amount of the capital contribution subscribed by each'[40] and that the parties 'shall share the profits, risks and losses in proportion to their respective contributions to the registered capital'.[41]

While existing legislation provides at least some indication as to the meaning of the corporate form mandated by the Joint Venture Law, the concept of 'legal person' has never been explicitly defined. According to Chinese officials, this matter will also be addressed in China's forthcoming Civil Code.[42] Chinese officials have indicated, however, that their definition of the concept will not diverge widely from that adopted by Western legal systems. According to one official, the basic components of the definition of 'legal person' will include the right to own, use and dispose of property; the right to carry out management and production activities independently; and the capacity to sue and be sued in a court of law.[43]

Few foreign investors would dispute the fact that a joint venture company incorporated in China should be subject to the jurisdiction of Chinese laws. Nonetheless this requirement has proved troublesome for many investors, largely because of the uncertainty that exists as to the impact of subsequently enacted legislation on the provisions contained in joint venture contracts.[44] At a time when China is actively engaged in the task of building a comprehensive legal framework, investors are justifiably concerned that their rights spelled out in contracts entered into today may be unfairly impaired by future legislative enactments.

The only official statement of the Chinese government's position on this issue is contained in a publication on foreign investment issued by MOFERT. This statement provides that,

> In accordance with generally accepted international practice, a contract signed before a new law is enacted should be bound by the new law. Nevertheless, execution of some provisions in the contract may continue even though these provisions run counter to the newly promulgated laws or regulations.[45]

In the light of this statement and continuing uncertainties surrounding the issue, many foreign investors have attempted to insert protective provisions in joint venture contracts. In general, explicit language to the effect that the contract shall prevail over subsequent legislation is not accepted by the Chinese authorities. However, 'renegotiation clauses' and similar provisions have been successfully negotiated in some cases. These generally provide that in the event that a new law is enacted which adversely affects the economic benefit of the contract to the foreign investor the new law shall be observed by the parties but the contract shall be renegotiated or other action taken on the Chinese side to ensure that the foreign investor's interest is not harmed.

In at least one area, taxation, developing Chinese practice indicates that the provisions contained in joint venture contracts will be permitted to prevail over subsequent legislation. One of the earliest joint venture agreements, approved before the enactment of the Joint Venture Income Tax Law, provided for an income tax rate of 31.5 per cent. When the tax law was put into effect a year later, the Chinese authorities agreed to abide by the contract rather than enforce the higher statutory rate.[46] More recently, new tax laws have extended preferential provisions to existing contracts, providing only that the new benefits will apply to the original contract period but not to any period of extension. To what extent this approach will be followed in other areas, however, is unclear.

B. Establishment

The Joint Venture Law, the Implementing Act and related regulations contain a number of provisions regarding the establishment of equity joint ventures. The major topics addressed by the laws include documentation, capitalization, external financing, approval procedures and registration.

i. Documentation

The Implementing Act contains specific rules regarding the documentation that must be produced by the parties during different stages of the negotiations for the establishment of a joint venture.[47] The Act provides that during the initial stage the Chinese party must submit to its superior unit a 'project proposal' and a 'preliminary feasibility study report' relating to the project. Once these documents have been agreed to and approved by the relevant approval authority, the Chinese party may then commence work with its foreign counterpart on the preparation of a formal feasibility study. Upon completion of the study, the parties are directed to negotiate and execute a joint venture agreement, the joint venture contract and the corporate charter.

To a large extent, the documentation requirements contained in the Act are a reflection of practices that have developed for the purpose of implementing internal Chinese approval procedures. As discussed earlier, these procedures involve the monitoring of business discussions between Chinese units and foreign companies with the aim of ensuring that only those projects that are included in the state plan are actually concluded and implemented. In addition, the documentation requirements serve the added function of allowing the Chinese authorities to assess at an early stage the various proposals of competitors. In general, only the most promising proposals will be permitted to proceed from the stage of the preliminary feasibility report to actual contract negotiations.

Despite the apparent formality of the documentary requirements set forth in the Implementing Act, in practice the situation is a good deal more flexible. The 'project proposal' and 'preliminary feasibility study report' may in fact be nothing more than a summary of an internal set of notes of meetings between the potential foreign investor and its Chinese host. Moreover, the Implementing Act itself allows that the joint venture 'agreement' (*xie yi*) — a non-binding document embodying the main points and principles of the proposed venture — may be dispensed with.[48]

The most important documents drawn up in connection with the establishment of a joint venture are the joint venture contract and the charter. In general, Chinese law views the contract (*hetong*) as the fundamental document which provides for the establishment of the venture by the parties and the charter as the company's code of governance, similar to the memorandum and articles of an English company. The Act contains detailed provisions regarding the topics that must be addressed in these documents and provides that in the event of conflict between the two, the provisions contained in the contract are to govern.[49] The Act also requires that both the joint venture contract and the charter must be written in Chinese.[50] However, a foreign language version of the documents may also be prepared, if the parties agree, in which event both language versions are to have 'equal validity'.[51]

Prior to the promulgation of the Implementing Act, two issues which were often the focus of contentious debate in joint venture contract negotiations were governing law and provisions for dispute settlement. With respect to the first issue, the foreign party typically argued that, as Chinese law was incomplete in many respects, the governing law of the contract should be the law of his home country or some other third country. These debates have now stopped, as the Implementing Act explicitly requires that 'the conclusion, validity, interpretation, and implementation of joint venture contracts and the resolution of disputes thereunder shall all be governed by Chinese law.'[52] As a matter of practice, however, the Chinese authorities have in some instances conceded ground on this issue and have permitted the inclusion of provisions allowing foreign arbitrators to supplement Chinese law with 'commonly accepted international commercial practices' where no existing Chinese rule addresses a particular issue.[53]

The second issue which often generated extended debate in joint venture negotiations pertains to dispute settlement. In general, foreign investors have preferred third-country arbitration while the Chinese have argued strongly for 'friendly discussions' and mediation, failing which the disputes should be referred to arbitration in China. The Implementing Act has now cast into law what had, during the three years prior to its promulgation, developed as the typical compromise on this issue.[54] Under the Implementing Act, friendly discussions and mediation are required as an initial step in attempting to resolve the dispute. If such efforts fail, however, the dispute may be submitted to arbitration, either in China, the country of the defendant, or a third country, depending on the agreement of the parties.[55] Interestingly, the Act also provides that in the absence of a written arbitration agreement, either party may bring suit in the Chinese courts.[56]

ii. Capitalization

The central concept employed by Chinese law in discussing the capitalization of equity joint ventures is 'registered capital' (*zhuce ziben*). According to the Implementing Act, registered capital refers to the total amount of the capital contribution subscribed by the parties to the joint venture which is registered with the Chinese registration authorities at the time the venture is formally established.[57] Therefore, registered capital is essentially the parties' equity in the venture and is to be distinguished from the concept of 'total investment' (*touzi zonge*) which includes external borrowings of the venture itself.[58]

The Joint Venture Law requires that the foreign party hold not less than 25 per cent of the registered capital of the joint venture.[59] No maximum is specified, leaving open at least the possibility that the foreign party may hold up to 99 per cent. In practice, however, the distribution of registered capital in most joint ventures established to date has been either 50:50 or 49:51, the majority position in the latter case usually being held by the Chinese side. In general, registered capital is to be expressed in renminbi, although foreign currency may be used if both parties agree.[60] Evidence of each party's ownership of its share of the company's registered capital is provided by the issue of 'certificates of capital contribution'. The certificates are issued by the company in accordance with a prescribed form after verification by a Chinese accountant that the contributions of both sides have been fully paid up.[61]

The Implementing Act contains a number of restrictions pertaining to the registered capital of a joint venture. For example, joint ventures are not permitted to reduce the amount of their registered capital during the term of the contract.[62] The registered capital may be increased but only if the board of directors has passed a formal resolution to this effect and the action is then approved by the original approval-granting authority.[63] A more significant restriction relates to transfer and assignment. The Act provides that a transfer or assignment of all or part of the registered capital owned by one party is not valid without the consent of the other party and the approval of the original approval-granting authority.[64] Moreover, if one party wishes to effect any such transfer or assignment, the other party is granted 'a pre-emptive right' to purchase the interest offered to the third party.[65] Finally, the Act provides that no assignment to a third party may be made on terms more preferential than the conditions for assignment to the other joint venture party.[66] Given such restrictions, it is unlikely that many foreign investors in equity joint ventures will be in a position to transfer their interests once the contract has been signed.

As noted earlier, the capital contributions of the parties that make up the registered capital of the joint venture may take a variety of forms, including cash, in-kind contributions, such as machinery, equipment, and intangible property, such as proprietary technology, trade marks and other industrial property rights. In addition, the Chinese side is permitted to contribute rights to the use of a site as part of its capital contribution.

The Implementing Act imposes a number of restrictions on in-kind contributions made by foreign joint venture partners. For example, machinery, equipment and other materials must meet all of the following criteria before they may be used as capital contributions : (1) they must be 'indispensable' to the production of the joint venture; (2) they must be items that China itself is not able to produce, or is able to produce but only at 'overly high' prices or under circumstances where supply and quality cannot be guaranteed; and (3) the foreign party's valuation of the items must not be higher than the international price for similar items.[67] Similar restrictions apply to industrial property rights or proprietary technology contributed by the foreign party as in-kind capital contributions. These must (1) enable the joint venture to produce products that China 'urgently needs' or that are suitable for export; (2) permit the joint venture to improve the quality and function of existing products and raise productivity; and (3) contribute to the conservation of energy and raw materials.[68]

One of the most vexing problems in negotiating the capital structure of joint ventures has been the valuation of in-kind contributions made by the parties. In general, Chinese negotiators have tended to adopt the strategy of first eliciting from the foreign side the proposed valuation of its in-kind contributions and then matching that amount by assigning an equal, and usually highly inflated, value to its contributions of factory buildings and land-use rights. Based on the principle of 'equality and mutual benefit', the Chinese will then demand reductions in the valuation proposed by the foreign side before they will accept a reduction in the value of their own contributions.

Under the Implementing Act, the foreign party is required to supply evidence of the basis for its valuation of intangible property provided as its capital contribution.[69] Such evidence includes patent and trade-mark registration certificates, documents indicating the state of validity, technical characteristics, and practical value of the property, and other information. In the event of a dispute regarding the valuation of intangibles, as well as other in-kind contributions of the parties, a third party agreed upon by the Chinese and foreign sides may be retained to make a binding assessment.[70] However, this procedure may not be applied in the case of the valuation of land provided by the Chinese side as part of its capital contribution.[71] Finally it should be noted that any valuation ultimately agreed to by the parties is subject to the approval of the Chinese party's 'higher authorities' and the formal approval-granting organ.[72]

iii. External Financing

Chinese law permits joint ventures to borrow funds from either the Bank of China or foreign banks to satisfy the financing requirements of the venture over and above the funds provided by way of the parties' capital contributions.[73] As a matter of practice, however, only a few joint ventures have been successful in arranging loans from foreign commercial banks.[74] In general, the Chinese party will prefer that the joint venture borrow from the Bank of China whose interest rates and other costs are in most cases lower than those offered by foreign commercial banks.

Borrowings by joint ventures from the Bank of China are governed by a specific set of rules contained in the Provisional Measures for Providing Loans to Joint Ventures Using Chinese and Foreign Investment by the Bank of China (hereafter cited as the Loan Measures).[75] The Loan Measures authorize the Bank of China to provide three different types of loans to joint ventures: working capital loans, loans for the settlement of accounts, and loans for the purchase of fixed assets.[76] Such loans may be extended in either renminbi or in a foreign currency and must be repaid by the borrower in the same currency in which they were advanced.[77]

The Loan Measures specify a number of requirements that must be fulfilled by a prospective borrower before its loan application can be approved.[78] For example, the joint venture must be approved and registered; it must abide by Chinese laws; it must have opened a bank account with the Bank of China; and it must be 'creditworthy and well managed'. The most important requirement relates to security. Under the Loan Measures, the joint venture must provide either a pledge of collateral as security for the loan or a guarantee acceptable to the Bank of China. As China has no formal system of mortgages applicable to property owned by joint ventures, the most common security device has been the guarantee. In general, the Bank of China has preferred either an unconditional and irrevocable letter of guarantee from the parent companies or a bank guarantee arranged by the parent companies in accordance with the ratio of capital contributions to the joint venture.

The procedures to be followed in applying for a loan include submission to the Bank of China of a formal application specifying the purpose for which the loan is to be used, together with a resolution of the board of directors of the joint venture ratifying the loan application, copies of the joint venture contract and other relevant documents.[79] Upon approval of the application, the parties are then to negotiate and sign the loan agreement and security documentation.

Interest on renminbi loans from the Bank of China is fixed in accordance with the rate set by the People's Bank of China.[80] In general, this rate is slightly higher than the rate normally charged to Chinese state-owned enterprises. The Loan Measures provide that the interest rate on foreign currency loans 'shall be set by the Bank of China'.[81] In practice, this rate has tended to follow closely the LIBOR rate. Interest penalties on overdue payments of principal and interest on Bank of China loans are calculated at a rate equal to the original interest rate plus twenty to fifty per cent of such a rate.[82]

iv. Approval Procedures

The Implementing Act provides that joint ventures must be approved by MOFERT.[83] However, as noted in Part I of this chapter, local authorities may in some instances be entrusted by MOFERT to exercise approval powers on its behalf. When applying for approval of a joint venture, the Chinese party is required to submit the following documents to the approval authority: (1) a formal application for approval; (2) a copy of the feasibility study; (3) executed copies of the joint venture agreement, the joint venture contract and the company charter; (4) a list of the names of the persons appointed to the board of directors of the joint venture; and (5) signed opinions regarding the establishment of the joint venture from the superior unit of the Chinese joint venture partner.[84] Within three months from the date of receipt of these documents, the approval authority must notify the parties of its disposition towards the application.[85] The approval authority is empowered to reject any application that contains 'improper points' and may demand that amendments be made to any of the documents, failing which an approval will not be granted.[86]

It should be noted that in cases where local approval authorities are empowered to approve joint ventures, the Implementing Act requires that a report be made by such an authority to MOFERT and that the actual certificate of approval be issued by MOFERT.[87] Although the Act states that such a report is merely provided 'for the record', in practice it allows MOFERT to exercise final review powers over the approval of the contract. There have been instances in the past where local authorities have approved the project but MOFERT has refused to issue a formal approval certificate unless certain amendments to the contract were made. Happily, however, this right is apparently only exercised in extraordinary circumstances.

v. Registration

Under the Implementing Act, joint ventures are required to register with the local bureau of the State Administration for Industry and Commerce at the place where their head office is located within one month of the issue of the formal certificate of approval.[88] The procedures for effecting registration are set forth in the Measures for the Registration of Joint Ventures Using Chinese and Foreign Investment (hereafter cited as the Registration Measures), promulgated by the State Council on 26 July 1980.[89]

When applying for registration, a joint venture is required by the Registration Measures to provide the following documents to the registration organ: (1) a completed application form, containing such information as the name of the joint venture, its scope of operations, the registered capital of the joint venture, a list of the names of the members of the board of directors and management personnel and the total number of employees; (2) a copy of the certificate of approval; (3) three copies each of the Chinese and foreign-language texts of the joint venture agreement, the joint venture contract and the company charter; and (4) a copy of the foreign party's business licence or other similar document issued by the authorities of its home country.[90] Upon approval of the application, and payment of a fee, the joint venture will then be issued a formal business licence.

Fees for the registration of joint ventures are levied in accordance with the Registration Fee Regulations.[91] Under these regulations, joint ventures with a registered capital of RMB 10,000,000 or less are required to pay a fee equal to 0.1 per cent of the registered capital; if the registered capital of the venture is in excess of this amount, the portion above RMB 10,000,000 is assessed at the rate of 0.05 per cent.[92]

The Registration Measures require that changes to previously registered items be notified to the registration organ and appropriate amendments be made to the registration records.[93] A fee of RMB 100 is imposed for each such change.[94] Moreover, if a joint venture increases its registered capital, a surcharge fee must be paid on the increased amount in accordance with the rates set forth in the preceding paragraph.[95]

C. Management Structure

The Joint Venture Law and the Implementing Act provide for a two-tiered system of management for joint ventures. At the first level is the board of directors which constitutes 'the highest organ of authority of a joint venture' and 'decides all major questions'.[96] The second level consists of the joint venture's managerial staff which is 'responsible for daily operational and managerial work'.[97]

Members of the board of directors are appointed by the parties to the joint venture and hold office for a term of four years.[98] According to the Implementing Act, the composition of the board of directors is to be determined 'by discussion' between the parties. The board must contain at least three members, but no maximum is specified by the law. The distribution of seats on the board is to be fixed 'by reference' to the ratio of capital contributions, leaving open at least the theoretical possibility that a foreign party holding a majority of the registered capital of a joint venture could control the board. However, the Act requires that the position of chairman be held by a Chinese appointee and provides that the vice-chairman may be appointed by the foreign side.

Joint ventures are required to convene meetings of the board of directors at least once a year.[99] The Act states that meetings are to be called by the Chinese chairman. However, many joint ventures stipulate in their charters that board meetings may also be convened upon the request of the foreign side's directors. The Act requires that a quorum of two-thirds of the directors present is required before a meeting of the board of directors may be convened. Directors unable to attend a meeting may issue a proxy authorizing a representative to act on their behalf.

Decision-making by the board of directors of joint ventures has tended to be a source of frustration for foreign investors. Under the Implementing Act, unanimity is required for certain fundamental decisions regarding the joint venture such as charter amendments, termination, changes in the registered capital of the joint venture and mergers.[100] All other decisions, however, may be made in the manner specified in the joint venture's charter.[101] The mechanism usually adopted is majority voting, but this has not generally proved to be workable. In practice, Chinese negotiators will usually insist that seats on the board be allocated equally between the parties. As a consequence, each side's appointees tend to vote as a block requiring, in effect, that all decisions made by the board be unanimous.

Decision-making at the managerial level has been no less problematic. Although the Joint Venture Law is silent on the matter, the Implementing Act mandates use of the deputy system whereby the various management positions of the joint venture each have a deputy.[102] What has evolved in practice is that in most joint ventures the foreign side appoints the top management positions, such as the President, and the Chinese side appoints the corresponding deputies, such as the Vice-President. As a result of this bifurcated structure, managerial decisions must generally be based on agreement between the expatriate manager and his deputy. Therefore, the scope for independent decision-making by foreign managerial personnel is usually quite limited.

In general, directors of a joint venture receive no fixed renumeration but are compensated by the joint venture for their travel costs, accommodation and other expenses incurred while attending board meetings. Under the

Implementing Act, the wage treatment of 'high-level' managerial personnel is to be decided upon by the board of directors.[103] The experience of most joint ventures has been that in determining wage levels for the company's managers the Chinese side will argue forcefully for the adoption of a policy of 'equal treatment' for both Chinese and expatriate personnel. Few foreign parties to joint ventures have been successful in overcoming Chinese insistence on this point, at least as regards acceptance of the principle. As a result, most efforts have been focused on attempting to limit its application to only the top rung of the venture's personnel or devising some other compromise solution.

D. Labour Management

Matters relating to staff and workers employed by joint ventures are governed by the Regulations on Labour Management in Joint Ventures Using Chinese and Foreign Investment (hereafter cited as the Labour Regulations), promulgated by the State Council on 26 July 1980.[104]

The Labour Regulations prescribe the use of a contract system for the employment of joint venture personnel.[105] The contract is required to contain provisions regarding employment terms, dismissal and resignation, wages, working hours, labour insurance, discipline and other matters, and must be approved by the labour management department of the local people's government where the joint venture is established. In general, the labour contract is to be signed between the joint venture and the labour union organization established by the staff and workers of the joint venture. In small-scale joint ventures, however, the contract may be signed between the venture and workers and staff members individually.

A major concern of foreign investors has been the extent to which joint ventures are permitted to exercise control over the hiring and firing of staff and workers. Under the Labour Regulations, a joint venture may either employ workers recommended by the local labour department or, with the consent of the labour department, recruit workers on its own.[106] In either case, the regulations provide that tests may be administered in the course of selecting personnel.[107] Despite these provisions, in practice most joint ventures have been staffed by personnel seconded by the Chinese side from its own unit. Although some joint ventures have been successful in implementing screening and other procedures to ensure that only qualified personnel are assigned by the Chinese side, most ventures have been pressured to accept the recommendations of the Chinese partner without instituting formal selection procedures.

With respect to the dismissal of joint venture personnel, the law provides that workers and staff members 'who have become redundant because of changes in production and technical conditions' and personnel who 'fail to meet the requirements of the enterprise after training and are not suitable for transfer to other types of work' may be released from employment.[108] In such cases compensation is to be paid to the dismissed workers and alternative employment is to be arranged for them by the local labour bureau.[109] Although seemingly encouraging, the practical effect of these provisions is muted by other stipulations contained in the Labour Regulations. These require that dismissals be reported to the local labour bureau for approval[110] and authorize the venture's labour union organization to lodge an objection to the dismissal with the board of directors.[111] If the matter cannot be resolved there through consultations, the aggrieved employee may request arbitration before the labour bureau.[112] If either party objects to the arbitration ruling, he may initiate a suit in a Chinese court.[113] As a result of these provisions, foreign investors have found that the dismissal of a joint venture employee is extremely difficult to enforce without the agreement of the Chinese partner.

The Labour Regulations provide that the wage levels for workers and staff members of a joint venture shall be set at '120 per cent to 150 per cent of the real wages received by workers and staff members of state-owned enterprises of the same trade in the same locality'.[114] In addition, joint ventures are required to pay for labour insurance, medical expenses and other subsidies provided to workers in state-owned enterprises.[115] As a result of these subsidies and other payments, the total renumeration paid to Chinese workers in a joint venture is often two to three times the amount of the worker's basic wage.

As noted earlier, the Labour Regulations contemplate the formation of a labour union organization consisting of the Chinese employees of joint ventures that operate on a relatively large scale. In practice, few joint ventures established to date have involved formation of such unions although this situation is likely to change in the future. Under the Implementing Act, joint venture labour unions are dealt with in some detail, a fact which presumably reflects an official policy of encouraging their formation.

The Implementing Act provides that joint venture employees 'have the right' to establish labour unions and to 'develop labour union activities' in accordance with Chinese labour laws.[116] Once established, the labour union is entrusted to 'represent the interests' of staff and workers and is charged with, among other tasks, supervising the implementation of labour contracts, organizing political, scientific and technical studies, and educating workers to observe labour discipline.[117] Under the Act, labour union representatives are granted the right to attend meetings of the board of directors of the joint venture and to voice their opinions with respect to production and operation activities, issues relating to wages and benefits provided to workers, and labour discipline.[118] Although union representatives are not permitted to vote at such meetings, the Act directs the board of directors to 'heed the opinions of the labour union' and obtain its co-operation.[119]

Joint ventures are required by the Act to 'actively support' the labour union formed by their employees.[120] Such support includes providing an office for the union and facilitating cultural and athletic activities. In addition, joint ventures are required to allocate, on a monthly basis, 2 per cent of the total amount of wages paid to staff and workers for payment into a labour union fund. The use of such funds is left to the discretion of the labour union, subject to regulations formulated by the All-China Federation of Labour Unions.

On 19 January 1984 China promulgated additional rules regarding labour matters in the form of Provisions for the Implementation of the Regulations on Labour Management in Joint Ventures Using Chinese and Foreign Investment. This law spells out in greater detail a number of provisions contained in the Labour Regulations, including remuneration and welfare schemes for joint venture personnel, labour protection, training and labour discipline. Among the provisions of the new law that go beyond clarification to impose new requirements on joint ventures are those that relate to the recruitment and dismissal of joint venture workers and staff members. Under the new law, joint ventures must formulate a 'labour plan' for approval by the Chinese labour authorities and inclusion in 'the state labour plan'. The apparent aim of this requirement is to ensure that Chinese labour is allocated to joint ventures in a co-ordinated way, and that emphasis be placed on satisfying the labour needs of joint ventures locally. The new law states that joint ventures must recruit workers within the localities stipulated by the labour authorities. Where qualified personnel are not available locally, the joint venture must obtain the consent of the local labour authority before it may recruit workers from the outside. In addition to restricting the freedom of joint ventures with respect to recruitment, the new law limits the circumstances under which joint venture personnel may be dismissed. For example, the law prohibits dismissal where workers and staff members are undergoing medical treatment due to a work-related ailment, or are in hospital. Dismissal is also not permitted in the case of women workers and staff members 'who are six months pregnant or more or are on maternity leave'. How these provisions will be applied in practice is unclear at present.

E. Operational Matters

The Implementing Act authorizes joint ventures to conduct their operational activities 'autonomously', subject to Chinese laws.[121] Among the most important Chinese legal stipulations that affect the operations of joint ventures are provisions dealing with the leasing of land, insurance and bank accounts, the purchase of raw materials, marketing and the licensing of technology by joint ventures.

i. Land Use

As mentioned previously in this chapter, the Chinese party to a joint venture may either supply the land needed by a joint venture for its plant and office facilities as part of its capital contribution, or the joint venture may lease a site from the local department in charge of land in the place where the joint venture conducts its operations. In either case, the joint venture obtains only a leasehold interest in the site and not ownership, and assignment of this interest to third parties is not permitted.[122]

If the site is leased by the joint venture directly, the Implementing Act requires that the venture enter into a lease contract with the local department in charge.[123] The standards for lease payments are to be determined in accordance with such factors as the proposed use of the site, its geographical and environmental conditions, whether or not expenses are incurred by the local government in requisitioning the site, and other factors.[124] In certain types of projects, such as those involving agriculture or animal husbandry, the joint venture may be permitted to pay land-use fees calculated as a percentage of the venture's income.[125] Special preferential treatment with respect to lease payments may also be granted to joint ventures that are established in economically underdeveloped areas.[126]

The Implementing Act requires that lease payments be made annually during the lease contract period.[127] During the first five years of the contract, lease charges are fixed.[128] Thereafter, the fees may be adjusted once every three years to take into account changes in the local economy, general geographic and environmental conditions, and factors relating to local supply and demand.[129]

ii. Insurance and Bank Accounts

Joint ventures are required to maintain appropriate insurance cover on their assets by securing policies with the People's Insurance Company of China.[130] Foreign insurance companies may only participate on the basis of reinsurance schemes entered into with the People's Insurance Company.

After having obtained a formal business licence, joint ventures are required to open foreign exchange deposit accounts and renminbi deposit accounts with the Bank of China.[131] Foreign exchange deposit accounts may also be opened with banks abroad or in Hong Kong and Macao upon the approval of the State General Administration of Exchange Control.[132]

iii. Purchasing

The Implementing Act grants freedom to joint ventures to purchase such items as machinery, equipment, raw materials, fuel, spare parts, office supplies and vehicles either in China or from sources abroad, provided that where conditions are equal priority is given to Chinese sources of supply.[133] With respect to the purchase of items on the Chinese domestic market, joint ventures are required to follow the procedures established for purchasing by Chinese state-owned enterprises which limit sources of supply to designated Chinese units.[134] Items to be purchased from abroad must fall within the scope of the joint venture's operations as specified in the joint venture contract. In the event that current Chinese regulations require an import licence for such items, the joint venture is required to prepare an annual import plan for approval by the relevant authorities and apply for the necessary licences on a six-month basis.[135]

The Implementing Act contains a number of stipulations regarding the pricing of necessary materials and services procured on the Chinese market.[136] Gold, silver, platinum, petroleum, coal and timber used in the production of export products are priced in accordance with prevailing international prices for such commodities, as determined by the State General Administration of Exchange Control or the relevant foreign trade department, as appropriate. Payments for such items may be made in either foreign exchange or renminbi. With respect to purchases of export or import commodities handled by Chinese foreign trade corporations, the prices are to be fixed by reference to international market prices and payment must be made in foreign exchange. Finally, joint ventures are granted equal treatment with Chinese state-owned enterprises with respect to the purchase price of coal used for fuel, oil for vehicles, and other items which are used for the production of goods to be sold in the Chinese domestic market, and for fees charged for water, electricity, gas, heating, goods transport and certain services provided to joint ventures by Chinese enterprises.[137]

Under the Act, purchases by joint ventures from Chinese enterprises should be conducted in accordance with China's Economic Contracts Law.[138] This law spells out the procedures for forming, implementing and enforcing contracts between Chinese entities and specifies the rights and responsibilities of the parties in the event of breach of contract. Contracts between a joint venture and foreign suppliers are also generally governed by Chinese law, although no specific regulations governing such transactions have yet been enacted. The Foreign Economic Contracts Law, which exists in draft form, is expected to be promulgated shortly and will presumably govern purchases by joint ventures from foreign suppliers in the future.

iv. Marketing

Joint ventures are 'encouraged' by the Chinese government to export their products, largely with the aim of earning foreign exchange and opening up international markets to Chinese goods. As a result, most joint ventures established to date have been obliged to gear their marketing efforts primarily towards foreign rather than domestic sales. The only circumstances under which Chinese law permits joint ventures to sell their products 'mainly' on the Chinese market are when the goods produced are items that China 'urgently needs' or when they serve a function as import-substitutes.[139]

The Implementing Act authorizes joint ventures to handle the export of their products in the manner decided by the parties.[140] Prices may be set by the joint venture itself, subject only to the requirement that such prices be reported to the Chinese price control authorities for the record.[141] By contrast, domestic sales must be carried out in accordance with the rules applicable to sales by Chinese state-owned enterprises.[142] These rules require that certain types of products that are subject to planned distribution be sold to designated

Chinese units for resale to end-users. In other cases, however, joint ventures may distribute their products directly. Prices for goods sold domestically must generally be fixed at levels determined by the state price control authorities. In some instances, however, international market prices may be adopted, provided that prior approval has been obtained from the price control department.

v. Technology Transfer

Most joint ventures involve the transfer of technology, either from the foreign joint venture party as part of its capital contribution or by means of a separate licensing agreement, or from a third party. The Implementing Act requires that all such agreements be approved by the relevant approval authority and conform to a specific set of stipulations.[143] These stipulations require that royalties generally be adopted as the form of payment, and that the royalty rate be 'fair and reasonable' and 'not higher than the common international level'. Unless otherwise agreed by the parties, the technology transfer agreement should not impose geographical, quantity or price restrictions on the marketing of the licensed product, and the joint venture is to have the right to purchase equipment, parts and raw materials from sources of its own choice. Of most importance, perhaps, are the stipulations requiring that the technology transfer agreement must generally not last for more than ten years and that upon expiry of the agreement the joint venture must be given the right to continue to use the technology. For foreign parties who license technology to joint ventures with a term longer than ten years these stipulations are particularly disadvantageous, as they constitute, in effect, a requirement that the foreign party contribute the technology free of charge during the later years of the venture's existence.

F. Foreign Exchange Controls

China's Foreign Exchange Control Regulations impose a number of stringent restrictions on joint ventures.[144] The most important of these is the requirement that all foreign exchange deposits and disbursements of a joint venture flow through the venture's bank account with the Bank of China or a bank approved by the Bank of China. Because the Chinese currency, renminbi, is not convertible into foreign exchange, the effect of these provisions is to require joint ventures to generate all foreign exchange necessary for the remittance of foreign exchange dividends and other distributions to the foreign joint venture party and the payment of all foreign exchange expenses incurred by the venture in the course of its operations.

The strictures imposed by this system have posed significant problems for investors who look upon joint ventures primarily as a vehicle for entry into the Chinese domestic market, and they are one of the major reasons why most joint ventures established to date have felt compelled to export all but a small portion of their products. As part of the Chinese government's efforts to enhance the attractiveness of joint ventures, these restrictions were liberalized to a certain extent with the promulgation in mid-1983 of the Detailed Rules for Foreign Exchange Control.[145] These rules dovetail with related rules contained in the Joint Venture Law's Implementing Act, providing joint ventures with greater access to the Chinese domestic market.

Under the new foreign exchange rules, foreign exchange may be used as the currency of settlement between joint ventures and Chinese domestic enterprises where the products sold by a joint venture are import-substitutes and the buyer is a Chinese unit engaged in foreign trade business; where the products constitute items required for the production of import or export goods handled by Chinese units engaged in foreign trade business; in construction contracts; and in other cases approved by the State General Administration of Exchange Control.[146] The Implementing Act gives further assurances to foreign investors by providing that where an approved contract permits a joint venture to sell its products 'mainly' on the domestic market, problems encountered by joint ventures in maintaining a foreign exchange balance are to be resolved by the local government in charge of the product or the State Planning Commission.[147]

G. Taxation

Equity joint ventures are subject to a variety of taxes, including an income tax, the Consolidated Industrial and Commercial Tax, customs duties and a Real Estate Tax. In addition, expatriate personnel assigned to work in a joint venture are required to pay individual income tax on their wages and salaries earned in China.

The most important tax legislation applicable to joint ventures is the Joint Venture Income Tax Law and the Detailed Implementing Rules issued thereunder.[148] The Joint Venture Income Tax Law taxes the net income of joint ventures at a flat rate of 33 per cent, comprised of a national tax of 30 per cent and a local surtax of 10 per cent of the amount of tax paid. In addition, the law imposes a 10 per cent withholding tax on dividends remitted outside China by the joint venture to the foreign party. Various forms of tax incentives and preferential treatment are provided to certain types of joint ventures engaged in relatively low-profit operations involving farming and forestry projects, and tax rebates may be obtained in certain circumstances by foreign parties to a joint venture who reinvest their profits in the venture. One of the most important incentives provided by the law are tax holidays. Pursuant to an amendment of the tax law in September 1983, joint ventures scheduled to operate for a period of at least ten years are eligible for an exemption from taxation during the first two profit-making years and may be taxed at only one half of the normal rate during the three subsequent years.

The Consolidated Industrial and Commercial Tax, a type of turnover tax, is imposed on imports by joint ventures and on their gross receipts from sales and service transactions.[149] Specific rates vary from item to item and range from 2.5 per cent to 69 per cent. Consolidated tax payments attributable to sales or service income may be deducted by the joint venture when computing taxable income under the Joint Venture Income Tax Law. In addition to the Consolidated Tax, customs duties are also levied on imports by joint ventures.

In mid-1983, the Chinese government issued new regulations providing for exemptions from the Consolidated Tax and customs duties with respect to certain items.[150] Under these regulations, exemptions may now be granted for imported machinery, equipment, spare parts and other materials related to the production activities of the joint venture that are provided by way of in-kind capital contributions or purchased with funds provided as part of the registered capital of the venture. In addition, items of the same type for which production or supply in China cannot be guaranteed may be imported free of the Consolidated Tax and customs duties when purchased with a joint venture's other funds. Finally, the regulations also provide tax exemptions for imported raw materials, auxiliary materials, components, spare parts and packaging materials used in connection with products produced by joint ventures for export. It should be noted that these exemptions do not apply to imported vehicles for office use, which continue to be subject to the levy of the Consolidated Tax and customs duties at ordinary rates.

The Real Estate Tax is imposed on factories or other buildings that have been provided by the Chinese side as part of its capital contribution to a joint venture.[151] The tax rate is 1.2 per cent per year and is levied on the value assigned to the property by a local appraisal committee. Where a joint venture leases a building the tax is usually paid by the Chinese lessor.

H. Accounting and Profit Distribution

The Joint Venture Law contains no specific provisions regarding the financial and accounting system that must be employed by equity joint ventures. It is known that Chinese officials have for some time been drafting a set of regulations intended to establish uniform accounting rules for joint ventures, but their promulgation has apparently been postponed. In the absence of these regulations, the Chinese government has been applying a number of internal guidelines to joint ventures, the main points of which are set forth in Chapter XI of the Implementing Act.

With respect to accounting mechanics, the Implementing Act requires joint ventures to adopt the calendar year as the fiscal year and mandates the use of the accrual system as the method for the keeping of accounts.[152] The Act also provides that renminbi should be used as the standard currency unit for accounting purposes, although a foreign currency may also be used if the parties agree.[153] Exchange losses and gains are required to be recorded in the joint venture's accounts as losses or gains in the year they are incurred.[154]

In most joint ventures, the accountant is appointed by the Chinese side and a deputy or assistant accountant is appointed by the foreign party. The accountants are responsible for preparing quarterly and annual accounting statements for distribution to the joint venture parties, the local tax office and other authorities, including the original approval-granting organ. Such statements must be audited by a Chinese registered accountant before they may be deemed valid.[155] In some joint ventures, the foreign party has been given the right to conduct at its own expense a separate audit of the joint venture's accounts, but such audits are not binding for the purposes of Chinese law unless they are conducted by a qualified Chinese accountant.

The system for distributing the profits of a joint venture is fixed by the Joint Venture Law, as supplemented by provisions contained in the Implementing Act.[156] This system is based on the computation of the after-tax net profit of the joint venture, from which are deducted amounts allocated to the joint venture's reserve fund, an incentive and welfare fund for the venture's employees, and an enterprise expansion fund. The actual amounts allocated to such funds may be decided by the board of directors and are usually calculated as a fixed percentage of the after-tax net profit. Amounts remaining after such deductions may be distributed to the joint venture parties in accordance with the ratio of their capital contributions. However, distributions are not mandatory and current profits may be retained for distribution in later years.

I. Term and Termination

Chinese law does not specify any fixed term for joint ventures. The Implementing Act provides only that 'in principle' the average term should be between 10 and 30 years, although longer terms may be permitted.[157] Moreover, the Act permits joint ventures to extend their life beyond the scheduled term, subject to the agreement of the parties and government approval. As a result, the actual duration of the venture is left to negotiation between the parties, taking into account the nature of the project, the wishes of the parties and the attitude of the Chinese government.

For most foreign investors, the scheduled duration of the venture is of less concern than the issue of what their rights and obligations will be upon termination and under what circumstances they will be permitted to end their participation in the joint venture prior to the expiration of its term. The Implementing Act permits early dissolution of a joint venture in the event of breach of contract by one of the parties, where the enterprise suffers heavy losses or is unable to attain its stated business goals, or upon the occurrence of other reasons stipulated in the joint venture contract.[158] In the event that the reason for termination is caused by a breach of contract which makes the joint venture unable to continue operations, the breaching party is liable to compensate the venture for the losses incurred thereby.[159]

Upon termination of the joint venture, the board of directors is required to establish a liquidation committee consisting of board members appointed by the parties.[160] This committee is entrusted with the task of compiling an inventory of the joint venture's assets and liabilities and formulating a plan for liquidation which must be ratified by the board of directors and implemented under the supervision of the Chinese department in charge of the joint venture. After clearance of the joint venture's debts, the remaining property may be distributed to the parties in accordance with the ratio of their capital contributions or some other method agreed to by the parties. In the event that the value of the remaining assets exceeds the amount of the joint venture's registered capital, the excess will be regarded as profit and will be subject to tax.[161] In addition, that portion of the distribution owing to the foreign party and remitted abroad which exceeds its original capital contribution will be subject to a 10 per cent withholding tax.[162]

Although the Implementing Act contemplates that joint ventures will be able to make distributions to the parties upon liquidation, a major fear of foreign investors has been that the Chinese side will prevent such a possibility from being realized. The fear is grounded in the belief that the Chinese members of the liquidation committee will insist on a low valuation of the company's assets and then arrange for their sale to a related Chinese entity, thereby permitting the Chinese side to continue the operations of the joint venture in a modified form. To diminish the likelihood that this will occur, many foreign investors have attempted to negotiate contract language that would require that the valuation of the joint venture's assets be performed by a foreign broker or at least be sold at auction in the international market. In other instances, language has been proposed that would permit the Chinese side to exercise a right of first refusal to purchase the foreign party's interest in the venture, calculated on the basis of the proportional value of the company's assets when viewed as part of a going concern with an additional value added to reflect the future profitability of the enterprise. These and similar attempts to ensure that liquidation will be conducted in a fair manner have met with varied success, although the Chinese willingness to accept such proposals has tended to increase over time.

V. Wholly-owned Foreign Investments

At present, the establishment of wholly-owned foreign enterprises in China is restricted to the Special Economic Zones (SEZs) located in Guangdong and Fujian Provinces. The only statutory basis that exists for this form of investment is the first article of the Regulations on Special Economic Zones in Guangdong Province (hereafter cited as the SEZ Regulations) which permits foreign investors 'to open up factories with their own investment' in the SEZs.[163] The legislative restriction on this investment form to 'factories' is presumably an oversight in drafting. In practice, a number of wholly-owned foreign enterprises have been set up by foreign investors in the service and other trades, in addition to the more common fields of production and assembly and processing of goods for export. By the end of 1982 more than 30 projects of this type were established, with a total investment of approximately US$200 million.[164]

The only formally promulgated legislation dealing with wholly-owned foreign investments are the SEZ Regulations and several sets of 'provisional' regulations dealing with the entry and exit of personnel, business registration, labour and wages, and land use issued pursuant to the SEZ Regulations. None of these laws deals exclusively with wholly-owned foreign investments as such, but they address matters relating to wholly-owned foreign enterprises in the context of investment in the SEZs in general. Therefore, all of the SEZ rules relating to joint ventures, such as tax rates, preferential customs rules, approval of registration of enterprises, labour regulations and land-use rules, are applicable to wholly-owned foreign enterprises as well. A detailed discussion of these provisions is found in Chapter 5 of this volume.

There are increasing signs that China is prepared to extend the permissibility of the wholly-owned foreign investment format to areas outside the SEZs. In early 1983, Chinese officials announced that they were actively reviewing a proposal by an American company to establish a wholly-owned plant in Shanghai.[165] Later in the same year, the Chinese press reported that plans were under way to permit foreign investors to set up wholly-owned enterprises in China's coastal regions.[166] According to MOFERT officials, legislation designed to implement these plans is now being drawn up. At the time of writing, however, it remains unclear when such legislation will be promulgated and what kinds of restrictions will be imposed on this form of investment.

VI. Conclusion

For a society that remains committed to Communist ideals, China has demonstrated an extraordinary degree of flexibility in permitting a variety of forms of foreign investment. Moreover, the efforts that have been made to date to establish a legal framework for the regulation of investment activities are admirable. Nonetheless, it is important to bear in mind that foreign investment is still relatively new to China and as such its future is to a large degree unpredictable. As a result, the ultimate test of China's commitment to foreign investment lies in how liberally it chooses to interpret and implement its newly established legal framework rather than in the strict letter of the laws themselves.

Notes

1. See 'China's Utilization of Foreign Capital, 1979–1982', *Intertrade*, October 1983, p.68.

2. The Constitution of the People's Republic of China, promulgated on 4 December 1982, Arts. 15 and 89.

3. The foregoing description of the foreign investment approval process is based on a speech entitled 'China Investment Needs Mutual Understanding' delivered by Gu Xiancheng, Vice-President of China International Economic Consultants, Inc. The speech was delivered in Tokyo and Hong Kong during 14–18 November 1983 at the China Update Conference, sponsored by the Institute for International Research.

4. Gu speech, note 3 above.

5. See The Law of the People's Republic of China on Joint Ventures Using Chinese and Foreign Investment, adopted at the Second Session of the Fifth National People's Congress on 1 July 1979 and promulgated on 8 July 1979, Art. 3 (hereafter cited as the Joint Venture Law). For an English translation of the Joint Venture Law, see F. Chu, M. Moser and O. Nee (eds.), *Commercial, Business and Trade Laws: People's Republic of China* (Dobbs Ferry, Oceana Publications Inc., 1982), Pt. 9, p.3.

6. See The Implementing Act for the Law of the People's Republic of China on Joint Ventures Using Chinese and Foreign Investment, promulgated by the State Council on 20 September 1983, Art. 8 (hereafter cited as the Implementing Act). All references to the Implementing Act are to an English translation on file with the author.

7. Gu speech, note 3 above.

8. For a discussion of the situation in the Guangdong Special Economic Zones, see Chapter 5 in this volume.

9. Gu speech, note 3 above.

10. See P. Torbert, 'China's Joint Venture Law: A Preliminary Analysis', *Vanderbilt Journal of Transnational Law*, No. 4, Fall 1979, p.822.

11. 'China's Utilization of Foreign Capital, 1979–1982', note 1 above.

12. The following discussion is based largely on *China: A Business Guide* (Tokyo, Japan External Trade Organization, 1979), pp.155–6; J. Cohen and O. Nee, 'All About Compensation Trade, Part I', *Asian Wall Street Journal*, 3 July 1979, p.4 and 'Part II', *Asian Wall Street Journal*, 4 July 1979, p.4; and Torbert, pp.822–7, note 10 above.

13. Provisional Regulations on Foreign Exchange Control of the People's Republic of China (hereafter cited as the Foreign Exchange Control Regulations), promulgated by the State Council on 18 December 1980, and Detailed Rules for Foreign Exchange Control for Enterprises with Overseas Chinese Capital, Enterprises with Foreign Capital and Chinese-Foreign Joint Venture Enterprises (hereafter cited as the Detailed Rules for Foreign Exchange Control), approved by the State Council on 19 July 1983 and promulgated by the State Administration of Foreign Exchange Control on 1 August 1983. All subsequent references to these two laws are to English translations on file with the author.

14. For a discussion of commodity inspection procedures, see Chapter 1 of this volume.

15. A detailed discussion of the Consolidated Industrial and Commercial Tax is set forth in Chapter 2 of this volume.

16. See Chapter 2 of this volume.

17. See Torbert, note 10 above.

18. See 'China's Utilization of Foreign Capital, 1979–1982', note 1 above.

19. The following discussion is based primarily on the table set forth on pp.52–3 in China International Economic Consultants, Inc. and Economic Information & Consultancy Co. (eds.), *Guide to Investment in China* (Hong Kong, Economic Information and Agency, 1983).

20. Joint Venture Law, Art. 5, note 5 above; and Implementing Act, Art. 25, note 6 above.

21. Implementing Act, Arts. 33 and 34, note 6 above.

22. Joint Venture Law, Art. 6, note 5 above.

23. Economic Contracts Law of the People's Republic of China, promulgated on 13 December 1981, Art. 2. An English translation of this law appears in Chu, Moser and Nee, Pt. 5, note 5 above.

24. The Income Tax Law of the People's Republic of China Concerning Joint Ventures Using Chinese and Foreign Investment (hereafter cited as the Joint Venture Income Tax Law), promulgated on 10 September 1980, and the Detailed Rules and Regulations for the Implementation of the Income Tax Law of the People's Republic of China Concerning Joint Ventures Using Chinese and Foreign Investment (hereafter cited as the Joint Venture Income Tax Detailed Rules), promulgated by the Ministry of Finance on 14 December 1980. English translations of both the Joint Venture Income Tax Law and the Joint Venture Income Tax Detailed Rules appear in Chu, Moser and Nee, Pt. 13, note 5 above.

25. The Income Tax Law of the People's Republic of China Concerning Foreign Enterprises (hereafter cited as the Foreign Enterprise Income Tax Law), promulgated on 13 December 1981. The Foreign Enterprise Income Tax Law has been supplemented by the Detailed Rules and Regulations for the Implementation of the Income Tax Law of the People's Republic of China Concerning Foreign Enterprises (hereafter cited as the Foreign Enterprise Income Tax Detailed Rules), promulgated by the Ministry of Finance on 21 February 1982. English translations of the Foreign Enterprise Income Tax Law and the Foreign Enterprise Income Tax Detailed Rules are set forth in Chu, Moser and Nee, Pt. 13, note 5 above.

26. See *Guide to Investment in China*, p.53, note 19 above.

27. For a discussion of China's individual income tax, see Chapter 2 of this volume.

28. See note 15 above.

29. See Regulations Regarding the Supervision and Control of and Levy and Exemption of Tax on Goods Imported and Exported by Chinese-Foreign Co-operative Ventures, promulgated on 31 January 1984 and put into effect on 1 February 1984. The original text and an English translation of this law are on file with the author.

30. See Part IV of this chapter.

31. See the Provisional Regulations on Standards for the Payment of Registration Fees by Joint Ventures (hereafter cited as the Registration Fee Regulations) issued in March 1982 by the General Administration for Industry and Commerce of the People's Republic of China, subsequently re-named the State Administration for Industry and Commerce of the People's Republic of China. The provisions referring to contractual joint ventures are set forth in Arts. 1 and 4.

32. See 'Creating a More Favourable Investment Environment for Foreign Investors', text of a speech prepared by Liu Yimin, Vice-Director, Department of Treaty and Law of the Ministry of Foreign Economic Relations and Trade. The speech was

delivered at a seminar held in Hong Kong on China's New Joint Venture Legislation, sponsored by Economic Information and Agency, on 11 November 1983.

33. Liu speech, note 32 above.

34. See 'Problems that Can Arise from Investment in China', text of a speech delivered by Kazuo Tomabechi, Managing Director of the Industrial Bank of Japan, at the China Update Conference held in Tokyo during 14–15 November 1983 under the sponsorship of the Institute for International Research. According to Mr Tomabechi, the investment environment in Taiwan, Korea, Indonesia, Malaysia and Singapore is far more attractive than in the People's Republic.

35. Liu speech, note 32 above.

36. Liu speech, note 32 above.

37. Joint Venture Law, Art. 4, note 5 above; and Implementing Act, Art. 19, note 6 above.

38. Implementing Act, Art. 2, note 6 above.

39. Implementing Act, Art. 2, note 6 above.

40. Implementing Act, Art. 19, note 6 above.

41. Joint Venture Law, Art. 4, note 5 above.

42. Liu speech, note 32 above.

43. Liu speech, note 32 above.

44. For a more extended discussion of this issue, see J. Cohen, 'Some Problems of Investing in China', in J. Cohen (ed.),*Legal Aspects of Doing Business in China 1983* (New York, Practising Law Institute, 1983), p.67.

45. Quoted in 'Questions and Answers Concerning Foreign Investment in China', *China Economic News* (Supplement 3), 12 May 1983, p.5.

46. The case referred to is the Schindler Elevator joint venture. See Cohen, p.82, note 44 above.

47. Implementing Act, Art. 9(1), note 6 above.

48. Implementing Act, Art. 13, note 6 above.

49. Implementing Act, Arts. 13, 14 and 16, note 6 above.

50. Implementing Act, Art. 9, note 6 above.

51. Implementing Act, Art. 9, note 6 above.

52. Implementing Act, Art. 15, note 6 above.

53. In general, however, the Chinese will require that these 'commonly accepted' practices also be acceptable to the Chinese party. A formulation that has been widely adopted in the petroleum area provides that: 'The validity, interpretation and implementation of the Contract shall be governed by the law of the People's Republic of China. Failing the relevant provisions of the law of the People's Republic of China for its implementation or interpretation of the Contract, the principles of the applicable laws widely used in petroleum resources countries acceptable to the CNOOC and the Contractor shall be applicable.'

54. Implementing Act, Arts. 109 and 110, note 6 above.

55. For a detailed examination of China's position regarding arbitration, see Chapter 11 of this volume.

56. Implementing Act, Art. 111, note 6 above.

57. Implementing Act, Art. 21, note 6 above.

58. Implementing Act, Art. 20, note 6 above.

59. Joint Venture Law, Art. 4, note 5 above.

60. Implementing Act, Art. 21, note 6 above.

61. Implementing Act, Art. 32, note 6 above.

62. Implementing Act, Art. 22, note 6 above.
63. Implementing Act, Art. 24, note 6 above.
64. Implementing Act, Art. 23, note 6 above.
65. Implementing Act, Art. 23, note 6 above.
66. Implementing Act, Art. 23, note 6 above.
67. Implementing Act, Art. 27, note 6 above.
68. Implementing Act, Art. 28, note 6 above.
69. Implementing Act, Art. 29, note 6 above.
70. Implementing Act, Art. 25, note 6 above.
71. Implementing Act, Art. 5, note 6 above.
72. Implementing Act, Art. 30, note 6 above.
73. Implementing Act, Art. 78, note 6 above.
74. For a discussion of the legal problems involved in commercial bank lending to Chinese entities, including joint ventures, see M. Moser, 'Documentation for Commercial Bank Loans to Chinese Borrowers: Some Legal and Practical Issues', in J. Cohen, p.251, note 44 above.
75. Approved by the State Council and promulgated by the Bank of China on 13 March 1981. For an English translation of the Loan Measures, see Chu, Moser and Nee, Pt. 9, note 5 above.
76. Loan Measures, Art. 2, note 75 above.
77. Loan Measures, Art. 3, note 75 above.
78. Loan Measures, Art. 4, note 75 above.
79. Loan Measures, Art. 7, note 75 above.
80. Loan Measures, Art. 6, note 75 above.
81. Loan Measures, Art. 6, note 75 above.
82. Loan Measures, Art. 8, note 75 above.
83. Implementing Act, Art. 8, note 6 above.
84. Implementing Act, Art. 9, note 6 above.
85. Implementing Act, Art. 10, note 6 above.
86. Implementing Act, Art. 10, note 6 above.
87. Implementing Act, Art. 8, note 6 above.
88. Implementing Act, Art. 11, note 6 above.
89. An English translation of the Registration Measures is included in Chu, Moser and Nee, Pt. 9, note 5 above.
90. Registration Measures, Art. 3, note 89 above.
91. See note 31 above.
92. Registration Fee Regulations, Art. 1, note 31 above.
93. Registration Measures, Art. 7, note 89 above.
94. Registration Fee Regulations, Art. 2, note 31 above.
95. Registration Fee Regulations, Art. 1, note 31 above.
96. Implementing Act, Art. 33, note 6 above.
97. Implementing Act, Art. 38, note 6 above.
98. This requirement, and the others referred to in this paragraph, are all contained in the Implementing Act, Art. 34, note 6 above.
99. The provisions referred to in this paragraph are contained in the Implementing Act, Art. 35, note 6 above.
100. Implementing Act, Art. 36, note 6 above.
101. Implementing Act, Art. 36, note 6 above.
102. Implementing Act, Art. 38, note 6 above.

103. Implementing Act, Art. 94, note 6 above.
104. An English translation of the Labour Regulations appears in Chu, Moser and Nee, Pt. 9, note 5 above.
105. Labour Regulations, Art. 2, note 104 above.
106. Art. 3, note 104 above.
107. Labour Regulations, Art. 3, note 104 above.
108. Labour Regulations, Art. 4, note 104 above.
109. Labour Regulations, Art. 4, note 104 above.
110. Labour Regulations, Art. 5, note 104 above.
111. Labour Regulations, Art. 6, note 104 above.
112. Labour Regulations, Art. 14, note 104 above.
113. Labour Regulations, Art. 14, note 104 above.
114. Labour Regulations, Art. 8, note 104 above.
115. Labour Regulations, Art. 11, note 104 above.
116. Implementing Act, Art. 95, note 6 above.
117. Implementing Act, Arts. 96 and 97, note 6 above.
118. Implementing Act, Art. 98, note 6 above.
119. Implementing Act, Art. 98, note 6 above.
120. Implementing Act, Art. 98, note 6 above.
121. Implementing Act, Art. 7, note 6 above.
122. Implementing Act, Art. 53, note 6 above.
123. Art. 47.
124. Implementing Act, Art. 49, note 6 above. According to an internal Chinese regulation issued by the State Council, land-use fees should be fixed within the range of RMB 5–300 per square metre per annum. See Provisional Regulations Concerning the Use of Land for Construction by Joint Ventures Using Chinese and Foreign Investment, issued on 26 July 1980.
125. Implementing Act, Art. 50, note 6 above.
126. Implementing Act, Art. 50, note 6 above.
127. Implementing Act, Art. 52, note 6 above.
128. Implementing Act, Art. 51, note 6 above.
129. Implementing Act, Art. 51, note 6 above.
130. Joint Venture Law, Art. 8, note 5 above.
131. Joint Venture Law, Art. 8, note 5 above; and Implementing Act, Art. 74, note 6 above.
132. Implementing Act, Art. 76, note 6 above.
133. Implementing Act, Art. 57, note 6 above.
134. Implementing Act, Art. 58, note 6 above.
135. Implementing Act, Art. 63, note 6 above.
136. Implementing Act, Art. 65, note 6 above.
137. Joint Venture Law, Art. 65 (3), note 5 above.
138. Implementing Act, Art. 67, note 6 above.
139. Implementing Act, Art. 61, note 6 above.
140. Art. 62.
141. Implementing Act, Art. 66, note 6 above.
142. Implementing Act, Art. 66, note 6 above.
143. Implementing Act, Art. 46, note 6 above.
144. See note 13 above.
145. See note 13 above.

146. Detailed Rules for Foreign Exchange Control, Art. 12, note 13 above.
147. Implementing Act, Art. 75, note 6 above.
148. See note 24 above. For a detailed discussion of the taxation of joint ventures see Chapter 2 of this volume.
149. See note 15 above.
150. Regulations for the Control of and Payment and Exemption of Taxes on Items Imported by Chinese-Foreign Joint Ventures, issued pursuant to the Document of the General Customs Office, the Ministry of Finance and the Ministry of Foreign Economic Relations and Trade, (83) *Shu Shui*, No. 377 (undated).
151. The Real Estate Tax is discussed in Chapter 2 of this volume.
152. Implementing Act, Arts. 83 and 84, note 6 above.
153. Implementing Act, Art. 55, note 6 above.
154. Implementing Act, Art. 56, note 6 above.
155. Implementing Act, Art. 90, note 6 above.
156. Joint Venture Law, Art. 7, note 5 above; and Implementing Act, Arts. 57 and 58, note 6 above.
157. Implementing Act, Art. 100, note 6 above.
158. Implementing Act, Art. 102, note 6 above.
159. Implementing Act, Art. 102, note 6 above.
160. Implementing Act, Arts. 103 and 104, note 6 above.
161. Implementing Act, Art. 106, note 6 above.
162. Implementing Act, Art. 106, note 6 above.
163. Promulgated on 26 August 1980 by the Standing Committee of the National People's Congress. For an English translation of the regulations, see Chu, Moser and Nee, Pt. 14, note 5 above.
164. 'China's Utilization of Foreign Capital, 1979–1982', note 1 above.
165. See 'SITCO Considers Proposal for Wholly-owned Foreign Venture', *China Market Intelligence*, February 1983, p.2.
166. See 'Foreigners Allowed to Open Businesses', *Beijing Review*, 24 October 1983, p.19.

5. Law and Investment in the Guangdong Special Economic Zones

MICHAEL J. MOSER

ONE of the most widely publicized aspects of China's post-Mao economic modernization programme has been the creation of *jingji tequ* or 'special economic zones' (SEZs). Of the SEZs established to date, the largest and most successful are the three zones located in the municipalities of Shenzhen, Zhuhai and Shantou in Guangdong Province.[1] Offering special incentives to foreign investors and various types of preferential treatment for enterprises established there, the Guangdong SEZs have begun to construct and implement a legal framework for investment that differs in many important respects from that which is applicable in China generally.

This chapter will describe the regulatory regime that has been established to govern investment and other economic activity in the Guangdong SEZs. Part I provides a background discussion focusing on the origins of the SEZs, government policy goals and investment patterns in the zones to date. Parts II and III examine the relevant laws and regulations affecting the conduct of business in the zones and discuss the major types of preferential treatment granted to SEZ enterprises. Part IV examines the special investment rules applicable to the Shekou industrial zone, a part of the Shenzhen SEZ, within the context of the general SEZ legislation.

I. Background

Although the roots of the 'special zone' concept can be traced back to the 1960s,[2] the present-day SEZs did not formally come into being until 1980. Searching for means to enhance the attractiveness of investment in China, the Chinese government, in early 1979, dispatched a number of teams of economists and planners abroad to conduct research on 'export' or 'free trade' zones.[3] Subsequently, in July of that year, the State Council issued a directive granting Guangdong Province wide-ranging powers to devise and implement flexible economic policies aimed at promoting tourism, foreign trade and investment.[4] One month later, in August 1979, Shantou Municipality in Guangdong announced that it had set up a 'trade and investment zone', and in September the bordering municipalities of Shenzhen and Zhuhai declared themselves 'special export zones'.[5] Finally, in August 1980, the Shantou, Shenzhen and Zhuhai zones were renamed 'special economic zones' and put under the unified management of the newly created Administrative Committee of the Special Economic Zones of Guangdong Province.[6]

China's decision to establish SEZs can be seen to have been motivated by a number of policy goals.[7] First, and perhaps foremost, is the aim to realize significant economic benefits from the zones. Like other developing countries which have set up 'free trade zones', 'special industrial estates' and similar zones on their borders, China has viewed the establishment of the SEZs as a useful means of accelerating the development of export-oriented enterprises while simultaneously increasing local employment and foreign exchange earnings.[8] In addition, the SEZs have been seen to be of value in serving more long-term goals. Unlike their counterparts in other developing countries, China's SEZs have not limited foreign investment to small-scale assembly and processing operations but have encouraged investment in major infrastructure projects such as the construction of roads, waterworks, airports and harbours.[9]

A second goal pursued by Chinese planners in establishing the SEZs has been to use the zones as a bridge for the introduction of foreign technology, know-how and management techniques to other parts of China.[10] Seen from this perspective, the promotion of regional economic development is only one aspect of government policy; in addition, the zones play a role in the national development plan, thereby serving China's overall socialist modernization drive.

A third, and somewhat related, function of the SEZs is to serve as centres for education and experimentation.[11] Isolated geographically, the SEZs are viewed as hothouses of economic development in which China is able, within a controlled environment, to gain experience in dealing with capitalist economies and to experiment with economic reforms which may be adopted elsewhere in China. Chinese publications have frequently elaborated on this theme, describing the SEZs as 'pilot projects' which, in the words of one writer, provide 'a testing ground for integrated economic development that co-ordinates development in infrastructure, regulation and law, industrial projects, construction, tourism and foreign investment.'[12]

In choosing Guangdong as the location for the first of China's SEZs, the nation's planners were prompted by a number of special considerations which tend to complement and support its policy goals.[13] Among the most important of these are geographical factors. First, being situated along the coast, the zones are ideally located to facilitate the importation of raw materials and the exportation of finished products to the international market. Secondly, Guangdong Province is the ancestral home for most overseas Chinese and therefore holds a special attraction for these investors. For many wealthy overseas Chinese the opportunity to assist in the development of the motherland and simultaneously turn a profit on their investments holds both a sentimental and a practical appeal. Finally the proximity of the Guangdong SEZs to Hong

Kong provides investors with easy access to the zones, and permits the SEZs to tap the infrastructural resources of one of the world's most important financial centres.

In addition, there is reason to believe that China's choice of Guangdong Province as the location for the first SEZs was also influenced by political considerations. The New Territories of Hong Kong, which border the Shenzhen SEZ, are scheduled to be returned to Chinese sovereignty when Britain's lease on the area expires in 1997.[14] By seeking to accelerate the pace of economic development on the Chinese side of the border and promote economic integration between Hong Kong and Guangdong, some commentators have suggested that China's ultimate goal is to develop a formula for reunification by which Hong Kong might retain its present economic system within the framework of a 'super SEZ' or at least to erase the economic boundary between the two areas and thereby facilitate the reunification process.[15]

The Shenzhen Special Economic Zone, located directly across the border from Hong Kong, is the largest of the SEZs. Consisting of an area of 327.5 square kilometres, the zone occupies approximately one-sixth of the total area of Shenzhen Municipality.[16]

Based on the zone's general development plan, the Shenzhen SEZ is divided into five districts.[17] At the western end of the zone, on the east coast of the Pearl River estuary, is the Shekou Industrial Zone.[18] During the period 1979–81, over US$20 million was invested in the district for site preparation.[19] As a result, Shekou enjoys a comparatively well-developed infrastructure featuring such facilities as a 600-metre dock capable of handling vessels of between 3,000 and 5,000 d.w.t.[20] and a microwave communications exchange which in the near future will provide direct-dial telephone and automatic telex links between the district and Hong Kong.[21] The district has also initiated a daily hydrofoil service to the British colony and has made extensive improvements to the highway connecting the district to central Shenzhen City.[22] As of the end of 1982, 35 agreements with a total investment commitment of approximately US$200 million had reportedly been signed with the Shekou authorities.[23] The projects include container manufacturing, flour-milling, steel-rolling, screw manufacturing and others.[24] The district does not welcome simple assembly and processing operations and hopes in the long term to concentrate on high-technology enterprises.[25] In addition, because of its strategic location, district planners expect to play an important role in China's offshore oil development programme.[26] The Chiwan Bay area adjacent to the district is under development by the Ministry of Petroleum Industry as a rear supply base to support oil exploration activities in the South China Sea.[27]

The other districts in the Shenzhen SEZ include the Shangbu District and the Luohu Commercial Area, both located in the middle section of the zone, a tourist district in the eastern sector and a residential district near the Shenzhen Reservoir. The Shangbu District is being developed as an industrial area focusing on electronics, textiles and other light industries and is the location of the American Pepsi Cola bottling plant, as well as numerous small assembly and processing operations.[28] The Luohu Commercial Area is being planned as the business centre for the zone.[29] Among nearly one hundred construction projects earmarked for the area is the 20-storey International Centre being constructed by Hong Kong investors which will provide office space for both foreign concerns and Chinese enterprises from areas outside the SEZ,[30] and a new railway station scheduled for completion in 1984.[31] Property development projects in the eastern sector are being geared mainly to the overseas Chinese and Hong Kong and Macao Chinese markets and consist largely of residential construction.[32] Tourist development projects range from co-operative ventures with Hong Kong tourist agencies for transport and package tours to the zone's scenic areas to larger projects such as the proposed development by a Swiss company of a large tourist complex and construction of a Holiday Inn.[33]

The Zhuhai Special Economic Zone, located across the border from the Portuguese enclave of Macao, is the second largest SEZ. Occupying a total of 6.8 square kilometres, the zone has been divided by planners into three sectors: the large, central sector earmarked for light industrial projects; the eastern sector, reserved for tourist and residential projects; and the western sector, slated for development as a residential area for employees of foreign oil companies engaged in petroleum exploration and development in the South China Sea.[34]

The major focus of activity in Zhuhai to date has been the scenic eastern sector where several tourist and residential projects have been completed and where others are under construction.[35] By contrast, industrial projects have lagged behind. Part of the reason for this can be attributed to the zone's inadequate infrastructure, particularly when compared to Shenzhen. Efforts are being made, however, to improve the facilities in Zhuhai, including the construction of a new cargo-handling port.[36]

The Shantou Special Economic Zone, consisting of only 0.8 square kilometres, is the smallest and least developed of the Guangdong SEZs.[37] Located along the north-east coast of Guangdong Province, the only link between the zone and Hong Kong is by ship or road. The zone has been plagued by persistent electricity and water supply problems and inadequate communications facilities.[38] As a result, Shantou remains at an early stage of development. The zone's development plans call for the establishment of a processing district, a district for agricultural projects, and a residential and tourist district.[39]

Since the establishment of the Guangdong SEZs investment has proceeded at a rapid pace. By the beginning of 1982 more than US$1.6 billion in foreign investment had been committed to projects in the SEZs, an amount which is equal to more than half of total direct investment in China as a whole.[40]

One of the major characteristics of investment in the SEZs has been the predominance of Hong Kong, Macao and overseas Chinese investment, a fact which has led some observers to remark that economic activity in the zones has become to a large extent a 'family affair'.[41] In Shenzhen, for example, reports indicate that as of February 1982 more than 95 per cent of total investment funds was pledged by Hong Kong businesses; the remainder was provided by overseas Chinese and by investors from the United States, Japan, Australia, Thailand and Singapore.[42]

Largely because of its size, its comparatively well-developed infrastructure and its proximity to Hong Kong, Shenzhen has succeeded in capturing the lion's share of investment in the SEZs so far. In February 1982 it was reported that agreements for more than 1,150 projects had been signed.[43] More than half of these projects have involved light industrial and small-scale processing and assembly operations.[44] In terms of investment, however, the bulk of the funds (approximately 72 per cent) pledged as of mid-1982 has been earmarked for real estate development.[45]

While the other zones are just beginning to gear up in their attempts to attract investment, Shenzhen has unveiled a detailed long-range development plan which calls for exports to reach US$5.2 billion per annum by 1990,[46] and annual industrial output to reach US$7.1 billion by the year 2000.[47] The draft plan, announced in September 1982, outlines a number of development projects in the areas of light industry, agriculture, tourism and transportation, and anticipates that before the end of the century foreign investment in these projects will top US$7.2 billion.[48] Under the plan, it is projected that more than 200 industrial projects will be in operation in the zone by 1985; by the year 2000, 1,500 enterprises employing more than 200,000 workers are expected.[49]

II. The 1980 SEZ Regulations

The basic regulatory framework for investment and other economic activity in the Guangdong SEZs is established by the Regulations on Special Economic Zones in Guangdong Province (hereafter cited as the SEZ Regulations).[50] Adopted by the Fifteenth Session of the Standing Committee of the Fifth National People's Congress on 26 August 1980,[51] the SEZ Regulations are the first piece of legislation promulgated specifically to govern business in the special zones. Consisting of only 26 brief articles, the law is nonetheless ambitious in scope. Apart from providing for the creation of the Guangdong SEZs, it establishes the administrative structure for managing and co-ordinating economic activity in the zones and sets forth the basic preferential terms offered to investors there.

At the outset it is important to note that the SEZ Regulations do not purport to establish a legal regime for the special zones which is separate and distinct from China's national legal system. The SEZ Regulations state that '[e]nterprises and individuals in the Special Zones must abide by the laws, decrees and relevant regulations of the People's Republic of China.'[52] The same article goes on to state that '[w]here specific stipulations are provided herein, such specific stipulations shall be implemented in accordance with these Regulations.'[53] Based on these provisions, national laws remain applicable in the zones at least to the extent that they have not been superseded, in whole or in part, by specific provisions contained in the SEZ Regulations.

A. Administrative Organization

The SEZ Regulations provide for the establishment of three different organizations, each of which plays a role in administering the zones. The most important of these is the Administrative Committee for the Special Economic Zones of Guangdong Province (ADCOM). The basic function of the ADCOM is 'to carry out unified management of the special zones on behalf of the Guangdong Provincial People's Government.'[54] To this end, the SEZ Regulations grant to the ADCOM a wide range of responsibilities and powers. These include the drawing up and implementation of development plans for the SEZs; approval of investment projects in the zones; control over matters relating to the registration of business enterprises and the allocation of land in the zones; the co-ordination of relations among taxation, customs, post and telecommunications, banking and other organizations in the SEZs; the supply of workers and staff members needed by enterprises established in the zones; the operation of educational, cultural, health and other public welfare facilities; and the maintenance of 'law and order' in the zones.[55] In addition to the foregoing, the ADCOM is responsible for the development of the local infrastructure, including land-levelling projects and the provision of public utilities.[56] The SEZ Regulations provide that 'when necessary' the ADCOM may utilize foreign investment to 'participate' in the development of such projects.[57]

In addition to the ADCOM, the SEZ Regulations provide for the establishment of a separate organization charged with developing and co-ordinating local investment activity. This organization, the Development Company for the Special Economic Zones in Guangdong Province, provides business facilitation services for foreign investors and is empowered to raise funds, engage in trust and investment activities, set up enterprises either independently or in co-operation with foreign investors, and act as agents on behalf of foreign investors in connection with the purchase from or sale of commodities to Chinese entities outside the zones.[58]

Finally, the SEZ Regulations also provide for the establishment in each of the zones of a local advisory committee comprised of 'experts in China and abroad and concerned individuals who are enthusiastic about China's modernization programme.'[59] The committees serve as consultative bodies to the ADCOM and the Development Company but have no administrative powers themselves.[60]

The administrative organization established by the SEZ Regulations has been generally well-received by investors in the zones, who reportedly encounter fewer bureaucratic entanglements than do investors engaged in projects elsewhere in China.[61] Nonetheless, indications exist that administrative authority has become increasingly diffused over time as the number of local administrative agencies has grown. As a result, investors in the zones are often uncertain as to where final administrative authority in a number of crucial areas actually rests. The problem has its genesis in the various supplementary regulations adopted subsequent to the SEZ Regulations which delegate to local agencies certain responsibilities which the SEZ Regulations had entrusted to the ADCOM. For example, under the SEZ Business Registration Regulations, registration is to be handled by the local administrative bureaux for industry and commerce.[62] The Shenzhen Land Regulations provide that municipal authorities shall issue land-use certificates and allot land within the zone to investors there.[63] Finally, the SEZ Labour and Wage Regulations grant to municipal labour bureaux in each of the zones responsibility over labour issues.[64] In each of these cases an apparent conflict exists with the provisions contained in the SEZ Regulations.[65] However, no attempts have been made thus far to clarify whether the local agencies named in the supplementary regulations are to act in conjunction with, under the supervision of, or independent of the ADCOM.

Another related issue which investors will wish to see clarified concerns the question of what approval is required for SEZ investment projects. Under the SEZ Regulations, the ADCOM is vested with the power to 'examine and approve' investment projects in the zones.[66] Although this provision was intended to streamline approval procedures by providing for a single approval-granting agency, it appears that in practice at least the ADCOM's approval powers are not exclusive. For example, the SEZ Business Registration Regulations imply that the municipal government in each of the zones, in addition to the ADCOM, has the power to issue approval.[67] Moveover, press reports indicate that the State Council's Office of SEZ Affairs in Beijing also has approval power over projects in the zones.[68] Although SEZ officials indicate that 'in most cases' only ADCOM approval is necessary,[69] questions remain as to when a municipal-level approval is by itself sufficient and when a central government approval is mandatory.

B. The Scope and Forms of Investment

The SEZ Regulations encourage investment in the zones by 'foreign citizens, overseas Chinese, compatriots in Hong Kong and Macao and their companies and enterprises.'[70] The law provides a wide scope for investment, including 'industry, agriculture, animal husbandry, fish breeding and poultry farming, tourism, housing and construction, research and manufacture involving high technologies and techniques. . .', as well as 'other trades of common interest to investors and the Chinese side.'[71]

Regarding the permissible forms of investment in the zones, the SEZ Regulations provide that projects may be undertaken by foreign investors 'with their own investment'[72] or 'by means of joint ventures with Chinese investment.'[73] The latter category is intended to include both equity and 'co-operative' or 'contractual' joint ventures.[74] In the case of equity joint ventures the law contains no provisions regarding minimum investment shares. Under China's national Joint Venture Law,[75] the share of foreign participants in equity joint ventures should 'in general not be less than twenty-five (25%) per cent' of the total equity of the venture.[76] In the absence of specific language regarding this issue in the SEZ Regulations, the same rule presumably applies to equity joint ventures established in the zones. The law's provision that investors may 'open factories with their own investment'[77] and 'independently operate their own enterprises'[78] has been particularly attractive to foreign business interests.[79] As of June 1983, the sole proprietorship investment pattern has not been permitted outside the SEZs, although indications exist that wholly-owned foreign ventures may be allowed on a selective basis in other parts of China in the future.[80]

C. Enterprise Operations

The SEZ Regulations contain several brief provisions regarding the operations of zone enterprises. Investors 'wishing to open factories or set up various economic enterprises' in the SEZs are required to register and obtain a land-use certificate.[81] Bank accounts are to be opened with the Bank of China branch in the SEZs or with 'other banks set up with China's approval' in the zones.[82] A similar provision relating to insurance for SEZ enterprises is also included.[83] Finally, upon termination of operations, an SEZ enterprise is required to 'report the reasons for termination' to the ADCOM and thereafter 'go through the procedures for termination and clear all debts.'[84] After these procedures have been completed, 'the assets of the enterprise may be transferred and its funds may be remitted out of China.'[85] Many of these provisions are dealt with in greater detail in subsequent SEZ legislation and regulatory policies described in Part III of this chapter.

D. Foreign Exchange

The SEZ Regulations provide that the 'lawful profits' of investors, as well as the wages and other 'legitimate income' of non-Chinese SEZ personnel, after payment of income tax, may be remitted out of China 'in accordance with the stipulations of the foreign exchange control measures of the Special Zones'.[86] At the time of writing, foreign exchange rules formulated specifically for the SEZs have yet to be announced. In the interim, the national foreign exchange control regulations are being applied in the zones.[87]

The only loosening in the national foreign exchange regulations which has occurred to date pertains to restrictions imposed on the possession of foreign exchange by Chinese residents in the SEZs. Workers in some SEZ enterprises are being permitted to receive a certain percentage of their wages in Hong Kong dollars or foreign exchange certificates.[88] In addition, under rules issued by the Bank of China, bank branches in Shenzhen and Zhuhai may accept Hong Kong dollar deposits from residents in the zones.[89] Funds may be withdrawn from such accounts in renminbi, foreign exchange certificates or Hong Kong dollars.[90]

E. Production, Marketing and Customs

The SEZ Regulations provide special encouragement for the use of Chinese 'machinery and equipment, raw and other materials and other goods' in production activities in the zones.[91] Under the regulations, enterprises that purchase Chinese production inputs will be granted 'preferential' prices based on the rates charged for similar commodities bound for export from China, provided settlement for such purchases is made in foreign exchange.[92] Since Chinese export prices are highly subsidized, SEZ enterprises will benefit from lower-cost production inputs by purchasing required items from Chinese suppliers.

In the event that SEZ investors choose to import production inputs, rather than purchase them domestically, the SEZ Regulations provide for favourable customs treatment upon entry. The law provides that imported 'machinery, equipment, spare parts, fittings, raw and other materials, transport vehicles and other materials required for production' shall be exempt from 'import taxes' provided they are 'necessary'.[93] Similar preferential treatment may also be granted to 'necessary' consumer goods imported for use by the personnel of SEZ enterprises.[94] Under Article 13, 'articles for daily use' may be exempt from import taxes, or subject to full or reduced duties, 'depending on the particular circumstances of the case'.

According to Chinese sources, 'import taxes' in this context has been interpreted to include both import duties and the Consolidated Industrial and Commercial Tax, a cascading excise tax imposed at various stages of production which is also applicable to the import of goods.[95] Whether an exemption from import duties and the consolidated tax is granted will presumably be left to the discretion of the Customs authorities. Under informal policy guidelines announced in August 1981, all imports into the zones must be approved in accordance with China's import licence regulations so that, theoretically at least, the preferential treatment provided under the SEZ Regulations could be denied.[96] In practice, however, this has not yet proved to be a problem with respect to production inputs, although a number of investors have continued to voice complaints about delays in clearing customs, especially in Shenzhen. With respect to consumer goods, the practice of the

Customs authorities in the zones has been to exempt most of such goods from import duties, the main exceptions being cigarettes and liquor which have been subject to duties levied at approximately one-half of the normal rate.

The basic philosophy which underlies the provisions granting preferential customs treatment to imports is that enterprises in the zones should be primarily export-oriented. Article 9 of the SEZ Regulations provides that the products of SEZ enterprises 'shall be sold in the international market' and permits domestic sales only after an approval has been obtained from the ADCOM.[97] According to one source, such approval must be applied for at the same time that the investment contract is submitted for approval.[98] Whether the application is granted is in large measure dependent on whether the SEZ authorities view the product as constituting a valuable import substitute. In the event that domestic sales are permitted, the SEZ Regulations provide that a 'supplementary payment' of customs duties and the consolidated tax must be made with respect to production inputs which had previously been allowed into the zones tax free.[99] Such a payment, of course, largely erases the customs benefits provided to investors in the SEZs.

F. Taxation

The SEZ Regulations also contain provisions relating to the tax treatment of enterprises established in the zones. Such treatment is considerably more favourable than that which is provided for under tax rules applicable in China generally.

Under China's national legislation, equity joint ventures are subject to a 30 per cent income tax on net profits.[100] In addition, such ventures must also pay a local income tax equal to 10 per cent of the amount of national income tax assessed.[101] In the case of 'co-operative' and 'co-production ventures' the net profits of the foreign party are subject to taxation at progressive rates, ranging from 20 to 40 per cent, under the Foreign Enterprises Income Tax Law (FEITL).[102] The FEITL also provides for payment of a local income tax of 10 per cent, calculated on the basis of taxable income.[103] Under Article 14 of the SEZ Regulations, the tax rate for 'enterprises' in the SEZs is set at 15 per cent. According to SEZ officials, the term 'enterprises' includes not only equity joint ventures but also wholly-owned foreign ventures and 'co-operative' or 'co-production' ventures.[104] Apparently, no local income tax is levied in the zones, unlike elsewhere in China.

In addition to offering a comparatively low rate of taxation, the SEZ Regulations promise investors a number of other tax incentives. For example, under Article 16 of the SEZ Regulations, enterprises that reinvest their profits in the zones for five years or more may be eligible for a reduction or exemption of income tax on such reinvested profits. Article 14 of the law promises 'special preferential treatment' to enterprises that have been set up within two years of the date of promulgation of the SEZ Regulations, enterprises with an investment of US$5 million or more, and enterprises involving 'higher technologies' or 'a longer financing cycle'.[105]

The SEZ Regulations fail to address specifically a number of important issues related to the taxation of enterprises and individuals in the zones. For example, the law is silent as to the method for computation of taxable income, as well as payment deadlines and procedures. At the moment such matters are apparently being handled in accordance with the provisions found in China's national tax legislation. An issue which will be of considerable importance to investors in the future relates to the 10 per cent tax imposed by the Joint Venture Income Tax Law on the after-tax profits due to the foreign party which are repatriated.[106] The SEZ Regulations fail to refer to this tax directly but do state that the 'lawful profits' of investors may be remitted out of the zones after payment of the 'income tax'.[107] Although this provision would seem to imply that the 10 per cent dividends tax is applicable to SEZ enterprises, tax authorities in the zones indicate that a final decision has yet to be made.[108]

G. Labour Management

The SEZ Regulations also contain special provisions relating to labour management in the zones. The law provides that local employees of SEZ enterprises may be recruited 'through the introduction of local labour service companies' established in each of the zones or by investors themselves.[109] In the event that recruitment of workers is done by investors independently the prior consent of the ADCOM must be obtained.[110] Regardless of the method of recruitment, workers may be 'tested and selected by the enterprise'.[111] The terms of employment — including wage levels, bonuses, labour insurance and other matters — are to be stipulated in labour contracts entered into between the enterprise and the individual worker 'in accordance with regulations' set by the ADCOM.[112] Workers may be dismissed or may resign of their own accord 'in accordance with the provisions contained in the labour contract'.[113]

H. Other Incentives

Finally, other types of preferential treatment for investors in the zones are also promised in the SEZ Regulations. For example, 'simplified entry and exit procedures' are promised 'for the convenience of foreign personnel, overseas Chinese and Hong Kong and Macao compatriots going in and out of the Special Zones.'[114] Land in the zones is provided to investors 'in accordance with actual needs' and 'specific measures' are promised to address such matters as the period of land use, fees and payment procedures, and other 'preferential treatment'.[115]

III. Subsequent Legislative and Regulatory Developments

The SEZ Regulations are not intended by themselves to provide a comprehensive legal regime for the Guangdong special zones. Like much of China's other investment legislation, in a number of areas the law provides little more than a statement of general principles and leaves the details to be filled in by supplementing regulations and implementing rules. Since the passage of the SEZ Regulations in 1980 the most important legislative and regulatory developments have concerned five issues: (1) access to and from the SEZs; (2) business registration; (3) labour management and wages for SEZ workers; (4) land use, construction and real estate transactions in the Shenzhen SEZ; (5) taxation; and (6) contracts and technology transfer.

A. Entry and Exit Regulations

A common complaint of foreign investors in China generally has concerned the nation's cumbersome and time-consuming visa regulations. As an incentive to investors, the SEZ Regulations promised 'simplified' procedures for businessmen travelling to and from the SEZs. Apparently intended to fulfill this promise, the Provisional Regulations of the Special Economic Zones in Guangdong Province Governing the Entry and Exit of Personnel (hereafter cited as the Entry and Exit Regulations)[116] were adopted on 17 November 1981 at the Thirteenth Session of the Standing Committee of the Fifth People's Congress of Guangdong Province. The Entry and Exit Regulations came into force on 1 January 1982.

Consisting of only 12 articles, the Entry and Exit Regulations apply only to 'foreigners, overseas Chinese, Hong Kong and Macao compatriots and Taiwan compatriots';[117] they are expressly made inapplicable to 'Chinese cadres, staff members, workers and other personnel working in the Special Zones' who are required to follow 'the existing regulations'.[118] Moreover, the regulations pertain solely to travel from outside China directly to the SEZs or from the SEZs directly to foreign countries. Individuals who merely pass through the SEZs on their way to or from other destinations in China must 'follow the procedures set forth in existing regulations'.[119]

Under the regulations, foreign passport holders are still required to obtain visas prior to entry into the SEZs. However, foreigners and overseas Chinese who 'have set up factories or various other kinds of business' or who 'have bought residences in or live in the Special Zones' and who need to enter and exit 'on a regular basis' may apply for multiple entry and exit visas on the strength of a 'letter of proof' from the SEZ Development Company.[120] With respect to residents of Hong Kong and Macao who travel to China holding 'home visit permits' or *hui xiang zheng*, the regulations provide for a simplification of existing entry procedures.[121]

The Entry and Exit Regulations also provide for the issue of group visas for individuals joining tour groups from Hong Kong or Macao to the SEZs.[122] In addition, the regulations permit transport vehicles to travel between the zones and Hong Kong or Macao after obtaining approval from the relevant municipal people's government and a pass from the local public security bureau.[123] Finally, the regulations seem to hold out the promise of a liberalization of customs procedures for personnel entering and exiting the SEZs. The regulations provide that such matters shall be handled in accordance with the 'customs regulations for the Special Zones' as opposed to the customs rules generally applicable in China.[124]

In general, the Entry and Exit Regulations have proved to be a disappointment to investors who had hoped for the promulgation of a more liberal entry/exit regime. In fact, in practical terms the regulations offer investors in the zones no greater benefits than those available to businesses in other parts of China. For example, as a result of a nationwide liberalization of visa procedures, most businessmen who travel frequently to China are now eligible for multiple-entry visas, the major concession provided by the regulations.

Another area where the Entry and Exit Regulations have not matched investors' expectations concerns the movement of transport vehicles between the zones and Hong Kong. Although Article 10 of the regulations specifically provides for such travel, the implementation of this provision has been restrictive. Under trial rules developed by the Hong Kong Government in co-operation with the SEZ authorities and announced in May 1982, cross-border vehicular permits have been limited to larger enterprises with active interests in the zones as opposed to property owners and small businesses.[125] Moreover, enterprises are restricted to obtaining only one permit applicable to one specific vehicle and one specific driver.[126] If the vehicle breaks down or the driver falls ill, the enterprise can be denied access to the zone.

Finally, although the Entry and Exit Regulations promised a liberalization of customs procedures at the SEZ border, investors have experienced little improvement.[127] Excessive delays apparently remain the rule, rather than the exception.

B. Business Registration Regulations

The SEZ Regulations impose a registration requirement on enterprises operating in the zones and specify certain procedures which are to be followed upon the termination of operations. The Provisional Regulations of the Special Economic Zones of Guangdong Province Governing the Registration of Business Enterprises (hereafter cited as the Business Registration Regulations),[128] which were adopted by the Thirteenth Session of the Standing Committee of the Fifth People's Congress of Guangdong Province on 17 November 1981 and which came into force on 1 January 1982, amplify and in some respects amend these provisions.

Under the Business Registration Regulations all foreign-owned enterprises, joint ventures and co-operative enterprises in the SEZs must register with the SEZ 'administrative organization for industry and commerce' and obtain a 'registration certificate' or 'business licence' prior to commencing operations.[129] When applying for registration, such enterprises are required to complete a detailed application form and submit copies of (1) the 'approval documents' issued by the municipal government or the SEZ administrative committee; (2) the 'agreement, contract and articles of association signed by the parties to the enterprise, together with a list of the names of the members of the board of directors'; and (3) the certificate of registration pertaining to the investor issued by the authorities in his home country together with evidence of the investor's creditworthiness.[130] The Business Registration Regulations also require enterprises setting up resident representative offices in the SEZs to register with the SEZ authorities and specify the procedures that must be followed to effect registration.[131]

SEZ enterprises and representative offices are deemed as established on the date of issue of the registration certificate.[132] Registration is normally effective for one year but may be renewed.[133] Once registered, enterprises and representative offices are required to open bank accounts with the Bank of China (or another approved bank) and register with the local tax authorities.[134]

When a registered enterprise changes any of the items appearing on the register — for example, when it changes its address, or extends the contract term or the amount of its registered capital — the enterprise must obtain approval from the municipal or SEZ administrative authorities and go through 'change of registration procedures' with the SEZ administrative organization for industry and commerce and the tax authorities.[135] To effect de-registration, an enterprise must cancel its original registration with the relevant authorities and return the registration certificate or business licence.[136]

The Business Registration Regulations authorize the SEZ administrative organization for industry and commerce to 'supervise and inspect' SEZ enterprises.[137] Violators of the regulations may be 'warned, fined or ordered to shut down operations' depending on the seriousness of the offence.[138]

Article 2 of the SEZ Business Registration Regulations provides that the registration procedures for foreign banks will be specified in 'separate regulations'. The only such regulations to be announced to date are the Provisional Regulations for the Establishment of Representative Offices in China by Overseas Chinese and Foreign Financial Institutions, issued by the People's Bank of China on 1 February 1983.[139] Under this law, foreign banks are only permitted to set up 'representative offices' in the SEZs and their scope of business is limited to 'non-profit' activities such as liaison, consulting and other services.[140] Additional regulations to allow the establishment of limited branch banking in the zones by foreign banks have been promised by the SEZ authorities but had not appeared at the time of writing.[141]

C. Labour and Wage Regulations

The SEZ Regulations contain four provisions which outline the labour management system in the zones. The Provisional Regulations of the Special Economic Zones of Guangdong Province Governing Labour and Wages for Business Enterprises (hereafter cited as the Labour and Wage Regulations),[142] which came into effect on 1 January 1982, expand upon these provisions and treat in detail many issues which the SEZ Regulations had addressed only indirectly.

Although the scope of the Labour and Wage Regulations includes foreign-owned enterprises and co-operative enterprises as well as equity joint ventures in the SEZs,[143] it is useful to consider the law's provisions alongside those contained in China's national legislation on labour management for joint ventures.[144] By comparison with the national labour rules, the SEZ Labour and Wage Regulations appear to provide for more favourable and flexible treatment of labour issues.

Under both the national joint venture labour rules and the SEZ Labour and Wage Regulations the basic terms for the employment of workers are to be specified in and governed by 'labour contracts'.[145] The national rules provide that, except in the case of small-scale ventures, the contract is to be signed between the enterprise and the trade union organization comprising all Chinese workers employed by the enterprise.[146] By contrast, the SEZ rules provide that labour contracts shall be entered into between the enterprise and each individual staff member and worker.[147] As a result, the Labour and Wage Regulations would appear to grant enterprises greater flexibility in determining the terms of employment for different workers as well as more direct control over individual employees.

Differences also appear in the provisions relating to the hiring of workers. While both the national rules and the Labour and Wage Regulations provide that workers may be hired either upon the recommendation of local labour departments or by the enterprise itself,[148] the SEZ rules appear to provide investors with greater flexibility with respect to workers provided by Chinese units. Under the Labour and Wage Regulations, such workers may be hired on a probationary basis of from three to six months thereby enabling enterprises to test their skills before a final employment decision is made.[149] In addition, the Labour and Wage Regulations contain a specific provision permitting the employment of non-Chinese citizens by SEZ enterprises.[150] The terms and conditions of employment of such personnel are to be determined by the enterprise itself.

Another difference between the national and SEZ labour rules relates to the provisions for the payment of wages and other benefits for workers. Under the national regulations, wage levels for workers in joint venture enterprises are to be set at 120–150 per cent of the wages paid to workers in state-owned enterprises engaged in the same type of business and in the same locality as the joint venture.[151] In addition, the regulations require that labour insurance, medical expenses and other kinds of government subsidies for workers shall be paid by the joint venture 'in accordance with the standards prevailing in state-owned enterprises'.[152] By contrast, the SEZ Labour and Wage Regulations appear to provide greater flexibility to investors. According to Article 7 labour service fees in the zones are not tied to wage levels prevailing in state-owned enterprises and are presumably subject to negotiations; the actual amounts are to be determined 'at the time the labour contract is signed according to the type of enterprise and the kind of work'.[153] In addition, the enterprise is free to choose the form of wages — hourly, weekly or piece-work — as well as the system to be adopted regarding bonuses and employee subsidies.[154]

Unlike the national labour rules the SEZ Labour and Wage Regulations contain specific rules for the allocation of labour service fees and related matters. Under the regulations, 70 per cent of the total amount of labour service fees is to be paid directly to the employee as wages; 5 per cent is to be retained by the enterprise for employee subsidies and other benefits; and 25 per cent is to be paid to the state for social labour and insurance and other subsidies.[155] The SEZ Labour and Wage Regulations also address the issue of wage raises in zone enterprises and provide that wages are to be increased on an annual basis by 5–15 per cent, the actual amount of the increase depending on 'the degree of technical and work proficiency' of the employee.[156] Finally, the SEZ rules also contain stipulations regarding the work schedule for enterprise employees. In general, SEZ enterprises are to operate on a six-day work week and an eight-hour day basis, with additional pay for overtime work.[157] In addition, the rules provide that SEZ enterprises are required to follow the system of legal holidays and leave stipulated by the Chinese state.[158]

The SEZ Labour and Wage Regulations also contain specific provisions dealing with two areas of special concern to investors — the resignation and discharge of enterprise employees. Like the national labour rules, the SEZ Labour and Wage Regulations provide that workers shall have the right to resign from an enterprise.[159] The SEZ rules go further than the national legislation, however, by addressing a matter which was left unresolved in the national labour rules, namely how to deal with the problem of workers who have been assigned to a venture merely to acquire free training and who, at the termination of their training period, resign from the enterprise to return — fully trained — to their original units. Under the SEZ Labour and Wage Regulations, if a worker has benefited from training of more than three months he may not ordinarily resign until the expiration of one year from the date of the completion of the training programme.[160] Otherwise, the worker is obliged to compensate the enterprise for the cost of his training.[161]

On the matter of dismissal of enterprise workers, the SEZ rules follow closely the language found in the national labour legislation. Under the SEZ Labour and Wage Regulations, enterprises enjoy the right to dismiss employees 'who have become redundant as a result of changes in production and technical conditions, (or) who fail to meet the requirements of the enterprises.'[162]

However, dismissal is only permitted if the affected worker, after training, cannot be transferred within the enterprise to other types of work.[163] Unlike the national labour rules, the Labour and Wage Regulations require SEZ enterprises to provide severance pay to dismissed employees, with the amount of each payment determined on the basis of the length of employment.[164] With respect to disciplinary measures, the SEZ rules grant enterprises the right to impose warnings, wage reduction and other measures, in addition to the discharge of workers.[165] However, workers who have been disciplined or dismissed by enterprises may appeal to the local labour bureau or institute a suit in the people's court.[166]

Despite the apparent advantages of the SEZ Labour and Wage Regulations, investors should be prepared to face a number of potential problems in their implementation. For example, although the rules prescribe a 'contract system' to govern the hiring and firing of workers, little is known about how this system will actually work. China's national Economic Contracts Law, passed in December 1981, does not apply to employment contracts between foreign and Chinese entities.[167] As a result, at present there is no legislation capable of providing guidance to investors on such issues as what actions constitute breach and what types of damages must be paid.

Another, and perhaps more important, problem relates to the degree of flexibility demonstrated by the local SEZ labour bureaux in administering and interpreting the rules. Under the regulations, these organizations must approve all labour contracts entered into between enterprises and workers and are required to give their consent if an enterprise chooses to hire workers on its own.[168] In addition, local labour bureaux must also approve the wage levels for workers and are empowered to 'examine' decisions taken by enterprises to dismiss employees or impose other disciplinary measures.[169] As a result of the wide-ranging powers granted to the local labour bureaux, whether or not investors actually receive the benefits provided by the regulations will in large measure depend on the attitudes and policies adopted by these units.[170]

Although the SEZ labour rules are relatively new, it appears that investors have on the whole been generally satisfied with their implementation thus far. However, conditions in the zones have tended to dampen the practical effect of some of the more attractive provisions contained in the rules. For example, although many enterprises would like to recruit their own workers the task has proved to be a difficult one, largely because no readily available pool of workers exists in the zones to choose from.[171] Given the difficulties imposed by China's household registration system in bringing in workers from outside the zones, most investors have had little alternative but to accept workers supplied to them by the labour bureaux. In addition, enterprises which have attempted to dismiss workers have encountered resistance from the SEZ authorities.[172] Even in circumstances where a labour bureau has agreed that dismissal may be justified, it has little incentive to approve the dismissal as the bureau must then fix alternative employment for the worker and continue to pay the worker's wages until such employment is found.[173]

D. Local Regulations Governing Land Use, Urban Construction and Real Estate Transactions

The SEZ Regulations provide that land in the zones will be supplied to investors 'in accordance with actual needs' and promise that 'separate stipulations' will be formulated to provide 'preferential treatment' to investors with respect to the period of land use, land-use fees and payment methods. As of January 1984 only the Shenzhen SEZ has issued regulations intended to fulfill this promise. The other two zones — Shantou and Zhuhai — are expected to issue their own regulations in the future.[174] However, until such rules are announced, it is likely that these zones will follow the general outlines of land-use policy established by the Shenzhen SEZ.

Under the Provisional Regulations Governing Land in the Shenzhen Special Economic Zone (hereafter cited as the Shenzhen Land Regulations),[175] land rights granted to investors are rights of usage only and not of ownership, and all forms of land sales are strictly prohibited.[176] Investors requiring the use of land in the zone must submit an application to the municipal planning department.[177] Once the application has been approved, the investor is required to make arrangements for payment of the land-use fee after which the land area will be demarcated and a 'Land-use Certificate' will be issued.[178] Within six months from the date of the certificate, the investor must submit the 'overall design drawing' and 'construction and production plans' relating to the project to the municipal authorities and within nine months from such date ground-breaking must occur.[179] In the event that these deadlines are not met, the regulations provide that the Land-use Certificate may be revoked and any fees paid prior to such date will not be refunded.[180] Delays in the production schedule of the project occurring after ground-breaking may also result in revocation of the Land-use Certificate, unless the delay can be justified to the municipal authorities and they agree to an extension of the term for project completion.[181] Finally, upon completion, the project must be inspected and approved by 'the responsible authorities' before operations may commence.[182]

The Shenzhen Land Regulations provide that the duration of land leases will differ depending on the nature of the project and 'actual needs'.[183] Nevertheless, the law does contain specific provisions that specify the maximum permissible duration for land leases. For example, land leases for industrial and tourist enterprises may be granted for up to 30 years; for agriculture-related and commercial enterprises (including restaurants) the limit is 20 years; and for marketable housing projects and educational, scientific or medical enterprises the limit is 50 years.[184]

The regulations also spell out the standards that will be applied in calculating land-use fees. Although actual fees will depend on the location and nature of the project, and the duration of the lease, industrial enterprises are required to pay RMB 10–13 per square metre per year; marketable housing projects will pay RMB 30–60; tourist projects will pay fees of RMB 60–100; and commercial projects will be billed at top rents of RMB 70–200.[185] Adjustments in the standard fee schedule will be made once every three years from the date of promulgation of the regulations, with increases not exceeding 30 per cent of the then-prevailing rates.[186] Fees may be paid in one lump-sum payment or on an instalment basis.[187] If paid by instalment, interest will be charged at a rate of 8 per cent per annum unless the entire amount is paid within two years in which case no interest will be charged.[188] Certain enterprises, such as educational, scientific and cultural institutions, will receive preferential treatment with respect to land-use fees, and non-profit projects and projects involving 'exceptionally advanced technologies' will be exempt from land fees.[189]

Investors attracted to the zones by promises of 'cheap land' should proceed cautiously. Certainly, the basic land fees in the SEZs are cheaper than prevailing rates in Hong Kong.[190] Moreover, they compare favourably with rates charged in similar 'special' zones in other parts of the world. For example, basic 'under roof' rates for factory space in Jamaica, Barbados, Columbia and the Dominican Republic range from US$2.50 to US$3.50 per square foot.[191] In reality, however, the apparent benefits of 'low' SEZ rates are partially offset by hidden costs.[192] For instance, Article 21 of the SEZ Regulations requires investors to pay the costs of linking up their power supply, water supply, sewer system and telecommunications lines within their land-use area to main lines outside. With these extra charges added on to the basic land-use fee, total land costs in the SEZs end up being comparable to costs incurred by investors in other parts of China.

The Shenzhen Land Regulations contain a number of provisions dealing with matters related to construction in the zone. The law states that all 'units and individuals' must abide by the zone's 'overall construction plan'[193] and empowers the Shenzhen municipal government to 'requisition, appropriate or nationalize' land within the zone 'based on construction needs'.[194] In the event land is 'requisitioned' or 'houses or other structures' are demolished 'due to construction requirements' compensation is to be paid.[195] Moreover, the regulations provide that investors must carry out construction in accordance with the municipal government's stipulations regarding 'space allocation ratios and greenery ratios'[196] and comply with 'Chinese building standards and fire prevention and safety requirements'.[197]

These and a number of other provisions relating to construction in the Shenzhen SEZ are further elaborated on in the Provisional Measures of Shenzhen Municipality Governing Urban Construction (hereafter cited as the Construction Measures), adopted on 1 July 1982 by the Shenzhen Municipal People's Government.[198] Consisting of 60 detailed articles, the Construction Measures address five different areas concerning construction activity in the zone.

The first topic dealt with by the measures is the management of land used for construction purposes. This section of the law sets forth the procedures for the requisitioning of land in the zone for construction projects, including the procedures to be followed by foreign investors who wish to obtain Land-use Certificates. In most important respects the provisions dealing with foreign investors follow those found in the Shenzhen Land Regulations. However, the Construction Measures do contain several new provisions regarding land use which will be of concern to investors.

The first of the new provisions contained in the Construction Measures provides that land that has been approved for construction may be 'readjusted' or 'withdrawn' at any time and without notice owing to 'urban construction requirements'.[199] Although the provision goes on to provide that 'reasonable compensation' will be paid in such cases, the law provides no indication of the kinds of circumstances under which 'readjustment' or 'withdrawal' may occur. The second provision states that where the urban plan calls for the development of 'complementary projects' — such as 'cultural, educational and public health facilities' — near a construction site, the investment for such projects shall be borne 'jointly' by the 'units located at that site'.[200] In this context 'units' presumably includes foreign investors and joint and co-operative ventures. How various units in the vicinity of a site are to bear the costs for complementary projects, and to what extent, is not specified by the law.

Among the other topics addressed by the Construction Measures are rules for construction work management, including the procedures to be followed to obtain building permits, and rules regarding the size, spacing and siting of buildings;[201] rules for the management of municipal projects, including road construction, the laying of telecommunication and electricity cables and pipelines, and related projects;[202] and rules for the management of survey and design work and the regulation of construction firms operating in the zones.[203] Regarding the latter topic, the law provides that wholly-owned foreign enterprises in the zone may entrust design work to foreign firms, but co-operative or joint venture enterprises must first obtain the approval of the Shenzhen SEZ's Office of the Chief Engineer before the services of foreign design or architectural firms may be retained for projects in the zone.[204] With respect to the performance of actual construction work, the Construction Measures specify that such work may only be undertaken by enterprises registered in the zone.[205] In the case of foreign construction companies, a performance guarantee must be provided before such registration is permitted.[206]

Commercial and residential property development projects in the Shenzhen SEZ have spawned an active market in local real estate transactions. In order to strengthen the legal basis for such transactions, the Guangdong Provincial People's Congress passed, on 15 November 1983, the Regulations of the Shenzhen Special Economic Zone On the Control of Commercial Real Estate (hereafter cited as the Real Estate Regulations).[207] The law contains provisions regarding the purchase, sale and other forms of transfer of property rights and sets forth a number of rules pertaining to the leasing of buildings in the zone. In addition, the law establishes a system for the registration of real property and the mortgage of real estate in the SEZ. Although the provisions contained in the law are brief and relatively unsophisticated, the Real Estate Regulations constitute an important first step toward the establishment of a comprehensive regulatory system for real estate transactions.

E. Enterprise and Individual Income Tax Rules

In addition to the formal legislative enactments which supplement the SEZ Regulations, the SEZ authorities have begun to implement a number of unpublished rules relating to the taxation of the income of SEZ enterprises and personnel.

The most important of the enterprise tax provisions being applied relates to tax holidays. According to Chinese sources, projects in the fields of transportation and communications, tourism and services, and production which have been established prior to 31 December 1982 are eligible for tax holidays of one, two, and three years, respectively.[208] In addition, the same sources indicate that tax holidays are being offered to ventures established in 1983 or after which are slated to have a duration of operation of at least five successive years. Under this scheme, projects in the transport and communications field will be granted a 50 per cent tax reduction during the first profit-making year; projects in the tourism and services sectors will receive a tax holiday of one year; and projects involving productive enterprises will be granted a two-year tax holiday.[209]

The unpublished SEZ rules indicate that longer tax holidays will be granted to various types of projects where total investment (Chinese plus foreign) exceeds US$5 million. Projects that meet this criterion in the fields of transport and communications, tourism and services, and production will be granted tax holidays of two, three, and five years, respectively.[210] In addition, 'sophisticated industries' with a slated duration of operation in excess of ten successive years are eligible for tax holidays of between five and seven years.[211]

Local SEZ tax authorities have also begun to provide favourable treatment with respect to individual income taxation of foreign personnel resident or working in the zones. Under the national Individual Income Tax Law,[212] monthly wages and salaries in excess of RMB 800 are taxed at progressive rates ranging from 5 to 45 per cent.[213] In the SEZs, however, tax officials have been applying a lower rate scale of from 3 to 30 per cent on the same monthly amounts.[214] Another area where the SEZ tax authorities have provided more favourable treatment than that which is provided for under the national tax law concerns foreign source income. Whereas the detailed regulations for the implementation of the Individual Income Tax Law require that foreigners resident in China for a period of five years or more pay tax on their worldwide income,[215] the SEZ authorities have indicated that non-China source earnings will be exempt from taxation in the zones regardless of the length of residence.[216]

F. Regulations Regarding Economic Contracts and Technology Transfer

In early 1984 the People's Government of Guangdong Province issued two sets of regulations which are likely to have a far-reaching impact on business and investment activity in the SEZs. These are the Regulations of the Shenzhen Special Economic Zone on Foreign Economic Contracts (hereafter cited as the SEZ Contracts Regulations), promulgated on 7 February 1984, and the Provisional Regulations of the Shenzhen Special Economic Zone on the Introduction of Technology (hereafter cited as the SEZ Technology Regulations), promulgated on 8 February 1984.[217]

The SEZ Contracts Regulations, consisting of 41 articles divided into 7 chapters, establish the general principles governing the conclusion, performance, amendment and termination of economic contracts. The law applies to contracts entered into among the various organizations and enterprises operating in the Shenzhen SEZ, including joint ventures, wholly-owned foreign enterprises and Chinese companies and governmental organizations, so long as such contracts are to be performed within the Shenzhen SEZ.[218] Among the provisions contained in the law is a list of the types of clauses that must be included in various kinds of contracts, including contracts for joint ventures, co-operative projects, compensation trade and assembly and processing transactions.[219] The law also includes a number of general provisions regarding compensation for breach of contract, joint and several liability, *force majeure*, and the rescission of invalid contracts.[220] Under the regulations, contracts may be altered or terminated for a variety of reasons such as breach, inability of one or both of the parties to perform under the contract, and 'change of circumstances'.[221] However, in such cases an approval must first be applied for and obtained from the Shenzhen Municipal Administration for Industry and Commerce, which is designated by the law as the organization responsible for supervising the performance of contracts.[222] In the event of disputes, the law permits the parties to submit to arbitration 'in accordance with the agreement of the parties', a phrase which apparently would permit foreign arbitration.[223] However, the regulations provide that contracts that 'have a close bearing on the sovereignty of China', such as investment contracts, must all be governed by Chinese law.[224] Moreover, only the Chinese-language text of a contract is viewed by the regulations as being legally binding.[225]

The SEZ Technology Regulations provide the statutory framework for the transfer of technology between foreign enterprises and Chinese enterprises in the Shenzhen SEZ. Consisting of 25 articles, the regulations contain provisions outlining the various clauses that must be included in a technology transfer contract and the procedures that are to be followed in applying for and obtaining approval for the transaction from the Shenzhen Municipal People's Government.[226] Under the regulations, the technology transfer may take place in the context of a variety of transactions, including compensation trade, licensing trade, co-operative arrangements, consultation services arrangements and equity joint ventures.[227] In the case of equity joint ventures, however, technology may be provided as part of the capital contribution up to a limit of 20 per cent of the total registered capital of the venture.[228] Moreover, regardless of the nature of the transaction, the law requires that all technology transfer contracts be limited to a term of five years, although they may be extended 'if both parties agree'.[229]

The SEZ Technology Regulations contain a number of provisions that are certain to cause concern among foreign investors. For example, the law requires the foreign transferor of technology to 'guarantee' that the Chinese party will 'master the entire technology and method of operation'.[230] In addition, the transferor must 'guarantee the legal effectiveness of the anticipated results of the introduced technology'.[231] Another provision that will likely prove troublesome to potential investors is the requirement that the products produced with the introduced technology have access to the international market. In the event the Chinese side incurs losses due to 'influence' on its product sales caused by the foreign party, the Chinese side may demand compensation.[232]

IV. Investment Rules for the Shekou Industrial Zone

The Shekou district of Shenzhen Municipality was designated as a separate special zone prior to the promulgation of the SEZ Regulations. In 1979 the China Merchants' Steam Navigation Company Ltd. (CMSN), a Hong Kong company under the control of the Ministry of Communications, received direct authorization from the State Council to develop the Shekou district as an 'industrial zone'.[233] Since then, the CMSN has invested large amounts of its own funds to develop the district and has played the key role in managing investment activity there. Although Shekou technically became a part of the Shenzhen SEZ after the passage of the SEZ Regulations in 1980, it has retained its independence to a large degree and has even issued its own rules to govern investment in the district.

The Shekou rules are contained in an 'investor's handbook' published by the CMSN which, among other things, sets forth the 'particulars of making investment' in the SEZ. The handbook was originally issued in January 1980[234] but was revised after the promulgation of the SEZ Regulations and republished in September 1981.[235] The legal status of the rules is clouded. They have apparently never been formally enacted by a Chinese legislative body although they are being applied in practice within the zone.[236]

Covering such matters as tax rates, land costs and labour management, the Shekou rules deal with many of the same topics addressed in the SEZ Regulations and related legislation. However, the treatment given to such issues by the Shekou handbook is far less detailed than that found in the SEZ laws. Moreover, disparities exist between the Shekou rules and the other SEZ laws regarding a number of issues. According to Shekou officials, the SEZ Regulations and related laws will be followed 'in principle' in the zone, but the Shekou rules will take precedence over those laws where the rules contain specific provisions at variance with provisions found in the general SEZ legislation.[237]

Like the SEZ Regulations, the Shekou rules provide a wide scope for foreign investors. Generally, 'all trades that have positive significance in international economic co-operation and technical exchanges' are welcome in the zone but particular emphasis is placed on 'trades that are rapidly developing or involve high technologies and techniques or are still non-existent in China at the present stage.'[238] However, certain types of projects may not be established in the zone. These include compensation trade and assembly or processing projects as well as projects that cause pollution, employ outmoded equipment or produce products that are subject to Chinese export quotas.[239]

The rules permit foreign investors to establish either wholly-owned enterprises or joint ventures in the zone.[240] Wholly-owned foreign enterprises are required to pay an annual 'management fee' to the CMSN, based on a certain percentage of the 'total turnover' of the enterprise.[241] The fee represents an additional cost of doing business in Shekou, as the SEZ Regulations do not require such payments from wholly-owned foreign enterprises in the other zones. Joint ventures are to be established between foreign investors and the CMSN; the rules do not contemplate joint ventures between foreigners and other Chinese organizations, although in practice minority equity participation by such organizations is permitted.[242] In general, a party's investment shall be not less than 25 per cent of the total.[243] The parties are free to determine the management structure of the venture, but the chairman of the Board of Directors is to be appointed by the CMSN.[244] The rules provide that the duration of the contract period for enterprises in the zone is to be determined according to 'the particular line of business of the enterprise'.[245] However, the rules stipulate an 'average term' of 25 years and provide for extensions of the scheduled term.[246]

The rules also address certain matters of a legal nature not dealt with by the SEZ Regulations or related legislation. The rules provide that in preparing the 'memorandum and articles of association' for enterprises in the zone 'reference' may be made both to Hong Kong and international practices.[247] The rules also provide for arbitration in the event of disputes between the parties. Arbitration may be conducted by an arbitral body in China or by another arbitral body 'agreed upon by the parties'.[248]

Enterprises requiring land in the zone are to apply to the Real Estate Company of the Shekou Industrial Zone, a subsidiary of the CMSN.[249] Land-use fees are charged at rates from HK$2 to HK$4 per square foot per year, somewhat lower than average rates in Shenzhen generally.[250] Power consumption in Shekou is charged at the same rates as charged in Hong Kong for electricity used for industrial purposes.[251] Water charges are collected at rates 20 per cent lower than prevailing rates in Hong Kong.[252]

Like the SEZ Regulations, the Shekou rules promise that 'entry and exit formalities will be simplified'.[253] The only significant benefit granted to foreign passport holders under the rules that is not found in the Entry and Exit Regulations relates to simplification of visa procedures. Under the Shekou rules, travellers to the zone by land may obtain visas within two days by presenting their passports to the CMSN directly.[254] Travellers by sea may obtain visas at the Shekou wharf prior to entry.[255]

With respect to import and export duties, the Shekou rules contain provisions which follow policies outlined in the SEZ Regulations. Imported means of production which are 'necessary' are exempt from import duties but may only be used inside the zone.[256] Similar provisions apply to consumer goods with the exception of cigarettes and liquor which are subject to 50 per cent of normal import duties.[257] Products of Shekou enterprises are exempt from export duties unless they are sold on the domestic market.[258]

The first issue of the CMSN's 'handbook' for investment in Shekou, issued prior to the promulgation of the SEZ Regulations, provided for a 'corporation profit tax' of 10 per cent.[259] The revised edition of the handbook, however, provides for a tax rate of 15 per cent, thus bringing Shekou into line with the tax rate applicable in the SEZs generally.[260] However, the revised rules provide that agreements signed prior to the promulgation of the SEZ Regulations when the 10 per cent rate was in effect continue to benefit from the earlier, lower rate.[261]

As regards tax holidays, the Shekou rules provide for a three- to five-year holiday for 'all enterprises'.[262] In addition, the rules provide 'special preferential treatment' for enterprises with an investment of US$5 million or more, those that employ 'higher technologies' or have a longer capital turnover cycle, and enterprises that have not yet been established in China.[263] Although this language echoes that found in the SEZ Regulations, Shekou officials maintain that the criteria for eligibility for larger tax holidays will be interpreted more flexibly in the zone than in the other SEZs.

Regarding labour management, the Shekou rules appear to be less liberal than the Labour and Wage Regulations applicable in the SEZs generally. The rules provide that all enterprises must hire workers and other personnel from the Shekou Labour Services Company;[264] unlike the Labour and Wage Regulations, there is no provision for independent recruitment by enterprises themselves. Moreover, under the Shekou rules labour contracts are signed between the enterprise and the Labour Services Company,[265] not between the enterprise and the individual worker as provided by the SEZ Regulations. Although enterprises in Shekou have the right 'to scrutinize' candidates for employment, and may dismiss employees who 'seriously violate' labour rules,[266] such rights will likely prove to be of little practical importance so long as the local Labour Services Company maintains a monopoly over labour supply.

With respect to the wage system in the zones, the rules provide that all enterprises shall pay wages to employees in Hong Kong dollars.[267] Average monthly wages are to be higher than wages paid by Chinese enterprises but lower than those paid in Hong Kong for the same type of enterprise.[268] The rules provide that a certain percentage of the total amount of wages may be drawn by the Labour Services Company and 'set aside' for employee welfare funds and medical benefits. Salaries and benefits for technicians or managerial personnel from Hong Kong and abroad are to be 'fixed separately'.[269]

The Shekou rules also contain several brief provisions regarding foreign exchange control. The rules provide that foreign currency shall be used for accounting and bookkeeping purposes by all enterprises in the zone and require that quarterly balance sheets be submitted to the Shekou Industrial Zone Administration.[270] The rules also state that foreign exchange may be 'freely remitted both inwards and outwards' provided that such transactions are conducted through banks in the zone.[271] What this means in practice is unclear. Shekou officials indicate that the procedures stipulated in China's national foreign exchange law must still be followed although the law itself will be interpreted 'more flexibly'.[272]

V. Conclusion

At present the legal framework for investment in the SEZs — like the zones themselves — is still in a formative stage of development. As is true for much of China's foreign investment legislation the SEZ Regulations and related rules are in many respects ambiguous and inconsistent. Moreover, gaps remain in a number of key areas. As a result, while the SEZ rules provide basic guidance for business activity in the zones a number of issues remain to be addressed.

With the aim of enhancing the attractiveness of investment in the zones, SEZ planners have called for a redoubling of efforts to put into place a more comprehensive regulatory regime. Included among the legislation reportedly now being drafted are rules intended to clarify the organizational structure of the zones, further detailed provisions regarding taxation, and special customs and foreign exchange rules.[273] Once this legislation has been put into place and greater experience has been gained with the implementation of existing SEZ rules investors will be in a better position to judge just how 'special' the special zones will be in the context of China's efforts to enlist foreign capital in its drive toward economic modernization.

Notes

1. As of August 1983 four SEZs have been officially established nationwide. The three Guangdong SEZs formally came into being in August 1980. The fourth SEZ

is located in Xiamen (Amoy) in Fujian Province. The Xiamen SEZ was set up in October 1980 but lags far behind the Guangdong SEZs in development. Regulations governing investment in the Xiamen SEZ have apparently been drafted but at the time of writing have not yet been promulgated officially. See 'The Xiamen Special Zone', *Beijing Review*, 14 December 1981, p. 20; and 'Xiamen Special Economic Zone Offers More Generous Terms', *Economic Reporter*, September 1981, p. 11. See also *Investor's Handbook: Xiamen Special Economic Zone of Fujian Province* (The Administration Commission of Xiamen SEZ, March 1983).

In addition to the four SEZs already in existence, plans are being developed or considered to create special zones in other parts of China, including Hainan, Shanghai, Guangzhou and Guangxi among others. See C. Clarke, 'Hainan', *China Business Review*, January–February 1983, p. 44; 'China Unveils Hainan Plan', *South China Morning Post*, 14 April 1983, p. 8; 'Plans Envisage Fast Development of Hainan Island', *China Daily*, 20 March 1983, p. 2; 'Shanghai Plans Concessions for Investors', *Asian Wall Street Journal*, 31 March 1983, p. 3; and T. Gelatt, 'China's Special Economic Zones' in J. Cohen (ed.), *Legal Aspects of Doing Business in China 1983* (New York, Practising Law Institute, 1983), p. 186.

2. See J. Kamm, 'Importing Some of Hong Kong . . . Exporting Some of China', *China Business Review*, March–April 1980, p. 29.

3. China reportedly investigated 30 such zones in over 40 countries. See F. Chi, 'China's Newborn SEZs and their Strategic Significance', *Economic Reporter*, August 1981, p. 11.

4. Kamm, p. 28, note 2 above.

5. Kamm, p. 28, note 2 above.

6. See 'NPC Approved Regulations on Guangdong Special Economic Zones', *China Economic News*, 1 September 1980, p. 2.

7. For Chinese views of the role to be played by the SEZs in the nation's economic development, see Chi, note 3 above; Stas, 'What's Going On In The SEZ's', *Economic Reporter*, August 1981, p. 14; D. Xu, 'China's Special Economic Zones', *Beijing Review*, 14 December 1981, p. 14; and 'Leader of State Administrative Commission on Import and Export Affairs on Development and Administration of Special Economic Zones', *China Economic News*, 29 June 1981, p. 3. See also D. Chu, 'The Costs of the Four SEZs to China', *Economic Reporter*, June 1982, p. 18.

8. See Xu, p. 16, note 7 above.

9. See J. Stepanek, 'China's SEZs: Terms in the Special Economic Zones Compare Well With Those in Other Parts of the World', *China Business Review*, March–April 1982, p. 39. Hopewell Holdings, the Hong Kong conglomerate, has announced plans to invest more than US$300 million to develop infrastructure in the Shenzhen area. One key Hopewell project is the planned construction of China's first modern highway from Hong Kong to Guangzhou via the Zhuhai and Shenzhen SEZs. See 'China's Enterprise Zones: Leaky Capitalist Enclaves', *The Economist*, 27 November 1982, p. 87; and 'Hopewell's HK$4.6 Billion Projects Marks Investment Trends in Key South China Special Economic Zone', *China Economic News*, 28 December 1981, p. 7.

10. See Xu, p. 15, note 7 above.

11. See Xu, p. 15, note 7 above.

12. Stas, p. 14, note 7 above.

13. Stas, p. 14, note 7 above.

14. For both legal and historical analyses of this issue, see P. Wesley-Smith,

Unequal Treaty 1898–1997: China, Great Britain and Hong Kong's New Territories (Hong Kong, Oxford University Press, 1980).

15. See Ho Li, '*Xin Xianggang? — Shenzhen Tequ Neiwang*' (A New Hong Kong? — An Inside View of the Shenzhen Special Economic Zone), *Qi Shih Nian Dai (The Seventies)*, March 1982, p. 16.

16. *Introduction to Shenzhen Special Economic Zone Investment Environment and Shenzhen SEZ Development Co.* (undated pamphlet published by Shenzhen Special Economic Zone Development Company), p. 16 (hereafter cited as the *Introduction to Shenzhen SEZ)*.

17. Ho, p. 16, note 15 above.

18. For a discussion of the origins of the Shekou Industrial Zone, see text, pp. 165–6.

19. T. Gorman, 'Deep Ditch and Snake Mouth: New Boom Towns in the Pearl River Delta', *Pacific*, 3 November 1982, p. 72.

20. Gorman, p. 72, note 19 above.

21. 'Shekou SEZ Begins to Show Its Advantages', *Economic Reporter*, December 1981, p. 22. See also Gorman, p. 72, note 19 above.

22. *Introduction to Shenzhen SEZ*, pp.16–17, note 16 above.

23. Gorman, p. 72, note 19 above.

24. Gorman, p. 72, note 19 above. See also L. Kraar, 'A Little Touch of Capitalism', *Fortune International*, 18 April 1983, p. 125.

25. See note 222 below and accompanying text.

26. Gorman, p. 72, note 19 above.

27. K. Woodward and R. Goodwin, 'Supplying Offshore Services', *China Business Review,* March–April 1982, p. 15.

28. See A. Li, 'Shenzhen Special Economic Zone', *Amcham,* October 1981, p. 21; F. Sum, 'Shenzhen SEZ: Hong Kong Money Moves North', *Pacific*, 3 November 1982, p. 68; F. Sum and S. Chapman, 'How to Move Your Money North', *Pacific*, 3 November 1982, p. 76; and F. Ching, 'China's Shenzhen Gives Capitalism A Shot at Success', *Asian Wall Street Journal*, 13 August 1982, p. 1.

29. 'Shenzhen — China's First Special Economic Zone', *Beijing Review*, 14 December 1981, p. 18.

30. 'Shenzhen — China's First Special Economic Zone', p. 18, note 29 above.

31. 'Hong Kong Businessman on Investment in New Luohu Railway Station', *China Economic News*, 20 December 1982, p. 1.

32. See Gorman, p. 71, note 19 above.

33. See S. Wong, 'Weekend Resorts; Shenzhen's Recreation Reservoirs', *Pacific*, 3 November 1982, p. 79.

34. See 'Two Other Special Economic Zones in Guangdong', *Beijing Review*, 14 December 1981, p. 19; T. Gelatt, 'Zhuhai Trip Report', *Amcham*, November 1982, p. 34; Stas, p. 17, note 7 above; and 'Zhuhai Zone to Draw More Foreign Investment', *China Daily*, 24 March 1983, p. 3.

35. Gelatt, p. 34, note 34 above.

36. Gelatt, p. 34, note 34 above.

37. 'Two Other Special Economic Zones in Guangdong', p. 20, note 34 above.

38. Stas, p. 18, note 7 above.

39. Stas, p. 18, note 7 above. See also 'Shantou Speeds Up Construction of Special Economic Zone', *China Economic News*, 27 September 1982, p. 10; and 'Shantou

Seeks Foreign Capital for 18 Projects', *China Economic News*, 27 September 1982, p. 10.

40. J. Stepanek, 'Direct Investment in China', *China Business Review*, September–October 1982, p. 25.

41. See Stepanek, p. 38, note 9 above.

42. See K. Yeung, 'Development in the Special Economic Zones' (unpublished paper presented at a Conference on Reassessing Business With China, 22–23 April 1982, Hong Kong).

43. Yeung, note 42 above. Other reports point to lower figures. See, for example, Ching, p. 1 (US$1 billion as of August 1982), note 28 above. Still others cite higher figures. See, for example, 'China's Enterprise Zones: Leaky Capitalist Enclaves', p. 88 (US$1.6 billion committed to 1,350 projects as of November 1982), note 9 above.

44. Yeung, note 42 above.

45. Yeung, note 42 above. See also, 'China's Enterprise Zones: Leaky Capitalist Enclaves', p. 87 ('Nearly 70% of foreign investment in Shenzhen is committed to the development of offices, hotels and other tourist facilities.'), note 9 above.

46. 'China's Enterprise Zones : Leaky Capitalist Enclaves', p. 87, note 9 above.

47. Gorman, p. 71, note 19 above.

48. See C. Zheng, 'Er Ling Ling Ling Nian De Shen Zhen' (Shenzhen in the Year 2000), *Qi Shih Nian Dai (The Seventies)*, March 1982, p. 26; and 'Shenzhen Zone Plan Wins Fresh Support', *China Daily*, 22 September 1982, p. 1.

49. See Gelatt, p. 156, note 1 above.

50. An English translation of the SEZ Regulations appears in F. Chu, M. Moser and O. Nee (eds.), *Commercial, Business and Trade Laws: People's Republic of China* (Dobbs Ferry, Oceana Publications, Inc., 1982), Pt.14.

51. The SEZ Regulations came into effect on the date of their promulgation.

52. SEZ Regulations, Art. 2, note 50 above.

53. SEZ Regulations, Art. 2, note 50 above.

54. SEZ Regulations, Art. 3, note 50 above.

55. SEZ Regulations, Art. 23, note 50 above.

56. SEZ Regulations, Art. 5, note 50 above.

57. SEZ Regulations, Art. 5, note 50 above.

58. SEZ Regulations, Art. 25, note 50 above.

59. SEZ Regulations, Art. 5, note 50 above.

60. SEZ Regulations, Art. 5, note 50 above.

61. But see Kraar, p. 125, note 24 above, quoting a manager of the Continental Grain Co.: 'What in other countries can be resolved with a simple letter or phone call takes a lot of time and discussion with officials. This is still China.'

62. See note 129 below and accompanying text.

63. See note 177 below and accompanying text.

64. See notes 168, 169 and 170 below and accompanying text.

65. See note 55 above and accompanying text.

66. SEZ Regulations, Art. 23, note 50 above.

67. See note 130 below and accompanying text.

68. See 'Special Zones Get Watchdog Office', *South China Morning Post*, 26 June 1982, p. 12. According to this report, the Office of SEZ Affairs has been 'charged with the task of examining major, costly projects'.

69. Moser, conversation with ADCOM official.

70. SEZ Regulations, Art. 1, note 50 above.
71. SEZ Regulations, Art. 4, note 50 above.
72. SEZ Regulations, Art. 1, note 50 above.
73. SEZ Regulations, Art. 4, note 50 above.
74. Moser, conversation with ADCOM official. For a discussion of the distinctions between the types of joint ventures see Chapter 4 in this volume.
75. Law of the People's Republic of China on Joint Ventures Using Chinese and Foreign Investment, adopted by the Second Session of the Fifth National People's Congress on 1 July 1979 and promulgated on 8 July 1979 (hereafter cited as the Joint Venture Law). An English translation of the Joint Venture Law appears in Chu, Moser and Nee, Pt. 9, note 50 above.
76. Joint Venture Law, Art. 4, note 75 above.
77. SEZ Regulations, Art. 1, note 50 above.
78. SEZ Regulations, Art. 10, note 50 above.
79. According to Chinese reports as of May 1983 there were 34 wholly-owned foreign businesses operating in China with planned investments totalling more than US$360 billion. See 'Meeting Discusses Use of Foreign Funds', *China Daily*, 12 May 1982, p. 2. In the Shekou Industrial Zone fully half of all agreements signed to date are for privately owned projects. See Gorman, p. 72, note 19 above.
80. See 'SITCO Considers Proposal for Wholly Owned Foreign Venture', *China Market Intelligence*, February 1983, p. 2, regarding 3-M Corporation's proposal to establish a wholly-owned plant in Shanghai.
81. SEZ Regulations, Art. 7, note 50 above.
82. SEZ Regulations, Art. 8, note 50 above.
83. SEZ Regulations, Art. 8, note 50 above. Insurance may be obtained 'from the People's Insurance Company of China in the Special Zones or other insurance companies set up in the Special Zones with China's approval'.
84. SEZ Regulations, Art. 11, note 50 above.
85. SEZ Regulations, Art. 11, note 50 above.
86. SEZ Regulations, Art. 15, note 50 above.
87. The central piece of legislation is the Provisional Regulations of the People's Republic of China Governing Foreign Exchange Control, promulgated by the State Council on 18 December 1980. An English translation of the law appears in Chu, Moser and Nee, Pt. 12, note 50 above. For a discussion of this law and other foreign exchange legislation see Chapter 8 in this volume.
88. See Kraar, p. 127, note 24 above.
89. The rules have not been made publicly available but are reported in 'Shenzhen, Zhuhai Residents May Have Accounts in HK Dollars', *Ta Kung Pao*, 4 April 1982, p. 5. See also, 'Shenzhen, Zhuhai Banks Offer Foreign Currency Accounts', *China Daily*, 11 April 1982, p. 2.
90. See note 89 above.
91. SEZ Regulations, Art. 17, note 50 above.
92. SEZ Regulations, Art. 17, note 50 above.
93. SEZ Regulations, Art. 13, note 50 above.
94. SEZ Regulations, Art. 13, note 50 above.
95. Moser, discusssion with Chinese tax official. See also Gelatt, p. 161, note 1 above. For a detailed description of the Consolidated Tax see Chapter 2 in this volume.
96. Gelatt, p. 161, note 1 above.

97. SEZ Regulations, Art. 9, note 50 above.
98. Gelatt, p. 160, note 1 above.
99. SEZ Regulations, Art. 9, note 50 above.
100. See The Income Tax Law of the People's Republic of China Concerning Joint Ventures Using Chinese and Foreign Investment, adopted by the Third Session of the Fifth National People's Congress on 10 September 1980, Art. 3 (hereafter cited as the JVITL). An English translation of the law appears in Chu, Moser and Nee, Pt. 13, note 50 above.
101. JVITL, Art. 3, note 100 above.
102. The Income Tax Law of the People's Republic of China Concerning Foreign Enterprises, adopted by the Fourth Session of the Fifth National People's Congress on 13 December 1981, Art. 3 (hereafter cited as the FEITL). An English translation of the law appears in Chu, Moser and Nee, Pt.13, note 50 above.
103. FEITL, Art. 4, note 102 above.
104. Moser, conversation with tax official. However, it should also be noted that the benefits of the lower SEZ tax rates are not available to an enterprise simply because such an enterprise has a presence in the zones; in addition, the income-producing activity of the enterprise must have a direct connection with the SEZs. Based on these principles, the Ministry of Finance has ruled that foreign oil companies that register offices in the SEZs but conduct exploration and production work, and thus derive their income from, outside the zones may not benefit from the 15 per cent profit tax provision. See V. Fung, 'China Clarifies Rules On Foreign Banks', *Asian Wall Street Journal,* 29 June 1983, p. 1.
105. SEZ Regulations, Art. 14, note 50 above.
106. JVITL, Art. 4, note 100 above.
107. SEZ Regulations, Art. 15, note 50 above.
108. Moser, conversation with tax official.
109. SEZ Regulations, Art. 19, note 50 above.
110. SEZ Regulations, Art. 19, note 50 above.
111. SEZ Regulations, Art. 19, note 50 above.
112. SEZ Regulations, Art. 21, note 50 above.
113. SEZ Regulations, Art. 20, note 50 above.
114. SEZ Regulations, Art. 18, note 50 above.
115. SEZ Regulations, Art. 12, note 50 above.
116. An English translation of the Entry and Exit Regulations appears in Chu, Moser and Nee, Pt.14, note 50 above.
117. Entry and Exit Regulations, Art. 2, note 116 above.
118. Entry and Exit Regulations, Art. 11, note 116 above.
119. Entry and Exit Regulations, Art. 2, note 116 above. Implicit in the Entry and Exit Regulations is an attempt to develop a scheme to isolate the SEZs from the rest of China. This scheme has now taken on a physical dimension at least in Shenzhen where a barbed-wire fence has been erected along the border of the municipality. This inner border is known as the 'second line', as distinct from the 'first line' which divides Shenzhen and neighbouring Hong Kong. See Ho, p. 17, note 15 above.
120. Entry and Exit Regulations, Art. 3(1), note 116 above.
121. Entry and Exit Regulations, Art. 3(2), note 116 above.
122. Entry and Exit Regulations, Art. 5, note 116 above.
123. Entry and Exit Regulations, Art. 10, note 116 above.
124. Entry and Exit Regulations, Art. 7, note 116 above.

125. See 'Border Procedures for Private Cars in Shenzhen', *China Trader Weekly Bulletin*, 9–15 May 1982, p. 4.
126. 'Border Procedures for Private Cars in Shenzhen', note 125 above.
127. See, for example, Kraar, p. 126, note 24 above, quoting a Pepsico Manager's complaints that the 19-mile trip from the company's Shenzhen plant to Hong Kong often takes four to five hours: 'It would take only an hour or two if not for the slow customs clearance at China's border'. See also M. Moser, 'Guangdong's SEZs: Four New Regulations Fill Important Gaps', *China Business Review*, March–April 1982, p. 40.
128. An English translation of the Business Registration Regulations appears in Chu, Moser and Nee, Pt. 14, p. 19, see note 50.
129. Business Registration Regulations, Art. 2, note 128 above. The 'administrative organization for industry and commerce' refers to the local unit of the General Administration for Industry and Commerce (GAIC). See R. Lutz, 'The General Administration for the Control of Industry and Commerce: Its Mandate Spans the Spectrum of Regulatory Functions', *China Business Review*, March–April 1983, p. 25. In mid-1983 the GAIC changed its name to the State Administration for Industry and Commerce of the People's Republic of China and is now commonly referred to in English as the SAIC.
130. Business Registration Regulations, Art. 3, note 128 above.
131. Business Registration Regulations, Art. 5, note 128 above.
132. Business Registration Regulations, Art. 6, note 128 above.
133. Business Registration Regulations, Art. 9, note 128 above.
134. Business Registration Regulations, Art. 7, note 128 above.
135. Business Registration Regulations, Art. 8, note 128 above.
136. Business Registration Regulations, Art. 11, note 128 above.
137. Business Registration Regulations, Art. 12, note 128 above.
138. Business Registration Regulations, Art. 12, note 128 above.
139. An English translation of the law appears in *China Economic News*, 21 February 1983, p. 1.
140. Provisional Regulations for the Establishment of Representative Offices in China by Overseas Chinese and Foreign Financial Institutions, Art. 8, note 139 above.
141. The Hong Kong-based Nanyang Commercial Bank opened a branch office in Shenzhen in 1982. However, this institution is a Bank of China affiliate, a fact which probably accounts for its preferred position. As of July 1983 five foreign banks have set up representative offices in Shenzhen. They include the Hongkong and Shanghai Banking Corporation, Chartered Bank, Banque Nationale de Paris, Takugin International (Asia) Ltd., and Banque de I'Indochine et de Suez. According to SEZ officials, once the Shenzhen banking regulations are promulgated foreign banks will be permitted to conduct 'normal banking business' and do 'whatever the Bank of China can do'. See V. Fung, 'China May Allow Foreign Banking in Shenzhen Zone', *Asian Wall Street Journal*, 5 July 1983, p. 1.
142. Adopted by the Thirteenth Session of the Standing Committee of the Fifth People's Congress of Guangdong Province on 17 November 1981 (hereafter cited as the SEZ Labour and Wage Regulations). An English translation of the SEZ Labour and Wage Regulations appears in Chu, Moser and Nee, Pt.14, note 50 above.
143. SEZ Labour and Wage Regulations, Art. 2, note 142 above.
144. Regulations on Labour Management in Joint Ventures Using Chinese and

Foreign Investment, promulgated by the State Council on 26 July 1980 (hereafter cited as the JV Labour Regulations). An English translation of the JV Labour Regulations appears in Chu, Moser and Nee, Pt. 9, note 50 above.
145. JV Labour Regulations, Art. 2, note 144 above; and SEZ Labour and Wage Regulations, Art. 2, note 142 above.
146. JV Labour Regulations, Art. 2, note 144 above.
147. SEZ Labour and Wage Regulations, Art. 2, note 142 above.
148. SEZ Labour and Wage Regulations, Art. 4, note 142 above; and JV Labour Regulations, Art. 3, note 144 above.
149. SEZ Labour and Wage Regulations, Art. 4, note 142 above.
150. SEZ Labour and Wage Regulations, Art. 19, note 142 above.
151. JV Labour Regulations, Art. 8, note 144 above.
152. JV Labour Regulations, Art. 11, note 144 above.
153. SEZ Labour and Wage Regulations, Art. 7, note 142 above.
154. SEZ Labour and Wage Regulations, Art. 9, note 142 above.
155. SEZ Labour and Wage Regulations, Art. 8, note 142 above.
156. SEZ Labour and Wage Regulations, Art. 7, note 142 above.
157. SEZ Labour and Wage Regulations, Art. 10, note 142 above.
158. SEZ Labour and Wage Regulations, Art. 11, note 142 above.
159. SEZ Labour and Wage Regulations, Arts. 15 and 16, note 142 above; and JV Labour Regulations, Arts. 4 and 7, note 144 above.
160. SEZ Labour and Wage Regulations, Art. 29, note 142 above.
161. SEZ Labour and Wage Regulations, Art. 29, note 142 above.
162. SEZ Labour and Wage Regulations, Art. 16, note 142 above.
163. SEZ Labour and Wage Regulations, Art. 16, note 142 above.
164. SEZ Labour and Wage Regulations, Art. 16, note 142 above.
165. SEZ Labour and Wage Regulations, Art. 17, note 142 above.
166. SEZ Labour and Wage Regulations, Art. 18, note 142 above.
167. Economic Contracts Law of the People's Republic of China adopted at the Fourth Session of the Fifth National People's Congress on 13 December 1981. An English translation of the law appears in Chu, Moser and Nee, Pt. 5, note 50 above.
168. SEZ Labour and Wage Regulations, Art. 4, note 142 above.
169. SEZ Labour and Wage Regulations, Art. 17, note 142 above.
170. See Moser, p. 42, note 127 above. See also 'Hiring and Firing In Guangdong's Special Economic Zones', *Business China*, 20 January 1982, p. 9.
171. See 'Seminar Offers Insights Into SEZs', *China Trader*, June 1982, p. 96.
172. 'Seminar Offers Insights into SEZs', note 171 above.
173. 'Seminar Offers Insights into SEZs', note 171 above.
174. See T. Gelatt, 'Land, Entry Laws in China's Economic Zones', *Asian Wall Street Journal*, 11 February 1982, p. 8.
175. Adopted by the Thirteenth Session of the Standing Committee of the Fifth People's Congress of Guangdong Province on 17 November 1981 and put into effect on 1 January 1982 (hereafter cited as the Shenzhen Land Regulations). An English translation of the Shenzhen Land Regulations appears in Chu, Moser and Nee, Pt.14, note 50 above.
176. Shenzhen Land Regulations, Art. 5, note 175 above.
177. Shenzhen Land Regulations, Art. 8, note 175 above.
178. Shenzhen Land Regulations, Art. 8, note 175 above.
179. Shenzhen Land Regulations, Art. 9, note 175 above.

180. Shenzhen Land Regulations, Art. 9, note 175 above.
181. Shenzhen Land Regulations, Art. 9, note 175 above.
182. Shenzhen Land Regulations, Art. 9, note 175 above.
183. Shenzhen Land Regulations, Art. 15, note 175 above.
184. Shenzhen Land Regulations, Art. 15, note 175 above.
185. Shenzhen Land Regulations, Art. 16, note 175 above. According to SEZ officials, during the four-year period 1982–5 special rate reductions of from 30 to 50 per cent will be granted to investors who lease land in the Luohu and Shekou industrial districts, the Shangbu, Reservoir and Shataukok areas and other designated parts of the Shenzhen SEZ. See *Introduction to Shenzhen SEZ*, p. 19, note 16 above.
186. Shenzhen Land Regulations, Art. 16, note 175 above.
187. Shenzhen Land Regulations, Art. 18, note 175 above.
188. Shenzhen Land Regulations, Art. 18, note 175 above.
189. Shenzhen Land Regulations, Art. 17, note 175 above.
190. See Moser, p. 44, note 127 above.
191. Stepanek, p. 38, note 9 above.
192. See 'Legal Framework for Investors to China's Special Economic Zones (SEZs)', *Economic Reporter*, February 1982, pp. 21 and 22.
193. Shenzhen Land Regulations, Art. 3, note 175 above.
194. Shenzhen Land Regulations, Art. 2, note 175 above.
195. Shenzhen Land Regulations, Art. 6, note 175 above.
196. Shenzhen Land Regulations, Art. 11, note 175 above.
197. Shenzhen Land Regulations, Art. 12, note 175 above.
198. The Chinese text of the law appears in *Shenzhen Tequ Bao (Shenzhen Special Zone News)*, 12 July 1982, p. 2. An English-language translation of the text is on file with the author.
199. Construction Measures, Art. 12, note 198 above.
200. Construction Measures, Art. 13, note 198 above.
201. Construction Measures, Arts. 19–25, note 198 above.
202. Construction Measures, Arts. 26–30, note 198 above.
203. Construction Measures, Arts. 31–49, note 198 above.
204. Construction Measures, Art. 33, note 198 above.
205. Construction Measures, Art. 42, note 198 above.
206. Construction Measures, Art. 43(5), note 198 above.
207. Original Chinese version and English translation on file with the author.
208. 'More on New SEZ Laws', *Economic Reporter*, September 1981, p. 9.
209. 'More on New SEZ Laws', p. 9, note 208 above.
210. 'More on New SEZ Laws', pp. 9 and 10, note 208 above.
211. 'More on New SEZ Laws', pp. 9 and 10, note 208 above.
212. Individual Income Tax Law of the People's Republic of China, adopted by the Third Session of the Fifth National People's Congress on 10 September 1980 and put into effect on the same date. An English translation of the law appears in Chu, Moser and Nee, Pt. 13, note 50 above.
213. Individual Income Tax Law, Art. 3, note 212 above.
214. See Gelatt, p. 178, note 1 above.
215. See Detailed Rules and Regulations for the Implementation of the Individual Income Tax Law of the People's Republic of China, adopted by the State Council on 10 December 1980 and promulgated by the Ministry of Finance on 14 December

1980, Art. 3. For an English translation of the law see Chu, Moser and Nee, Pt. 13, note 50 above.

216. See Gelatt, p. 179, note 1 above. It should be noted that the national tax rules regarding this issue have also recently been relaxed to some extent. Under a document issued by the Ministry of Finance, non-China source income of a foreigner whose presence in China is due to employment there will not be taxable in China regardless of the length of residence and regardless of whether such income is remitted into China. See Notice Concerning the Exemption from Reporting and Payment of Individual Income Tax for Income Earned Outside China by Personnel of Foreign Nationality Working Within China (Document (83) *Cai Shui* No. 62), issued by the Ministry of Finance on 7 March 1983. An English translation of this document is on file with the author.

217. Both laws came into effect on the date of promulgation. All references to the SEZ Contracts Regulations and the SEZ Technology Regulations are to English-language translations of the laws on file with the author.

218. SEZ Contracts Regulations, Art. 2, note 217 above.

219. SEZ Contracts Regulations, Arts. 15, 16, 17, 18 and 19, note 217 above.

220. SEZ Contracts Regulations, Arts. 21, 22, 23, 24 and 25, note 217 above.

221. SEZ Contracts Regulations, Art. 27, note 217 above.

222. SEZ Contracts Regulations, Arts. 27 and 31, note 217 above.

223. SEZ Contracts Regulations, Arts. 34 and 35, note 217 above.

224. SEZ Contracts Regulations, Art. 35, note 217 above.

225. SEZ Contracts Regulations, Art. 40, note 217 above.

226. SEZ Technology Regulations, Arts. 15, 16 and 17, note 217 above.

227. SEZ Technology Regulations, Art. 4, note 217 above.

228. SEZ Technology Regulations, Art. 23, note 217 above.

229. SEZ Technology Regulations, Art. 19, note 217 above.

230. SEZ Technology Regulations, Art. 10, note 217 above.

231. SEZ Technology Regulations, Art. 11, note 217 above.

232. SEZ Technology Regulations, Art. 12, note 217 above.

233. 'Shekou SEZ Begins to Show Its Advantages', p. 22, note 21 above.

234. See *Investor's Handbook 'The Shekou Industrial Zone in Shenzhen' under China Merchants' Steam Navigation Co., Ltd. of Hong Kong* (January 1980) (hereafter cited as the First Shekou Handbook).

235. See *Investor's Handbook (Revised and Enlarged Edition) China Merchants' Shekou Industrial Zone in Shenzhen Special Economic Zone in Guangdong Province* (September 1981) (hereafter cited as the Shekou Handbook).

236. See 'Guangdong Zone Rules Cloud More Issues Than They Clarify', *Business China*, 24 September 1980, p. 137; and T. Gelatt, 'Laws for China's Economic Zones are Unclear', *Asian Wall Street Journal*, 10 February 1982, p. 12.

237. Moser, conversation with CMSN official. See also Gelatt, p. 180, note 1 above.

238. Shekou Handbook, p. 22, note 235 above.

239. Shekou Handbook, p. 22, note 235 above.

240. Shekou Handbook, p. 21, note 235 above.

241. Shekou Handbook, p. 11, note 235 above.

242. Moser, conversation with CMSN official.

243. Shekou Handbook, p. 22, note 235 above.

244. Shekou Handbook, p. 22, note 235 above.

245. Shekou Handbook, p. 22, note 235 above.
246. Shekou Handbook, p. 22, note 235 above.
247. Shekou Handbook, p. 22, note 235 above.
248. Shekou Handbook, p. 24, note 235 above.
249. Shekou Handbook, p. 22, note 235 above.
250. Shekou Handbook, p. 22, note 235 above; and Gelatt, p. 181, note 1 above.
251. Shekou Handbook, p. 24, note 235 above.
252. Shekou Handbook, p. 24, note 235 above.
253. Shekou Handbook, p. 23, note 235 above.
254. Shekou Handbook, p. 23, note 235 above.
255. Shekou Handbook, p. 23, note 235 above.
256. Shekou Handbook, p. 23, note 235 above.
257. Shekou Handbook, p. 23, note 235 above.
258. Shekou Handbook, p. 23, note 235 above.
259. First Shekou Handbook, p. 13, note 234 above.
260. Shekou Handbook, p. 23, note 235 above.
261. Shekou Handbook, p. 23, note 235 above.
262. Shekou Handbook, p. 23, note 235 above.
263. Shekou Handbook, p. 23, note 235 above.
264. Shekou Handbook, p. 23, note 235 above.
265. Shekou Handbook, p. 23, note 235 above.
266. Shekou Handbook, p. 23, note 235 above.
267. Shekou Handbook, p. 23, note 235 above.
268. Shekou Handbook, p. 23, note 235 above.
269. Shekou Handbook, p. 24, note 235 above.
270. Shekou Handbook, p. 24, note 235 above.
271. Shekou Handbook, p. 24, note 235 above.
272. Moser, conversation with CMSN official.
273. Reports indicate that the SEZ foreign exchange rules may include the issue of a special SEZ currency. See 'Comment: SEZ Currency — More Funny Money?', *China Trader Weekly Bulletin*, 10–16 January 1982, p. 4; and 'China Mulling Issue of Shenzhen Money', *Asian Wall Street Journal*, 26 October 1983, p.3.

6. Offshore Oil Exploration and Development in China: The Current Regulatory Regime

MICHAEL J. MOSER

WITH oil reserves estimated at between 30 billion and 100 billion barrels, China's continental shelf is believed to contain the largest untapped oil deposits remaining in the world today.[1] As onshore production levelled off in the late 1970s, China's leaders decided to embark on a programme to develop the nation's offshore reserves in co-operation with foreign oil companies.[2] By so doing, China not only hopes to bring its offshore production onstream within the shortest possible time, but also seeks to gain training, technology and managerial experience from its foreign partners. It is anticipated that most of the production from China's offshore wells will be used to satisfy burgeoning domestic demand, although a portion of crude production may be exported to earn foreign exchange.[3]

The first phase in China's programme to involve foreign companies in the development of its offshore oil began in 1979. During that year foreign oil companies were invited to enter into geophysical survey agreements with the China National Oil and Gas Exploration and Development Corporation (CNOGEDC), opening up blocks in the South China Sea and the South Yellow Sea to initial exploration activity.[4] The costs of the surveys were borne by the foreign parties who were obliged, under the terms of their agreements with the CNOGEDC, to turn over all seismic information and interpretation. In exchange, participating foreign companies were given assurances that they would be granted bidding rights to selected blocks to be opened up for joint Chinese-foreign exploration and development in the near future.

Prior to the opening of competitive bidding, China moved forward in negotiations for exploration and development contracts with selected companies. On 29 May 1980, the CNOGEDC signed three contracts: one with the Japan National Oil Corporation for exploration and development in the Bohai Gulf; another with France's Société Nationale Elf Aquitaine, also for exploration and development in the Bohai; and a third with the Compagnie Française des Petroles (Total) of France for the Beibu Gulf area in the South China Sea.[5] At the same time negotiations were conducted with the Atlantic Richfield Company (ARCO) and Santa Fe International of the United States for an exploration and development contract in a 9,000-square-kilometre area in the

Ying Ge Hai Basin off the south coast of Hainan Island. After substantial delays, these negotiations finally bore fruit with the signing of a contract in September 1982.[6]

The years 1982 and 1983 saw a flurry of activity which put China's offshore oil development programme into high gear. First, in January 1982, the State Council promulgated the Regulations of the People's Republic of China on the Exploitation of Offshore Petroleum Resources in Co-operation with Foreign Enterprises (hereafter cited as the Petroleum Regulations) which provide the legal framework for exploration and development activities involving foreign entities.[7] Several weeks later, on 15 February 1982, the China National Offshore Oil Corporation (CNOOC) was created and granted exclusive authority to negotiate and sign contracts with foreign oil companies.[8] On the following day, the CNOOC announced that 43 blocks totalling more than 150,000 square kilometres would be opened for competitive bidding.[9] Soon after, invitations were issued to 46 foreign companies that had participated in China's earlier seismic survey programme.[10] By April, 40 of these companies had responded positively to the invitation and had indicated an interest in submitting formal bids.[11] On 10 May these companies were invited by the CNOOC to Beijing to collect the 'bidding documents package', including a copy of China's 'Model Contract' which was intended to be the starting point for negotiations.[12] When the bidding deadline arrived on 17 August 1982, a total of 33 companies had submitted 102 formal bids to the CNOOC, thus indicating a desire to pursue detailed negotiations.[13] However, not until 10 May 1983 did the CNOOC sign the first exploration and development contract, with a consortium led by British Petroleum (BP) and including participants from Australia, Brazil and Canada.[14] This contract was soon followed by others, including those signed by Exxon, Shell, Occidental, Texaco and Chevron.[15]

This chapter is intended to provide an overview of the most important elements of the legal framework established to permit and regulate the participation of foreign enterprises in the exploration and development of China's offshore oil and gas resources. Part I describes the main provisions of the Petroleum Regulations and Part II examines the Model Contract. Part III focuses on Chinese tax laws applicable to offshore oil activities. Finally, Part IV reviews several miscellaneous regulations affecting the operations of foreign companies involved in offshore oil activities, including registration rules, special tax and customs provisions and environmental protection rules.

I. The Petroleum Regulations

The Petroleum Regulations provide the basic statutory foundation for China's policy to develop its offshore oil and gas resources in co-operation with foreign enterprises. Consisting of 31 articles, the law addresses five major topics: (1) the general principles under which China's co-operative offshore oil development programme is to be carried out; (2) the organization of the nation's oil bureaucracy; (3) the rights and obligations of the parties to petroleum contracts; (4) the conduct of petroleum operations, including exploration, development and production activities; and (5) dispute settlement and enforcement measures.

A. General Principles

The first task accomplished by the Petroleum Regulations is to provide a broad statement of purpose or legislative aims. Article 1 provides that the law has been formulated 'to permit foreign enterprises to participate in the co-operative exploitation of offshore petroleum resources' in order to 'develop the national economy' and 'expand international economic and technical co-operation'. In addition, the article states that the law is intended to safeguard China's 'national sovereignty and economic interests'.[16] At the outset, therefore, the Petroleum Regulations provide the necessary legal basis for China's negotiations with foreign oil companies and establish the basic principle that foreign participation in the nation's offshore oil development programme will be regulated so as to protect China's perceived economic and political interests.

Like China's other foreign investment legislation, the Petroleum Regulations provide that the activities, share of profits and other 'legitimate rights and interests' of foreign enterprises making investments in China will be protected, 'in accordance with law', by the Chinese government.[17] In return, foreign enterprises are required to comply with Chinese 'laws and decrees' as well as 'relevant stipulations of the State'.[18] In addition, the Petroleum Regulations require that all persons and enterprises engaged in oil exploration, production and development activities in China be subject to 'inspection and supervision by the relevant competent authorities of the Chinese government'.[19]

Finally, the Petroleum Regulations also contain a statement of general principles relating to the ownership of China's petroleum resources and an assertion of legal jurisdiction over petroleum operations conducted within the nation's territory. The law provides that all oil and natural gas deposits located within China's internal and territorial waters and on its continental shelf, as well as deposits in other waters that are under China's control, are 'owned by' the People's Republic of China.[20] In addition, the law provides that China has jurisdiction over all buildings, structures and vessels established or operating within such waters in order to serve the petroleum operations.[21] What the Petroleum Regulations fail to make clear, however, is the precise extent of such jurisdiction, a matter which is the subject of some dispute with China's neighbours.[22]

B. The Organization of China's Oil Bureaucracy

Article 4 of the Petroleum Regulations designates the Ministry of Petroleum Industry (MOPI) as the 'competent government authority in charge of the exploitation of offshore petroleum resources in co-operation with foreign enterprises.' The responsibilities and powers granted to the MOPI under the regulations are far-reaching. They include determining the forms of co-operation to be undertaken with foreign enterprises; demarcating concession areas within the zones designated by the state for co-operative development; developing plans for the co-operative exploitation of petroleum resources in accordance with the state's long-term economic programme; and formulating operational and management policies, as well as examining and approving 'the overall development programme' for offshore petroleum and gas fields.[23]

The Petroleum Regulations also provide for the creation of the CNOOC to handle the 'business' aspects of China's co-operative offshore oil development programme. Under the law, such tasks are to be 'unified under the full responsibility of' the CNOOC.[24] In addition, the regulations grant the CNOOC the power to call for bids, establish 'regional companies, specialized companies and overseas representative offices', and enter into contracts with foreign enterprises.[25] All contracts signed by the CNOOC in connection with the co-operative exploitation of China's oil and gas resources must be approved by the Foreign Investment Bureau of the Ministry of Foreign Economic Relations and Trade.[26]

The legal nature of the CNOOC has been a source of concern for a number of foreign oil companies.[27] The Petroleum Regulations shed little light on this question, except to state that the CNOOC is a 'state corporation with the qualification of a juridical person which has the exclusive right to explore, develop, produce and market petroleum within the zones of co-operation with foreign enterprises.'[28] However, in January 1984 the CNOOC had still not made public its Articles of Incorporation or corporate charter (if indeed any such documents exist), which might clarify the extent of the company's legal powers.

Since the promulgation of the Petroleum Regulations, the organizational structure for offshore operations has become rather complex. At the apex of this structure, the CNOOC headquarters in Beijing has established 12 specialized departments dealing with foreign co-operation and contracts, foreign liaison matters, exploration and development, production operations, planning, personnel, finance, education, engineering, marketing, services, and general administration.[29] At the local level, the CNOOC has established four branch corporations.[30] The Bohai Oil Corporation, based in Tanggu, will be responsible for petroleum operations in the Bohai Gulf, and the South Huang Hai Oil Corporation, headquartered in Shanghai, will take charge of operations in the South Yellow Sea concession areas. In the South China Sea region two branch corporations have been established, the Nanhai (West) Oil Corporation and the Nanhai (East) Oil Corporation. The geographical boundary for the division of responsibility between the Nanhai (West) and Nanhai (East) corporations will be the 113° 10′ line of longitude, which falls just west of Guangzhou.

With the focus of petroleum exploration and development activity now on the south, the CNOOC's operations there have grown in importance. The Nanhai (West) corporation has established its headquarters and rear support base in Zhanjiang and is developing front bases in Wushi and Sanya on Hainan Island.[31] The Nanhai (East) branch, with its headquarters in Guangzhou, is developing front bases in the Shekou–Chiwan area and in Shantou.[32] In addition, the CNOOC has formally entered into a co-operative venture with Guangdong Province in the form of the China-Nanhai Oil Joint Services Corporation (CNOJSC), which is intended to be the main service and supply organization for operations in both the western and eastern sectors of the South China Sea.[33] The CNOJSC itself is divided into a number of specialized subsidiaries, some of which are wholly owned by the CNOJSC and others which are owned jointly with other Chinese organizations.

The CNOOC has also begun to move to establish at least a limited presence in oil and supply centres outside China proper. In January 1983, the CNOOC established a representative office in Hong Kong with the aim of co-ordinating oil-related activities of Hong Kong-based Chinese companies and foreign supply and service companies. Prior to this it was widely expected that the Chinese would attempt to exclude Hong Kong from any major back-up role in offshore oil development, particularly as the Petroleum Regulations require that service and supply bases must be located within the People's Republic.[34] It is anticipated that CNOOC representative offices similar to the office set up in Hong Kong will be established in the future in foreign oil centres, including Houston, Singapore and, perhaps, Stavanger, Norway.

C. The Rights and Obligations of Parties to Petroleum Contracts

In addition to setting forth the basic principles governing, and the organizational framework for, China's co-operation with foreign enterprises, the Petroleum Regulations provide a general outline of the form such co-operation should take. Under Article 7 of the law, the terms of such co-operation are to be specified in the 'petroleum contract' entered into between the CNOOC and foreign oil companies. Unless otherwise provided by the MOPI or in the contract, the foreign contractor is required to undertake all exploration operations and must provide all exploration investment and bear all risks associated therewith.[35] Once a 'commercial' oil or gas field is discovered, the field is to be developed by the CNOOC and the foreign contractor jointly, with both parties providing the necessary investment.[36] The law also provides that the foreign contractor bear responsibility for both 'development operations' and 'production operations', at least until such time as the CNOOC assumes responsibility for production operations pursuant to the terms of the contract.[37] Finally, the law states that foreign contractors shall be permitted to recover their investment and expenses and receive renumeration from the petroleum produced.[38] Petroleum received by foreign contractors may be exported, and sums attributable to investment recovery, profits and 'other legitimate income' may be remitted abroad.[39]

The Petroleum Regulations also contain a number of provisions dealing with the operations of foreign contractors, subcontractors, and other foreign enterprises engaged in activities related to the development of offshore oil. For example, Article 11 requires that foreign contractors open a bank account in accordance with China's foreign exchange regulations. Article 9 requires enterprises engaged in petroleum operations, together with their employees, to pay taxes in accordance with Chinese law. Article 10 promises 'preferential' customs treatment for imported equipment and materials used in petroleum operations. And finally, the law requires that both contractors and subcontractors establish a 'subsidiary or branch or representative office' in China at places to be determined through 'consultation' with the CNOOC.[40]

In the course of implementing the petroleum contract with the CNOOC, the Petroleum Regulations require that the foreign contractor assume a number of responsibilities. For example, the foreign contractor must employ 'appropriate and advanced' technology and managerial experience and must transfer such technology and experience to the Chinese side.[41] The contractor must also give priority to Chinese personnel when employing workers for the implementation of the contract and must 'keep the percentage of Chinese steadily rising' and 'train Chinese personnel in a planned way'.[42] Finally, the law also requires the foreign contractor to keep accurate and complete records and data regarding the petroleum operations and to 'regularly submit' such information together with technological, financial, accounting and administrative reports to the CNOOC.[43]

D. Petroleum Operations

The fourth set of provisions contained in the Petroleum Regulations deals with matters pertaining to 'petroleum operations', defined as 'all exploration, development and production operations and other related activities carried out in the implementation of the petroleum contract.'[44] The provisions are essentially a group of requirements imposed on foreign operators, contractors and subcontractors in connection with the conduct of such activities.

The first requirement set forth in the law pertains to operators, that is the foreign oil companies that are responsible for performing petroleum operations pursuant to the petroleum contract. With the aim of maximizing potential recovery, Article 16 requires operators to formulate an 'overall development plan' for oil and gas fields within their concession blocks. In addition, operators are required to carry out production operations — including extraction, processing, storage, transportation, lifting of crude oil, and so on — in accordance with the Petroleum Regulations and other 'relevant rules' promulgated by the MOPI.[45]

The Petroleum Regulations contain several provisions requiring that preference be given to Chinese entities or materials in the conduct of petroleum operations. For example, Article 18 provides that Chinese design corporations must be given priority by operators when they subcontract for overall designs and engineering designs required for implementation of the petroleum contract, provided that the terms offered by such Chinese corporations are competitive. Article 19 requires that operators give priority to Chinese manufacturers and engineering companies when concluding subcontracts for such facilities as platforms, buildings and other structures, provided the Chinese companies are competitive in 'quality, price, terms of delivery and services'. Under Article 20, priority must also be given to Chinese equipment and materials, again provided that these are competitive. Finally, Article 21 requires that operators and subcontractors give priority to Chinese enterprises when concluding subcontracts and service contracts, such as contracts for geophysical prospecting, well-drilling, diving, aircraft, vessels and bases. Again, the preference for Chinese enterprises is only required where such enterprises are competitive in price, efficiency and service.

The Petroleum Regulations also address briefly the question of ownership of tangible and intangible property used or acquired by foreign contractors in the course of petroleum operations. The law provides that assets purchased or built by a foreign contractor in order to implement the petroleum contract shall become the property of the CNOOC after the foreign party has recovered its investment in accordance with the terms of the contract.[46] In addition, the law provides that the CNOOC shall be the owner of all 'data, records, samples, vouchers and other original information' connected with the petroleum operations and requires that the use, transfer, sale or publication of such information shall be controlled in accordance with rules formulated by the MOPI.[47]

Another requirement imposed on foreign contractors by the Petroleum Regulations concerns the landing of petroleum. Article 25 provides that in general all petroleum produced within a contract area must be landed in Chinese territory and exported from designated points, although exceptions to this rule may be granted by the MOPI. In the event of war, or threat of war, or 'other emergency circumstances', the Petroleum Regulations empower the Chinese government to 'requisition by purchase or requisition for use' all or a part of the petroleum obtained or purchased by a foreign contractor.[48]

Finally, the Petroleum Regulations also require that foreign operators and subcontractors comply with Chinese environmental protection and safety laws and generally conduct their operations 'with reference to international practice'.[49]

E. Dispute Settlement and Enforcement

The Petroleum Regulations include two general provisions regarding the settlement of disputes between foreign and Chinese enterprises engaged in the co-operative exploitation of China's offshore oil reserves and the enforcement of the regulations. Regarding dispute settlement, Article 27 prescribes 'friendly consultations' as the first step in resolving conflicts. If a solution is unattainable, settlement may be attempted through mediation or arbitration in China, or through arbitration by 'another arbitration body agreed upon by both parties' which presumably includes third-country arbitration. With respect to enforcement, Article 28 of the law empowers the MOPI to handle violations of the Petroleum Regulations. The MOPI may issue warnings, make demands for remedial action, and even order a termination of operations. Economic losses in such cases are to be borne by the responsible parties. The law also provides that the MOPI may fine or bring suit against parties who are responsible for 'serious violations' of the regulations.

II. The Model Contract

The Model Contract, which has served as the starting point for the negotiation of China's concession contracts, is in many respects a lawyer's longhand version of the Petroleum Regulations. Consisting of 30 articles and 4 annexes spread over more than 120 pages, the Model Contract sets forth in detail the Chinese vision of the legal and business relationship between the CNOOC and the foreign oil companies which is outlined in the Petroleum Regulations. Reportedly developed after close study of petroleum contracts and arrangements in other countries, especially Indonesia and Norway,[50] the Model Contract calls for the establishment of a form of co-operation between the CNOOC and foreign oil companies which resembles something approaching a cross between a production-sharing arrangement and a co-operative or contractual joint venture. The most important features of this relationship are described as follows.

A. The Basic Structure of Co-operation

The bulk of the Model Contract is concerned with the basic terms under which the CNOOC and the foreign contractor will co-operate in the development of offshore oil and gas resources within the blocks won by the foreign company in the bidding process. The contract divides the term of such co-operation into three periods — exploration, development and production — which in total shall generally not exceed thirty years. Each of these periods carries with it different rights and responsibilities for the parties.

During the exploration period all responsibility is to be borne by the foreign contractor. It must provide all of the funds required and bears all risks associated with the exploration activities. The contract also requires that the foreign contractor fulfill a 'minimum exploration work programme' including completion of a minimum number of kilometres of seismic lines, and drilling and completion of a minimum number of metres of wildcat wells. In addition, the contractor must spend at least a fixed amount of funds as a 'minimum expenditure obligation' during the exploration period. The extent of the minimum work programme and expenditure pledged by contractors was one of the areas open to bidding by foreign oil companies and, presumably, was a major factor considered by the CNOOC in the award of contract areas.

The duration of the exploration period is dependent upon the size of the area awarded to the foreign contractor. Where the contract area is less than 2,000 square kilometres, the exploration period consists of a term of five years, divided into an initial phase of three years and a second phase of two years. In the case of a contract area of 2,000 square kilometres or more, the exploration period is fixed at seven years, divided into three phases of three years, two years and two years.

Upon the completion of each phase of the exploration period the contractor is required to relinquish a certain portion of the contract area. For example, in the case of a contract area in excess of 2,000 square kilometres the foreign contractor must give up 25 per cent of the total area at the end of the third year of the exploration period. At the end of the fifth year the contractor must relinquish 25 per cent of the remaining contract area after deducting the area of oil and gas fields that have been discovered and designated for development. Finally, at the end of the seventh year, the remaining contract area, excluding fields designated for development, must be relinquished. As a result of these requirements, the foreign contractor is forced to move quickly to assess which areas within its designated concession blocks are most promising, and thus warrant further exploration, and which should be given up.[51]

Upon the expiration of each phase prior to the last phase of the exploration period, the foreign contractor is given the option of either proceeding with exploration and entering the next phase or of terminating the contract. Therefore, if exploration operations have not been promising the foreign party may withdraw from the co-operation and sustain a loss equal to the total amount of exploration costs incurred to date. In addition, the contract provides for automatic termination upon the expiration of the full term of the exploration period if no commercial oil or gas reservoir has been discovered within the contract area during that time.

In the event that the contract is not terminated prior to or at the expiration of the exploration period, the operations move into the development phase. The period begins on the date of approval by the MOPI of the 'overall development plan', prepared by the foreign contractor or operator, which sets forth the plan for the development of oil and gas fields discovered within the contract area and the time schedule for development.

In general, the costs required for the development operations are to be shared by the parties in proportion to their 'participating interests', fixed in the contract at 51 per cent for the CNOOC and 49 per cent for the foreign contractor. However, the CNOOC has the option of not participating in the development of any field or of participating at a level of less than 51 per cent. Such an option must be exercised by notice in writing to the foreign contractor within ninety days from the date of approval of the overall development plan. In the event that the CNOOC chooses not to participate in the development of a field or chooses to participate at a reduced level, the foreign contractor is required to provide all or the remaining part of the funds necessary for development of the field.

The production period of an oil or gas field begins on the 'date of commencement of commercial production' and may last for up to 15 years. The 'date of commencement of commercial production' is defined in the contract to mean the date on which a cumulative total of not less than 100,000 metric tons of crude oil, in the case of an oil field, or not less than 100,000,000 cubic metres of natural gas, in the case of a gas field, has been extracted and delivered from the field in accordance with normal procedures.

The Model Contract sets forth a rather complex formula for the allocation of crude oil produced from a field during each calendar year of the production period. Under this formula, 17.5 per cent of annual gross production is paid in kind to the Chinese authorities as a royalty and as payment of the Consolidated Industrial and Commercial Tax.[52] Next, 50 per cent of annual gross production is deemed 'cost recovery oil'. Finally, the remaining 32.5 per cent is designated as 'profit oil'.

Under the Model Contract, 'cost recovery oil' is first used to compensate the CNOOC and the foreign contractor for operating costs actually paid by them during the calendar year. Payment is made in kind after operating costs have been converted into an amount of crude oil in accordance with a pricing formula that is based on 'the prevailing price in arm's length transactions of similar quality crude oil on the main world markets'.

The remainder of the 'cost recovery oil', after payment of operating costs, is deemed by the contract as 'investment recovery oil'. This amount is first used as payment to the foreign contractor for the reimbursement of exploration costs which have been incurred during the exploration period but which have not yet been fully recovered. Unrecovered exploration expenses in any calendar year are carried forward to succeeding years for recovery from the 'investment recovery oil' portion of annual gross production for such years. In the year during which exploration costs are recovered in full, the remainder of the 'investment recovery oil' for that year may be used as payment to the CNOOC and the foreign contractor for the recovery of development costs incurred but not yet fully recovered by them, together with 'deemed interest' on the amount of such costs calculated at the rate of 9 per cent. Payment to the parties is made in proportion to their respective participating interests in the oil fields from which production is being allocated. Payment is made in kind, in accordance with the same price conversion formula that is used for payment of operating costs. Like unrecovered exploration costs, unrecovered development costs and 'deemed interest' thereon may be carried forward to succeeding calendar years until fully recovered. In the event that full recovery is not achieved by the date of expiration of a field's production period, unrecovered costs are deemed to be losses, borne by the parties in proportion to their respective participating interests. If full recovery is achieved prior to the date of expiration, however, any remaining 'investment recovery oil' is to be regarded as 'profit oil'.

The amount of annual gross production of crude oil designated as 'profit oil' is divided by the Model Contract into two components: 'share oil' and 'allocable profit oil'. The 'share oil' portion is paid only to the Chinese party and the remainder is divided between the CNOOC and the foreign contractor in proportion to their respective participating interests in the development costs attributable to the field. In general this will entail a split of 51 per cent for the CNOOC and 49 per cent for the foreign contractor, unless the CNOOC has opted not to participate in development or to participate at a lower percentage level, in which case the allocation will be in accordance with the parties' actual participation.

How much of the annual 'profit oil' is to be divided between the parties as 'allocable profit oil' is determined by multiplying the total amount of the 'profit oil' attributable to a field by an 'x factor' proposed by the foreign contractor as part of the competitive bidding process prior to the signing of the contract. The 'x factor' for each oil field is applied on an incremental basis in accordance with eight tiers of annual gross production ranging from 500,000 metric tons or less in tier one to over 10,000,000 metric tons in tier eight. Based on this system, then, the amount of 'allocable profit oil' is calculated by applying the tier one 'x factor' to the amount of 'profit oil' equal to or less than 500,000 metric tons; the tier two 'x factor' to the amount from 500,000 to 1,000,000 metric tons; the tier three 'x factor' to the amount from 1,000,000 to 2,000,000 metric tons; and so on.

The Model Contract, echoing the Petroleum Regulations, provides that the foreign contractor is free to export from China and sell on foreign markets all crude oil received by it, whether as 'cost recovery oil', 'investment recovery oil', or 'allocable profit oil'. However, the contract also stipulates that the CNOOC reserves the right to regulate any such export sales by prohibiting transport by the foreign contractor to 'destinations which infringe on the political interest of the People's Republic of China'.

B. Management Organization

The Model Contract calls for the creation of a management organization by which the Chinese party is able to exercise firm control over both long-range budgeting and planning as well as everyday operations. The heart of this management organization is the Joint Management Committee (JMC). Both the CNOOC and the foreign contractor have the right to appoint three to five representatives to the JMC. The chairman of the JMC is the chief representative designated by the CNOOC and the vice-chairman is the chief representative designated by the foreign party. JMC meetings must be held at least four times a year, once each calendar quarter, but they may also be called at any time by either party.

The JMC's duties and powers are far-reaching. They include reviewing the work programme and budget proposed by the foreign party; determining the commerciality of each oil and/or gas field; reviewing the overall development programme and budget for each oil and/or gas field; approving certain expensive items for procurement and excess budget expenditures; determining 'the date of commencement of commercial operations' with respect to oil and/or gas fields; and other matters. The contract requires that decisions of the JMC be made 'unanimously through consultation'. In the event that unanimity cannot be achieved, the contract merely states that 'the Parties may convene another meeting and shall attempt to find another solution based on the principle of mutual benefit.'

The Model Contract calls for the creation of several other organizations under the JMC. One of these is the secretariat, which serves as the administrative arm of the JMC. The others are the various 'expert groups' created to deal with specialized issues that arise in the course of the petroleum operations. Like the JMC itself, both the secretariat and the expert groups are composed of equal numbers of Chinese and foreign appointees.

Apart from the creation of a formal organizational structure consisting of the JMC, the secretariat and the expert advisory groups, the Model Contract provides for Chinese penetration and control over management of the petroleum operations in other ways as well. The contract states, for example, that the CNOOC shall have the right to assign its own 'professional representatives' to 'all sectors' of the foreign contractor's administration, thereby creating a Chinese counterpart organization. Such Chinese personnel are to have access to all activities and information, and the foreign staff are required to discuss their work with them on a regular basis. All costs and expenses relating to such Chinese staff members are to be paid initially by the foreign contractor but may be recovered out of commercial production together with other expenses.

C. The Obligations of the Parties

The Model Contract imposes a number of specific obligations on the foreign operator and the CNOOC. In essence these require that the operator bear primary responsibility for carrying out the exploration, development and production operations within the contract area and that the CNOOC provide assistance to the operator in the performance of these tasks.

In the course of carrying out the petroleum operations the operator is required to apply 'appropriate and advanced technology and business managerial experience' so that the operations are performed 'reasonably and economically according to sound international practice'; to prepare and, after approval, implement the budget and work programme; to assume responsibility for procurement and subcontracting; to prepare and, after approval, implement a personnel training programme; to develop an insurance programme; to issue cash call notices for financial contributions by the parties; to maintain accounting records in accordance with the accounting procedures stipulated in the contract; to make all preparations for JMC meetings; to inform all subcontractors and expatriate employees of their duty to abide by Chinese laws; and to report all aspects of its work to the JMC. In addition, the operator is required to grant the CNOOC access to all information, samples and reports pertaining to the petroleum operations.

The CNOOC's main obligation under the Model Contract is to assist the contractor so as to enable him to carry out 'expeditiously and efficiently' the petroleum operations. Specifically, the CNOOC is to assist the contractor to: obtain necessary licences and approvals to open accounts with the Bank of China; go through foreign exchange, visa and customs formalities; obtain office space, supplies, transportation and communications facilities; obtain permits to export samples and data for analysis or processing; and contact relevant Chinese departments as required. Expenses incurred by the CNOOC in providing such assistance are to be paid by the contractor.

The Model Contract contemplates that production operations within the contract areas are to be gradually assumed by the CNOOC. Prior to the recovery of development costs, transfer to the CNOOC of production operations is permissible only with the agreement of the contractor. However, the contract grants to the CNOOC a unilateral right to take over production operations 'at any time' after development costs have been recovered by the foreign contractor in full. In such an event, most of the obligations imposed by the Model Contract on the operator are transferred to the CNOOC.

D. Procurement

The Model Contract specifically provides that the procurement activities of the contractor shall be subject to the preference provisions set forth in the Petroleum Regulations. Therefore, the contractor is required to give priority to Chinese suppliers of goods and services provided they are 'competitive' with those provided by foreign suppliers. In order to monitor the contractor's procurement activities and ensure that the preference provisions are being respected, the Model Contract provides that the CNOOC shall have the right to appoint its own representatives to work with the contractor's procurement staff. Such representatives shall inform the contractor of Chinese companies able to supply goods and services required for procurement and shall have the right to 'take part in' the bidding process, including the evaluation of bids and the award of contracts.

E. Personnel Training and Technology Transfer

In accordance with the Petroleum Regulations, the Model Contract requires that the contractor give priority to the employment of Chinese personnel in the petroleum operations and that it transfer technology and managerial experience to such personnel. The 'scope, approach and objective' of the contractor's programme for the training of Chinese personnel and technology transfer are to be determined by the parties during the negotiations and incorporated in an annex to the final contract prior to signing.

With respect to training, the Model Contract requires the contractor to develop a training programme proposal and submit the same to the JMC for approval prior to the commencement of each of the exploration, development and production periods. The programme is to include training for a wide range of Chinese personnel, including technical personnel, managers, economists and lawyers. The expenses of the programme are to be paid by the contractor but may be charged as exploration costs, development costs or operating costs, as the case may be. Upon the expiry of the training programme, the contractor is obliged to employ 'qualified' Chinese personnel. Candidates for positions are to be recommended by the CNOOC but may be tested by the contractor prior to employment.

F. Miscellaneous Provisions

In addition to the provisions described above, the Model Contract contains a number of miscellaneous articles worthy of note. For example, the contract reiterates language found in the Petroleum Regulations providing that the CNOOC shall be the owner of all data obtained in the course of the petroleum operations. Ownership of physical assets acquired with budgeted funds are to revert to the CNOOC after recovery in full by the contractor of the development costs. Assignment of the contractor's rights and obligations under the contract is permissible, provided that the CNOOC has consented to such assignment. By contrast, the foreign party's consent is not required if the CNOOC assigns its interest in the contract to a third party. In accordance with the Petroleum Regulations, the contract provides for 'consultations' between the parties as the primary dispute settlement medium. In the event that consultations fail, the dispute may be referred to arbitration in China or 'another arbitration party agreed' by the parties. Finally, the Model Contract provides that Chinese law shall be the governing law as regards matters relating to the validity, interpretation and implementation of the contract.

G. Problem Areas

When the Model Contract was issued, it was greeted with little enthusiasm by foreign oil companies. The consensus among potential bidders was that the terms proposed by China were tough and that substantive changes to the document would have to be negotiated before agreement could be reached.

One area of concern to foreign companies relates to the repatriation of profits. As noted previously, both the Petroleum Regulations and the Model Contract provide that foreign contractors will be permitted to repatriate crude oil received by them as either profit or cost recovery oil by selling it in the international market. However, the Petroleum Regulations also require that contractors establish accounts with the Bank of China and be subject to China's foreign exchange control laws. Many companies have been fearful that if earnings from their oil were forced to go through the Bank of China, the bank could through its control over exchange rates effectively restrict the earnings of foreign contractors and the amounts they are able to remit abroad in foreign exchange. In a letter addressed to foreign bidders dated 23 June 1982, the State General Administration for Exchange Control (SGAEC) informed companies that they would be permitted to deal freely with their oil profits abroad without remitting them to the Bank of China. However, the legal effect of such a letter is unclear and many foreign oil companies have remained concerned about how the implementation of China's foreign exchange laws will affect their business operations.[53]

Another source of concern to foreign oil companies is the CNOOC itself. Apart from the lack of clarity regarding the CNOOC's legal status referred to earlier, many companies are uncertain whether the CNOOC and the MOPI have sufficient clout to ensure that petroleum operations can be conducted efficiently.[54] Conflicting organizational claims among different ministries and between central and local authorities could hinder the CNOOC from providing contractors with the assistance — from obtaining visas for foreign personnel to securing export licences for crude oil — that is required under the Model Contract in order to operate in China.

Control is another area that has been the subject of intense negotiations. Many foreign companies have complained that the Model Contract permits the Chinese effectively to control day-to-day operations even during the exploration phase when the foreign party bears all risks. Moreover, it is generally felt that the JMC system is unwieldy and expensive and, in the event of dispute between the parties, could lead to a paralysis of operations. Therefore, many companies have sought in the negotiations to clarify and restrict the JMC's mandate and generally reduce the CNOOC's role in everyday operational decision-making.

Dissatisfaction has also been voiced with provisions relating to training and technology transfer. Many companies feel it is unfair that they are required to bear the huge expense that training Chinese personnel will entail but are not paid any royalties for the transfer of technology. Foreign companies have also been concerned that the scope of the training requirement is too broad. Under the Model Contract a wide range of technology and experience must be transferred to Chinese personnel. Some observers have interpreted this obligation to include all types of technology that belong to the foreign contractor and not simply those which are used in Chinese petroleum operations.[55] In attempting to deal with these problems in the negotiations, foreign oil companies have tried to reduce the scope and extent of the training and technology transfer obligations to acceptable limits.

A final problem area concerns the preference provisions found in the Model Contract. Oil companies have viewed the requirements that they give priority to the use of Chinese personnel, and pay them at international wage rates, as unfair in view of the fact that experience and performance levels are not on a par with expatriate petroleum professionals. Many foreign companies have also feared that the preference requirements for service and supply contractors will force them to accept outdated Chinese equipment and services of poor and unreliable quality, despite the literal wording of the Petroleum Regulations that the preference only applies where Chinese goods and services are 'competitive' in the world market.[56] These fears have been assuaged somewhat by the formation of a number of joint ventures between the CNOOC and other Chinese organizations and foreign supply and service companies.[57] As Chinese juridical persons, these joint ventures qualify as 'Chinese companies' for purposes of the preference provisions, and the technology and level of services that they provide are in many cases up to world standards. Despite this, many foreign contractors remain concerned about the degree of freedom they will enjoy in practice to employ service and supply subcontractors of their own choosing and fear that they may be forced to use Chinese-foreign joint ventures and other Chinese companies. These fears were heightened when the CNOOC issued, on 1 July 1983, the Circular Concerning the Contracting Out of Petroleum Operations in the Exploration Phase. This document requires operators to employ the services of Chinese companies and joint ventures in the fields of aviation, navigation and radio control; positioning; communications; and supply vessels and bases. Other provisions in the Circular attempt to strengthen the preference requirement for services outside these mandatory categories.

IV. Taxation of Offshore Oil Activities

Both the Petroleum Regulations and the Model Contract require that foreign companies engaged in oil and gas-related activities in China pay taxes in accordance with Chinese law. The principal tax laws affecting the activities of foreign companies in China are (1) the Income Tax Law of the People's Republic of China Concerning Foreign Enterprises (hereafter cited as the FEITL),[58] and (2) the Consolidated Industrial and Commercial Tax Regulations of the People's Republic of China (hereafter cited as the Consolidated Tax).[59]

A. The Foreign Enterprise Income Tax

The FEITL provides for an income tax of general application to the activities of foreign enterprises in China. The law states that income tax is to be levied on 'income derived from production, business and other sources by any foreign enterprise operating in the People's Republic of China.'[60] The broad scope of the law is confirmed by provisions contained in the implementing regulations for the FEITL (hereafter cited as the Implementing Regulations), issued by the Ministry of Finance.[61] These regulations provide that 'production' and 'business' are to be interpreted to include a wide range of profit-making activities, and 'income from other sources' is to include passive income such as dividends, rentals, royalties, interest and 'other income' as defined by the Ministry of Finance.[62]

The FEITL, together with the Implementing Regulations, establish what are in effect three separate tax regimes. The first is a progressive tax on net income, the second is a gross receipts tax on passive income and the third is what is commonly referred to as a tax on 'deemed profits'. In the following sections each of these tax regimes will be discussed in turn, focusing on their application in the context of offshore oil activities.

i. The Progressive Tax

The FEITL's progressive tax applies to enterprises that have 'establishments' in China. Under the Implementing Regulations, establishments are defined as 'organizations, places or business agents engaging in production or business operations which are established by foreign enterprises in China' and include 'management organizations, branch organizations, representative organizations and factories, places where natural resources are being exploited and places where construction installation, assembling, exploration and other projects are being undertaken.'[63] Given that foreign contractors are required by both the Petroleum Regulations and the Model Contract to set up establishments in China in order to carry out the petroleum operations, it is clear that they will be subject to the progressive tax.

Taxable income under the progressive tax is akin to the American notion of 'net income', that is annual gross income minus allowable deductions. The rates provided for in the law range from 20 to 40 per cent.[64] In addition, the FEITL provides for a local income tax of 10 per cent on the same taxable income amount.[65]

Under the FEITL's Implementing Regulations, foreign companies engaged in co-operative activities with Chinese enterprises for the exploitation of China's offshore oil resources are deemed to receive income 'at the time they receive their share of crude oil.'[66] The law requires that the amount of such income be computed on the basis of 'a price which is adjusted periodically according to the international market price of crude oil of similar quality.'[67] As noted earlier, however, under the Model Contract a different standard is stipulated for computing the price of crude oil received by foreign parties. This standard involves reference to 'the long-term contract sales price of similar quality crude oil in the main world markets'. In an internal document issued by the Ministry of Finance in response to a request from the MOPI for clarification of the discrepancy between the two pricing formulae, the Ministry of Finance has implied that the Model Contract's pricing mechanism will be acceptable for tax purposes.[68]

The FEITL and the Implementing Regulations permit taxpayers to deduct a number of kinds of expenses when computing taxable income. Among the most important costs to foreign oil companies are interest expenses incurred on loans borrowed by their contracting entities in China from banks or affiliated companies during the production and development phases. Under the Implementing Regulations such expenses may be deducted if the local tax authorities have determined that the underlying interest rate on the loan is 'reasonable' and that the loan is a 'normal loan'.[69] Although Chinese tax officials have not yet stated what tests will be used to determine whether a loan is 'normal', they have indicated that an interest rate will be deemed 'reasonable' if it is based on the London Interbank Offered Rate (LIBOR) for dollars, even where the loan itself is provided by an affiliate of the borrower.[70]

Another issue of concern to foreign oil companies is the deductibility of certain payments made by the China-based contracting entity to its head office. Although the law disallows a deduction for royalties paid to head offices,[71] 'administrative expenses' paid to the head office 'for services directly provided' by it may be deductible, provided such expenses are 'reasonable' and are supported by adequate documentation and a certified accountant's report and are approved by local tax authorities.[72] Interestingly, the Model Contract takes a different approach to the issue of head office expenses for accounting purposes.[73] Under the Model Contract's accounting procedure there is a limitation on the amount of head office overheads that may be charged to the joint interest account. During the exploration phase charges may not exceed a specific percentage of annual exploration costs; separate limitations are to be negotiated for the development and production phases. Although the issue remains unclear at present, it is likely that the tax authorities will take such limitations into account when determining whether the amount of head office expenses meets the 'reasonableness' test of the tax laws.

Generally speaking, the FEITL and the Implementing Regulations adhere to international tax practices with regard to the types of expenses that are disallowed as deductions.[74] However, the law's blanket provision that 'income tax payments and local tax payments' are not deductible expenses will cause problems for foreign contractors.[75] In normal practice, agreements with service subcontractors generally require that all payments be free of tax and that the contractor 'gross up' in the event that taxes are imposed. Whether such gross-up payments will be viewed as a part of the normal operating expenses of a contractor, and hence deductible, or as non-deductible tax payments, is a question that has yet to be resolved by Chinese tax officials.

The FEITL's Implementing Regulations provide that the 'entire investment' of a foreign oil company during the development phase may be capitalized using the oil or gas field as the reference unit, and that allocable expenses may be recovered from commercial production of crude oil from the field.[76] In addition, 'reasonable exploration expenses' incurred within a contract area may also be capitalized and may be recovered from any oil or gas field within the contract area once it begins commercial production.[77] Fixed assets acquired by foreign oil companies for petroleum operations during and after the development phase may be depreciated on a composite basis over a period of not less than six years, and losses may be carried forward and amortized for a period not exceeding five years.[78]

A number of foreign oil companies either presently are or will likely be involved in both onshore and offshore operations, or, if exclusively offshore, may operate in a number of different areas. Hence, an issue of concern to such companies is the extent to which their various operations may be consolidated for tax purposes. The Chinese have indicated that consolidation of onshore and offshore petroleum operations will not be permitted, although consolidation will be allowed to a limited extent for income and losses within different contract areas offshore.

According to Chinese tax officials, as a general rule a foreign oil company must calculate and pay income tax separately with respect to each contract area. If a company holds, and operates in, two contract areas, it may consolidate income and losses only if it 'terminates' operations in one of the areas.[79] Termination in this context is interpreted to mean abandonment of the area, not simply a temporary stoppage of operations. Therefore, only if a contract area is abandoned may losses and unamortized exploration and other expenses incurred in connection with such an area be applied or amortized against income derived from another contract area.

Finally, mention should be made of certain unresolved issues relating to accounting. Under the FEITL, foreign enterprises are required to submit their 'financial and accounting system' to local tax authorities 'for reference', but if the taxpayer's accounting methods conflict with provisions contained in the tax law the latter will govern.[80] Chinese tax authorities have yet to issue a clear statement regarding the acceptability for tax purposes of the accounting procedures mandated by the Model Contract. The issue is, of course, in no way an academic one for important differences exist between the FEITL and the Model Contract with respect to accounting. One basic difference between the two relates to the accounting method employed by the taxpayer, the Model Contract requiring use of a 'cash basis' method and the FEITL Implementing Regulations calling for accounting on the 'accrual basis'.[81] Although the issue has been resolved by some foreign oil companies in the course of negotiations with the Chinese, reliance on the clear language of the tax law and the Model Contract would seem to require oil companies to maintain separate accounting systems for petroleum operations and tax payment.

ii. The Withholding Tax on Passive Income

The second tax regime created by the FEITL is set forth in Article 11 of the law. This article provides that foreign enterprises that do not have establishments in China shall pay income tax at a flat rate on income obtained from dividends, interest, royalties, rentals and other income 'the source of which is from China'. This tax on passive income is imposed on the gross amount of income received and is collected by means of withholding. For oil companies, the most important areas of application of the withholding tax will be interest payments made to foreign banks and affiliates as well as payments of royalties, rentals and other fees to either affiliated companies or unrelated third parties.

Under the FEITL, the withholding tax on passive income is imposed at a rate of 20 per cent.[82] However, rules issued in 1983 effectively amend the FEITL to provide for a reduction of the withholding tax to 10 per cent or a total exemption from the tax in certain circumstances. These rules are contained in the Provisional Regulations of the Ministry of Finance of the People's Republic of China Regarding the Reduction and Exemption of Income Tax Relating to Interest Earned by Foreign Businesses From China (hereafter cited as the Provisional Interest Tax Regulations) and the Provisional Regulations of the Ministry of Finance of the People's Republic of China Regarding the Reduction and Exemption of Income Tax on Fees for the Use of Proprietary Technology (hereafter cited as the Provisional Technology Tax Regulations).[83]

The Provisional Interest Tax Regulations were issued by the Ministry of Finance on 7 January 1983 but came into force as of 1 January 1983. The new rules do not apply to contracts that have been signed and became effective prior to 1 January 1983. However, the parties to such contracts may take advantage of the concessions provided under the new rules during any extension period of such contracts. Basically, the rules provide for three different kinds of tax concessions which are of interest to foreign oil companies: (1) a provisional reduction of the income tax on interest; (2) specific exemptions from the interest income tax; and (3) favourable treatment for income tax on leasing fees.

The interest income tax reduction provided for in the Provisional Interest Tax Regulations amounts to 50 per cent, which effectively reduces the withholding tax on interest income of foreign enterprises from 20 to 10 per cent. The tax reduction applies to interest earned by foreign companies from 'loans, advances and deferred payments' made pursuant to credit or trade contracts with Chinese companies signed between 1983 and 1985. In order to qualify for the reduction, the relevant contract need only be signed during this period; all payments of interest made during the period of the contract's effectiveness, not simply the period between 1 January 1983 and 1 January 1985, will be subject to the reduced withholding rate.

The second type of tax concession provided under the new regulations consists of five specific exemptions from income tax on interest. The exemptions provided for under the Provisional Interest Tax Regulations are in addition to those already specified in the FEITL and the Implementing Regulations.[84] The first exemption applies to interest income from loans made by foreign banks to China's state banks at an international interbank loan rate. According to Bank of China officials, this rate is intended to refer to a LIBOR, SIBOR or HIBOR rate plus a slight margin. The same officials indicated that in general the guidelines that will be applied in determining 'permissible' margins are as follows: not more than 0.25 per cent for loans with a maturity of less than 12 months; not more than 0.375 per cent for loans with a maturity of less than 24 months; and not more than 0.5 per cent for loans with a maturity of more than 24 months.[85] The second exemption applies to interest income from loans made by foreign banks to the China National Offshore Oil Corporation, provided the interest rate of such loans does not exceed the interest guidelines described above. The third exemption applies to interest on deferred payments by Chinese companies to foreign suppliers for the import of technology, equipment and commodities financed by means of seller's credits provided by the foreign supplier's state bank. In order to qualify for the exemption, the rate of interest charged under the seller's credit cannot exceed the rate that would be charged under buyer's credits that would be provided to the Chinese side. The fourth exemption applies to interest earned by foreign banks and individuals on deposits placed with China's state banks, provided the rate of interest paid on such deposits is *lower* than the interest rate on deposits in the home country of such foreign banks or individuals. Finally, the fifth exemption applies to compensation trade arrangements.

The Provisional Interest Tax Regulations also provide favourable treatment for income derived from 'leasing fees' which are defined as fees paid by Chinese companies for 'equipment and related articles' supplied by foreign leasing companies by means of the 'lease-trade method'. The regulations conceive of such fees as consisting of three elements: (1) equipment cost; (2) the basic interest charge or cost of funds; and (3) the lessor's 'special' or service charge. Under the regulations, taxable income derived from leasing fees consists only of elements (2) and (3), that is the portion of the total amount of fees remaining after deducting the equipment cost. Tax is levied on this amount at a reduced rate of 10 per cent. However, if the contract and other supporting documentation can demonstrate that the rate of interest ('cost of funds' element) meets the criteria for exemption from tax applicable to seller's credits (described above), then the basic interest element may be exempt from tax and the amount remaining after the deduction of such interest (that is the 'spread' or 'service charge' element) shall be subject to the reduced 10 per cent rate as described above. It should be noted that, as in the case of the interest income tax reduction, the reduced tax rate for income from leasing fees is to be applied on a 'provisional' basis and benefits only those contracts signed within the two-year period between 1 January 1983 and 1 January 1985. Moreover, it should be emphasized that the new provisions apply only to lease-sale type arrangements, not rentals, the latter presumably still being subject to the 20 per cent withholding tax rate.

The major concessions provided under the Provisional Technology Tax Regulations[86] are tax reductions and exemptions with respect to income earned by foreign companies which take the form of 'fees for the use of proprietary technology'. Under Article 11 of the FEITL, foreign companies that do not have establishments in China are subject to a 20 per cent withholding tax on 'royalties' earned from China. The FEITL Regulations define 'royalties' in Article 27 to include 'income from all types of patents, *proprietary technology*, copyrights, etc. provided for use in China' (my italics). It is unclear why the Provisional Technology Tax Regulations appear to have abandoned the concept of 'royalties' in favour of 'proprietary technology' fees particularly as the latter term has never been defined. Nonetheless, a close reading of the Provisional Technology Tax Regulations leads one to believe that 'proprietary technology' is an inclusive term, encompassing the items included in the FEITL Regulations' definition of 'royalties', as well as such items as fees for blueprints and documentation, technical service fees and personnel training fees paid in connection with the transfer of technology. These latter items are specifically included within the scope of 'proprietary technology' pursuant to the Provisional Technology Tax Regulations.

The Provisional Technology Tax Regulations provide for a reduced withholding tax of 10 per cent on income from fees earned by foreign enterprises without China establishments in connection with the transfer of certain types of 'proprietary technology' to Chinese entities. The types of technology fees eligible for the tax reduction include those received in connection with the transfer of technology for 'China's key construction projects in exploring for energy ...'. Moreover, a total tax exemption may be granted where 'the technology is advanced and the terms are preferential'. According to discussions with MOPI officials, the determination of whether a particular type of technology is 'advanced' will be based not on some abstract notion of international standards but on whether the particular technology, when compared with other available technology, best meets the needs of the Chinese party that will use it.[87] As to what criteria will be used to determine whether the terms of transfer are 'preferential', Chinese tax officials cited three factors: (1) the cost of the technology in comparison with that of the foreign supplier's competitors; (2) whether the foreign supplier/seller will provide free training to Chinese personnel for the initial use and operation period; and (3) whether the Chinese user will be permitted to continue to use the technology without the payment of an additional fee upon the expiration of the contract period.[88]

In addition to the tax exemptions available for fees earned in respect of technology which falls within the five categories mentioned above and which meets the two requirements of being 'advanced' and transferred on 'preferential terms', the Provisional Technology Tax Regulations also provide for exemptions from the FEITL's withholding tax for certain types of income which do not arise in connection with technology transfer arrangements. The types of income eligible for the exemption are set forth in detail in the regulations and include certain kinds of service fees, technology instruction fees, technical assistance fees and technical service fees.[89]

iii. The Deemed Profits Tax

Companies that provide services to the offshore oil industry on a subcontract basis are by nature extremely mobile and often work in different parts of a country for varying periods of time. As a result, calculating the taxable income of such subcontractors can be a difficult task. In order to facilitate tax administration, the Ministry of Finance has determined that foreign offshore oil subcontractors operating in China may pay tax in accordance with Article 24 of the FEITL's Implementing Regulations. This article provides that the profit rate and taxable income of foreign subcontractors shall be determined 'on the basis of the total income from the project', such deemed profit then being taxed in accordance with the FEITL's progressive rates. At present the deemed profit margin fixed by the Ministry of Finance for offshore oil subcontractors is 10 per cent.[90]

Whether the FEITL's deemed profit system will be mandatory for all subcontractors, or merely an option, has apparently not yet been resolved. Although the Tax Commissioner stated publicly in June 1982 that the system will be applied to all subcontractors,[91] in more recent, private discussions Ministry of Finance officials have indicated otherwise. According to these officials, where subcontractors have an establishment in China and are able to calculate net income and support their calculations with adequate documentation they may apply to the local tax authorities to pay tax on a net income basis.

B. The Consolidated Tax

Unlike the FEITL, which applies only to foreign enterprises, the Consolidated Tax is applicable to both foreign and Chinese entities engaged in business transactions in China. The structure of the tax differs significantly from the FEITL tax regimes.[92] Basically, the Consolidated Tax is a type of cascading turnover tax assessed on gross receipts arising from the sale or transfer of products. Tax liability arises at each level in the distribution system and the tax is paid by the seller or transferor. In the case of crude oil, for example, the tax would be paid by the producer upon production, by the refiner upon transfer of the refined product, and by the retailer upon sale to the consumer. The tax is also applicable to purchases of foreign goods, or imports. In such cases, however, the tax is imposed on the importer instead of the foreign exporter.

Items taxable under the Consolidated Tax are divided into two general categories: (1) industrial and agricultural products, and (2) commercial retailing, communications and transportation and other service trades. Although the first category includes a list of more than 100 specific products, there is no list for petroleum or petroleum products as such. Rather, these items are classified under the last heading of 'other industrial products' and are taxed at a rate of 5 per cent. The second category contains a list for 'service trades' which includes most offshore oil subcontractor services. The tax rate applicable to such activities is 3 per cent.

C. Tax Administration

On 12 June 1982 the Ministry of Finance submitted to the State Council a Petition Regarding the Establishment of the Offshore Oil Taxation Bureau (hereafter cited as the Petition).[93] The Petition took note of the fact that business activities in connection with offshore oil development were marked by 'special characteristics' and that financial, accounting and other matters were 'comparatively complex.' Therefore, the Petition proposed the establishment of a specialized bureau to handle tax matters related to offshore oil exploration and development activities, and went on to detail the scope of duties of such a bureau, issues relating to organization and staffing, and other matters. Subsequently, on 7 August 1982 the State Council issued Document No.(82) *Guo Han* 159 (hereafter cited as the Document No.159), addressed to the Ministry of Finance and the people's governments of Beijing, Shanghai and Tianjin municipalities and Guangdong Province.[94] Document No.159 sanctioned the creation of the Offshore Oil Taxation Bureau (OOTB) and specifically approved the proposals set forth in the Petition regarding the OOTB's functions, organizational structure and staffing. The OOTB officially commenced its work in December 1982.

The Petition sets forth five main functions for the OOTB. These include:

(1) 'to thoroughly implement the state's tax laws', and specifically to exercise 'unified management' and 'unified taxation and collection' with respect to the various taxes imposed in connection with offshore oil activities;
(2) 'to research and draft supplementary regulations regarding offshore oil taxation, and to provide explanations of the relevant tax laws';
(3) 'to gather information, to grasp in a timely manner an understanding of the situation regarding the source of taxes and to make decisions regarding the calculation of taxes on the prices of oil and natural gas';
(4) 'to grasp the economic activities of taxpaying enterprises and individuals, and to solve problems regarding the handling of financial and accounting matters of taxable enterprises in a reasonable manner and in the light of international practice'; and
(5) 'to formulate measures regarding tax management, to strengthen the investigation and supervision of tax payment, to verify tax amounts and to organize in a timely manner work regarding the deposit of tax proceeds in the treasury'.

Despite the OOTB's involvement in offshore oil activities it is not related directly to the MOPI. Rather, in terms of China's bureaucratic organization, it falls under the supervision of the General Taxation Bureau of the Ministry of Finance (GTB). In fact, ties between the GTB and the OOTB are extremely close and most OOTB employees have been seconded from the GTB.

The headquarters of the OOTB are based in Beijing. In addition, branches have been established in those areas where the China National Offshore Oil Corporation has established local operations, namely Shanghai, Tianjin, Guangzhou and Zhanjiang. Although it is difficult to establish the exact number of OOTB employees nationwide, commonly accepted estimates range from 35 to 45.

According to the OOTB, in general OOTB policies are formulated by the GTB in consultation with the MOPI. Branch organizations are 'guided by' the OOTB headquarters and are not permitted to act independently with respect to policy formulation and implementation. Finally, according to the OOTB, decisions of the OOTB with respect to tax matters relating to offshore oil activities take precedence over those of municipal and provincial tax bureaux.

Whether the OOTB's vision of clear lines and demarcations of authority will be realized in practice is difficult to judge at this early stage. Indications do exist, however, that the OOTB's branches, which are staffed largely by provincial tax bureau officials, have not always bowed to the wishes of the Beijing headquarters on matters of policy. Moreover, different branches have at times taken different approaches to specific tax issues with, generally speaking, Zhanjiang taking an aggressive approach and the Tianjin authorities being somewhat more lenient.

V. Other Regulatory Developments

The Petroleum Regulations, the Model Contract and China's tax laws provide the foundation of the regulatory regime for offshore oil exploration and development activity. In addition, a number of other laws have a bearing on the operations of foreign companies involved in offshore work. The most important of these include rules governing the registration of foreign contractors and subcontractors, special rules providing preferential customs treatment to companies engaged in offshore oil activities, and legislation concerning environmental protection.

A. Registration Regulations

Both the Petroleum Regulations and the Model Contract require foreign contractors and subcontractors to register with the appropriate Chinese authorities, but neither document specifies the procedures by which registration is to be accomplished. This task is fulfilled by a notice (the Registration Notice) issued on 12 March 1983 by the State Administration for Industry and Commerce (SAIC) which came into effect on 1 April of the same year.[95]

According to the Registration Notice, all foreign contractors must apply to the headquarters of the SAIC in Beijing. The application process consists of filling in a form and submitting copies of the contract and the related Chinese approvals. Companies must also submit certificates pertaining to their legal status and creditworthiness and information relating to service and supply subcontractors that they employ. Once the application has been approved by the SAIC the foreign contractor will be issued with a 'business licence'.

The Registration Notice provides that fees for the registration of foreign contractors are to be assessed in accordance with the standards set forth in regulations made public by the SAIC in March 1982 for the payment of registration fees by joint ventures.[96] Based on these standards, oil companies with a registered capital of RMB 10 million will pay a fee equal to the sum of 0.1 per cent of the registered capital for the portion under RMB 10 million and 0.05 per cent for the portion above that amount. According to the SAIC, no company will be required to pay registration fees in excess of RMB 30,000 even if computation in accordance with the above formula yields a higher amount. Moreover, the rules themselves provide for 'preferential treatment' for oil companies during the exploration period when, under the terms of the Model Contract, they are to bear all financial risks. Registration fees during this period are fixed 'provisionally' at RMB 2,000. Once commercial production begins, however, the foreign contractor must re-register with the SAIC and pay fees based on the standards described above.

The Registration Notice also requires all foreign subcontractors operating in China to register. The registration requirement applies not only to 'first-tier' subcontractors — that is, service and supply companies in a direct contractual relationship with the foreign contractor. It also applies to companies that have entered into contracts with subcontractors — that is, 'second-tier' and 'third-tier' subcontractors.[97] According to the SAIC, these companies are also subject to the registration requirement so long as their services are performed within China.

The Registration Notice provides that subcontractors ordinarily should go through registration procedures at local bureaux of the SAIC authorized to handle registration. However, if a subcontractor performs operations in several provinces or localities simultaneously, it should register with the central bureau in Beijing. According to the SAIC, the registration requirement applies no matter how long it takes a subcontractor to perform its job and registration must be effective before work can begin.[98] In addition, the registration will be valid only for a specific subcontract.[99] Therefore, if a subcontractor is engaged by foreign contractor X to perform a job with a duration of two weeks, it must register before commencing work, de-register upon expiration of the subcontract, then re-register before beginning a new job with foreign contractor Y.

When applying for registration, the subcontractor must fill out an application form, signed by its chairman or president, describing the scope of operations and the subcontract project and attaching data related to China-based employees during the contract period. In addition, applicants must submit copies of the subcontract together with a certificate of the local branch of the CNOOC at the place where the subcontract is being performed. Once approved, the applicant will be issued with a registration certificate.

Fees for subcontractor registration are calculated in accordance with a modified version of the system used for the calculation of fees for foreign contractors.[100] Under this system, 20 per cent of the total subcontract amount is to be taken as the base amount for fee collection purposes. If this base amount is the equivalent of RMB 10 million or less, then the registration fee will be charged at the rate of 0.1 per cent. If the base amount is more than RMB 10 million, the fee will be calculated at 0.1 per cent of the base amount for the portion under RMB 10 million and at 0.05 per cent for the portion above that amount. The maximum fee for each single registration is RMB 30,000.

B. Customs Provisions

To facilitate the conduct of the petroleum operations, the Chinese Customs authorities have issued a number of regulations and directives providing favourable customs treatment for foreign companies and their employees engaged in oil exploration and development activities. For example, under a 1981 regulation foreign contractors and subcontractors may import machinery, equipment and other 'production materials' without having first to obtain a formal import licence, provided such items have been confirmed by the Customs authorities as being 'within the scope of the project' concerned.[101] The same regulation also stipulates that 'foreign engineers and technical personnel' who come to China to engage in petroleum operations shall be granted the same favourable customs treatment as is extended to 'foreign experts' invited to work in China by the Chinese government. In general, the application of this standard will provide duty-free treatment for many personal items of daily use imported by or for such personnel.

Another important set of provisions are contained in regulations promulgated jointly by the General Administration of Customs and the Ministry of Finance on 1 April 1982.[102] These regulations provide for an exemption from export duties and the Consolidated Industrial and Commercial Tax for crude oil received by foreign contractors in accordance with the provisions set forth in the Model Contract and exported from China. In addition, the regulations exempt a wide range of imported items from import duties and the Consolidated Industrial and Commercial Tax, subject to 'verification and approval' by the

Customs authorities. These include machinery, equipment, spare parts and other materials used directly in exploration and development activities as well as parts, components and materials necessary for the manufacture of machinery and equipment in China for petroleum operations. In addition, the regulations exempt from taxation all 'machinery and other construction equipment' that is imported temporarily and guaranteed to be exported by the foreign party upon completion of the project for which it is being used.

C. Environmental Protection

The Petroleum Regulations and the Model Contract both contain provisions requiring that the petroleum operations be carried out in compliance with China's environmental protection laws. The most important of these laws as regards offshore oil activity is the Marine Environmental Protection Law of the People's Republic of China (MEPL).[103]

The MEPL is by its terms applicable to all enterprises and individuals engaged in exploration, development, production and other activities within the maritime areas under the jurisdiction of China. In addition to imposing a general obligation on such enterprises and individuals to 'protect the marine environment' and to 'supervise and report' activities harmful to the environment, the MEPL contains in Chapter III a number of specific provisions relating to the prevention of pollution and damage to the maritime environment due to oil exploration and development activities offshore. Among the most important of these provisions is one that requires enterprises engaged in offshore oil activities to prepare a written environmental impact study, including a report on measures to be taken to prevent pollution.[104] The report and study are to be submitted to the environmental protection department of the State Council for 'examination and ratification' which presumably must be obtained before operations can commence. The MEPL also requires that 'appropriate anti-pollutant facilities and equipment' be installed on vessels, platforms and other structures operating offshore when exploring for or developing oilfields, and that 'technical measures' be taken to prevent blow-outs and oil leakage.[105] In the event of a well blow-out, contractors are required to inform the relevant authorities, take interim measures to control the damage and submit to an investigation by the maritime authorities. Enterprises and individuals found to be in violation of the law may be fined, ordered to pay compensation, or may be subject to criminal sanctions in serious cases.[106]

VI. Conclusion

China's programme to develop its offshore oil resources in co-operation with foreign enterprises has necessitated the establishment of a regulatory regime that is in many ways distinct from that which has been put into place for other types of foreign investment activity. As the pace of activity offshore quickens a number of new laws are likely to be enacted.[107] Among those reportedly now being considered are special labour management rules for personnel engaged in offshore work, safety regulations, and rules designed to implement the preference provisions of the Petroleum Regulations. Like the Model Contract and China's existing petroleum-related legislation, it can be expected that any new laws will reflect China's determination to exercise firm control over oil exploration and development activities and to enhance her own capabilities to conduct future offshore oil operations independent of, but on a technological par with, the major foreign oil companies.

Notes

1. C. Brown, 'Tough Terms for Offshore Oil', *China Business Review*, July–August 1982, p.34. See also S. Carlson, *China's Oil: Problems and Prospects* (Washington, DC, Georgetown University Center for Strategic and International Studies, 1979); Chen Senqiang, 'General Survey of Geological Structure and Prospects in Oil and Gas of the Continental Shelf in the Northern Part of the South China Sea', *Economic Reporter*, December 1981; and B. Knoll, 'China Oil: Looking Forward to a Better Future Offshore', in *China Energy Report* (Hong Kong, Energy Committee of the American Chamber of Commerce, 1982).

2. According to official Chinese statistics, onshore production reached a peak of 106.15 million tons in 1979 and has declined steadily since then. Production in 1980 was 105.95 million tons, decreasing to 101.22 million tons in 1981. See B. Knoll, p.40, note 1 above. For background on China's offshore oil development policy see K. Fountain, 'The Development of China's Offshore Oil', in N. Ludlow (ed.), *China's Petroleum Organization and Manpower* (Washington, DC, The National Council for U.S.–China Trade, 1980), pp. 63–76.

3. See 'China's Crude Oil Export Prospects, 1979–90', in Ludlow, p. 77, note 2 above.

4. For a discussion of China's geophysical survey programme and a legal analysis of the survey agreements, see M. Hoyt, 'Current Developments in Petroleum Exploration Offshore China', in *Energy Law 1979* (London, International Bar Association, 1979), topic I, paper 3.

5. For a synopsis of the terms of these contracts, see D. Jones, 'China's Offshore Oil Development: Japanese and French Contracts Offer Some Insights, Some Confusion', *China Business Review*, July–August 1980, pp.51–6.

6. See *The New York Times*, 20 September 1982, p.34.

7. The Petroleum Regulations were adopted by the State Council on 12 January 1982 and promulgated on 30 January 1982. An English-language translation of the law appears in F. Chu, M. Moser and O. Nee (eds.), *Commercial, Business and Trade Laws: People's Republic of China* (Dobbs Ferry, Oceana Publications, Inc., 1982), Pt. 10.

8. *China Daily*, 17 March 1982, p.1.

9. See F. Ching, 'China Opens Offshore Oil Bidding', *Asian Wall Street Journal*, 17 February 1982, p.1; 'Bidding for Offshore Petroleum Exploitation', *Peking Review*, 22 February 1982, p.5; and 'China's Offshore Oil Now Up for International Bidding', *Economic Reporter*, March 1982, pp.8–10.

10. The invitations, or more accurately 'letters of notification of bidding', were issued in two groups at an interval of one month. Invitations issued on 16 February 1982 covered the Pearl River basin area and blocks in the northern part of the South Yellow Sea. Invitations sent on 16 March 1982 covered areas in the southern parts of the South Yellow Sea and the Beibu Gulf basin as well as the western part of the Ying Ge Sea basin. See 'New Offshore Oil Corporation's Chief on Oil Exploitation Bidding in Interview with CEN', *China Economic News,* 22 February 1982, p.2.

11. The deadlines for expressions of interest were 30 March 1982, for companies that had been issued invitations on 16 February, and 25 April 1982, for companies that had been invited to bid in the second phase on 16 March. Companies that expressed an interest in bidding were required to pay a fee of between US$10,000–40,000, depending on the location and number of blocks. Upon payment of the fee, companies were issued with a 'Certificate of Qualified Bidder' by the CNOOC which certified that the holder was entitled to participate in the competitive bidding.

12. See '40 Foreign Oil Companies Receive Documents on Offshore Oil Bidding', *China Economic News*, 17 May 1982, p.3.

13. According to the CNOOC, 25 of the 33 companies submitting bids organized themselves into 13 separate bidding groups and 8 companies bid independently. See '33 Foreign Oil Companies Forward Bid Proposals on Joint Exploitation of China's Offshore Petroleum Resources', *China Economic News,* 23 August 1982, p.12.

The 33 foreign oil companies are: Agip (Overseas) Ltd. (Italy); Amoco Orient Petroleum Company (USA); Ampol Exploration Ltd. (Australia); Berkeley Exploration & Production Ltd. (UK); BP Petroleum Development Ltd. (UK); Broken Hill Proprietary, Ltd. (Australia); Chevron Orient Inc. (USA); Cities Service Orient Petroleum Co. (USA); Cluff Oil Ltd. (UK); CSR Ltd. (Australia); Esso Exploration Inc. (USA); Getty Oil International (Orient) Inc. (USA); Hispanica de Petroleos S.A. (Spain); Hunt Sedco International (USA); Indemitsu Oil Development Co. Ltd. (Japan); Japan National Oil Corporation (Japan); Mobil Oil Corporation (USA); Natomas (Far East) Ltd. (USA); Occidental Eastern Inc. (USA); Pecten Orient Co. (USA); Pennzoil Far East Ltd. (USA); Petrobras International S.A. (Brazil); Petro Canada Exploration Inc. (Canada); Phillips Petroleum International Corporation Asia (USA); Ranger Oil (Canada) Ltd. (Canada); Shell Exploration China Ltd. (UK); Société Nationale Elf-Aquitaine (France); Sun Orient Exploration Company (USA); Texaco Orient Petroleum Co. (USA); Texas Eastern Corporation (USA); Total Exploration (France); Tricentrol North Sea Ltd. (UK); and Union Oil Orient Ltd. (USA).

14. The consortium consists of five members with the following shareholdings: BP (45 per cent), Broken Hill Proprietary Ltd. (20 per cent), Petrobras International S.A. (15 per cent), Ranger Oil (Canada) Ltd. (10 per cent), and Petro-Canada Exploration Inc. (10 per cent). BP will act as operator for the consortium which will explore and develop five contract blocks totalling 14,086 square kilometres in the Pearl River mouth basin and the South Yellow Sea. For further discussion, see

'CNOOC Says More Offshore Oil Contracts to Follow BP's Lead, Drilling in 2nd Half of 1983', *China Economic News*, 23 May 1983, p.1.

15. For a complete list of offshore exploration and development contracts signed between the CNOOC and foreign oil companies in 1979–83, see 'Offshore China Contracts 1979–1983', *Petroleum News*, January 1984, p.16.

16. Petroleum Regulations, Art. 1, note 7 above.

17. Petroleum Regulations, Art. 3, note 7 above.

18. Petroleum Regulations, Art. 3, note 7 above.

19. Petroleum Regulations, Art. 3, note 7 above.

20. Petroleum Regulations, Art. 2, note 7 above.

21. Petroleum Regulations, Art. 2, note 7 above.

22. Conflicting jurisdictional claims over offshore resources exist among China, Japan and Korea in the north, and between China and Vietnam in the south. Among others, Chinese-Vietnamese claims in the Beibu Gulf and Yingge Sea area south-west of Hainan Island could have a direct impact on petroleum operations in the South China Sea, particularly in light of the deterioration of relations between the two countries since the late 1970s. For general background on territorial disputes and their effect on offshore oil activities in Asia, see S. Harrison, *China, Oil and Asia: Conflict Ahead?* (New York, Columbia University Press, 1978).

23. Petroleum Regulations, Art. 4, note 7 above.

24. Petroleum Regulations, Art. 5, note 7 above.

25. Petroleum Regulations, Arts. 5 and 6, note 7 above.

26. Petroleum Regulations, Art. 6, note 7 above.

27. Among other issues, the question of the CNOOC's authority to conclude binding contracts was reportedly a major stumbling block in the ARCO negotiations.

28. Petroleum Regulations, Art. 5, note 7 above.

29. For an organization chart of the CNOOC's headquarters, see *China Market Intelligence*, March 1983.

30. See 'Four Regional Oil Corporations Set Up', *China Economic News*, 30 May 1983, p.8; and 'China Sets Up Four Regional Oil Corporations', *Xinhua News Bulletin*, 17 May 1983, p.21.

31. See 'How the Zhanjiang Oil Support Base Is Shaping Up', *Business China*, 16 June 1982, pp.82–3; and 'Offshore Service Opportunities Tied to JVs with CNOOC', *Business China*, 13 April 1983, pp.49–51.

32. See K. Woodward and R. Goodwin, 'Supplying Offshore Services', *China Business Review*, March–April 1982, pp.17–18.

33. For a description of the CNOJSC and its subsidiaries, see 'China Nanhai Oil Service Corporation', *China Market Intelligence*, May 1983, p.5; and D. Denny, 'The Quest for Control', *China Business Review*, May–June 1983, pp.28–9.

34. Petroleum Regulations, Art. 17, note 7 above.

35. Petroleum Regulations, Art. 7, note 7 above.

36. Petroleum Regulations, Art. 7, note 7 above.

37. Petroleum Regulations, Art. 7, note 7 above.

38. Petroleum Regulations, Art. 7, note 7 above.

39. Petroleum Regulations, Art. 8, note 7 above.

40. Petroleum Regulations, Arts. 14 and 15, note 7 above.

41. Petroleum Regulations, Art. 12, note 7 above.

42. Petroleum Regulations, Art. 12, note 7 above.

43. Petroleum Regulations, Art. 13, note 7 above.

44. Petroleum Regulations, Art. 29(5), note 7 above.
45. Petroleum Regulations, Arts. 16 and 29(8), note 7 above.
46. Petroleum Regulations, Art. 22, note 7 above.
47. Petroleum Regulations, Art. 23, note 7 above.
48. Petroleum Regulations, Art. 26, note 7 above.
49. Petroleum Regulations, Art. 24, note 7 above.
50. The Norwegian state-owned oil company, Statoil, has played an important role in the formulation of China's offshore oil policies in general and in the drafting of the Model Contract in particular. See 'The Norwegian Experience and China's Oil Policy', *Petroleum News*, November 1980, pp.39–43.
51. Brown, p.35, note 1 above.
52. See note 59 below and accompanying text.
53. For recent developments, see p. 257 in this volume.
54. See Denny, pp.25–31, note 33 above; and S. Green, 'The Offshore Oil Race', *China Business Review*, July–August 1981, p.57.
55. Brown, p.37, note 1 above.
56. For an overview of Chinese capabilities in the oil supply and service sector, see Woodward and Goodwin, pp.8–19, note 32 above.
57. The first such joint venture, China-GECO Geophysical Company, was established in September 1982 by the CNOOC and the Geophysical Company of Norway A/S (GECO). Since then similar ventures have been established in a wide variety of fields. See 'Offshore Service Opportunities Tied to JVs With CNOOC', *Business China*, 13 April 1983, pp.49–51.
58. Adopted at the Fourth Session of the Fifth National People's Congress on 13 December 1981, and promulgated by an order of Ye Jianming, Chairman of the Standing Committee of the National People's Congress, on 13 December 1981. The law came into effect on 1 January 1982. An English-language translation of the FEITL appears in Chu, Moser and Nee, Pt. 13, note 7 above.
59. Adopted in draft form by the Standing Committee of the National People's Congress on 11 September 1958 and promulgated on 13 September 1958. The law came into effect on the date of promulgation. An English-language translation of the Consolidated Tax regulations appears in Chu, Moser and Nee, Pt. 13, note 7 above.
60. FEITL, Art. 1, note 58 above.
61. Detailed Rules and Regulations for the Implementation of the Income Tax Law of the People's Republic of China Concerning Foreign Enterprises. The Implementing Regulations were approved by the State Council on 17 February 1982 and promulgated by the Ministry of Finance on 21 February 1982, but are retroactively effective to the effective date of the FEITL, 1 January 1982. For an English-language translation of the Implementing Regulations, see Chu, Moser and Nee, Pt. 13, note 7 above.
62. Implementing Regulations, Art. 4, note 61 above.
63. Implementing Regulations, Art. 2, note 61 above.
64. FEITL, Art. 3, note 58 above.
65. FEITL, Art. 3, note 58 above.
66. Implementing Regulations, Art. 26, note 61 above.
67. Implementing Regulations, Art. 26, note 61 above.
68. Document of the Ministry of Finance No.(82) *Cai Shui* 98, dated 20 March 1982, reads in part as follows: '[i]f the crude oil pricing method determined in a co-operative exploitation petroleum contract, after being examined by the relevant tax

authorities, conforms to the principle of pricing method stipulated in Article 26 of the Tax Regulations, the corresponding pricing method in the petroleum contract will be allowed to compute the amount of income.'

69. Article 12 of the Implementing Regulations provides as follows: 'Interest paid by a foreign enterprise on loans may be listed as an expenditure at a reasonable interest rate when backed by documents certifying such loans and interest payments and after having been examined and verified by the local tax authorities as being normal loans.'

70. These remarks were made by Mr Liu Zhicheng, Commissioner of Taxation, in a speech entitled 'Salient Features of the New Foreign Enterprises Income Tax Law' delivered at a seminar arranged by Price Waterhouse and held in Houston, Texas, on 30 June 1982.

71. Implementing Regulations, Art. 10(9), note 61 above.

72. Implementing Regulations, Art. 11, note 61 above.

73. See O. Nee, 'Taxation of the Offshore Oil and Gas Industry in China' (unpublished paper on file with the author).

74. Implementing Regulations, Art. 10, note 61 above.

75. Implementing Regulations, Art. 20(4), note 61 above.

76. Implementing Regulations, Art. 16, note 61 above.

77. Document of the Ministry of Finance No.(82) *Cai Shui* 98, dated 20 March 1982, para. 5.

78. Implementing Regulations, Art. 18, note 61 above; and FEITL, Art. 6, note 58 above.

79. Document of the Ministry of Finance No.(82) *Cai Shui* 98, dated 20 March 1982, para. 4.

80. FEITL, Art. 9, note 58 above.

81. Implementing Regulations, Art. 38, note 61 above.

82. FEITL, Art. 11, note 58 above.

83. English-language translations of the Provisional Interest Tax Regulations and the Provisional Technology Tax Regulations are on file with the author.

84. See FEITL, Art. 11, note 58 above; and Implementing Regulations, Arts. 29, 30 and 31, note 61 above.

85. Personal communication to the author by Bank of China officials.

86. The Provisional Technology Tax Regulations were issued on 13 December 1982 and came into effect on 1 January 1983. Contracts signed prior to the effective date of the regulations are not eligible for the tax benefits provided therein, although the parties to such contracts may take advantage of the tax concessions during any extension period of the contract.

87. Personal communication to the author by MOPI officials.

88. Personal communication to the author by Ministry of Finance officials.

89. It is important to note that the exemption for these non-technology transfer fees relates only to the FEITL's withholding tax. Paragraph 11 of the Provisional Technology Tax Regulations makes it clear that in the event that the income recipient maintains an establishment in China, tax will be levied on income earned by such an establishment in accordance with the progressive tax set forth in Articles 3 and 4 of the FEITL. Therefore, if a foreign enterprise were deemed by Chinese tax authorities to have established a 'site' in China in connection with technology instruction or personnel training, instruction fees and training fees paid to the foreign enterprise

would be taxable on an establishment, as opposed to a withholding, basis, thus denying the taxpayer the benefits of the exemption provisions.

90. See Ministry of Finance Document No.(82) *Cai Shui* 103, dated 6 April 1982 (original Chinese version on file with the author). At the end of 1983, Chinese tax officials were known to be considering an increase in the deemed profit rate to 15 or possibly even 20 per cent.

91. The remarks were made by Commissioner Liu in the speech referred to in note 70 above.

92. For a detailed discussion of the Consolidated Tax, see Chapter 2 of this volume.

93. A copy of the original Chinese version of the Petition is on file with the author.

94. A copy of Document No.159 is on file with the author.

95. State Administration for Industry and Commerce Notice Concerning the Registration of Foreign Companies that Come to China to Engage in Co-operative Development and Contract Projects (original Chinese-language version on file with the author). For a discussion of the Registration Regulations, see M. Moser, 'China's Registration Rules for Foreign Oil Companies', *Asian Wall Street Journal*, 21 June 1983.

96. See Provisional Regulations on Standards for the Payment of Registration Fees by Joint Ventures Using Chinese and Foreign Investment, Art. 1. An English-language translation of the law appears in Chu, Moser and Nee, Pt.9, note 7 above.

97. This interpretation is contained in a document entitled Explanations Regarding the Notice Concerning the Registration of Foreign Companies that Come to China to Engage in Co-operative Development and Contract Projects, issued by the State Administration for Industry and Commerce on 4 May 1983 (hereafter cited as the Explanations). A copy of the original Chinese version of the Explanations is on file with the author.

98. Explanations, para. 3, note 97 above.

99. Explanations, para. 3, note 97 above.

100. Explanations, para. 3, note 97 above.

101. See Provisional Measures of the Customs Authorities Concerning the Supervision and Control of Imports and Exports Required in the Co-operative Exploration and Development of Offshore Petroleum and Baggage and Articles of Engineers and Technical Personnel, issued by the General Administration of Customs of the People's Republic of China on 1 October 1981. An English-language translation of the law appears in Chu, Moser and Nee, Pt. 10, note 7 above.

102. Regulations of the General Administration of Customs and the Ministry of Finance Concerning the Levy and Exemption of Customs Duties and the Consolidated Industrial and Commercial Tax on Imports and Exports for Chinese and Foreign Exploitation of Offshore Petroleum, approved by the State Council on 28 February 1982. For an English-language translation of these regulations see Chu, Moser and Nee, Pt. 10, note 7 above.

103. The MEPL was adopted at the Twenty-fourth Session of the Standing Committee of the Fifth National People's Congress on 23 August 1982.

In addition to specific provisions contained in the MEPL, a number of other Chinese environmental protection laws will be of relevance to the operations of foreign contractors and subcontractors. For a general discussion of these laws, see J. Gresser, 'The Principle of Multiple Use in Chinese Environmental Law', in J. Cohen (ed.), *Legal Aspects of Doing Business in China 1983* (New York, Practising Law Institute, 1983).

104. MEPL, Art. 10, note 103 above.

105. MEPL, Art. 17, note 103 above.
106. MEPL, Arts. 41, 42, 43 and 44, note 103 above.
107. Many of the new laws and regulations are likely to be issued by the MOPI pursuant to Article 30 of the Petroleum Regulations. This article grants the Ministry the power to formulate 'detailed rules and regulations' for the implementation of the Petroleum Regulations.

7. Contract Law in the People's Republic of China

PRESTON M. TORBERT

I. Introduction

MANY aspects of China's economic policy since 1978 have attracted the attention of foreign firms interested in doing business with China, particularly the new laws and regulations concerning joint ventures, representative offices, taxation and other features of foreign economic contacts. However, the new legislation has affected mainly the most innovative and complex transactions. Whilst these transactions are significant in that they define the limits of what can be done, they are not generally representative of the experience of most foreign firms in China, for whom the negotiation of their contract is the most important contact with China's new economic policy. Since China has not yet promulgated a Civil Code or a contract law applicable to foreign transactions, foreign firms must look primarily to their contract as the source of their legal rights. Of the contracts that foreign firms sign with Chinese entities those for purchase or sale are the most common, followed by licensing and compensation trade agreements. Joint venture agreements are rarer, although they are perhaps the most interesting by nature of their complexity. The discussion that follows deals with recent contract practice as a whole, but refers to these different types of contracts where appropriate.

II. Standard-form Contracts

Any discussion of contracts in China must begin with the standard forms used by Chinese entities in their economic relations with foreign parties.[1] In a socialist economy, all transactions with foreign parties are conducted by state entities and therefore involve the interests of the state. In order to insure that the state's interests are adequately protected, standard-form contracts are widely used. Now, as in the past, foreign parties doing business with socialist countries, including China, must generally sign the standard-form contracts for the most common transactions.

China's practice regarding standard-form contracts, however, has been influenced by changes in the country's policy towards foreign economic relations in the last ten years. Especially since 1979, under the leadership of Deng Xiaoping, China's economic policy has emphasized foreign trade and investment as a major element in China's modernization.[2] As a result, China's contacts with foreign companies have increased considerably. The monopoly of the Ministry of Foreign Trade on almost all economic contacts with foreign countries has been broken, and other ministries, provinces and municipalities now have the authority to deal with foreign companies directly.[3] This decentralization of authority has had contradictory effects. In some respects it has resulted in more flexibility in the use of standard forms, since local enterprises may be more willing to negotiate amendments to them. However, it has also reinforced the use of standard forms. Due to the lack of lawyers or legal experts in China and the larger numbers of entities now involved in foreign trade, the use of standard-form contracts is an important means of protecting China's interests while allowing enterprises to engage in foreign economic relations without legal assistance.

Nevertheless, neither the standard forms used for the most common and simple transactions nor those used for licensing agreements appear to have changed substantially in the last decade, although it is now easier to negotiate changes in certain provisions, such as arbitration. Nor are major changes in the agreements expected in the future, although such a possibility exists. The Economic Contracts Law (which applies to transactions between domestic Chinese enterprises) refers in Article 55 to the preparation of a Foreign Economic Contracts Law that will apply to contracts between Chinese and foreign entities and indicates that the new law will be based on the principles of the Economic Contracts Law and 'international practice'.[4] It may be that the Foreign Economic Contracts Law, which is purported to be in the drafting stage, will require changes in some of China's standard-form contracts to conform with 'international practice' as interpreted in the future law.

At present, as in the past, the foreigner engaging in business activities in China will invariably meet the standard-form contracts in simple purchase and sales negotiations. In more complex transactions Chinese entities, sometimes those who have only recently engaged in foreign trade, tend to be more flexible. They may have a standard form, but they do not always insist that it be used for the particular transaction if the foreigner has his own standard form. This is most often the case in licensing, joint venture, co-operation and compensation trade contracts. For example, the China National Offshore Oil Corporation has reportedly drafted a 'model' contract for offshore petroleum equity joint ventures which it offers to potential foreign joint venture partners. In many cases, the new entities engaging in foreign trade seem to have received copies of standard-form contracts from the foreign trade corporations, such as the China National Technical Import Corporation (Techimport). However, in licensing, joint venture, compensation trade and co-operation contracts the idiosyncrasies of any particular project are often sufficient to assure that any standard form will not be appropriate. In such cases, which are increasing with the growing complexity of China's economic contracts with foreign countries, an appropriate contract is generally drawn up by the two parties together, often based on a draft prepared by the foreign party.

III. The Authority of the Contracting Party

The decentralization of foreign trade in China has raised significant questions for foreign companies signing contracts with Chinese enterprises. As noted above, in 1979 China abolished the monopoly of the Ministry of Foreign Trade over China's economic contacts with foreign countries. The eight Chinese foreign trade corporations[5] are no longer the only parties in China authorized to sign contracts with foreign companies. Now entities at the provincial, municipal or even lower levels may conduct trade directly with a foreign firm.[6] In addition, many of the national ministries have their own foreign trade companies.[7] This decentralization has achieved its purpose of expediting foreign trade by giving the initiative to local or ministerial entities, but it has also presented foreigners with the problems of choosing among competing Chinese organizations and determining which Chinese entity is the most appropriate one to do business with. An important part of the answer to such problems is whether the relevant Chinese entities are in fact authorized to engage in the contemplated transaction.

Previously, foreign firms could rely on tradition and experience in signing contracts with the eight foreign trade corporations, all of whom were well-known to foreign parties. Therefore, even though these foreign trade corporations might refuse to supply any documentation that indicated their authority to engage in foreign trade, such as their articles of incorporation, foreign companies entered into contracts with them without great concern. But foreign firms have not been so willing to accept at face value the assertions of lawful authority by new corporations. On the one hand, this is due in part to an outdated belief that in China there can only be one organization authorized to deal with a particular product. If a foreign trade corporation still exists to handle a particular product, then some foreigners may suspect that any other organization claiming to deal with that product is not authorized to do so. On the other hand, this is due in part also to the fact that one Chinese organization may assert that it is the only organization in China authorized to deal with a particular product, thus contributing to the foreigner's misunderstanding.

The matter of the authority of the contracting party raises three principal issues. Firstly, there is the question of whether the Chinese entity which has invited the foreign party to China for contract negotiations has the authority to discuss and sign contracts with foreign entities generally. Such authority would normally be contained in the articles of incorporation or in the business licence of the Chinese entity issued by the State Administration of Industry and Commerce. Some Chinese entities, such as the China International Trust and Investment Corporation and the Shanghai Investment and Trust Corporation, have published their articles of incorporation and are happy to provide them to foreign parties. Most Chinese organizations, however, will not provide such documentation when requested. A recent example of this reportedly occurred in May 1982 when a major foreign oil company negotiated with the China National Offshore Oil Corporation (CNOOC) for concessions in the offshore petroleum sector. It seems that the company insisted that the CNOOC present some documentation other than the Regulations of the People's Republic of China on the Exploitation of Offshore Petroleum Resources in Co-operation with Foreign Enterprises to prove that it had the authority to sign the contract. The company reportedly suggested that the Ministry of Petroleum co-sign the contract. The CNOOC, however, refused and the contract was apparently signed by the CNOOC and the company without any additional written evidence by the CNOOC of its authority.

The second issue concerns the necessity in many cases of submitting a signed contract to a higher authority for approval. Here again the foreign party will probably not be able to obtain any document that clearly states the necessity of such approval and that lists the organizations which are entitled to grant it. This question is generally handled by making the contract's effectiveness subject to the approval of the appropriate 'Chinese governmental authorities'. Because the approval process is considered an 'internal' matter by the Chinese entity, it is generally unwilling to reveal which authorities must approve the contract and what standards will be applied in the approval process. Thus, the specific Chinese organizations which will approve or disapprove the contract are not mentioned. It is common knowledge among foreign companies doing business with China that contracts must often be approved by higher authorities, generally the particular ministry and, in certain cases, the Ministry of Foreign Economic Relations and Trade. The foreign party, however, has no way of knowing whether a contract has in fact been referred to the 'authorities' and whether it has been approved or disapproved. Presumably, any Chinese organization which misleads a foreign party as to the approval would be subject to disciplinary measures. But since the foreign party often either does not know which organization will approve or disapprove the contract, or does not wish to risk its goodwill with the Chinese party by approaching the approving organization directly, it is impossible to verify that the organization has approved or disapproved the contract. There is no known case of a Chinese organization misleading a foreigner. However, if a Chinese organization were to do so, it is doubtful whether the foreign party would ever come to hear of it. Thus, the secrecy practised by Chinese organizations with regard to the approval process may cause foreign companies uneasiness, given their complete reliance on the Chinese party to the contract for news of the granting or refusal by higher authorities of approval. Some foreigners find consolation in the fact that the Chinese party often stands, in practice, in much the same position regarding the foreign company's representations as to export control approvals in the foreign country.

The third issue concerns the presence in licensing agreements of an intermediary. In such cases, the entity signing the contract is an intermediary which negotiates the commercial terms on behalf of the Chinese factory that will implement the technology. The intermediary signing the contract generally does not present any evidence of its authority to act on behalf of the factory, nor any evidence of its authority, if necessary, to make the factory observe the terms of the contract, particularly those relating to non-disclosure of the technology to third parties. In most cases, the foreign party is not able to obtain documentary evidence indicating the relationship between the signatory of the contract and the factory and must rely on experience and appearances to reassure himself on these points.

It is interesting to note that the question of the authority of the contracting party is one which has occurred not only to foreign entities, but also to the Chinese themselves. In some cases Chinese enterprises have requested from foreign entities written evidence, such as a power of attorney, of the foreigners' authority to conduct negotiations and sign contracts. Foreign contract negotiators should be aware, therefore, that if they do press the Chinese side for evidence of their authority, the Chinese may well request similar documentation from them.

In addition to requesting documentation from the Chinese party itself, foreign companies that desire confirmation of the authority of the Chinese party to conduct negotiations and execute foreign economic contracts may contact trade organizations such as the National Council for US–China Trade in the United States, or the China Council for the Promotion of International Trade or China International Economic Consultants, Inc., in China for assistance. Another possible alternative, the notarization of contracts, has not been used in the past but may be appropriate in some cases.[8]

IV. The Enforcement of Contracts

A. The Enforceable Contract

Under American law a contract is generally considered to be an agreement between two parties which is enforceable in accordance with its terms.[9] Usually 'enforceable' is understood to mean enforcement directly through the courts. However, contracts signed with Chinese entities are not generally enforceable directly through the courts, but through arbitration. Furthermore, disputes are generally resolved by conciliation or friendly discussions even prior to arbitration. In fact, there appear to be few, if any, non-maritime cases in which a Chinese party to a foreign trade contract has gone to arbitration outside China.

Given China's preference for conciliation and arbitration, it is interesting to note that the Law on Civil Procedure of the People's Republic of China (hereafter cited as the Civil Procedure Law), promulgated for trial implementation on 8 March 1982, has a special chapter dealing with litigation involving foreigners. It allows foreigners to bring contractual disputes to the economic chambers of the people's courts. Article 192 of the law provides that disputes involving foreign economic relations, trade, transportation and maritime matters can be referred to the Chinese courts. Access to the courts in handling such disputes is limited to cases where there is no written agreement between the parties providing for arbitration in China.[10] Since Chinese entities almost uniformly insist on an arbitration clause in the contracts they sign with foreign companies, resort to the economic courts by foreigners for enforcement of their contracts may not be generally available. Unless China's desire for arbitration clauses declines, the bringing of contractual disputes to court in China will continue to be rare.

It should be noted, however, that although an arbitration clause does generally preclude resort to court, this may not be so in all cases. In some jurisdictions preliminary protective measures, such as an injunction, are available through the courts to parties who have entered into an agreement containing an arbitration clause. For example, under Swedish law either party may apply to a court for protective measures before or during the arbitration proceedings.[11] It is unclear whether this would be permissible in China under the Civil Procedure Law if the relevant arbitration clause called for arbitration in Stockholm under the Stockholm Chamber of Commerce rules.[12] Some jurisdictions also allow a party to an arbitration agreement to sue in court to have an arbitration award overturned in certain circumstances.[13] In China, Article 193 of the law provides that such judicial review is not available for arbitration awards rendered by Chinese arbitration organizations.

While China's policy in favour of arbitration rather than litigation has been consistent over the last decade, this does not mean that the provisions in Chinese foreign trade contracts for arbitration have remained the same. Previously, Chinese standard-form contracts provided for, and Chinese foreign trade entities generally insisted upon, arbitration in Beijing under the rules of the Foreign Trade Arbitration Commission of the China Council for the Promotion of International Trade.[14] Over the last decade Chinese entities have agreed to alter the standard-form contracts to provide for arbitration in third countries under the rules of foreign arbitral bodies. A review of arbitration clauses in a number of contracts between American and Chinese parties indicates that Sweden and Switzerland are popular sites for arbitration, that the local arbitration rules of the site of arbitration are often used, and that Chinese entities sometimes request the use of the Arbitration Rules of the United Nations Commission on International Trade Law (UNCITRAL). Chinese entities generally oppose a provision for arbitration under the

International Chamber of Commerce rules because Taiwan is a member of the Chamber, while China is not.

B. The Retroactive Effect of Laws and Regulations

Another question related to the enforceability of a contract executed in China is the retroactive effect of subsequent laws and regulations. Since China is in the process of promulgating many new laws and regulations relating to foreign trade and investment, it is natural that subsequent legislation may affect the provisions of the contract. The general policy in this regard has been very favourable towards foreign parties. In the area of tax in particular, China has allowed preferential tax treatment provided for in contracts to continue to apply even in the face of subsequent legislation. One example of this is the Schindler joint venture contract (between the China Construction Machinery Corporation, Schindler Holding AG and Jardine Schindler (Far East) Holdings, S.A.), dated 19 March 1980, that provided for a maximum tax rate of 31.5 per cent,[15] while the Joint Venture Income Tax Law promulgated subsequently provided for a maximum rate of 33 per cent.[16] Another example is a Ministry of Finance ruling of 29 March 1982 entitled 'Concerning the Problem of Taxation of Technology Transfer, Loans, Leasing and Other Contracts Approved Before the Promulgation of the Tax Law', which grants 'grandfather clause' status to clauses in agreements providing for the Chinese entity to take care of all taxes in China related to the transaction.[17] More recently, in Shanghai, the Minhang and Hongqiao Development Corporation has not yet promulgated regulations concerning the Minhang Hongqiao Development Zone, but has assured investors that the terms of any agreement which they negotiate will be given effect regardless of the provisions of subsequent regulations.[18]

The retroactive effect of subsequent laws has not proved to be a substantial problem in China, although each time new laws and regulations are promulgated which apply to transactions for which contracts have already been signed the question arises of how the new provisions will apply to existing contracts.

C. The Effect of Acts of Government on Contracts

Another aspect of enforceability is the impact of acts of government on executed contracts. On the Chinese side this question most often occurs in the context of changes in economic policy and the state economic plan. The first question is whether a contract that violates the state economic plan at the time of signing would be enforceable. With regard to transactions between Chinese domestic enterprises, the Economic Contracts Law provides in Article 7(a) that such a contract would be null and void. Presumably, the same rule would apply to contracts involving foreign parties. Execution of a contract that would violate the state plan, however, is more a hypothetical than a practical problem. What is more likely is that an executed contract may be affected by a subsequent change in the state economic policy or plan. Examples are the contracts for the Baoshan Iron and Steel Complex and the international trade centre in Beijing which are discussed below. In contracts between Chinese enterprises, the Economic Contracts Law provides that in such cases the contract may be amended or terminated, but such alteration or termination must be reported for prior approval to the relevant business department handing down the plan. It is interesting to note that the law does not treat a revision or cancellation of the state plan as a case of *force majeure*. *Force majeure* is a separate ground permitting the amendment or termination of a contract.

It seems safe to assume that the future Foreign Economic Contracts Law will probably contain provisions excusing failure to perform due to certain causes. Whether these will include provisions for a contract that violates laws, regulations or public policy, or changes in the state economic plan, is not yet clear. In foreign economic contracts Chinese organizations have generally not allowed acts of government, whether those of the foreign country or of China, to be regarded as instances of *force majeure* for the purposes of excusing contractual performance, even though prior to the promulgation of the Economic Contracts Law alterations in the state plan were considered for domestic purposes as incidents of *force majeure* excusing Chinese enterprises from fulfilling contractual obligations.[19] In addition, in at least one case the Chinese have reportedly not allowed foreign bidders to make their contractual obligations subject to the granting of an export licence by the United States government. Accordingly, some American companies which were successful bidders suffered the risk of paying substantial sums under performance bonds that they were required to post if they were subsequently unable to obtain United States export licences for products to be supplied to China.

Perhaps the best-known example of the difficulties caused by a change in the state plan is the Baoshan Iron and Steel Complex. This steel complex near Shanghai, originally designed as a state-of-the-art plant modelled on Nippon Steel's Oita complex, was part of China's ambitious development plans unveiled in 1978. The economic readjustment instituted shortly thereafter, however, caused changes in the state economic plan and criticism of the scale and cost of new construction projects, including the Baoshan iron and steel plant. In contrast to the earlier Baoshan contracts, in this case the contracts had come into force.[20] They did not contain any cancellation or penalty clauses. The Chinese entered into negotiations with the suppliers, primarily Japanese and German firms, and eventually agreed to pay substantial amounts for compensation to them for their losses.[21] Another example of changes in the state plan was the cancellation of a US$250-million foreign trade centre in Beijing in 1980. After an agreement had been signed and the foreign parties had incurred some preliminary costs, the project was cancelled due to a conflict of views between Chinese entities as to the practicality of the project. Again, the Chinese agreed to pay compensation to the foreign parties involved.

While foreign companies dealing with China should be aware of the potential problems of changes in the state economic plan affecting their contracts in China, Chinese entities are also aware of the danger of action by foreign governments affecting contracts that they sign with foreign companies. The United States government has, for example, imposed restrictions on the export of certain scarce materials, such as ferrous scrap in 1973,[22] and has at times revoked export licences for exports to Communist countries, as in 1982 for exports to the Soviet Union of equipment related to a natural gas pipeline.[23]

The growing stability in China's economic planning and the recent loosening of restrictions on American export licensing procedures[24] may resolve some of the problems relating to the influence of subsequent government acts on contracts between Chinese and foreign parties. Whether China's policy on how such government acts should be treated for executed contracts will change is unclear. This policy has not changed significantly in the last ten years, and it is open to question whether it will change in the future under the Foreign Economic Contracts Law. Until China's policy does change, foreign firms will try to protect themselves by negotiating larger down payments or inserting cancellation and penalty clauses in their contracts with the Chinese.

V. The Interpretation of Contracts

The interpretation of contracts signed between foreign and Chinese enterprises is governed in large part by three factors: the Chinese view of contracts, the choice of governing law, and the choice of governing language. Lawyers are often familiar with the latter two factors, but not with the first.

Chinese parties have strongly held views about contracts which influence their interpretation of them. These beliefs are not so much legal concepts as commercial ones, and are familiar to foreign visitors who have conducted negotiations in China. The terms which Chinese parties often use in their contract discussions, such as 'long-term relationship', 'friendship', and 'equality and mutual benefit', reflect these beliefs. As these phrases indicate, the view of the Chinese is that contracts are not one-off transactions. They reflect the long-term, friendly relationship between the parties. This relationship is a beneficial one to both parties and one of essential equality between the parties. Thus, any disputes about a contract must be put into the perspective of the parties' desire for a long-term business relationship. The Chinese parties are willing, therefore, to make short-term concessions in the interests of long-term benefits. They expect the foreigner to do the same. For example, if a shipment of Chinese products does not conform with the terms of the agreement, and the foreign purchaser requests damages, the Chinese party will try to negotiate a settlement by which discounts or 'friendly' prices will be offered on future orders.

In some cases the Chinese emphasis on a long-term, friendly relationship can lead them to overestimate the commitment of the foreign party. In such cases a Chinese party to a contract, particularly one involving the import of technology, will look to the foreign supplier as the authoritative source for all information on the technology, including its implementation in China. The Chinese entity, thinking in terms of 'friendship' and a 'long-term relationship', may assume that under the contract the foreign party will do everything necessary to make the transfer of technology successful, regardless of the particular language in the contract. The foreign party is sometimes viewed, therefore, almost as a guarantor of the entire transaction by the Chinese. This is a point which foreign suppliers should be aware of and which they must handle with the greatest delicacy.

More familiar to lawyers are the problems of choice of law and choice of language. The standard-form contracts which Chinese enterprises use have in the past not included any choice of law clause or any other language in the contract allowing a third party to determine what law should be used to govern the contract.

This is still generally the practice, although governing law clauses are now beginning to appear in some contracts, such as ones prepared by Techimport. Also, Article 15 of the new Implementing Act for Joint Ventures provides that the joint venture document, the articles of incorporation, and so on, must be governed by Chinese law. The absence of a governing law provision in the standard-form contract does not mean that the Chinese will allow the insertion of foreign law. On the contrary, the foreigner who demands a clause calling for foreign law as the governing law of the contract will probably be met with a demand by the Chinese party for the use of Chinese law. As a result, most contracts negotiated with China do not provide for any governing law. Where the contracts negotiated with Chinese entities have generally provided for the resolution of disputes in the last resort by arbitration in China, the application of Chinese law to govern the contract is probably inevitable. Now that Chinese contracts signed with foreign entities often contain arbitration clauses calling for arbitration in third countries, the lack of a governing law clause adds uncertainty to the interpretation of the contract.

If a contract without a choice of law clause were referred to arbitration in a third country, it seems likely that the arbitrators would apply the choice of law rules of the jurisdiction where the arbitration was being held. The result of such an application of the choice of law rules could differ according to the site of the arbitration. In Sweden, for example, the choice of law rules applied would be similar to the British 'closest connection' test.[25] Since, in many cases, the contracts are negotiated, signed and largely performed in China, it seems that Chinese law would be applied to interpret the contract by application of the 'closest connection' choice of law rule. In fact, it has been suggested that the Chinese desire for negotiation and signature of the contract in China is related to this fact. However, an increasing number of Chinese entities are now conducting contract negotiations and even signing contracts abroad. In such cases, the results under the choice of law rules turn on the particular facts of each situation.

In a few exceptional cases foreign parties have been able to have foreign law inserted in the contract as the governing law. The most notable example of this is in the lease contract between a foreign firm and the Civil Aeronautics Administration of China (CAAC) for a Boeing 747 SP. In that contract the CAAC reportedly agreed not only to the application of New York law to govern the contract, but also agreed to submit to the jurisdiction of the courts in New York for the purposes of service of process, thus allowing resort to court, rather than arbitration, in the case of a dispute. In a few other cases the application of foreign law has been allowed, principally the law of the third country where arbitration proceedings are to be held. One question which arises in such cases is whether the foreign party should be content with a simple reference to the application of the law of the jurisdiction, or whether it should insist that the substantive, rather than procedural or choice of law, rules of the jurisdiction be applied. Under the legal concept of *renvoi* the mere reference to the law of the jurisdiction without further clarification could result in the application merely of the choice of law rules of the jurisdiction which, as noted above in the case of Sweden, could result in the application of Chinese substantive law to interpret the contract.

The choice of language question is one which often does not arise until the very end of contract negotiations. In most cases where the Chinese have prepared a standard-form contract for the basis of the negotiation, they are willing to accept the English version of the contract, on which the negotiations are based, as the only binding version. In such cases, there is no problem with regard to the governing language of the contract since the Chinese will sign the English version and will not insist that the Chinese translation be signed by the foreigner. In some cases, such as the standard-form sales or purchase contracts, there are interlinear Chinese translations of the contract. The use of the English language as the sole governing language of the contract is, in fact, one of the advantages of using the Chinese standard forms.

If the foreigner is fortunate enough to convince the Chinese side that the foreigner's draft contract be used as the basis of negotiations, then the choice of language question is posed. In such cases, the Chinese will negotiate from the contract prepared by the foreigner but will almost always insist that a clause be inserted at the end of the contract indicating that both the English and the Chinese versions of the contract be equally valid and binding. Unfortunately, this problem often arises at the very end of negotiations when the foreign party is not prepared to have the two versions compared for accuracy. In many cases, the foreign party has no choice but to concede and sign both versions. But substantial discrepancies between the two versions can occur and may relate to important aspects of the foreign party's obligations, such as guarantees. The reasons for such inaccuracies are twofold. Firstly, the

Chinese translators are often extremely busy when preparing the Chinese version of the contract and are unable to translate as carefully as they would like. Secondly, the translators and the negotiators may be unfamiliar with legal or commercial concepts used in international transactions for in some cases no standardized translations for such terms exist in Chinese. Examples are the concept of 'need to know' in regard to the disclosure of proprietary technology and the 'per diem' payments made to a licensor for the value of technical services. From a technical point of view, the foreign party might have an advantage in arbitration relating to a discrepancy in the language of the contract in a third country where English, but not Chinese, was widely spoken. Presumably, the arbitrators would give preference to the English version if they were able to read it and not the Chinese version. Still, to avoid disputes regarding the obligations in the contract, it would be best for foreign parties to verify the Chinese version of the contract, if necessary, during the negotiations.

VI. Conclusion

In its economic relations with foreign companies China has experienced both continuity and change in contract practice. In the most common purchase and sales contracts, China continues to use, and foreign parties continue to sign, without significant amendments standard-form contracts prepared by the Chinese party. In the more interesting and complex licensing, compensation trade and joint venture contracts, however, there is evidence of greater flexibility and creativity. This has been true in the past and will continue to be so in the future. The more complex contracts should become relatively more common and important if China's policy of encouraging foreign trade and investment continues with the same vigour that it has displayed in recent years. New legislation, such as the Patent Law,[26] and legislation now being drafted such as the Foreign Economic Contracts Law and the Civil Code, will force changes in some of these complex contracts if not in the simpler standard-form contracts as well. Nevertheless, it seems likely that foreign firms entering into contracts with Chinese entities will face many of the issues that they have faced in the past and will continue to try to resolve them by negotiating appropriate provisions in their contracts.

Notes

1. The basic provisions of these contracts as they existed in the 1970s have been described by several commentators: E. Theroux, *China's Standard Form Contracts and Related Legal Issues in US–China Trade* (Special Report No. 13 of the National

Council for US–China Trade, June 1973); Note, 'Legal Aspects of China's Foreign Trade Practices and Procedures', *Journal of International Law and Economics*, No. 12 (1977–8), p. 105; K.R. Shaney, 'Selected Legal Aspects of China's Conduct of Foreign Trade', *International Lawyer*, No. 11 (1977), p. 641; A.H. Smith, 'Standard Form Contracts in the International Trade of the People's Republic of China', *The International and Comparative Law Quarterly Review*, No. 21 (1972), p. 133; and Note, 'An Analysis of Chinese Contractual Policy and Practice', *Wayne Law Review*, No. 27 (1980–1), p. 1229.

2. See generally Chen Muhua, 'Prospects for China's Foreign Trade in 1983', *Beijing Review*, No. 6 (1983), p. 14; and 'Interview/Wei Yuming', *Far Eastern Economic Review*, 25 December 1981, p. 46.

3. See generally V.K. Fung, 'China's Decentralization of Foreign Trade', *Asian Wall Street Journal*, 24 November 1982, p. 6; and Li Shude, 'General Review on China's Structural Reform of Foreign Trade System' (speech at a seminar organized by the Commission of the European Communities on the Reform of China's Foreign Trade System, Brussels, 7 and 8 July 1982). Mr Li Shude is Director of the Third Department, Ministry of Foreign Economic Relations and Trade.

4. Economic Contracts Law of the People's Republic of China, promulgated on 13 December 1981 and put into effect on 1 July 1982 (hereafter cited as the Economic Contracts Law).

5. The eight Chinese foreign trade corporations are the China National Chemicals Import and Export Corporation; China National Native Produce and Animal By-Products Corporation; China National Light Industrial Products Import and Export Corporation; China National Textiles Import and Export Corporation; China National Cereals, Oils and Foodstuffs Import and Export Corporation; China National Machinery Import and Export Corporation; China National Metals and Minerals Import and Export Corporation; and China National Technical Import Corporation. The China National Chartering Corporation and the Chinese Foreign Trade Transportation Corporation are also sometimes considered to be foreign trade corporations. See Theroux, note 1 above.

6. Li Shude, in his speech (see Li Shude, note 3 above), said: 'Since 1980, special policies and flexible measures concerning foreign trade have been adopted in [the] provinces of Guangdong and Fujian. These two provinces are entitled, under the guidance of unified foreign trade principles and planning, to manage on their own export of all the local products, with the exception of crude oil, refined oil, and some other products which are handled by the head offices of relevant national import and export corporations. A certain percentage of the foreign currency earnings are kept by the provinces at [*sic*] their own disposal.

'To give full play to the advantages of the provinces and cities and to expand further China's foreign trade, foreign trade corporations were set up in Beijing, Shanghai and Tianjin in 1980, and were given more power to manage import and export business. It was further decided earlier this year that the provinces, municipalities and autonomous regions, which are located along the sea coast and with necessary conditions, can manage in principle foreign trade business on the basis of independent accounting and bearing their own profits or losses.

'Independent management of foreign trade has also been approved to other provinces, municipalities and autonomous regions to various extent[s], with the power to negotiate directly with foreign companies.'

7. Examples of such trading companies are the China Electric Import and Export Corporation; China North Industries Corporation; China Atomic Energy Industry Corporation; China National Aerotechnology Import and Export Corporation; China State Shipbuilding Corporation; China Great Wall Industry Corporation; China Precision Machinery Import and Export Corporation; China Xinshidai Company; China Xiao Feng Company; China Metallurgical Import and Export Corporation; China Seeds Company; China Forest Seeds Import and Export Corporation; China Breeding Stock Import and Export Corporation; and China Oriental Scientific Instruments Import and Export Corporation.

8. See the Provisional Regulations of the People's Republic of China on Notarization, promulgated by the State Council on 13 April 1982, and the major treatise on notarization, He Mingfu, *Gongzheng Jiben Zhishi (Basic Knowledge of Notarization)* (Beijing, The Masses Publishing Co., 1982).

9. According to the Restatement of Contracts, a contract is a promise or a set of promises for the breach of which the law gives a remedy, or the performance of which the law in some way recognizes as a duty. Restatement (Second) of Contracts (1979), §1. The Uniform Commercial Code, §§1–201(3), defines contracts as the total legal obligation which results from the parties' agreement as affected by the code and any other applicable rules of law.

10. Presumably the same rule would apply where the contract provided for arbitration abroad.

11. See Provisional Security Measures in An Introduction to International Arbitration in Sweden by the Arbitration Institute of the Stockholm Chamber of Commerce.

12. Article 194 of the Civil Procedure Law states that 'a PRC foreign arbitration organization' can apply to a people's court for such protective measures in certain circumstances, but it is unclear whether this applies only to arbitration proceedings in China or to those conducted abroad as well.

13. Different countries have varying practices with respect to judicial review. In England, under the Arbitration Act of 1979, parties to international contracts, other than those concerning maritime, insurance, or commodities matters, may foreclose judicial review by an exclusion agreement in the commercial contract. However, prior to the effective date of the Act (1 August 1979), English courts could intervene extensively in arbitrations held in England and Wales. In Zurich and Geneva the judiciary may examine the merits of a dispute submitted to arbitration where one side believes that the arbitrator has committed an error. In the Netherlands, Sweden and the United States, a *laissez-faire* approach is adopted, where error as such is not subject to review. France has an optional approach to arbitrator error, where the parties may choose whether or not to prohibit an appeal on the merits of the case (Park, 'Judicial Supervision of Transnational Commercial Arbitration: The English Arbitration Act of 1979', *Harvard Law Review*, No. 21 (1980), p. 37).

14. Since 1980 the Foreign Trade Arbitration Commission has been renamed the Foreign Trade and Economic Arbitration Commission.

15. See Article 8(2) of the Agreement on the Establishment of a Joint Venture Elevator Company in the People's Republic of China (1980).

16. The Income Tax Law of the People's Republic of China Concerning Joint Ventures Using Chinese and Foreign Investment, promulgated on 10 September 1980.

17. General Bureau of Taxation of the Ministry of Finance (ed.), *Zhongguo Duiwai*

Shuiwu Shouce (Handbook of China's Foreign Taxation) (Beijing, China Financial and Economic Publishing House, 1983), p. 37.

18. P.M. Torbert, 'Shanghai Moves Ahead, Receives Greater Authority to Conduct Foreign Trade and Investment', *East Asian Executive Reports,* 15 October 1983, p. 12.

19. R. Pfeffer, *The Role of Contracts in China* (1970), pp. 54–5.

20. Y. Yamada, 'The Problems of China's Suspending Plant Import Contracts', *China Newsletter,* No. 22 (July 1979), p. 16.

21. 'Chinese Credibility on the Line Due to Baoshan Cancellation', *Business Asia,* 6 March 1981, p. 75.

22. Federal Regulations, Vol. 38, p. 17817, 3 July 1973.

23. Federal Regulations, Vol. 47, p. 141, 1982 (to be codified in CFR, Parts 379, 385 and 399, p. 15).

24. Federal Regulations, Vol. 48, pp. 53064–71, 1983 (to be codified in CFR Parts 368–99, p. 15).

25. See J. Wetter, *Arbitration in Sweden* (1977), pp. 45–9.

26. For a discussion concerning China's Patent Law see Chapter 12 of this volume.

8. Banking and Finance in the China Trade

Franklin D. Chu

China has greatly expanded its international commercial ties in recent years, but the amount of business it has concluded with foreign banks and financial institutions has remained small for a country with one-quarter of the world's population. This reflects caution and restraint that is hardly surprising given China's economic readjustment programme announced in 1979 to curb government spending; distaste for borrowing funds except on concessionary terms; inefficient bureaucratic structures; sensitivity to making mistakes; and lack of familiarity with many international financial practices.

However, China's fiscal restraint has enabled the country to accumulate reserves so that in 1984 China seems poised to increase significantly imports of the technology, plant and equipment that she lacks and to construct the infrastructure necessary to absorb much greater foreign investment. In 1983, 1982 and 1981 China had trade surpluses of US$3.86 billion, US$4.6 billion and US$1.4 billion respectively.[1] At the end of 1983 China had US$14.392 billion in foreign exchange reserves (larger than the reserves of any developing country except Saudi Arabia), as well as 12.67 million troy ounces of gold, which is sufficient to cover imports for about 8 months.[2] In comparison to its reserves China's foreign debt is small. The Ministry of Finance reported that at the end of 1981 China had only US$4.7 billion in foreign debt, which approached US$6 billion in mid-1982 and decreased sharply to US$3.02 billion at the end of 1983.[3]

As a developing country, China is in the unusual position of being a net creditor to the world. At the end of 1981 China had an estimated net credit position of US$0.5 billion and its large 1982 current account surplus strengthened this position to US$6–7 billion at the end of 1982.[4]

Foreign banks have lost no time in demonstrating their eagerness to penetrate the China market. As of the end of 1983, approximately 45 foreign banks have established representative offices in Beijing, 7 have sub-representative offices in Shanghai, 4 have long-established branch offices in Shanghai, 8 have established sub-representative offices in Guangzhou, 9 have established representative offices in the Shenzhen Special Economic Zone across the border from Hong Kong and 2 have established representative offices in the Xiamen Special Economic Zone in Fujian Province. In each of these locations other foreign banks are still in the waiting line.[5] Thus far, few of these banks are reaping significant profits, but all seem committed to developing their long-term business relationships with China.

China's financial institutions, Chinese business and financial practices, and Chinese laws and regulations applicable to banking transactions are in the process of evolution, which is likely to continue for the forseeable future. This chapter focuses on banking and finance in the China trade from the late 1970s to the present. Four major areas will be discussed: (1) the organization of China's banking system with an emphasis on those institutions engaged in international financial and investment activities; (2) the activities of foreign banks in China; (3) Chinese trade financing practices in connection with letters of credit and export credits; and (4) China's foreign exchange control system and its impact on international business transactions.

I. The Organization of China's Banking System

China's banking system includes as major units the People's Bank of China, five specialized banks, the People's Insurance Company of China, the State General Administration of Exchange Control, and the China International Trust and Investment Corporation, all of which are to some extent under the direction of the State Council, which is the highest executive organ of government. Outside this core group the Ministry of Finance and the State Capital Construction Commission exercise certain supervisory and regulatory functions, and numerous trust and investment corporations have been authorized to engage in specified banking activities. In addition, the banking system has close links with 12 so-called 'sister' banks in Hong Kong and another in Macao and has two major affiliates in Hong Kong. China is also a member of several international financial organizations.

A. Domestically Oriented Units

i. The People's Bank of China (PBOC)

The PBOC is China's central bank and acts as a state administrative organ for the regulation of finance under the leadership of the State Council.[6] In the Chinese government hierarchy it enjoys ministry-level status.

On 14 July 1982 the State Council approved five primary roles for the PBOC: (1) to formulate national financial regulations and policies, to determine interest rates for renminbi deposits and loans and to implement such rates after State Council approval; (2) to print and issue currency and to regulate the circulation of currency in accordance with the plan approved by the State Council; (3) to co-ordinate and implement in a comprehensive manner credit plans and to allocate credit funds in a unified manner; (4) to examine the establishment, termination and consolidation of financial organs, to determine the division of operations and to co-ordinate and examine the business of financial organs, to administer financial markets, to examine and approve the establishment and winding up of foreign financial institutions in China and to supervise such foreign financial institutions according to law; and (5) to administer in a unified manner China's foreign exchange and bullion, to manage foreign exchange and gold reserves, to determine the exchange rates of the renminbi against foreign currencies and to engage in related international activities on behalf of the government.[7] In addition to its banking activities, the PBOC oversees the activities of the People's Insurance Company of China.

In practice, certain of the PBOC's functions are carried out by other banking units under the PBOC's supervision. For example, applications of foreign banks to establish representative offices in China are usually screened and examined by the Bank of China and afterwards are sent to the PBOC for formal approval. The Bank of China also engages in the management and utilization of foreign exchange in both trade and non-trade areas.

On 17 September 1983, the State Council decided that the PBOC would henceforth restrict its functions to those of the country's central bank and not engage in the issue of credit funds to either enterprises or individuals. The PBOC, however, continues to exercise control over the specialized banks and other financial institutions, including the country's insurance companies, through economic measures supplemented by necessary administrative measures. As part of the recent reorganization the PBOC has set up a policy-making council, composed of the PBOC's president (who acts as the council chairman) and vice-presidents, several advisors and specialists, a vice-minister of the Ministry of Finance, a vice-minister of both the State Planning Commission and the State Economic Commission, the presidents of the specialized banks and the general manager of the insurance company. If the council does not reach a unanimous agreement on matters discussed, the chairman is authorized to adjudicate, while important issues are submitted to the State Council for decision.[8]

ii. The Industrial and Commercial Bank of China (Industrial and Commercial Bank)

The Industrial and Commercial Bank was established on 1 January 1984 as a specialized bank to take over part of the PBOC's former activities with respect to the management of industrial and commercial credits and related payments. The primary tasks of the Industrial and Commercial Bank are the handling of savings deposits of industrial and commercial enterprises; extending loans for working capital and technical transformation; managing payments; controlling working capital of industrial and commercial enterprises; and handling savings deposits in cities and towns.[9]

iii. The Agricultural Bank of China (Agricultural Bank)

The Agricultural Bank is directly subordinate to the State Council but its supervisory management is entrusted by the State Council to the PBOC.[10] At times in its history the Agricultural Bank has operated as a department of the PBOC, but in 1979 it was reinstituted as an independent entity and assumed supervision over the rural offices of the PBOC.[11] The Agricultural Bank's principal tasks are examining, issuing and utilizing state funds in support of agriculture and cash deposits for the purchase of agricultural products by the state; managing savings deposits and credit business for rural commune and production brigade enterprises, state-run agricultural enterprises and organizations, agricultural-industrial-commercial joint enterprises and supply and marketing co-operatives; managing savings deposits and credit business for offices, people's organizations, schools, enterprises and other units set up by the state in the countryside, as well as the settlement of accounting and cash control in the urban and rural areas; and supervising rural credit co-operatives.[12]

iv. The People's Construction Bank of China (Construction Bank)

The Construction Bank is also directly subordinate to the State Council but its supervisory management is entrusted by the State Council to the Ministry of Finance and, to a lesser degree, to the PBOC and the State Capital Construction Commission.[13] The responsibilities of the Construction Bank include administering government appropriations and loans for capital construction; managing the deposits, loans and final accounting of such units as construction and installation enterprises, geological prospecting units and enterprises which supply and market goods and materials for capital construction; and controlling capital funds related to capital construction.[14]

v. Ministry of Finance (MOF)

The MOF is an independent body reporting directly to the State Council and is in charge of fiscal management, the collection of most taxes and annual and long-term planning of the state budget. In the banking sector the MOF provides financial guidance to the Construction Bank and the Investment Bank of China.[15]

B. Internationally Oriented Units

i. The Bank of China (BOC)

By far the most important Chinese entity involved in international banking and finance is the BOC. According to its Articles of Association, which were approved by the State Council on 22 September 1980, the BOC is a state-owned socialist enterprise and is the foreign exchange bank of the People's Republic of China.[16] Supervisory management of the BOC is generally carried out by the PBOC on behalf of the State Council. Under this arrangement the BOC will refer important business and administrative matters to the PBOC for resolution, although in some cases the BOC may also refer matters directly to the State Council for resolution. Day-to-day administration and business management of the BOC are conducted by the bank itself.[17]

The authorized activities of the BOC cover a broad range of international banking activities including the international settlement of accounts, interbank deposits and loans; handling international remittances, foreign currency deposits and loans, and deposits and loans in renminbi that are related to foreign exchange and have been approved by the PBOC; buying and selling foreign exchange and gold; organizing and participating in international lending syndicates; establishing banks and other financial institutions abroad; issuing foreign currency bonds and other securities that have been authorized by the state; and providing trust and advisory services and other banking services approved by the state.

The authorized capital of the BOC is at present RMB 1 billion, all appropriated by the government.[18] In addition, the MOF and the PBOC appropriate certain amounts of renminbi and foreign exchange as the BOC's working capital.[19] In 1982, the assets of the BOC were RMB 119 billion and its net income was RMB 1.06 billion, an increase of 29.2 per cent and 50.1 per cent respectively over 1981.[20]

The Board of Directors and Council of Supervisors of the BOC (whose members are appointed by the State Council) function as the bank's leading bodies and the President and the several Vice-Presidents act as chief executive officers.[21] The head office in Beijing is staffed by more than 500 personnel in the following departments: Administration and Secretariat, Personnel, General Co-ordination, International, Foreign Exchange and Funds, Credit, Accounting, and Research.[22] Each department is headed by its own General Manager and Deputy-General Managers.

At the end of 1980 the BOC had 34 branches and 41 sub-branches in the capitals of each province and autonomous region and in major cities, ports and border areas where international business is concentrated.[23] The BOC presently has overseas branches in London, New York, Singapore, Hong Kong and Luxembourg and representative offices in Paris and Tokyo. In addition, it has over 1,000 correspondent banks in about 150 countries and regions.

One foreign legal expert has questioned whether the BOC is legally part of the Chinese state or whether it is a distinct legal person separate from the Chinese government.[24] The Chinese themselves appear to look upon the BOC as part of the Chinese government for some purposes and as an independent enterprise for others, although where the line is drawn is unclear. On the one hand, the Articles of Association of the BOC state that it is a state-owned socialist enterprise, which implies it is an independent legal person responsible for its own assets and liabilities that can sue and be sued in its own name.[25] On the other hand, in an official notice describing the relationship between the PBOC and China's specialized banks, the State Council confirmed that the BOC is an 'economic unit at the general administrative level',[26] which implies that it is part of the Chinese government.

The legal status of the BOC is, of course, an important factor for foreign bankers in assessing credit risks and determining lending limits to single borrowers. The BOC itself has represented to both the United States Federal Deposit Insurance Corporation and the Export-Import Bank of the United States that its obligations are backed by the full faith and credit of the People's Republic of China.[27] While it is highly unlikely that the BOC would make such a representation if it had any doubts on the matter, there is at present no legislation passed by the National People's Congress that spells this out. According to press reports, the Japanese government in 1983 refused to accept a BOC guarantee in connection with the proposed issue of bonds by Fujian Province in the Japanese market unless the State Council endorsed the BOC's guarantee.[28] The Chinese parties reportedly did not consent to this request. It is clear, however, that the obligations of many other state-owned enterprises are not backed by the full faith and credit of the Chinese government. Certain Chinese officials have expressed the opinion that in the event such other enterprises default on their obligations, the Chinese government would recognize only a moral obligation to assume payment.

The authority of the BOC's branches is another important consideration, as foreign banks frequently enter into transactions directly with branches of the BOC rather than with its head office. The scope of authority granted to the BOC's branches, however, is unclear and generally considered *neibu* or an internal matter not to be disclosed to foreigners. According to sketchy public information provided by the BOC with respect to its application to establish a New York branch, prior approval of the BOC head office is necessary for 'certain major matters, including the annual budget of the New York branch, loans or syndicated loans to companies located outside the United States and loans to United States customers in excess of an approved limit, to be established.'[29] As is the case with foreign banks though, not all BOC branches exercise the same authority; foreign BOC branches appear to exercise greater authority than domestic branches. There are also differences among the domestic branches. For example, in 1981 branches in the provinces of Guangdong and Fujian and the municipalities of Beijing, Shanghai and Tianjin had independent authority to extend foreign currency loans up to US$5 million, while 7 other 'first-level' branches had ceilings of US$3 million and 17 'second-level' branches had ceilings of US$1 million.[30] In practice, foreign banks generally have assumed that the major BOC branches in Beijing, Shanghai and Tianjin and in Guangdong and Fujian Provinces would not enter into transactions with foreign banks unless they had the requisite authority, and foreign banks generally have not required evidence of head office approval unless the amount involved is very substantial.

Apart from the issue of the authority of its branches, the question remains whether the BOC is responsible for its branches' liabilities. Under general concepts of Western banking law a bank is responsible for the liabilities of all its branches.[31] Unless certain exceptions or contractual provisions apply, refusal or inability to honour an obligation by a branch entitles a creditor to receive payment from the head office of the bank. There presently exists no

Chinese law or regulation that addresses this question with respect to Chinese banks or other entities. The issue also has never arisen in an actual case involving the BOC. Should such a case arise, it would seem unlikely that the BOC would as a general matter disclaim responsibility for the liabilities of its branches although other Chinese enterprises that do not have the same stature and international reputation as the BOC might have greater leeway to act otherwise.

In the last few years the BOC has significantly expanded its own international banking activities and the services it offers to Chinese-foreign joint ventures and domestic entities involved in export trade. The most significant of these activities for foreign banks and companies are discussed below.

a. Participation in Syndicated Loans

One of the most welcome new activities of the BOC is its participation, principally through its London branch, in Eurocurrency syndicated loans. Motivated by a desire to gain experience in international syndications and to take advantage of high interest rates in 1981 and 1982, as well as the necessity to recycle some of its increasing reserves, the BOC participated in at least 15 Eurocurrency syndicated loans in 1982 alone.[32] Borrowers for these loans range from the Danish Export-Import Bank and the Ente Nationale Idrocaburi, the Italian national oil company, to the Veneer Hotel, a Singapore enterprise.[33]

The BOC has also begun to participate in syndicated loans for projects in China. In early 1983, the BOC agreed to participate in an international syndicate for a US$10,000,000 loan to the Xian Golden Flower Hotel Company, a Chinese-foreign joint co-operative enterprise.[34] By mid-1983, the BOC had gained sufficient experience to arrange as lead managers with its affiliate, CCIC Finance Ltd., a HK$700 million syndicated loan to Garden Hotel Holidays Ltd. to finance a hotel and office complex in Guangzhou.[35]

b. Loans to Foreign Companies for Projects in China

The BOC has also announced that it will provide loans to foreign companies involved in projects in China provided that the foreign company has a registered office in China and certain unspecified guarantees are obtained.[36] According to the BOC, from 1980 to the beginning of 1983 it made loans totalling US$50 million and RMB 60 million to 54 Chinese-foreign joint ventures.[37] It is unclear whether these loans were made to the joint venture itself or to the Chinese partner as part of its equity contribution.

Both foreign companies and joint ventures operating in China may find it cheaper to borrow from the BOC than from foreign banks since the BOC, unlike foreign banks, is not subject to the withholding tax on China-source interest income. This does not mean, however, that other terms of loan agreements that joint ventures sign with the BOC will be equally advantageous. Under current regulations, a joint venture must provide the BOC with a pledge of collateral security or a guarantee from a guarantor acceptable to the BOC.[38] The BOC has recently begun consideration of accepting contractual mortgages over certain types of assets. But until Chinese laws and regulations relating to mortgages or other security arrangements are adopted, a parent company or bank guarantee generally would have to be provided which lessens the appeal of a BOC loan. In addition, the regulations provide interest penalty payments ranging from 20 per cent to 50 per cent of the original interest rate, which are far in excess of the standard range of default interest rates set by foreign banks.

c. Foreign Exchange and Renminbi Loans to Chinese and Other Entities

Of much greater magnitude are the foreign exchange and renminbi loans that the BOC provides to domestic entities engaged in foreign trade, communications, transportation and energy development, and to small and medium-sized enterprises (particularly those manufacturing export products). Between 1979 and June 1982, the BOC is reported to have approved foreign exchange loans totalling US$13.266 billion to domestic entities of which US$10.256 billion was drawn down;[39] it is also reported that the BOC issued US$630 million of foreign exchange loans to Chinese small and medium-sized enterprises from January to November 1983. These include a US$2.94 billion loan to the Ministry of Communications to finance several hundred new ocean-going ships, a US$500 million loan to improve harbours, a loan to the Civil Aviation Administration of China to buy Boeing 747 aircraft, a US$2 billion low-interest buyer's credit for oil and coal production, and US$1.547 billion in loans to small and medium-sized enterprises.[40] In early 1983 it was reported that the BOC decided to allot US$2 billion in foreign exchange between 1983 and 1985 for loans at preferential rates to small and medium-sized enterprises for the import of advanced equipment and technology;[41] and in early 1984 it was further reported that such preferential loans (preferential interest rates were reduced from 10–12 per cent in early 1983 to 7.5–8.5 per cent in early 1984) would be made not only to Chinese enterprises and other Chinese financial institutions, but also to enterprises with Chinese-foreign investment, or overseas Chinese funds or sole foreign capital and also to Chinese factories, cultural, educational, medical, scientific research and tourist organizations and corporations for contracting engineering projects overseas. The BOC's foreign exchange loans are made in US dollars, Japanese yen, Hong Kong dollars, British pounds and French francs; in addition, the BOC has recently drawn up Instructions on Foreign Exchange Loans, defining the categories of its foreign exchange loans available to borrowers, application procedures and the use of such loans.[42]

The BOC has also started to finance jointly with foreign banks projects in China. For example, the BOC, Shanghai branch, has jointly financed with Deutsche Bank AG the setting up of the Shanghai Shipyard Container Factory.[43]

The BOC's foreign exchange loans are sometimes used by Chinese borrowers to pay for the down-payment portion of imported plant and equipment, the remainder of the cost of which is financed by export credits provided by foreign banks. For example, this pattern was followed in a US$50 million note purchase facility provided by a syndicate of foreign banks to the Yan Shan Petrochemical General Corporation and guaranteed by the Beijing Economic Development Corporation. It is noteworthy that officials from the BOC's Beijing branch assisted the borrower in the negotiations with the foreign banks, a service the BOC is providing to an increasing number of Chinese borrowers. The BOC's participation in loan negotiations can be extremely helpful, particularly for obtaining necessary government and foreign exchange approvals for the transaction.

d. Export Credits

The BOC is also reported to have decided to offer export credits. A national conference of BOC managers held in January 1983 apparently concluded that the BOC should make available export credits totalling US$500 million over the next three years to encourage exports of machinery and ships. A pilot scheme is to be implemented first in Beijing and then in the port cities of Tianjin, Shanghai and Dalian.[44] Details of the plan have yet to be released. Chinese bankers, however, seem to have a very broad notion of what constitutes export credits. For example, some Chinese bankers have considered as an export credit a loan made at subsidized interest rates to a Chinese shipyard for machinery to construct a ship to be purchased by a foreign buyer. Sometimes deferred payment arrangements offered by Chinese manufacturers to foreign purchasers are referred to as export credits. For example, in 1982 the China State Shipbuilding Corporation offered to a Norwegian shipping company deferred payment terms for 80 per cent of the price of Chinese-built ships calling for 12 semi-annual instalments at an interest rate of 9 per cent.[45] It remains to be seen whether the BOC will offer export credits involving long-term financing at subsidized rates to a foreign party. Certainly the BOC is gaining more experience in this area through its participation in the export credit programmes that other countries have offered to China, which are discussed below.

e. Direct Investment in Chinese Entities and Chinese-Foreign Joint Ventures

The BOC has also begun to make direct investments in projects in China. For example, the BOC has made two direct investments in the Shanghai Offshore Petroleum Engineering Corporation. The BOC Shanghai Branch is reported to have invested in the Shanghai-Pilkington Glass Co., Ltd., and the Shanghai Offshore Oil Engineering Joint Corporation, initialled a joint investment agreement with respect to the Shanghai Global Toy Co., Ltd., and accelerated a feasibility study of an automobile production joint venture between Shanghai Tractor and Automobile Corporation and Volkswagenwerk AG. The BOC's general practice reportedly is to purchase a 10–25 per cent share in these joint ventures.[46]

f. International Trust and Consultancy Services

In 1980 the BOC began providing international trust and consultancy services, activities already engaged in by many other Chinese entities. The

BOC's trust operations, which have little relation to the traditional trust services provided by foreign banks except for receiving inheritances from overseas Chinese, are primarily directed at raising and utilizing foreign capital for China's modernization programme in line with the state plan. By the end of 1981, the BOC and its branches had established 38 trust departments and companies involved in joint ventures, international leasing, transfers of surplus foreign exchange among Chinese units, compensation trade, processing and assembling arrangements, acting as business or purchase and sales agents, and supplying information on the credit standing of foreign companies.[47] In addition, by the beginning of 1984 the BOC had signed agreements on co-operation in trust and consultancy business with 42 foreign banks and companies. Generally, these are no more than short, one- to two-page agreements providing for co-operation between the parties and cross-referral of clients. Most recently the BOC has established the Bank of China Trust and Consultancy Company, which is a socialist state enterprise and an affiliate of the BOC, with a registered capital of RMB 600 million.[48]

g. Activities in Hong Kong

Of the BOC's overseas operations, those in Hong Kong are by far the most extensive. In addition to its own 10 branches in Hong Kong, the BOC controls 12 affiliated banks, known as 'sister' banks, that operate through some 168 branches in Hong Kong.[49] Eight of these banks — Bank of Communications; Kwangtung Provincial Bank; Sin Hua Trust, Savings and Commercial Bank, Ltd.; Kincheng Banking Corporation; China and South Sea Bank Ltd.; China State Bank Ltd.; National Commercial Bank Ltd.; and Yien Yieh Commercial Bank Ltd. — are incorporated and have their head offices in China. The other four — Nanyang Commercial Bank; Hua Chiao Commercial Bank Ltd.; Chiyu Bank Corporation Ltd.; and Po Sang Bank Ltd. — are incorporated in Hong Kong. The Nanyang Commercial Bank recently opened branches in the Shenzhen Special Economic Zone and in San Francisco.[50] The Kwangtung Provincial Bank Ltd. has a branch in Singapore. A thirteenth sister bank, Banco Nam Tung, is incorporated and operates in Macao.[51]

The BOC and its 12 sister banks in Hong Kong provide a full range of banking services, including their traditional trade-financing business, and are conservatively estimated to control at least one-quarter of Hong Kong dollar bank deposits.[52] In contrast to China's cautious approach in other international markets, the BOC and its sister banks aggressively expanded their loan portfolios between 1979 and 1981, with considerable exposure in Hong Kong's speculative property market. It is estimated that 40 per cent of the affiliated banks' HK$43 billion in loans at the end of 1981 had been granted to real estate developers.[53]

In the wake of the major downturn in Hong Kong's property market in 1982, the BOC and its affiliates have apparently suffered serious losses as have many foreign banks heavily involved in Hong Kong property loans. It seems that because of poor co-ordination between the BOC and its affiliates, the Chinese-controlled banks sometimes took a major share of a single syndicated loan to a property developer. It has been reported that the Chinese-controlled banks accounted for about one-quarter of the HK$2 billion in credits extended to Eda Investments Ltd., which recently went into receivership in Hong Kong, and its chairman, C.M. Chung.[54] In addition, it has been reported that the Chinese-controlled banks loaned HK$477.4 million to third parties guaranteed by Mr Chung and the companies he controls.[55]

As a result of such events, much more restrictive lending practices have been adopted. Participation in any major loan or syndication by one of the sister banks must now be approved by the group's business committee, which is composed of senior officials of the BOC and the chairmen of the 12 sister banks. Under the new policies, loans to local Hong Kong property developers and loans secured only by personal guarantees will be extremely difficult, if not impossible, to obtain.[56]

Aside from its sister banks, the BOC has two major affiliates which were established in Hong Kong in 1980. The first is CCIC Finance Ltd., a merchant bank formed by the BOC with the First National Bank of Chicago, the Industrial Bank of Japan and China Resources Co. Ltd., which has been China's major import-export agent in Hong Kong. The three banks each hold a 30 per cent interest and China Resources 10 per cent. CCIC Finance Ltd. recently increased its authorized capital by 300 per cent to HK$100 million and its paid-up capital by 200 per cent to HK$75 million.[57] In its first fiscal year CCIC Finance Ltd. enjoyed a modest HK$2.74 million profit and as of October 1981 had assets of HK$990 million.[58] In addition to developing its activities as a merchant bank, CCIC Finance Ltd. will concentrate on financing projects in accordance with China's economic policies in energy, communications and light industry, and serving as a bridge for trade and finance between China and the United States and Japan.[59] Of particular note is CCIC Finance's role as financial consultant to both the China National Offshore Oil Corporation (CNOOC), which has overall responsibility for developing China's offshore petroleum resources, and China Nanhai Oil Joint Services Corporation, a joint venture between the CNOOC and Guangdong Province which has responsibility for providing certain services for the exploration and development of petroleum resources in the South China Sea. CCIC Finance Ltd. has also reached agreements with over a hundred foreign banks for credit lines totalling several hundred million US dollars to be used for development financing in China, Hong Kong and the Asian-Pacific region.[60]

Aside from CCIC Finance Ltd., the BOC has a 10 per cent interest in Kincheng-Tokyo Finance Company, a Hong Kong-incorporated finance company and merchant bank that was set up with Kincheng Banking Corporation (one of the sister banks) and the Bank of Tokyo. Kincheng-Tokyo Finance Company has an authorized capital of HK$5 million and provides trade financing, investment advice and assistance to joint ventures in China.[61]

ii. The Investment Bank of China (Investment Bank)

The Investment Bank was established in December 1981 as a specialized bank for borrowing funds from international financial institutions to lend to small and medium-sized Chinese enterprises and to finance Chinese-foreign joint ventures.[62] The Investment Bank has an authorized capital of RMB 4 billion of which approximately 10 per cent has been paid in by the Chinese government.[63] As of the first quarter of 1983, the Investment Bank's only source of foreign funds was a US$70 million loan from the World Bank, consisting of a US$40 million loan for 20 years with an interest rate of 11.43 per cent and a US$30 million soft loan of 50 years which is interest-free but carries a service fee of 0.75 per cent.[64] The World Bank loan will be used for the renovation and transformation of existing small and medium-sized enterprises. Significantly, Investment Bank loans will be granted only after approval of feasibility studies and the Investment Bank will monitor the financed projects. According to one Investment Bank official, only small loans of up to US$8 million initially will be approved.[65]

iii. The State General Administration of Exchange Control (SGAEC)

The SGAEC was established in early 1979 and is the administrative organ of China in charge of foreign exchange control. Other than the BOC, no financial institution may engage in foreign exchange business without the approval of the SGAEC.[66]

In theory the SGAEC reports directly to the State Council, but it is subordinate to the PBOC with respect to exchange-rate policy guidance and seems to function as an adjunct to the BOC. Indeed, the staff of the SGAEC are largely seconded from the BOC's foreign exchange departments and both the head office and branch offices of the SGAEC are housed in BOC offices.

The head office of the SGAEC has three departments. The first undertakes the planning of China's foreign exchange policies, the second drafts and implements China's exchange control regulations and the third works with the BOC and the PBOC in setting China's foreign exchange rates.[67] The regulatory functions of the SGAEC are discussed below.

iv. The China International Trust and Investment Corporation (CITIC) and Other Special Organizations

The CITIC is a state-owned socialist enterprise established in 1979 under the direct leadership of the State Council.[68] Its chairman is Rong Yiren, a Shanghainese, who is perhaps China's best-known former capitalist. In general, the CITIC functions both as a consulting firm and as a merchant bank, and its business operations have recently come under the control and supervision of the PBOC.[69]

According to its statutes, the CITIC is permitted to engage in the following activities: (1) to assist foreign companies and individuals, as well as Chinese entities, to negotiate and enter into joint venture and technological co-operation agreements and related contracts in China; (2) to accept funds from foreign companies and individuals and to raise funds abroad by issuing debentures or bonds for investment in China; (3) to provide consulting services to both foreign and Chinese entities on legal matters, taxation, foreign exchange control, labour wages, accounting and auditing; (4) to act as the agent of foreign companies in business activities relating to advanced technology and equipment; and (5) to engage in joint ventures and to invest in projects inside and outside China.[70]

By the end of 1981, the CITIC had signed agreements with some forty foreign banks for credit facilities amounting to approximately US$1 billion. Currently, the CITIC is reported to be seeking investors for a US$1 billion two-year industrial modernization programme, as well as export credits from major banks in supplier countries to finance the projects.[71] The CITIC has formed equity joint ventures with domestic entities such as the Yizhen Chemical Fibre Corporation, Ltd. and the China Leasing Company Ltd. and, along with other Chinese entities, has established Chinese-foreign joint ventures such as the China Orient Leasing Company Ltd. with the Japanese Orient Leasing Company S.A., and the Guang-Mei Foods Company Ltd. with Beatrice Foods. The CITIC has also invested some US$300 million in projects involving the production of chemical fibres, linen textiles, phosphate fertilizer, castings and gelatine, as well as in non-ferrous metal mines and shipping companies. In January 1982 the CITIC became the first Chinese entity to issue bonds abroad through a 10 billion-yen private placement in Japan and is considering tapping the Eurobond market.[72]

In early 1983 CITIC investment missions were sent to foreign countries to investigate equity investments in foreign companies operating in the resources field. The areas that reportedly most interest the Chinese include foreign products, fertilizers, iron-ore mines and the aluminium and fisheries industries.[73]

The CITIC has the flexibility to offer a potential tax advantage to foreign lenders that many other Chinese borrowers are unable to provide. China's tax laws generally impose a 10–20 per cent withholding tax on interest earned by foreign enterprises that do not have an 'establishment' in China.[74] But the laws exempt from such withholding tax interest income earned with respect to loans from foreign banks, carrying an interest rate equal to the interbank offered rate, to China's state banks and to trust and investment companies approved by the State Council to engage in foreign exchange business.[75] The CITIC is one of the trust and investment companies approved by the State Council to engage in foreign exchange business within the scope permitted by the SGAEC.[76] To circumvent the withholding tax for loans destined for other Chinese borrowers, several foreign banks have inquired whether the CITIC would act as an on-lending vehicle. Up to now, however, it appears that the CITIC will only serve in this function in projects in which the CITIC itself will take an equity participation.

In addition to the CITIC some 15 regional trust and investment corporations have been established to engage in many of the same activities as the CITIC. The most active of these corporations include the Beijing Economic Development Corporation, the Shanghai Trust and Investment Corporation, the Tianjin International Trust and Investment Corporation and the Guangdong International Trust and Investment Corporation.

C. China's Participation in International Financial Organizations

China's participation in international financial organizations revived in October 1979 when it borrowed US$15 million from the United Nations Development Programme. In mid-January 1980 China joined the United Nations' International Fund for Agricultural Development.

By far the most significant development in this area came when China joined the International Monetary Fund (IMF) and the World Bank on 17 April and 15 May 1980, respectively. In 1981 China's quota in the IMF totalled 1.8 billion special drawing rights (SDRs), which represented approximately 3.02 per cent of the total quota, and its voting power in the IMF was 2.89 per cent of the total.[77] An extra seat on the IMF's executive board was created so that China could be represented without diminishing the number of seats of any other countries. As of 31 January 1982 China had drawn 759.2 million SDRs from the IMF.[78]

China's voting power in the World Bank is 12,250 votes or 3.55 per cent of the total. China was also given a seat on the World Bank's Executive Board which was increased from 20 to 21 members to accommodate China. By the second quarter of 1983, China and the World Bank had signed the following loan agreements providing for loans both from the World Bank's hard loan source, the International Bank for Reconstruction and Development (IBRD), and from the World Bank's soft loan source, the International Development Association (IDA): (1) US$200 million for instruments, computer equipment and training at 26 key Chinese universities, consisting of a US$100 million hard loan and a US$100 million soft loan; (2) US$60 million for the control of waterlogging and soil salinity in a three-province region in the North China plain, consisting entirely of a soft loan; (3) US$124 million for the expansion of three Chinese ports at Shanghai, Tianjin and Huangpu; (4) US$75.4 million for agricultural education and research, consisting entirely of a soft loan; (5) US$80 million for building a land reclamation and grain production centre in the northernmost province of Heilongjiang, consisting of a US$45 million soft loan and a US$35 million hard loan; and (6) US$70 million for the Investment Bank of China, consisting of a US$40 million hard loan and a US$30 million soft loan.[79] Soft loans from the IDA generally carry only a 0.75 per cent annual service fee with a term of 50 years, while hard loans from the IBRD generally are for 20 years at market rates (currently 11.43 per cent per annum).

In the near future China and the World Bank are expected to reach agreement on several additional loans including: (1) US$160 million for oil-field equipment for the Daqing oil field; (2) US$120 million for the Zhongyuan (formerly called Dongpu) oil field; (3) US$150 million for the construction of a hydroelectric power project in Yunnan Provine at Lubuge; and (4) US$240 million for the development of two fully mechanized, longwell, underground coal mines in Shanxi Province. According to A.W. Clausen, President of the World Bank, China is expected to borrow about US$1 billion from the World Bank during its 1984 fiscal year.[80]

China has also expressed its desire to join the Asian Development Bank (ADB), but an accommodation has yet to be worked out by the ADB's members which presently include Taiwan.

II. The Activities of Foreign Banks in China

A. The Registration of and Restrictions on Representative Offices

China does not currently allow foreign banks to operate branches in China other than the four long-standing foreign bank branches in Shanghai. Thus at present the only available alternative for foreign banks is to establish a representative office.

Until 1 February 1983 foreign banks were subject to the same general registration regulations as other foreign enterprises. On that date, however, the PBOC issued the Provisional Regulations for the Establishment of Representative Offices in China by Overseas Chinese and Foreign Financial Institutions (hereafter cited as the Registration Regulations).[81] As before, the application procedures for establishing a bank representative office under the Registration Regulations remain simple. The applicant bank first fills out a short application form, which is obtainable from the PBOC and must be signed by the applicant's chairman or chief executive, and attaches copies of the bank's charter or business licence; articles of association; by-laws; latest balance sheet and profit and loss statement; a list of the bank's directors; a power of attorney given to the chief representative that must be signed by the chairman or chief executive; and the curricula vitae of the chief representative and other representatives of the bank. The application is then submitted for approval directly to the PBOC or through a relevant financial institution, which for foreign banks is the BOC. Generally, approval will only be granted upon favourable recommendation by the BOC.

After obtaining the approval certificate of the PBOC, the applicant bank goes through routine registration procedures with the local administrative bureau for industry and commerce and obtains a registration certificate. If there are no problems, the entire process can be completed in as little as two months, although some banks have waited considerably longer.

The Registration Regulations permit the establishment of representative offices in Beijing and/or any of China's Special Economic Zones (SEZs), and subordinate representative offices in other designated cities such as Shanghai and Guangzhou. Before a foreign bank may establish a subordinate representative office, however, it must first establish a representative office in Beijing.[82]

In assessing whether it will recommend approval for an application to establish a representative office in Beijing, the BOC apparently applies three criteria. The first, which rarely presents a problem, is whether the applicant bank's home country grants reciprocal rights to Chinese banks. The second reflects a desire to maintain a rough geographical balance in the numbers of banks from various countries. Although the optimum number of banks from any one country depends on the volume of its bilateral trade with China and the importance China attaches to their economic relations, it is clearly easier to obtain approval as the first bank from a particular country rather than as the fifth. The last criterion involves political considerations concerning the then current state of relations between China and the applicant's home country.[83]

Article 8 of the Registration Regulations restricts representative offices to carrying out 'non-profit activities such as . . . business negotiations, acting as liaison, providing consultancy and other services'. Representative offices 'shall not engage in any direct-profit making activities'.[84] Furthermore, representative offices in an SEZ are limited to engaging in such non-profit activities within the confines of the SEZ. These restrictions would seem to preclude a limited branch-banking licence in the SEZs which several foreign banks hope to obtain. Nevertheless, both a Vice-Mayor and the Secretary-General of Shenzhen Municipality recently stated that the municipal government is considering upgrading the representative offices of foreign banks in that SEZ to branch level.[85] At present only one 'foreign' bank, the Nanyang Commercial Bank, which is one of the BOC's sister banks incorporated in Hong Kong, operates a branch in the Shenzhen SEZ.

The extent of the restrictions in Article 8 of the Registration Regulations has also been called into question by another set of regulations promulgated after the Registration Regulations but which came into force on 1 January 1983. Article 4 of the Provisional Regulations of the Ministry of Finance of the People's Republic of China Regarding the Reduction and Exemption of Income Tax Relating to Interest Earned by Foreign Businesses from China (hereafter cited as the Interest Income Tax Regulations) is intended to give foreign banks with representative offices in China preferential treatment with respect to China's withholding tax on interest income.[86] Under China's tax laws a foreign enterprise with an 'establishment' in China is subject to tax on net income at progressive rates from 20 per cent to 40 per cent of net taxable income and a local income tax equal to 10 per cent of the same taxable income.[87] A foreign enterprise without an establishment is generally subject to a 20 per cent withholding tax on the gross amount of passive income such as interest, although interest income earned with respect to loan agreements signed between 1983 and 1985 is subject to a reduced rate of 10 per cent.[88]

Prior to promulgation of the Interest Income Tax Regulations, local tax officials informed foreign bank representative offices that they would not be liable for any income tax because such representative offices engage only in liaison activities and earn no income. Under the Interest Income Tax Regulations, however, bank representative offices do constitute establishments and will be deemed to receive as taxable income 15 per cent of the amount of interest income earned in connection with loan agreements that such offices sign with Chinese borrowers.[89] This appears to give banks with representative offices a definite tax advantage. For example, a bank making a US$10,000,000 loan at a 10 per cent interest rate will be liable for US$100,000 in withholding tax if the agreement is not signed by a representative office in China. But profit tax on the same loan concluded by a representative office in Beijing would amount to approximately US$46,500.[90] Moreover, if a representative office in the Shenzhen SEZ signs the same loan agreement it would only be subject to a profit tax of US$22,500 due to the lower rate of taxation in the SEZs. The crucial question, however, is whether the prohibition in Article 8 of the Registration Regulations against representative offices engaging in any direct profit-making business activities will preclude foreign banks from taking advantage of this favourable tax treatment. To date no written ruling has been issued by Chinese officials, but a recent report indicates that foreign banks' representative offices in China may sign loan agreements with Chinese enterprises if authorized by their head offices.[91]

Assuming that representative offices are permitted to sign loan agreements, further questions arise regarding the breadth of Article 4 of the Interest Income Tax Regulations. For example, may a representative office sign a loan agreement on behalf of a syndicate, whose members do not all have representative offices in China, and be permitted to pass on the tax advantage to each syndicate member? Preliminary discussions with Chinese officials indicate this will not be permissible. The tax advantage apparently is intended only to benefit banks that have established representative offices in China.

B. Banking Business with China

From 1978 to 1981 foreign banks concentrated their marketing efforts on extending loans to China. Such loans generally carry an interest rate of one-half of one per cent over the London interbank offered rate for periods of three or six months, although a three-eighths of one per cent spread has been offered for short-term credits. Front-end fees were rarely obtained. During this period roughly US$10 billion in commercial credits was offered to China, but only around US$3 billion was actually drawn down.[92]

A combination of conservative borrowing policies and high interest rates were in part responsible for the relatively small amount utilized. Another significant impediment to the utilization of any type of foreign credit is that

Chinese borrowers generally must not only demonstrate that the proposed project will produce sufficient foreign exchange to repay foreign debts but must also justify the use of scarce domestic funds, materials and facilities. China has a strong preference for low-interest or no-interest loans from foreign governments and international financial organizations and for subsidized government export credits.[93] Even with respect to loans at preferential interest rates, China has adhered to a conservative approach and has permitted availability deadlines to expire rather than borrow for hastily conceived projects. It is estimated that as of June 1981 China utilized only US$2.04 billion of some US$16.8 billion of such official credits offered to China.[94] Moreover, China announced in May 1983 that it would repay in 1983 the entire 450 million in SDRs borrowed in March 1981 from the IMF which China was scheduled to begin repaying in March 1984.[95]

In 1982 China literally stopped borrowing private commercial credits. Indeed, flush with a growing trade surplus, China took the opportunity to prepay much of its existing commercial debt to the disappointment of many foreign bankers. For example, in early 1982 the BOC prepaid after two years the entire sum — US$150 million — it had drawn down from the US$300 million syndicated loan led by the Union des Banques Arabes et Françaises.[96] The BOC has also refinanced at lower interest rates and for longer terms loans from foreign banks to other Chinese borrowers. This was the case for a US$35.2 million loan to the China International Travel Service, Nanjing Branch, for the construction of the Jinling Hotel in Nanjing that was arranged in 1980 by Wardley Ltd., a unit of The Hongkong and Shanghai Banking Corporation.[97]

The curtailment of lending to China in 1982 resulted also from the imposition of China's withholding tax on interest, which became effective on 1 January 1982. As a result, a significant portion of the loans made in 1982 were redirected to Hong Kong companies controlled by Chinese entities and to their Hong Kong branches.

In the future, commercial banks are likely to concentrate their China-related lending efforts on participation in export credit facilities and project financing of oil, gas, coal, phosphorus, non-ferrous metals and certain rare metals, as well as on financing foreign parties involved in the exploitation of China's offshore petroleum resources.[98]

As opportunities for direct lending to domestic Chinese borrowers have subsided, foreign banks have gone back to promoting trade financing, traditionally the major source of their China profits. Typically, foreign banks open letters of credit for their customers to purchase Chinese imports and advise letters of credit for sales to China. Chinese practices in trade financing are discussed in detail below. Foreign banks have also focused greater attention on equipment-leasing both direct to Chinese lessees and in conjunction with Chinese organizations such as the CITIC, and on providing financial consulting services to Chinese entities as well as foreign companies. A small number of banks are even considering equity investments in China.[99]

As mentioned above, four foreign banks operate branches in Shanghai: The Hongkong and Shanghai Banking Corporation, the Chartered Bank, the Overseas Chinese Banking Corporation and the Bank of East Asia, Ltd. The primary business of these Shanghai branches is advising letters of credit, although they are permitted to accept foreign currency deposits from non-residents and handle inward remittances. Such branches are not permitted to open letters of credit for Chinese entities, make loans at commercial rates, handle outward remittances or accept any renminbi deposits.

III. Chinese Trade Financing Practices

China utilizes a variety of methods to settle foreign trade transactions including barter trade, counterpurchase, compensation trade, cash settlement, buyer and supplier credits, private commercial credits and official government credits. This section focuses on Chinese practices with respect to two methods not discussed elsewhere in this volume, namely letters of credit and government-subsidized export credits.

A. Letter of Credit Financing of Exports and Imports

Traditionally, China's trade with foreign countries has been in the form of cash transactions paid through letters of credit. China is not a member of the International Chamber of Commerce (of which Taiwan is a member) and thus does not officially adhere to that body's Uniform Customs and Practice for Documentary Credits. Although the BOC and other Chinese entities generally follow these rules, in some instances they do not and special Chinese practices have developed over the years to which foreign companies and banks should pay particular attention.[100]

i. The Export of Chinese Goods to Foreign Buyers

The general procedure for letters of credit used in connection with Chinese exports usually follows the sequence described below:

(1) The Chinese seller and foreign buyer agree to the terms of the underlying contract, which generally provides for payment by an irrevocable and transferable letter of credit opened by the foreign buyer's bank and payable through sight drafts upon the presentation of documents. The letter of credit is usually opened soon after the contract is signed (particularly if the contract involves the manufacture of new products) since the Chinese party generally will not start production until the

letter of credit is opened. Such a letter of credit remains valid for at least ten days following the shipment date. Generally, the opening bank must be a correspondent of the BOC, and if it is not, the letter of credit must be advised through a correspondent bank, adding to the cost of the transaction.

(2) After the foreign buyer's bank opens the letter of credit, it instructs the advising bank located in China and specifies the documents to be presented. The advising bank is usually a domestic BOC branch, although in Shanghai the four foreign bank branches also perform this function. BOC regulations require, however, that each foreign bank branch report, and supply a copy of, all incoming documentary credits and amendments thereto to the BOC, Shanghai Branch. It is of crucial importance for the foreign buyer to understand that all charges incurred in China, including reimbursement and interest charges, are for the opener's account. A letter of credit that does not conform to this condition will be rejected by the advising bank.

Another problem that occasionally arises is determining whether a letter of credit has arrived at the BOC branch and whether it has been accepted by the Chinese seller. The BOC reportedly can be quite slow in responding to inquiries.

(3) Upon acceptance of advice from the BOC, the Chinese seller will obtain the documents required under the letter of credit. Over the years Chinese suppliers have developed the types of documents generally acceptable in international commerce and in certain cases will even obtain special documents required by the opener (for example, documents in Spanish rather than English) although this will take more time. The following points, however, should be noted:

(a) Documents certified by a Chamber of Commerce or consular office are generally unavailable.

(b) Documents requiring notarization or other forms of legalization are difficult to obtain, although documents may be certified by the China Council for the Promotion of International Trade.

(c) Unless the documentary credit specifically stipulates otherwise, BOC and foreign bank branches are required to accept documents chopped with a Chinese seal rather than signed by a handwritten signature and to accept combined documents (for example, combined invoice and certificate of origin). Separate documents, however, are generally obtainable.

It should also be noted that China almost always prefers to sell C.I.F. Specific restrictions in the letter of credit as to carrying vessels are generally not permitted (such as 'shipment should be made by Conference Line vessel'), but general restrictions may be included (such as 'carrying vessel should not be more than 15 years old'). A typical insurance clause calls for an insurance policy covering Ocean Marine Cargo Clauses All Risks (including

Warehouse to Warehouse Clauses) and War Risks Clauses (1/1/1976) of the People's Insurance Company of China. Supplementary risks such as strikes, riots and civil commotion and rejection may also be covered.

(4) After obtaining all the necessary documents the Chinese seller will present them to the BOC branch or foreign bank branch. If the advising bank finds that the documents conform to the letter of credit, it will seek to effect payment from the issuing bank. In recent years most of the underlying sales contracts with Chinese entities have provided for payment in foreign exchange, a development that eliminates exchange risks for foreign buyers. The primary problem in effecting payment is one of timing. If the letter of credit is opened in Hong Kong, the BOC will grant a six-day 'grace' period after negotiation of the sight drafts by the domestic BOC branch or the foreign bank branch for payment to be received from the issuing bank. The grace period is extended to 12 days if the letter of credit was issued outside Hong Kong. After this grace period interest will be charged to the issuing bank and hence to the foreign supplier.

Unless the underlying contract calls for telegraphic transfer (TT) reimbursement to the advising bank from the issuing bank, the BOC generally airmails the documents to the issuing bank and this can delay payment beyond the applicable grace period. Any delay in the payment will result in an interest charge to the foreign buyer who may have thought that he had already arranged for timely payment in full to the Chinese seller.

ii. The Import of Foreign Goods by Chinese Buyers

The following procedures generally apply to letters of credit used in the import of foreign goods:

(1) The underlying contracts always require that the BOC open all letters of credit. The BOC head office in Beijing usually issues such letters of credit although some domestic BOC branches will do so, particularly if the buyer is a local entity. Standard procedure calls for the BOC to issue an irrevocable letter of credit upon notification by the foreign seller that the shipment is ready. Such letters of credit almost always require that sight drafts be drawn on, and documents be presented to, a specified domestic BOC branch. In the past only foreign sellers with considerable bargaining power, such as grain suppliers, have been able to arrange for presentation of documents and payment outside China.

All charges incurred in China with respect to the letter of credit are always for the account of the beneficiary.

(2) After the letter of credit is opened, the foreign seller's bank will advise the letter of credit assuming that it is a BOC correspondent bank. If it is not, a bank that is a correspondent will have to advise the letter

of credit. BOC letters of credit, however, are not confirmed by foreign banks since, given its position as a state-owned bank, the BOC considers a request for confirmation as an affront. This poses a major problem for foreign suppliers since all negotiations will have to be with the BOC in China.

(3) China prefers to buy F.O.B. so that Chinese shipping companies will transport the goods. To ensure this, BOC letters of credit generally require for F.O.B. shipments a 'certificate issued by the shipping agents that the vessel is chartered or booked by the China National Foreign Trade Transportation Corporation, Beijing or China National Chartering Corporation, Beijing (Charter-party Bills of Lading are acceptable)'. In the rare cases where foreign goods are sold C.I.F. or C & F, BOC letters of credit contain as documentary requirements the 'Shipping Company's scheduled itinerary showing that the carrying vessel, prior to its arrival at destination, will not touch any port(s) of the Taiwan Area' and/or the letter of the foreign seller 'attesting that the nationality of the carrying vessel has been approved by the buyers'.

(4) Inherent risks for the foreign supplier arise after the foreign seller provides the documents to his bank for presentation to the BOC in China. Until the documents are negotiated, the foreign seller has neither possession of the goods or the documents nor payment. Several difficulties can be encountered. First, it is sometimes a problem to determine whether the documents have arrived at the BOC. Foreign bankers based in China can spend a considerable portion of their time checking on the status of letters of credit. One foreign bank before it established a representative office in China even resorted to an interim arrangement with a foreign trading company based in Beijing to deliver documents to the BOC and to follow through until the BOC issued its payment instructions. Second, even after the BOC acknowledges receipt of the documents it will normally permit Chinese buyers to review the documents for compliance if they so request. This can frequently result in a one- or two-day delay and there have been reports that the BOC has in certain cases delayed payment until the goods have arrived and the Chinese buyer has inspected them to insure that the underlying contract has been fulfilled. Finally, even after the documents have been found to be in order, payment instructions are usually sent by airmail, unless the underlying contract stipulates that the foreign seller's bank is entitled to receive TT reimbursement. Until it receives payment, the foreign supplier in effect will be extending interest-free credit to the Chinese buyer and, if there is any substantial delay, the loss of interest can wipe out slender profit margins.

At present there is no indication that the BOC will dramatically reform its letter of credit practices. The BOC is, of course, aware of these problems and in 1980 announced that it was considering measures to raise efficiency in examining letters of credit.[101]

B. Export Credit Financing

Broadly speaking, an export credit is extended to China whenever a Chinese buyer of foreign goods or services is allowed to defer payment for a period of time. There are two types of export credit. Under a supplier credit arrangement the exporter extends credit to the overseas buyer and is itself usually financed by its bank, whereas under a buyer credit a bank in the exporter's country provides finance direct to the overseas buyer with the exporter receiving payment from the financing bank. Subsidized export credits arise when a government export credit agency in the exporter's country participates in the financing through an insurance programme and/or through a direct extension of credit so that preferential interest rates and long-term repayment of principal can be extended to the overseas buyer.

Both supplier and buyer credits with and without the participation of a foreign government export credit agency have been offered to China. It can be expected, however, that China will primarily utilize subsidized buyer credits. In general, a buyer credit is considered a more appropriate mechanism for larger and more complex contracts of sale that require commissioning and other post-shipment responsibilities, whereas a supplier credit is considered more appropriate for financing contracts that involve little more than a straight supply of goods or equipment. Chinese buyers prefer the lower interest rates offered by subsidized export credits, a very large amount of which has not yet been utilized. To date many foreign governments, including those of France, Great Britain, Italy, Japan, Belgium, West Germany, Canada, Argentina and the United States, have negotiated agreements with China providing for a wide range of direct credits and subsidized commercial bank credits designed to stimulate Chinese purchases of foreign goods. The majority of credit lines negotiated thus far are tied to long-term government-to-government bilateral trade agreements. China is under no obligation, however, to draw down these lines of credit.

These government export credit programmes basically work in the same manner with respect to China as they do in connection with other countries. The major difference, however, is the active participation of the BOC in all phases from approval of the export credit, to the draw-down of funds, to repayment. Government-subsidized buyer credits generally require complicated documentation. In China any single document tends to be simpler and shorter, but because of the BOC's involvement the number of documents tends to be greater.

The overall framework for utilization of government export buyer credits is set forth in credit agreements with the BOC, which acts as a conduit for on-lending to the ultimate borrower (either a Chinese entity or, in some cases, a Chinese-foreign joint venture or co-operative enterprise). In contrast to other countries, such credit agreements are not concluded directly with Chinese borrowers. The foreign parties to such agreements are generally either a group of participating commercial banks from the relevant country in the case of insurance-oriented export credit programmes (for example, those sponsored by Great Britain's ECGD, France's COFACE and West Germany's HERMES), or the export credit agency itself in the case of bank-oriented export credit programmes (for example, those offered by the US Eximbank or Eximbank of Japan).

Such credit agreements contain general provisions covering the maximum amount of credit offered; the availability period; utilization procedures and conditions to be fulfilled prior to utilization; the types of supply contracts and the percentage of the contract price eligible for financing; prepayment; taxes and related costs; events of default; and dispute settlement.[102] The repayment period, interest rate and fees are generally set each time the BOC applies for a utilization of the funds under the credit agreement for particular supply contracts.

The underlying supply contract between the foreign supplier and the Chinese buyer must be approved by the BOC, the foreign government export credit agency and commercial lenders to ensure that it falls within the terms and conditions of the basic credit agreement. One of the principal difficulties with these supply contracts is that they are frequently negotiated between foreign suppliers and Chinese buyers without adequate attention to financing requirements.

Based on previous transactions with which this author has been involved, it is recommended that any foreign company or its bank contemplating export credit financing for a supply contract should involve the BOC in the contract negotiations when financing is discussed. Preferably, officials from the BOC's head office should be involved since they, and not BOC branch officials, will be most familiar with the requirements of available export credit facilities. In the case of Chinese-foreign joint ventures and co-operative enterprises, the BOC apparently decides on a case-by-case basis whether it will make export credit lines available and what procedures are to be followed. In the past, the BOC has required joint ventures to provide for the BOC's own internal planning purposes a pro forma breakdown of the amount and country of origin of each group of items to be procured abroad. This will be difficult to provide if the procurement is to be done through international bidding. Rather than complain about the difficulties of providing such a breakdown, it is better simply to provide it on the understanding that it is subject to the results of the bidding.

Two additional agreements generally will be required when Chinese-foreign joint ventures and co-operative enterprises wish to utilize export credit financing. First, the joint venture or co-operative enterprise will have to sign a loan agreement with the BOC for each supply contract to be financed through the on-lending of funds that the BOC obtains pursuant to an export credit agreement. Although BOC practice may differ in connection with export credits utilized by domestic Chinese entities, it has in the past charged joint ventures a spread of approximately one per cent as a fee for its services. Second, the BOC requires a counter-guarantee from a foreign bank or syndicate of banks of the amount borrowed by the joint venture or co-operative enterprise. These requirements increase the complexity of documentation, the time for negotiation and the cost of utilizing export credits.

A substantially different structure that did not involve the BOC as a party was used in the 1981 syndicated note purchase facility provided to the Yan Shan Petrochemical General Corporation to finance the purchase of primarily Italian-origin plant and equipment. In that transaction, the foreign banks purchased Yan Shan's negotiable promissory notes (which are guaranteed by the Beijing Economic Development Corporation) from the Italian supplier on a non-recourse basis. The foreign banks will hold the notes, which cover both principal and interest, until they mature, and in the interim will collect both fees and an interest make-up from the Italian government's Mediocredito Centrale. Furthermore, by purchasing the notes on a non-recourse basis from the Italian supplier and not obtaining a guarantee from an Italian government agency, the lenders were able to lower the cost of the financing and obtain a pure China risk with respect to the notes.

Whether the Yan Shan transaction will serve as a precedent for future transactions is unclear. A major obstacle is the great reluctance of Chinese buyers to issue negotiable promissory notes, the payment of which is not tied to the performance of the underlying supply contract.

IV. China's Exchange Control System and Its Impact on International Transactions

Every trade, investment and banking transaction with China must comply with China's foreign exchange control system. A variety of state plans, approval and licence procedures, rules and regulations define the contours of this system, but its foundation is set forth in the Provisional Regulations of the People's Republic of China Governing Foreign Exchange Control (hereafter cited as the Foreign Exchange Regulations)[103] which came into effect on 1 March 1981. The Foreign Exchange Regulations implement 'a policy of centralized control and unified management of foreign exchange by the State' and designate the State General Administration of Exchange Control (SGAEC) and its branch offices as the administrative organ in charge of foreign exchange control.

A. The Administration of Control

The SGAEC and its branch offices are granted specific approval authority over certain foreign exchange activities of Chinese domestic organizations; the remittance out of China of foreign exchange by Chinese and certain foreign individuals; the conversion into foreign currency of visa and certification fees received in renminbi by foreign diplomatic missions and consulates in China; and the repatriation abroad by foreign partners in Chinese joint ventures of their portion of the net profits and capital.

The SGAEC and its branch offices, however, do not exercise sole authority over foreign exchange activities. All foreign exchange retained by Chinese domestic organizations, non-trade foreign exchange and foreign exchange under compensatory trade received in advance for late payments, funds borrowed in convertible foreign currency and other foreign exchange held with the approval of the SGAEC must be placed in foreign currency deposit accounts or foreign currency quota accounts opened with the BOC and must be used within the scope prescribed by, and are subject to the supervision of, the BOC. The BOC is granted specific authority to certify the remittance of foreign exchange retained by Chinese and certain foreign individuals residing in China and of the foreign exchange required by foreign experts, staff members and workers employed in Chinese domestic organizations.

The organizational boundary between the SGAEC and the BOC is blurred since the staff of the SGAEC are largely seconded from the BOC's foreign exchange departments and both the head office and branch offices of the SGAEC are housed in the BOC's offices. Where the SGAEC does not have a branch, the local BOC branch acts as its agent.

Certain foreign exchange activities are outside the authority of both the SGAEC and the BOC and must be approved by the State Council. For example, no Chinese domestic organization may issue securities with a foreign exchange value inside or outside China without the approval of the State Council. Furthermore, the State Council alone has the authority to approve plans drawn up by provincial and local governments for loans to Chinese domestic organizations. It should also be noted that the CITIC, six other international trust and investment corporations and the four foreign bank branches in Shanghai are authorized to engage in designated foreign exchange transactions.

Foreign exchange transactions are generally made in accordance with China's foreign exchange plan. The Ministry of Foreign Economic Relations and Trade prepares those parts of the plan relating to foreign trade and external assistance and loans by China. The Ministry of Finance prepares the foreign exchange budgets of other government departments. The SGAEC compiles that part of the plan covering local and provincial non-trade transactions, receipts from overseas Chinese and individual receipts. The SGAEC also co-ordinates the overall foreign exchange plan and, after it has been reviewed and reconciled with other plans by the State Planning Commission, submits it to the State Council for approval. After approval the plan is sent back to the various subordinate organs for implementation under the supervision of the BOC.[104]

B. The Impact of Exchange Controls on International Transactions

The basic pattern of control is set forth in Article 4 of the Foreign Exchange Regulations:

> All Chinese and foreign organizations and individuals residing in the People's Republic of China must, unless otherwise stipulated by law or decree or in these regulations, *sell* their foreign exchange proceeds to the Bank of China. Any foreign exchange required is to be sold to them by the Bank of China in accordance with the quota approved by the State or with relevant regulations [105] [my italics].

As discussed below, Chinese-foreign joint ventures and foreign and overseas Chinese enterprises and individuals in China enjoy somewhat greater flexibility in their foreign exchange dealings.

i. Trading Operations

Foreign trade is conducted in accordance with the annual foreign trade plan which is drawn up by the Ministry of Foreign Economic Relations and Trade in conjunction with the State Planning Commission and approved by the State Council. Input for the plan is provided by all foreign trade corporations and foreign trade bureaux in the provinces, municipalities and autonomous regions which draw up lists of needed imports and goods available for export.

In addition to complying with the annual foreign trade plan, all import and export transactions require a licence issued by the Ministry of Foreign Economic Relations and Trade. The Foreign Exchange Regulations require banks handling import and export transactions to check the foreign exchange receipts and payments of domestic Chinese organizations against the import or export licence duly verified by the Customs or against the Customs declaration forms for imports or exports.[106] Part of the proceeds of some exports may be retained by domestic organizations in a foreign exchange deposit or foreign exchange quota account with the BOC, and such foreign exchange must be used within the scope prescribed therefor and be subject to the BOC's supervision. All other foreign receipts must be sold to the BOC unless specific approval is granted by the SGAEC. The BOC provides foreign exchange for imports subject to the issue of an import licence and approval of the SGAEC.

In buying and selling foreign exchange with the BOC, Chinese entities are frequently required to use an internal settlement rate. In recent years the internal settlement rate was approximately RMB 2.8 to US$1.00, but as the US dollar appreciated against other foreign currencies the internal settlement rate has been increased to over RMB 3 to US$1.00, which is substantially higher than the official rate. On 23 April 1984 the official rate of the renminbi against the US dollar was approximately RMB 2.09 to US$1.00. The internal settlement rate is formed by adding an 'equalization price' to the official rate and its objective is to promote exports and constrict imports. The internal settlement rate applies to all trade-related transactions including transactions in invisibles such as shipping and insurance. The official rate remains in effect for all other transactions in invisibles and for all settlements that are denominated in renminbi with Chinese-foreign joint ventures, foreign enterprises and individuals.[107]

To utilize more efficiently surplus foreign exchange the BOC has established an experimental trading system for foreign exchange in a few areas, including Beijing, Guangdong, Hefei, Shanghai and Tianjin. National enterprises that have been permitted to retain foreign exchange are permitted to sell such foreign exchange to other national enterprises that have a quota for spending foreign exchange. The BOC itself neither participates in this trading system on its own account nor does it provide foreign exchange. According to the IMF, the BOC acts merely as a broker and levies a commission of 0.1–0.3 per cent on both sides of the transaction.[108] All transactions in this market are spot transactions and use the then prevailing internal settlement rate. Most transactions are in US dollars although pounds sterling and Hong Kong dollars are also traded.

ii. Loans to Chinese Organizations

In order for Chinese entities to borrow from foreign banks, such loans must be in the annual plans for loans prepared by the departments under the State Council and people's governments of provinces, municipalities and autonomous regions. These plans must be submitted for examination to the SGAEC and the Foreign Investment Bureau within the Ministry of Foreign Economic Relations and Trade and are then forwarded to the State Council for approval.

The Foreign Exchange Regulations state that measures for examining and approving loans to Chinese organizations from foreign banks and companies shall be stipulated separately,[109] but such measures have yet to be promulgated. Although the existing Foreign Exchange Regulations make specific reference only to loans, it would be highly imprudent to conclude that contingent obligations like guarantees are not subject to the examination and approval of the appropriate authorities. One high-ranking BOC official has told this author that guarantees given by Chinese entities with respect to loans from both foreign and domestic sources would be subject to approval.

It is important to understand that foreign exchange approval of a loan or a contract by the SGAEC or other relevant Chinese authorities does not mean that foreign exchange will definitely be made available to pay the obligation when due to the foreign bank or company. The only method of assuring payment in foreign exchange is to obtain a BOC guarantee.

iii. Chinese-Foreign Joint Ventures, Enterprises with Overseas Chinese Capital and Enterprises with Foreign Capital

Rules for the Implementation of the Foreign Exchange Regulations have recently been published for enterprises with overseas Chinese capital, enterprises with foreign capital and Chinese-foreign joint ventures (hereafter cited as the Foreign Exchange Implementation Rules).[110] These rules expand on the Foreign

Exchange Regulations and in certain circumstances provide for preferential treatment for such enterprises, especially for foreign enterprises engaged in co-operative exploitation of offshore petroleum resources in China.

As a general rule, joint ventures and enterprises with overseas Chinese or foreign capital should open both renminbi and foreign exchange deposit accounts in China with the BOC or any other bank approved by the SGAEC or its branch offices; payments and receipts in such accounts are subject to the supervision of the bank where such accounts have been established.[111] Such enterprises are also generally required to deposit all foreign exchange receipts in, and make all foreign exchange payments from, their accounts in banks in China.[112]

Moreover, such enterprises must submit periodically to the SGAEC or its branch offices the following statements: (1) before 31 March of each year its balance sheet as of 31 December of the previous year, profit and loss statement, statement of receipts and payments of foreign exchange for the previous calendar year and the audit report by an auditor registered in China; and (2) before 1 December of each year its budget of foreign exchange receipts and payments for the coming year.[113] The SGAEC and its branch offices are authorized to request such enterprises to provide information about their business activities involving foreign exchange and to inspect their foreign exchange income and expenditure.[114]

Preferential treatment is granted under the Foreign Exchange Implementation Rules to enterprises engaged in co-operative exploitation of offshore petroleum resources in China. Such enterprises may deposit their solely-borne exploration funds and co-operative production funds in banks in foreign countries or in Hong Kong or Macao that are agreed upon by their Chinese partners and after approval has been granted by the SGAEC or its branch offices. Such enterprises shall submit to the SGAEC or its branch offices quarterly statements of payments into, and withdrawals from, such accounts outside China within 30 days after the end of each quarter.[115]

In order to implement their petroleum operations specified in their contracts with Chinese enterprises, foreign oil companies may also pay directly outside China wages, salaries, the cost of procurements, labour costs and service charges to foreign workers and staff members and foreign subcontractors and suppliers, who shall remain obligated, however, to pay Chinese income tax on taxable income earned in China.[116] In addition, joint ventures and enterprises with overseas Chinese or foreign capital that are engaged in the co-operative exploitation of resources such as offshore petroleum, coal and other co-operative and joint ventures, whose costs are recovered and profits are taken in products in accordance with their contracts, may send such products out of China on the condition that taxes and other required payments are remitted back to China.[117]

Under the Foreign Exchange Regulations all Chinese-foreign joint ventures and enterprises with overseas Chinese or foreign capital must use renminbi in the settlement of accounts with Chinese entities, enterprises and individuals residing in China. But the Foreign Exchange Implementation Rules provide three exceptions to this general rule. Provided that the prior approval of Chinese foreign trade authorities has been granted and the seller and buyer have reached agreement, such enterprises may use foreign currencies in the pricing and the settlement of accounts for (1) sales of products to Chinese entities or enterprises engaged in foreign trade which would otherwise have to import such products, and (2) purchases, for the sake of production, of commodities exported or imported by Chinese entities engaged in foreign trade. In both cases, the prices of such products and commodities are to be commensurate with current world market prices. As a third exception, such enterprises may use foreign currencies in the payment for, and in the settlement of accounts related to, construction work performed by Chinese construction entities provided that prior approval has been obtained from the SGAEC or its branch offices.[118]

One of the more onerous requirements of the Foreign Exchange Regulations and Foreign Exchange Implementation Rules is that joint ventures and enterprises with overseas Chinese or foreign capital must generate sufficient foreign exchange earnings to pay all their foreign exchange expenditures. This requirement has been mitigated to some extent by the Implementing Act for the Law of the People's Republic of China on Joint Ventures Using Chinese and Foreign Investment (hereafter cited as the Joint Venture Implementation Regulations). Article 75 of the Joint Venture Implementation Regulations provides that when a joint venture whose products are mainly sold on the domestic market under its approved feasibility study report and contract has an imbalance of foreign exchange income and expenses, the imbalance shall be solved by the people's government of the relevant province, autonomous region or municipality directly under the central government or the department in charge under the State Council from their own foreign exchange reserves; and in case it cannot be so resolved, it shall be resolved after examination and approval by the Ministry of Foreign Economic Relations and Trade together with the State Planning Commission.[119]

The language of the Foreign Exchange Regulations and Foreign Exchange Implementation Rules leaves several questions unanswered. For example, Article 4 of the Foreign Exchange Regulations prohibits the mortgage of foreign currency. Does this prohibition extend to commonly used security arrangements such as a pledge of foreign currency receivables? This question has not been generally addressed by the SGAEC, although in one transaction foreign lenders were permitted to obtain a pledge of rentals received in foreign exchange by a Chinese-foreign joint co-operative enterprise and deposited in its foreign exchange deposit account with the BOC.

Second, will a foreign investor that terminates its participation in a joint venture or other enterprise, whether because the term of co-operation has expired, heavy losses have been incurred or a major dispute cannot be resolved, be permitted to remit in foreign exchange its share of the net book value of the joint venture or enterprise? Article 24 of the Foreign Exchange Regulations directs foreign investors to apply to the SGAEC or its branch offices for transferring foreign exchange capital abroad by debiting the foreign exchange deposit account of the joint venture or enterprise. But the word capital may include only the capital originally invested and not retained earnings. Even if retained earnings may be remitted, this will be small comfort to the foreign investor if the foreign exchange deposit account does not contain an amount sufficient to cover the proposed outward remittance. Unless joint ventures and enterprises with overseas Chinese or foreign capital are permitted to purchase foreign exchange to cover their liabilities or broadly come under the protection of Article 75 of the Joint Venture Implementation Regulations cited above, foreign investors may have to obtain insurance coverage for foreign exchange convertibility.

Another question left unanswered by the foreign exchange regulations and rules is whether a foreign investor that has entered into several joint ventures with different Chinese partners will be permitted to pool the foreign exchange accounts of its joint ventures, so that the joint ventures as a group or the foreign investor individually may remit foreign exchange not exceeding the aggregate amount in such accounts. Such an arrangement would probably require the approval of several Chinese organizations in addition to the SGAEC.

A final problem for joint ventures and enterprises with overseas Chinese or foreign capital concerns the foreign exchange earnings of their foreign employees. Article 25 of the Foreign Exchange Regulations limits such personnel to remitting an amount not exceeding 50 per cent of their net wages and other legitimate earnings after tax. The limitation should not prove a problem for foreign oil companies engaged in co-operative exploitation of offshore petroleum resources, since under the new Foreign Exchange Implementation Rules they are permitted to pay directly outside China the wages and salaries of foreign workers and staff members. The new Foreign Exchange Implementation Rules also ease, but to a lesser extent, this restriction for the personnel of other enterprises with foreign or overseas Chinese capital and of Chinese and foreign joint ventures. The personnel of such entities may remit amounts exceeding 50 per cent of their wages and legitimate earnings after tax deductions if approved by the SGAEC or its branch offices and as long as such excess amounts are debited to the foreign exchange deposit accounts of the employing enterprise.[120] A further relaxation is granted under Article 79 of the Joint Venture Implementation Regulations to foreign personnel working for joint ventures who, after payment of Chinese individual income taxes, may apply to the BOC for permission to remit outside China all of the remaining foreign exchange after deduction of their living expenses in China.[121] There is no restriction on the remittance of earnings of foreign resident representatives of foreign companies with representative offices in China.

iv. Transactions with the Special Economic Zones

Projects in China's SEZs are generally subject to more flexible regulations providing for preferential treatment. Regulations in force for the SEZs in

Guangdong Province refer to the foreign exchange control measures of the special zones,[122] but these have yet to be promulgated.

V. Conclusion

Banking and financial transactions with China have become increasingly sophisticated in recent years. It can be expected that they will be somewhat easier to conclude in the future as China develops its legal system and gains more experience in international financial practices. The dollar volume of such transactions will also significantly increase in the long term, but in the short to medium term China will concentrate on using its own foreign exchange reserves and the financial assistance of foreign governments and international financial organizations.

Notes

1. *South China Morning Post*, *Business News*, 31 January 1983, p. 8; and 'China's 1983 Imp-Export Volume Up 2.2% to US $40.14 Billion', *China Economic News*, 12 March 1983, pp. 4–5.

2. 'China has "Mountain of Reserves" ', *South China Morning Post*, *Business News*, 12 December 1983, p. 1; 'China's foreign exchange keeps upward trend', *China Daily*, 4 April 1984, p. 2; and 'China's Foreign Currency Reserves and Gold Total About $19 Billion', *Asian Wall Street Journal*, 5 April 1984, p. 3. Of China's foreign exchange funds, approximately US$4.5 billion is placed abroad in Eurodollar deposits according to figures of the Bank for International Settlements. See 'China shy of commercial loans', *Hong Kong Standard*, 25 May 1983, Business News Section, p. 1.

3. F. Chu, 'Foreign Banks' Business Prospects in China', *International Financial Law Review*, June 1983, p. 35; 'Banks eager to give China credit, if . . .', *South China Morning Post*, 25 May 1983, p. 3; 'China has "Mountain of Reserves" ', note 2 above; and 'China's Foreign Currency Reserves and Gold Total About $19 Billion', note 2 above.

4. These estimates were provided by the Economics Section of the United States Embassy in Beijing.

5. 'Listing of offices set up by foreign financial groups', *China Daily*, 27 July 1983, p. 2; 'Seven Foreign Banks Set Up Offices in Shanghai', *China Economic News*, 9 January 1984, pp. 6–7; and 'Foreign Banks set up offices in Guangzhou, Shenzhen, Xiamen', *China Economic News*, 13 February 1984, p. 10.

6. The role of the People's Bank of China is set forth in two Chinese language documents, Notice of the State Council Approving and Transmitting the Request for Instruction by the People's Bank of China Concerning the Function of the People's Bank as the Central Bank and its Relationship with other Specialized Banks, and Request for Instruction by the People's Bank of China Concerning the Function of

the People's Bank as the Central Bank and its Relationship with other Specialized Banks, which are published in *Zhonghua Renmin Gongheguo Guowuyuan Gongbao* (hereafter cited as the *State Council Gazette*), No. 13, 15 September 1982, p. 582.

7. *State Council Gazette*, p. 583, note 6 above.

8. 'China's Financial Organizations, Their Business and Mutual Relations', *China Economic News*, 5 March 1984, pp. 6–8; and 'China's Centralized Banking System Being Set Up, How System Works Explained by Official', *China Economic News*, 16 January 1984, pp. 4–5.

9. 'China's Financial Organizations, Their Business and Mutual Relations', p. 7, note 8 above.

10. P. Reynolds, *China's International Banking and Financial System* (New York, Praeger, 1982), p. 29.

11. Reynolds, p. 29, note 10 above.

12. 'China's Financial Organizations, Their Business and Mutual Relations', p. 7, note 8 above.

13. 'China's Financial Institutions', *China Business Review*, July–August 1980, p. 17; and 'China's Financial Organizations, Their Business and Mutual Relations', pp. 7–8, note 8 above.

14. 'China's Financial Organizations, Their Business and Mutual Relations', p. 7–8, note 8 above.

15. 'China's Financial Organizations, Their Business and Mutual Relations', p. 8, note 8 above.

16. Articles of Association of the Bank of China, Art. 1. A translation appears in *Euromoney*, December 1980, pp. 109–10.

17. Application of Bank of China Dated 25 March 1981 to Establish A Federal Branch to the Comptroller of the Currency, p. 8 (hereafter cited as the N.Y. Branch Application). On public file with the United States Comptroller of the Currency.

18. N.Y. Branch Application, p. 34, note 17 above.

19. N.Y. Branch Application, p. 34, note 17 above.

20. 'BOC Net Assets Up 25.6% to US$48.5 bn', *China Economic News*, 9 May 1983, p. 3.

21. Articles of Association of the Bank of China, Chap. IV, note 16 above.

22. N. Ludlow and J. Stepanek, 'Inside the Bank of China', *China Business Review*, July–August 1980, p. 9.

23. N.Y. Branch Application, p. 6, note 17 above.

24. J. Cohen, 'The Bank of China Clears Up Its Legal Status', *Euromoney*, December 1980, p. 108.

25. Cohen, p. 108, note 24 above.

26. *State Council Gazette*, p. 583, note 6 above.

27. Application of Bank of China Dated 25 March 1981 to the Federal Deposit Insurance Corporation, Supplemental Information, p. 6 (on public file with the United States Federal Deposit Insurance Corporation); and Loan Agreement Dated 8 May 1981 Between the Bank of China and Export-Import Bank of the United States, Art. 6.

28. V. Fung, 'Fujian Bonds Hit Roadblock in Japan, Fall Flat at Home', *Asian Wall Street Journal*, 28 April 1983, p. 1.

29. N.Y. Branch Application, p. 20, note 17 above.

30. Z.Z. Zhong, 'BOC's New Role as Sole Foreign Exchange Bank', *Economic Reporter*, June 1981, p. 9.

31. With respect to the United States see Vishipco Line v. Chase Manhattan Bank, N.A. 660 F.2d 854, p. 860 (2d Cir. 1981) *cert. denied* 103 S. Ct. 313 (1982); United States v. First National City Bank, 379 U.S. 378 (1965); Sokoloff v. National City Bank of New York, 130 Misc. 66, 224 N.Y.S. 102 (sup 1927), *aff'd* 223 App. Div. 754, 228 N.Y.S. 907 (1st Dept. 1928), *aff'd* 250 N.Y. 69, 164 N.E. 745 (1928); 1917 F.R.B. 198.

32. E. Lachica, 'China's Lending Expands as Reserves Balloon', *Asian Wall Street Journal*, 24 November 1982, p. 1.

33. Lachica, p. 1, note 32 above.

34. *Asian Wall Street Journal*, 13 January 1983, p. 3.

35. V. Fung, 'China to Extend its Biggest Loan Yet for Venture', *Asian Wall Street Journal*, 24–25 June 1983, p. 1.

36. F. Ching, 'China Considers Loans To Foreign Companies For Projects in China', *Asian Wall Street Journal*, 17 December 1982, p. 1.

37. *China Daily*, 13 March 1983, p. 2.

38. Provisional Measures for Providing Loans to Joint Ventures Using Chinese and Foreign Investment By the Bank of China, Art. 4(4). A translation of these measures appears in F. Chu, M. Moser and O. Nee (eds.), *Commercial, Business and Trade Laws: People's Republic of China* (Dobbs Ferry, Oceana Publications, Inc., 1982), Pt. 9, pp. 21–5.

39. 'Growing BOC Credit Facilities Mirror Future PRC Foreign Exchange Spending Patterns', *China Economic News*, 17 January 1983, p. 1; and 'BOC Extends US$630 Million Foreign Exchange Loans to Chinese Enterprises', *China Economic News*, 16 January 1984, p. 5.

40. 'Growing BOC Credit Facilities Mirror Future PRC Foreign Exchange Spending Patterns', p. 2, note 39 above.

41. 'BOC National Conference on New Expanded Role as Sole Foreign Exchange Bank', *China Economic News*, 7 February 1983, p. 2; and 'BOC Extends US$630 Million Foreign Exchange Loans to Chinese Enterprises', p. 5, note 39 above.

42. 'Growing BOC Credit Facilities Mirror Future PRC Foreign Exchange Spending Patterns', p. 2, note 39 above. A translation of the Instructions of the Bank of China on Foreign Exchange Loans appears in *China Economic News*, 30 January 1984, pp. 3–4.

43. M.N. Shi, 'Briefing on the Business of the Bank of China, Shanghai Branch', speech given at the Celebration of the Second Anniversary of the Establishment of SITCO, Seminar, Session 10, 27 July 1983, p. 3.

44. 'Update on the BOC Push to Expand Its Banking Clout', *Business China*, 23 February 1983, p. 27.

45. 'Shanghai Begins Giving Low-interest Loans to Overseas Ship Buyers', *China Economic News*, 27 September 1982, p. 5.

46. Shi, p. 4, note 43 above; and 'BOC Shanghai Bank Invests in Joint Ventures', *China Economic News*, 2 January 1984, p. 4.

47. 'BOC's Fledgling International Trade and Consultancy Business Reviewed', *China Economic News,* 13 September 1982, p. 2.

48. 'BOC Signs Trust Consulting Agreements with 42 Overseas Banks, Companies', *China Economic News*, 2 January 1984, pp. 3–4; and 'Articles of Association of the Bank of China Trust and Consultancy Company', *China Economic News*, 2 January 1984, pp. 4–5.

49. Reynolds, p. 56, note 10 above.

50. *South China Morning Post, Business News,* 31 January 1983, p. 1.

51. Reynolds, p. 58, note 10 above.

52. This estimate was provided by several foreign bankers based in Hong Kong.

53. V. Fung, 'Peking Banks to Trim Property Loans in Colony', *Asian Wall Street Journal,* 11 November 1982, p. 1.

54. Fung, p. 1. note 53 above.

55. Fung, p. 1, note 53 above.

56. Fung, p. 1, note 53 above.

57. 'CCIC Finance Boosts Its Authorized Capital', *Asian Wall Street Journal,* 7 July 1983, p. 3.

58. 'The First Sino-American-Japanese Finance Joint Venture Chalks Up Initial Success, Eyes Future Opportunities', *Economic Reporter,* June 1982, p. 20.

59. 'The First Sino-American-Japanese Finance Joint Venture', p. 20, note 58 above.

60. 'The First Sino-American-Japanese Finance Joint Venture', p. 20, note 58 above.

61. N.Y. Branch Application, p. 7, note 17 above.

62. 'China Investment Bank Raises Funds for Selected Projects', *China Economic News,* 1 March 1982, p. 3.

63. F. Ching, 'Investment Bank in China Begins to Assess Loans', *Asian Wall Street Journal,* 4–5 March 1983, p. 1.

64. 'World Bank Lends US$70 Million to China Investment Bank', *China Economic News,* 10 January 1983, p. 1.

65. Ching, note 63 above.

66. Provisional Regulations of the People's Republic of China Governing Foreign Exchange Control, Art. 3 (hereafter cited as the Foreign Exchange Regulations). A translation of these regulations appears in Chu, Moser and Nee, Pt. 12, pp. 3–15, note 38 above.

67. Reynolds, pp. 32–3, note 10 above.

68. Statutes of China International Trust and Investment Corporation, Art. 1 (hereafter cited as the Statutes). A translation of these statutes appears in China International Economic Consultants, Inc. and Economic Information & Consultancy Co., *Guide to Investment in China* (Hong Kong, Economic Information & Agency, 1982), pp. 169–73 (hereafter cited as the *Investment Guide*).

69. 'China's Financial Organizations, Their Business and Mutual Relations', p. 8, note 8 above.

70. Statutes, Arts. 6–11, note 68 above.

71. T. Roth, 'China Bank Scours Europe for Investors', *Asian Wall Street Journal,* 9 May 1983, p. 4.

72. *Investment Guide*, pp. 168–9, note 68 above; and 'CITIC Official on Utilizing Foreign Capital in Economic Construction', *China Economic News*, 1 November 1982, p. 9.

73. M. Fenton-Jones, 'Chinese Mission Seeks Equity in Canadian Firms', *South China Morning Post, Business News*, 16 April 1983, p. 8.

74. See The Income Tax Law of the People's Republic of China Concerning Foreign Enterprises, Art. 11 (which generally imposes a 20 per cent withholding tax), and Interim Provisions of the Ministry of Finance of the People's Republic of China Regarding the Reduction and Exemption of Income Tax Relating to Interest Earned by Foreign Businesses From China, Art. 1 (hereafter cited as the Interest Income Tax

Regulations) (which reduces the withholding tax to 10 per cent on interest obtained from loans, advances and deferred payments under credit agreements signed between 1983 and 1985). A translation of the tax law appears in Chu, Moser and Nee, Pt. 13, pp. 41–7, note 38 above; a translation of the interim provisions appears in *China Economic News*, 21 March 1983, pp. 1–2.

75. Interest Income Tax Regulations, Art. 11 (1), note 74 above.

76. *China Economic News*, 1 November 1982, p. 10.

77. K. Berney and D. Jones, 'China's Activities in the IMF and World Bank', *China Business Review,* March–April 1981, p. 47.

78. *Hong Kong Standard*, Business Section, 21 May 1983, p. 1.

79. For reports of these loans see, for example, 'World Bank Support for PRC Agriculture', *Business China*, 30 June 1982, p. 95; 'World Bank Loans US$60 Million for Agricultural Development in North China Plain', *China Economic News*, 12 July 1982, p. 1; 'World Bank to Loan China US$80 Million for China's Agricultural Development', *China Economic News*, 1 November 1982, p. 11; 'World Bank, China to Sign Loan Agreement For Agricultural Education and Research', *China Economic News*, 22 November 1982, p. 5; 'More World Bank Projects', *China Market Intelligence*, December 1982, p. 1; N. Ludlow, 'China and the World Bank', *China Business Review*, November–December 1982, p. 12; 'Equipment for China's 7 New Container Berths to be Financed by World Bank Loan', *China Economic News*, 31 January 1983, p. 6; and 'World Bank extends US$80M Loan for N.E. China Farm Project, Open Bids on Farm Equipment to be invited in May', *China Economic News*, 18 April 1983, p. 10.

80. 'World Bank Chief Says China to Get $1 Billion', *Asian Wall Street Journal*, 27 May 1983, p. 3.

81. Provisional Regulations for the Establishment of Representative Offices in China by Overseas Chinese and Foreign Financial Institutions (hereafter cited as the Registration Regulations). A translation appears in *China Economic News*, 21 February 1983, pp. 1–3.

82. Registration Regulations, Art. 2, note 81 above.

83. Chu, note 3 above.

84. Registration Regulations, note 81 above.

85. *South China Morning Post, Business News*, 21 May 1983, p. 1; V. Fung, 'China May Allow Foreign Banking in Shenzhen Zone', *Asian Wall Street Journal*, 5 July 1983, p. 1.

86. Interest Income Tax Regulations, Art. 4, note 74 above.

87. The Income Tax Law of the People's Republic of China Concerning Foreign Enterprises, Arts. 1, 3 and 4, note 74 above.

88. The Income Tax Law of the People's Republic of China Concerning Foreign Enterprises, Art. 11, and Interest Income Tax Regulations, note 74 above.

89. Interest Income Tax Regulations, Art. 4, note 74 above.

90. F. Ching, 'China Softens Its Tax Regulations On Income By Foreign Companies', *Asian Wall Street Journal*, 14 March 1983, p. 1.

91. V. Fung, 'China Clarifies Rules on Foreign Banks', *Asian Wall Street Journal*, 29 June 1983, p. 1.

92. Lachica, note 32 above; and Chu, note 3 above.

93. M. Bu, 'China's Financial Relations with Foreign Countries', *Beijing Review*, 20 April 1983, p. 21; and Chu, note 3 above.

94. Lachica, note 32 above.

95. *Asian Wall Street Journal*, 20–21 May 1983, p. 1.
96. 'UBAF Loan's Surprise for Bank', *Business China*, 28 April 1983, p. 63.
97. V. Fung, 'China Bank Takes Over Foreign Loan for Hotel', *Asian Wall Street Journal*, 9 December 1982, p. 1.
98. Chu, note 3 above.
99. V. Fung, 'U.S. Banks Map New Strategy with China', *Asian Wall Street Journal*, 20 October 1982, p. 1.
100. The analysis of Chinese letter of credit practices is based on discussions with Chinese and foreign bankers and businessmen and examination of standard-form contracts used by Chinese trading corporations and standard-form letters of credit issued by the BOC.
101. 'Bank of China Quickens Account Clearing Processes in Foreign Trade', *China Economic News*, 20 October 1980, p. 9.
102. See, for example, Loan Agreement Dated as of 8 May 1981 Between the Bank of China and the Export-Import Bank of the United States; and Credit Agreement Dated as of 9 May 1979 among a group of French banks and the Bank of China to finance part of the contracts signed by French suppliers and corporations of the People's Republic of China for delivery of French capital goods, industrial complexes and services.
103. Foreign Exchange Regulations, note 66 above.
104. International Monetary Fund, *Annual Report on Exchange Arrangements and Exchange Restrictions 1982*, p. 120.
105. Foreign Exchange Regulations, Art. 4, note 66 above.
106. Foreign Exchange Regulations, Art. 10, note 66 above.
107. International Monetary Fund, p. 120, note 104 above.
108. International Monetary Fund, p. 120, note 104 above.
109. Foreign Exchange Regulations, Art. 8, note 66 above.
110. Rules for the Implementation of Exchange Control Regulations Relating to Enterprises with Overseas Chinese Capital, Enterprises with Foreign Capital, and Chinese and Foreign Joint Ventures, which were approved by the State Council on 19 July 1983 and promulgated by the SGAEC on 1 August 1983 (hereafter cited as the Foreign Exchange Implementation Rules). A translation appears in *China Daily*, August 1983, p 2. Article 2 of these rules defines: (1) 'enterprises with overseas Chinese capital' to mean 'corporations, enterprises or other economic entities registered in China with overseas Chinese capital or capital of compatriots in Hong Kong and Macao areas, and managed independently or jointly with Chinese enterprises'; (2) 'enterprises with foreign capital' to mean 'corporations, enterprises or other economic entities registered in China with foreign capital, and managed independently or jointly with Chinese enterprises'; and (3) 'Chinese and foreign joint ventures' to mean 'enterprises jointly established, owned and run in China by corporations, enterprises, other economic entities or individuals with overseas Chinese capital, capital of compatriots in Hong Kong and Macao areas or foreign capital and Chinese corporations, enterprises or other economic entities.'
111. Foreign Exchange Implementation Rules, Art. 4, note 110 above.
112. Foreign Exchange Implementation Rules, Art. 7, note 110 above.
113. Foreign Exchange Implementation Rules, Art. 9, note 110 above.
114. Foreign Exchange Implementation Rules, Art. 9, note 110 above.
115. Foreign Exchange Implementation Rules, Arts. 6 and 7, note 110 above.
116. Foreign Exchange Implementation Rules, Art. 8, note 110 above.

117. Foreign Exchange Implementation Rules, Art. 14, note 110 above.
118. Foreign Exchange Implementation Rules, Art. 12, note 110 above.
119. A translation of the Implementing Act for the Law of the People's Republic of China on Joint Ventures Using Chinese and Foreign Investment (hereafter cited as the Joint Venture Implementation Regulations) is on file with the author.
120. Foreign Exchange Implementation Rules, Art. 15, note 110 above.
121. Joint Venture Implementation Regulations, Art. 79, note 119 above.
122. Regulations on Special Economic Zones in Guangdong Province, Art. 15. A translation of these regulations appears in Chu, Moser and Nee, Pt. 14, pp. 3–11, note 38 above.

9. Trade-mark Law in the People's Republic of China

JESSE T. H. CHANG AND CHARLES J. CONROY

I. Introduction

THE concept of using trade marks in China to identify the source of manufacture can be traced back to the early days of Chinese society. The pottery wares of a famous craftsman in the Northern Zhou dynasty (AD 556–580) carried a mark to distinguish his products from those of other craftsmen.[1] Today, objects of art with trade marks of manufacturers dating back to the Song dynasty (AD 960–1279) can be found on display at the Museum of Chinese History in Beijing.[2]

In 1904, these early developments in the trade-mark area were followed by the promulgation by the Qing government of China's first formal trade-mark law, the Trial Regulations for Trade-mark Registration (hereafter cited as the Trial Regulations). However, the Trial Regulations were both drafted and, in practice, administered by foreigners, who at that time assumed control over much of China's trade. Accordingly, it was not surprising that foreign trade marks received adequate protection under the provisions of the Trial Regulations. In fact, the Trial Regulations went so far as to provide that the settlement of trade-mark disputes was within the jurisdiction of the foreign consulates in China.

Two major trade-mark laws were promulgated between 1911 and 1949. The first was the Trade-mark Law of 1923 which made few improvements to the Trial Regulations and continued to vest the authority for settling trade-mark disputes with the foreign consulates. A revised Trade-mark Law was promulgated by the Nationalist regime in 1931, but its provisions were essentially adopted without significant changes from the trade-mark laws of other countries. Reflecting the influence which foreign trade-mark practice exerted over Chinese practice, the goods classification table used during the period was identical to the Japanese goods classification table.[3]

Shortly after the formal founding of the People's Republic of China (PRC), the PRC's first trade-mark law was released in 1950. Since that time, trade-mark legislation in China has undergone significant changes, with new laws being introduced in 1963 and 1983. These developments in China's trade-mark legislation, including China's present trade-mark law, are discussed in further detail below.

II. The Early Trade-mark Laws

A. The 1950 Provisional Regulations

The Provisional Regulations Governing Trade-mark Registration (hereafter cited as the 1950 Provisional Regulations) were promulgated by the Government Administration Council on 28 August 1950.[4]

Although the Regulations were rather brief and uncomplicated, they were nevertheless important as they introduced the concept of trade marks to socialist China. The Regulations recognized the monopolistic right of a party to use a trade mark, a right that seemed perilously close to capitalist principles. Indeed, Article 1 of the Regulations went so far as to provide that the Regulations '. . . are enacted for the protection of the rights of exclusive use of trade marks by general industry and commerce'.

B. The 1963 Trade-mark Laws

On 10 April 1963, the State Council promulgated the Regulations of the People's Republic of China Governing the Control of Trade Marks (hereafter cited as the 1963 Trade-mark Regulations). Shortly thereafter, the Central Administration for Industry and Commerce (CAIC) promulgated the Detailed Implementing Rules of the 1963 Trade-mark Regulations (hereafter cited as the 1963 Implementing Rules).[5]

The most important aspect of the 1963 legislation was the recognition that the trade-mark law could be used as a means of controlling the quality of products. This concept of using trade marks as a means of quality control over goods has been cited by Chinese legal scholars as the rationale for adopting a trade-mark registration system in socialist China.[6] Thus, in contrast to the 1950 Regulations, which emphasized the connection between trade marks and exclusive use, the focus of the 1963 Trade-mark Law was on quality control.

The concern of the 1963 Trade-mark Law with quality control is evidenced by the definition of a trade mark as '. . . a distinctive sign representing the quality of the goods bearing it . . .'.[7] The 1963 Trade-mark Law also stipulated that the authorities concerned shall exercise supervision and control over the quality of the goods using trade marks.[8] In addition, it provided for mandatory registration of all trade marks used by any enterprise in China. Even if an enterprise did not display trade marks on its products, it had to indicate its name and address on the goods or packages in order to facilitate control by the CAIC.[9] The right of registration was granted to the first applicant.[10] No rights were accorded to first users as they are in most common law jurisdictions.

Another important aspect of the 1963 Trade-mark Law was the omission of the requirement of 'prior use' or 'intention to use in the future'. In addition to the concern for quality control, this feature has come to characterize Chinese trade-mark law.

Initially, foreign parties had only limited opportunities to register trade marks in China. Only those foreign parties with home registration and whose countries had reciprocal registration agreements with China were permitted to apply for registration.[11] These requirements of home registration and reciprocal registration agreements were subsequently waived in 1978, presumably to promote China's trade with foreign countries. Those foreign applicants who met the registration requirements had to use the Trade-mark Registration Agency of the China Council for the Promotion of International Trade (CCPIT) as their agent in filing the registration documents with the CAIC.[12]

III. The 1983 Trade-mark Law

A. Introduction

In order to attract more foreign investment to China, the People's Republic announced its general intention to adopt an 'open-door' policy in 1978. As part of this effort, the Chinese leadership recognized the need to introduce more complete laws to govern and protect foreign investment in China. As discussed elsewhere in this volume, laws relating to joint ventures and taxation began to be promulgated for the first time in 1979. At the same time, it was clear that some of the existing laws, such as the 1963 Trade-mark Law, needed to be revised or replaced in order to accommodate the concerns of foreign businesses.

Accordingly, in 1983, two important pieces of trade-mark legislation were released to replace the 1963 Trade-mark Law. The first is the Trade-mark Law of the People's Republic of China (hereafter cited as the Trade-mark Law) which was passed on 23 August 1982 by the Twenty-fourth Meeting of the Standing Committee of the Fifth National People's Congress and became effective on 1 March 1983. The second is the Detailed Implementing Rules of the Trade-mark Law of the People's Republic of China (hereafter cited as the Implementing Rules) which were also promulgated and came into effect on 10 March 1983.[13]

At present, China's Trade-mark Law only provides for registration and protection of marks for goods, and not 'service marks' or marks of service institutions such as banks.[14] Many countries, such as the United Kingdom, are now considering adopting a system for registering service marks. It is uncertain whether China will also move in this direction.

As with the 1963 Trade-mark Law, there is no requirement of prior use or intention to use in the future for the purpose of filing trade-mark applications. Prior use may, however, become important in order to establish priority between competing applications.[15]

B. The Trade-mark Bureau

The Trade-mark Bureau, an agency consisting of about 200 personnel within the State Administration for Industry and Commerce (SAIC),[16] is responsible for trade-mark registration and control throughout China. Matters relating to the use or issue of trade marks are therefore within the jurisdiction of the Trade-mark Bureau. However, the task of actually enforcing the Trade-mark Law rests with the local departments of the Administration for Industry and Commerce (AIC).[17]

C. Quality Control

As in the 1963 Trade-mark Law, the present Law emphasizes the importance of the relationship between trade marks and quality control. Article 1 of the Trade-mark Law expressly states that the Law '. . . is specially enacted in order to strengthen trade-mark control, to protect the right of exclusive use of trade marks, to impel producers to guarantee the quality of goods and uphold the reputation of trade marks, thereby safeguarding the interests of consumers . . .'. The interests of consumers are further advanced by a provision of the Trade-mark Law which states that trade-mark users must bear responsibility for the quality of the goods that bear their trade marks.[18]

It is interesting to note that the right of exclusive use is also clearly recognized by the new Law. The Law does so, in part, by defining a trade mark approved for registration by the Trade-mark Bureau as '. . . a registered trade mark [for which] the registrant of the trade mark enjoys the right of exclusive use of the trade mark and receives legal protection'.[19]

D. Other Provisions

Words and designs used for trade marks, or their composition, must be distinctive.[20] Goods displaying registered trade marks shall be marked with the Chinese words for 'Registered Trade-mark'(注册商标) or marked with the symbols ® or ㊟.[21] No penalty is specified in the Trade-mark Law for failure to comply with this requirement. However, CCPIT trade-mark officials have expressed their intention to impose a penalty in the near future for non-compliance.[22]

Unlike the 1963 Trade-mark Law, which provided for compulsory trade-mark registration, trade-mark registration is generally voluntary under the Trade-mark Law. However, under Article 5 of the Trade-mark Law, certain goods may not be sold on the market unless and until they use registered trade marks.

For example, the Implementing Rules, in Article 4, impose such a requirement for the sale of pharmaceuticals.[23] Also, in registering trade marks for pharmaceuticals, a document certifying approval of production issued by the relevant local health authorities must be appended to the application materials.[24]

Where goods are sold in violation of Article 5 of the Trade-mark Law, the local departments of the AIC are empowered to prohibit the goods from being sold on the market, confiscate unregistered trade-mark signs and order an application for registration within a stated period.[25] In addition, these departments may fine the infringing party up to renminbi (RMB) 1,000.[26]

In addition to the provisions contained in the Trade-mark Law, the Tobacco Monopoly Regulations of the People's Republic of China (hereafter cited as the Tobacco Monopoly Regulations) require that cigarettes and cigars must have registered trade marks before they are sold on the market.[27] This requirement imposed by the Tobacco Monopoly Regulations is analogous to the quality control restriction imposed by the Trade-mark Law on pharmaceutical sales and appears to be directed towards the general protection of the consumer.

E. Foreign Applicants

Foreign individuals or companies applying to register trade marks in China are subject to the Trade-mark Law. The promulgation of the Law is certainly a step forward, as foreign parties investing in or doing business with China can now rely upon a trade-mark registration system for their goods which is more consistent with common international trade-mark practice.

As in the past under the 1963 Trade-mark Law, foreign applicants are not allowed to file their applications directly with the Trade-mark Bureau, the agency actually responsible for consideration of trade-mark applications. Rather, they must appoint the Trade-mark Registration Agency of the CCPIT as their agent to process their applications.[28] The CCPIT is a government organization with its headquarters in Beijing. Its Trade-mark Registration Agency in Beijing has a staff of about 30 personnel and monopolizes the business of trade-mark registrations for foreign parties in China.

For an agency fee of RMB 350 for each trade-mark application, the CCPIT processes the application materials for submission to the Trade-mark Bureau. Foreign applicants are required to submit their application forms and materials in Chinese.[29] If foreign applicants fail to provide the application materials in Chinese, the CCPIT will perform any necessary translation services for an additional fee.

Foreign parties are also required to appoint the CCPIT as their agent for 'handling other trade-mark matters'.[30] The precise type of assistance which falls within the category of 'other trade-mark matters' is not clear. However, the CCPIT has been known to assist some American multinational companies in settling amicably trade-mark disputes with Chinese entities.

F. Application Procedures

In applying for registration of a trade mark, applicants must complete and submit an application form with the class and name of the product using the trade mark in accordance with China's goods classification table.[31] The goods classification table presently in use has not changed since 1963.[32] It is not necessary to have the application form notarized or legalized.

A separate application must be made for each of the classes in which the applicant proposes to register a given trade mark.[33] Unlike international practice, a separate application must be filed where the applicant wishes to use a registered trade mark on another product even though it may be in the same class.[34]

If it becomes necessary to change the words or design of a registered trade mark, the owner must make a new application for registration.[35] Similarly, it is necessary to file an application for alteration where the name or address of the registrant changes.[36]

Foreign applicants, in addition to completing and submitting the trade-mark application form, must submit a power of attorney form.[37] The power of attorney form is required to be notarized, but whether legalization is necessary depends on the principle of reciprocity.[38] The requirement of legalization is generally waived for applicants from developed countries, such as the United States, West Germany and Japan, most of which have reciprocal arrangements with China. The power of attorney form appoints the CCPIT as the agent for the foreign applicant in processing the application.

The CCPIT charges a fee of RMB 450 for each trade-mark application in each class. This fee consists of the Trade-mark Bureau's application fee of RMB 20, the CCPIT's agency fee of RMB 350, and a registration fee of RMB 80. The registration fee of RMB 80 is payable upon application and is not refundable if the mark is rejected. The total fee must be submitted together with the application form, power of attorney form and the trade-mark specimens. The Trade-mark Bureau and the CCPIT require ten and five specimens of the trade mark, respectively.[39] The time required to obtain a trade-mark registration is generally between one and two years from the date of the application.

G. Rejection

Certain contents are prohibited in both registered and unregistered trade marks, including: those that are the same or similar to the state name, national flag, national emblem, military flag or medals of the PRC or of other foreign countries; the commonly used name or design of the goods in question; words or designs directly expressing the quality, main raw materials, functions, use, weight, quantity and other characteristics of the goods; those that exaggerate and are of a deceptive nature; and those that are harmful to the customs of socialist morality or have other 'bad influences'.[40]

Foreign applicants have generally found that the Trade-mark Bureau adopts a very broad interpretation of the criteria 'harmful to the customs of socialist morality or [having] other bad influences'. The Trade-mark Bureau has been known to have rejected on these grounds many registration applications of foreign trade marks which were registered in other jurisdictions.

H. Examination and Re-examination

The Trade-mark Bureau performs the task of examining trade-mark applications. Once the application conforms to the requirements of the Trade-mark Law, preliminary approval is granted by the Trade-mark Bureau and a public announcement of the preliminary approval is made.[41] However, the application is rejected and no public announcement is made in cases where an application for registration does not conform to the relevant requirements of the Trade-mark Law, or is the same as or similar to a trade mark which is already registered, or which has been preliminarily approved after examination.[42] In all such cases, the Trade-mark Bureau notifies the applicant in writing.[43]

If the applicant does not agree with the decision of the Trade-mark Bureau, he may apply for a re-examination within fifteen days of receiving the notification.[44] For this purpose, the applicant needs to submit a copy of the Application Form for Re-examination of Rejected Trade Marks to the Trade-mark Review Committee,[45] which is responsible for handling trade-mark-related disputes.[46] The applicant is notified in writing by the Committee of its decision, which is to be final and binding.[47]

Anyone who opposes the granting of the preliminary approval has three months from the date of the public announcement to 'raise objections' with the Trade-mark Bureau.[48] In raising objections, opponents must submit the Objections to Trade Marks Form to the Trade-mark Bureau.[49] The Trade-mark Bureau is to consider the facts and reasons stated by both the objector and the applicant and shall, after investigation and verification, render a decision.[50]

If a party does not agree with the decision of the Trade-mark Bureau, he may, within fifteen days of receiving notification, apply to the Trade-mark Review Committee for re-examination by submitting the Application Form for Re-examination of Objections to Trade Marks.[51] The Trade-mark Review Committee shall notify the parties of its final ruling in writing.[52] If there are no objections to the preliminary approval of the Trade-mark Bureau or any objections are overruled by the Trade-mark Review Committee, the trade mark is to be registered.

Objections may also be raised to registered trade marks.[53] Within one year of the registration of a trade mark, an objection may be brought for a ruling by the Trade-mark Review Committee provided that the same objection has not been raised and ruled upon during the period for objections to preliminary approvals. Opponents of trade marks already registered need to submit to the

Trade-mark Review Committee an Application Form for a Ruling on Disputes on Registered Trade Marks.[54]

I. Competing Applications

Where two or more applicants apply for registration of the same or a similar trade mark on the same or a similar type of product, preliminary approval is granted by the Trade-mark Bureau after examination and public announcement are made of the trade mark which was applied for first.[55] In cases where the applications are made on the same day, preliminary approval is granted after examination and public announcement are made of the trade mark first used.[56] Neither the Trade-mark Law nor the Implementing Rules provides any guidance on how the principle of use is to be interpreted by the Trade-mark Bureau. Nevertheless, Chinese trade-mark officials have unofficially stated that the principle of use is not restricted to within China and includes use outside China. The proof required of such use is the date on which the product is sold on the market, within or outside China.[57]

The Trade-mark Bureau is prohibited from approving, within one year of the date of the revocation or cancellation of a registered trade mark, any application for trade-mark registration which is the same or similar to the cancelled trade mark.[58]

J. Extensions

A registered trade mark is valid for ten years from the date of approval of registration, and not from the date of the filing of the application as is the case in international practice.[59] An application for the extension of registration of an additional ten years can be made six months before or on the expiry of the basic ten-year term.[60] In cases where such an application is not made by the end of the ten-year validity period, the registered trade mark in question is no longer valid and is cancelled.[61]

K. Licensing and Assignment

In a significant improvement to the 1963 Trade-mark Law, the Trade-mark Law provides for the first time for the licensing of the right to use a registered trade mark in China.[62] Although the Trade-mark Law does not require the licensor or the licensee to obtain approval from the Trade-mark Bureau for licensing trade marks, it does provide that licensing agreements must be filed with the Trade-mark Bureau 'for the record'.[63]

Licensors, such as those foreign parties engaged in technology transfer agreements in China which include the licensing of the right to the use of registered trade marks in China, shall 'supervise' the quality of the goods on which the licensees use their registered trade marks.[64] The licensees, in turn, shall 'guarantee' the quality of the goods on which they use the registered trade marks.[65] As the Trade-mark Law does not specify the precise nature of the responsibility required from the licensing parties, this aspect of the law remains to be clarified through experience.

In cases of assignment of registered trade marks, the assignor and the assignee must jointly file an application for the assignment to the Trade-mark Bureau.[66] The assignee must 'guarantee' the quality of the goods which use the relevant registered trade mark.[67]

L. The Powers of the Trade-mark Bureau on Misconduct

Independent of third-party applications, the Trade-mark Bureau is empowered in some circumstances by the Trade-mark Law to order trade-mark registrants who breach the law either to correct their behaviour or face the possibility of having their registered trade marks revoked by the Trade-mark Bureau.[68] These circumstances include the changing of the words or design, or the assigning, of a registered trade mark without following the stipulated procedures of the law, and non-use of a trade mark for three consecutive years.[69]

A party which disagrees with the decision of the Trade-mark Bureau in revoking its registered trade mark may apply for re-examination of the decision by the Trade-mark Review Committee within fifteen days of receiving the Trade-mark Bureau's notification.[70] The Trade-mark Review Committee is obliged to render a final decision in writing to the applicant.[71]

In other situations where registrants carry on conduct in violation of the Trade-mark Law such as when goods are '. . . manufactured in a rough and slipshod way, the inferior being passed off as good, deceiving consumers . . .',[72] the relevant departments of the AIC are authorized '. . . to order rectification within a stated period and to circulate a notice on the matter or impose fines, . . .'.[73] In such cases, if the circumstances of the offence are minor, 'criticism education' is to be conducted and rectification demanded by the relevant local AIC departments.[74] However, where the circumstances are serious, 'self-criticism' is to be ordered and either a notice is to be circulated or a fine of up to RMB 2,000 is to be imposed by the local departments of the AIC.[75] The Trade-mark Bureau may also independently revoke the relevant registered trade mark.[76]

If a trade-mark owner, in using unregistered trade marks for the sale of certain goods, represents the mark as a registered trade mark or violates any of the provisions of the Trade-mark Law regarding the contents of the trade mark,[77] the local departments of the AIC are authorized to prohibit the goods in question from being sold on the market, to stop any advertisement of the goods, to confiscate the trade-mark signs and order rectification within a stated period.[78] Such AIC departments may also, according to the seriousness of the circumstances, either circulate a notice on the matter or impose a fine of up to RMB 2,000 on the violator.[79]

A party who is fined by the local AIC for misconduct under the Trade-mark Law may appeal in the people's courts within fifteen days of receiving notification of the fine.[80] However, if the fifteen-day period has elapsed and the violating party has neither appealed nor taken remedial action, the local AIC department is to apply to the people's courts for compulsory execution of the fine.[81]

M. Infringement

The Trade-mark Law has filled a major gap in China's previous trade-mark legislation by providing a system of civil remedies for trade-mark infringement. Trade-mark infringement is defined broadly under the Trade-mark Law to include one of the following types of conduct:

(1) using, without obtaining the licence of the registered trade-mark owner, on the same or a similar type of product a trade mark which is the same as or similar to the owner's registered trade mark;
(2) unauthorized manufacture or sale of another's registered trade-mark sign; or
(3) causing other damage to another's right of exclusive use of a registered trade mark.[82]

The Trade-mark Law provides an aggrieved registrant with a choice of remedies. Where his fundamental right of exclusive use of the registered trade mark has been infringed, he may bring a suit directly in the people's court or request the local AIC department to order the infringer to cease immediately the infringing conduct and to compensate him for his losses.[83] Where the circumstances of the infringement are serious, fines may also be imposed on the infringing party by the local department of the AIC.[84]

However, aggrieved foreign parties cannot complain of infringement directly to the local AIC departments. Instead, foreign parties wishing to lodge infringement complaints must request that the CCPIT handle the matter with the relevant departments of the local AIC. Moreover, if litigation in the people's courts is required, the Legal Counsel Office of the CCPIT is to be retained.[85]

If the registrant chooses to seek the administrative relief available from the local department of the AIC but does not agree with the amount of the fine imposed by the local AIC department, he may appeal before the people's court within fifteen days of receiving notification of the imposition of the fine.[86] The accused infringer, however, is also entitled to appeal to the people's court for disputes regarding the amount of the fine imposed. However, where a suit has not been brought before the court by either the registrant or the accused party within the fifteen-day period and where the infringing conduct has not ceased and compensation has not been paid, the local AIC has the right to apply to the people's court for compulsory execution.[87]

In cases of counterfeiting of another's registered trade mark, which includes the unauthorized manufacture or sale of another's registered trade-mark sign, the infringing party is liable to pay compensation to the registrant for his losses and faces the possibility of additional fines. Moreover, the criminal responsibility of the person(s) directly responsible for the infringement is to be 'investigated according to law by the judicial organs'.[88]

IV. Conclusion

In tracing the history of Chinese trade-mark law since 1949, it is obvious that significant improvements have been made. Although China has not yet joined the Paris Convention, the 1983 Trade-mark Law has brought China's trade-mark system much closer to common international practice.

The Trade-mark Law's consideration of many areas of concern to foreign trade-mark owners which were not previously covered by the earlier trade-mark law demonstrates the advancement of trade-mark law in China. The most important examples of these changes are provisions in the 1983 Law relating to the licensing of the exclusive right to use registered trade marks and the offering of a range of civil remedies for infringements.

There have also been improvements with regard to the administration of the Law. For example, although not yet fully tested, the time required for registration under the new Law is anticipated to remain between one and two years. This compares favourably with the length of time required for trade-mark registration in European countries and in Australia.

Nevertheless, some areas of administration still require improvement. Many foreign applicants have urged the Trade-mark Registration Agency of the CCPIT, in its role as the sole agent for foreign applicants, to keep them better informed of the progress of their applications. Foreign applicants would also welcome any efforts which the CCPIT makes in generally providing a better bridge of communication between foreign clients and the Trade-mark Bureau.

Notes

1. See Han Shaoyou, *Jurisprudence* (Shanghai), October 1982, p.37.
2. Han, p.37, note 1 above.
3. For this paragraph and the preceding paragraph, see Han, p.38, note 1 above.
4. The Government Administration Council was subsequently renamed the State Council.

5. The 1963 Trade-mark Regulations and the 1963 Implementing Rules will in this chapter be collectively referred to as the 1963 Trade-mark Law.

6. See, for example, Li Hongxiang, *China Finance and Trade Journal,* April 1983, p.35.

7. 1963 Trade-mark Regulations, Art. 3.

8. 1963 Trade-mark Regulations, Art. 3.

9. 1963 Trade-mark Regulations, Art. 2.

10. 1963 Trade-mark Regulations, Art. 7.

11. 1963 Trade-mark Regulations, Art. 12.

12. 1963 Implementing Rules, Art. 15.

13. Unless otherwise specified in this chapter, a reference to the Trade-mark Law will include the Trade-mark Law as supplemented by the Implementing Rules.

14. Under the Trade-mark Law, foreign banks will be able to register their trade marks for tangible goods such as bank publications. Protection will, however, not be extended to banks' names and logos. See T. A. Gelatt and T. Y. Chan, 'China's New and Improved Trademark Law', *Asian Wall Street Journal,* 22 October 1982, p.6.

15. See 'Competing Applications', p. 274 in this volume, for a more detailed discussion of prior use.

16. Previously, under the 1963 Trade-mark Regulations, the SAIC was known as the GAIC. The SAIC is under the direct supervision and jurisdiction of the State Council.

17. Trade-mark Law, Art. 6.

18. Trade-mark Law, Art. 6.

19. Trade-mark Law, Art. 3.

20. Trade-mark Law, Art. 7.

21. Trade-mark Law, Art. 7; and Implementing Rules, Art. 8.

22. This information is based on discussions held between the authors and CCPIT Trade-mark Registration Agency officials in Beijing in June 1983.

23. According to a circular issued in July 1983 by the Ministry of Public Health, the State Pharmaceutical Administration and the SAIC, the term pharmaceuticals covers all pharmaceuticals, new patent drugs, traditional Chinese patent drugs and medicinal liquors.

24. The July 1983 circular, see note 23 above, requires foreign enterprises to submit certificates approving production from their own governments.

25. Implementing Rules, Art. 22.

26. Implementing Rules, Art. 2. US$1.00 equals approximately RMB1.98 (January 1984).

27. See Article 16 of the Tobacco Monopoly Regulations. These regulations became effective on 1 November 1983.

28. Implementing Rules, Art. 29.

29. Implementing Rules, Art. 31.

30. Implementing Rules, Art. 29.

31. Trade-mark Law, Art. 11.

32. For more details, see I. J. Kaufman, 'Trademark Protection in the People's Republic of China', in Jerome A. Cohen (ed.), *Legal Aspects of Doing Business in China 1983* (New York, Practising Law Institute, 1983), p.436.

33. Trade-mark Law, Art. 12.

34. Trade-mark Law, Art. 13.

35. Trade-mark Law, Art. 14.

36. Trade-mark Law, Art. 15; and Implementing Rules, Art. 7.

37. Implementing Rules, Art. 30.

38. Implementing Rules, Art. 31.

39. The specimens must be on glossy durable paper of a size not exceeding 10 × 10 centimetres. The specimens may be photocopies of the mark. However, if the mark is in colour, the specimens need also to be in colour, and an additional black and white ink draft of the mark is also required. The specimens must also be accompanied by an explanation of the meaning and derivation of the mark, unless the mark has no particular meaning in which case no explanation is necessary. See Implementing Rules, Art. 3.

40. Trade-mark Law, Art. 8. It is interesting to note that one of the most well-known beers in Beijing uses the registered trade mark 'Wuxing', meaning 'five-star', which must be close to violating the national emblem prohibition. The five-star symbol is the national emblem of the People's Republic of China.

41. Trade-mark Law, Art. 16.

42. Trade-mark Law, Art. 17.

43. Foreign applicants only receive the CCPIT's written advice which generally provides only the decision of the Trade-mark Bureau, and not any of the arguments which the CCPIT might have presented on behalf of the foreign applicant nor any of the counterarguments which it might have received from the Trade-mark Bureau.

44. Trade-mark Law, Art. 21; and Implementing Rules, Art. 10. At meetings with the authors, CCPIT trade-mark officials have unofficially expressed their concern for the time limitation imposed on foreign applicants by the fifteen-day requirement. In their opinion, foreign applicants should be granted an extension beyond the fifteen-day period.

See also C. L. Gholz, 'China's New Trade-mark Law', *China Law Reporter*, Vol. II, No. 2, Summer 1982, p.106.

45. Implementing Rules, Art. 10.

46. Trade-mark Law, Art. 20.

47. Trade-mark Law, Art. 21.

48. Trade-mark Law, Art. 19.

49. Implementing Rules, Art. 11.

50. Trade-mark Law, Art. 22. As yet, it is not clear in practice whether the Trade-mark Bureau intends to notify the relevant parties of its decision in writing.

51. Trade-mark Law, Art. 22; and Implementing Rules, Art. 11.

52. Trade-mark Law, Art. 22.

53. Trade-mark Law, Art. 27.

54. Implementing Rules, Art. 12.

55. Trade-mark Law, Art. 18.

56. Trade-mark Law, Art. 18.

57. This information is based on meetings between the authors and CCPIT Trade-mark Registration Agency officials in May and June 1983.

58. Trade-mark Law, Art. 32.

59. Trade-mark Law, Art. 23.

60. Trade-mark Law, Art. 24.

61. Trade-mark Law, Art. 24.

62. Trade-mark Law, Art. 26.

63. Trade-mark Law, Art. 26.

64. Trade-mark Law, Art. 26.
65. Trade-mark Law, Art. 26.
66. Trade-mark Law, Art. 25.
67. Trade-mark Law, Art. 25.
68. Trade-mark Law, Art. 30.
69. Trade-mark Law, Art. 30.
70. Trade-mark Law, Art. 35; and Implementing Rules, Art. 28.
71. Trade-mark Law, Art. 35.
72. Trade-mark Law, Art. 34(3).
73. Trade-mark Law, Art. 34.
74. Implementing Rules, Art. 21(1).
75. Implementing Rules, Art. 21(2).
76. Implementing Rules, Art. 21(2).
77. Trade-mark Law, Art. 34(1) and (2).
78. Implementing Rules, Art. 23.
79. Implementing Rules, Art. 23.
80. Trade-mark Law, Art. 36; and Implementing Rules, Art. 25.
81. Trade-mark Law, Art. 36; and Implementing Rules, Art. 25.
82. Trade-mark Law, Art. 38.
83. Trade-mark Law, Art. 39. The amount of compensation is stipulated by Article 39 of the Trade-mark Law to be either the profits gained by the infringer or the losses suffered by the registrant during the period of infringement as a result of the infringing conduct.
84. Trade-mark Law, Art. 39. The local AIC departments appear to have discretion on the amount of fines which may be imposed as this is not specified in Article 39 of the Trade-mark Law.
85. This information is based on the advice of the CCPIT Trade-mark Registration Agency given to the authors in August 1983.
86. Trade-mark Law, Art. 39; and Implementing Rules, Art. 25.
87. Trade-mark Law, Art. 39; and Implementing Rules, Art. 25.
88. Trade-mark Law, Art. 40.

10. Representative Offices in China: Legal Aspects of Registration and Control

CLARK T. RANDT, JR.

MUCH has changed since the stately clipper ships of the nineteenth century made their semi-annual journeys up the Pearl River to the foreign factories and trading houses in a restricted area of Guangzhou. Yet China's suspicion of, and consequent desire to control, the foreign commercial presence within her borders remains an important element of contemporary Chinese policy. The dilemma of how to build a strong, modern China without sacrificing cultural identity or compromising internal security weighs as heavily on the nation's current leaders as it did on officials of the Qing dynasty. On the one hand, the presence of foreigners in China — bringing with them modern technology, know-how, managerial skills and foreign exchange — is to be encouraged. On the other hand, the foreign presence is to be controlled and the activities of foreigners regulated so as to lessen the risk that they might contaminate China's disciplined and comparatively austere socialist society.

At present the principal vehicle by which foreign companies are permitted to maintain a presence in China is the resident representative office (*changzhu daibiao jigou*). As of the beginning of 1983, 512 representative offices had been established in Beijing, Shanghai, Guangzhou and other major Chinese cities by enterprises from 29 countries and Hong Kong and Macao.[1] The registration and operational activities of these offices is governed by a number of regulations. The basic legislative framework is provided by a national statute promulgated in 1980, the Provisional Regulations of the State Council of the People's Republic of China Concerning the Control of Resident Representative Offices of Foreign Enterprises (hereafter cited as the Registration Regulations).[2] The Registration Regulations were subsequently supplemented by a Circular Concerning the Registration Procedures for Resident Offices of Foreign Enterprises by the General Administration for Industry and Commerce of the People's Republic of China (hereafter cited as the Circular), issued on 8 December 1981;[3] by the Measures of the State Administration of Industry and Commerce of the People's Republic of China Regarding the Control of Registration of Long-term Representative Offices of Foreign Enterprises (hereafter cited as the SAIC Measures), issued on 15 March 1983;[4] and by various municipal announcements and notices which will be discussed later.

In addition, Guangdong Province has promulgated its own rules governing representative offices established there, and separate regulations have been issued by the People's Bank of China concerning representative offices established by foreign banks and insurance companies.[5]

This chapter will provide a description and analysis of the legal aspects of registration and control of foreign resident representative offices in China. The first part will discuss the registration requirement imposed on foreign companies maintaining a presence in China and the second part will describe the procedures to be followed when registering a representative office. The third part will describe various control aspects of the registration rules. Finally, the fourth part will examine the main features of the Guangdong registration rules and the regulations applicable to foreign financial institutions.

I. The Registration Requirement and Benefits of Registration

The Registration Regulations do not make clear under what circumstances registration is mandatory or optional. Although the law does state that 'a foreign enterprise that has not obtained an approval and registered may not commence the business activities of a registered office',[6] the Chinese authorities have never provided any explicit guidance to foreign companies as to what types of activities or behaviour will be deemed to constitute 'the business activities of a resident office'. Moreover, the Registration Regulations themselves do not specify any penalties for failure to register. As a result, at the time the Registration Regulations came into effect in late 1980, many companies that were already operating in China through makeshift hotel room offices ignored the new rules. According to Chinese press reports at the time, one month after the promulgation of the Registration Regulations less than one out of four foreign firms operating in China had obtained official approval to do so.[7]

Subsequently, efforts have been made by the Chinese authorities to clarify the scope of the registration requirement established by the Registration Regulations. In mid-1981, the General Administration for Industry and Commerce of the People's Republic of China issued an internal circular to Chinese organizations informing them that foreign companies operating in China that had not yet registered should not be permitted (1) to put up signs or nameplates before any hotel rooms or other space they may lease in China; (2) to refer to themselves as having an 'office' in China; (3) to use a seal identifying the company's 'office' in China; (4) to open accounts at banks in China; or (5) to 'engage in the business operations of resident offices'.[8] The implication of this circular was clear: a company may be deemed to be engaged in the 'business operations of a resident office' if it acts in the manner of such an office — by putting up signs, opening bank accounts, and so on — without being registered.

With the promulgation of the SAIC Measures in 1983, foreign enterprises acting in violation of the registration requirement became subject to sanctions for the first time. Under the SAIC Measures, foreign companies that 'engage without authorization in the business activities of a resident representative office' may be ordered to terminate their business activities in China and may be fined not more than RMB 10,000.[9] As if to underscore the seriousness of the SAIC Measures with an example, a mere two weeks after their initial publication the China-Swiss Group Co. Ltd., in a much publicized case, was banned from China and subjected to the maximum fine for carrying out business operations without having registered.[10]

Although the threat of sanctions provides an incentive to foreign companies to register formally their presence in China, a more powerful incentive is provided by the fact that registration can greatly facilitate the everyday operations of a company. Among the privileges extended to, and technically reserved for, registered representative offices and their representatives are the ability to enter into long-term office and room leases; to obtain long-term multiple-entry visas; to import office equipment and supplies; to import the personal effects of the resident representative duty-free, except for certain electronic entertainment equipment such as video cassette recorders; to import an automobile or vessel for office use; to open bank accounts; to hire Chinese employees; to request visas for visitors to China; to rent telecommunications lines and equipment; and to display signs and use business cards identifying the company's presence in China.

More recently, in the autumn of 1983, pursuant to announcements by municipal governments and notices from the municipal branches of the State Administration of Industry and Commerce (SAIC), registration also entitles the representatives and Chinese employees of foreign resident representative offices to identification cards and employee identification cards respectively.[11] These cards are required by the representatives and Chinese employees of representative offices to hold meetings and discussions with Chinese organizations and to carry on the work of a representative office. Chinese organizations will request to see these cards unless the persons seeking contact are already known to them.

II. Registration Procedures

The initial step in the registration of a resident representative office is to secure a formal approval document *(pizhunshu)* from the appropriate Chinese sponsor (*jiedai danwei*).[12] Without the support of such a Chinese sponsor the establishment of a representative office is impossible. Which Chinese units, then, are the appropriate sponsors for a given foreign company? Article 4 of the Registration Regulations provides that:

(1) traders, manufacturers and shipping agents shall apply to the Ministry of Foreign Economic Relations and Trade (MOFERT);
(2) ocean shipping companies and ocean shipping agents shall apply to the Ministry of Communications;
(3) air transport companies shall apply to the Civil Aviation Administration of China; and
(4) others shall apply to the appropriate commission, ministry or bureau 'in accordance with the nature of their work'.

Examples of this last category are oil companies, which are sponsored by the Ministry of Petroleum Industry; computer companies, which are sponsored by the Ministry of Electronics Industry; accounting companies, which are sponsored by the Ministry of Finance; and foreign tour operators, which are sponsored by the China National Tourism Administration.

The statutory standard by which potential Chinese sponsor organizations determine whether a foreign company merits their support and approval is 'genuine need'.[13] In view of the limited number of locations available for foreign offices and the scarcity of support facilities at present, representative office applications exceed China's current capacity to accommodate them. Therefore, to justify the issue of an approval document, the Chinese organization in practice must assess its own 'genuine need' for the representative office which has applied to it. Practice, in this respect, does not conform with the actual language of the Registration Regulations, which implies that it is the need of the foreign applicant, rather than any Chinese organization, which is determinative.[14] Justification of an approval may apparently tend to be based on historical business volume or, in the case of foreign companies whose names, products or services are well known to the Chinese, on potential business volume.

To obtain the approval document, an application letter signed by the chairman or the president of the company requesting registration and containing general information regarding the company should be submitted to the prospective Chinese sponsor organization together with (1) a copy of the applicant's official licence to conduct business in its home jurisdiction; (2) a letter of creditworthiness issued by the applicant's bank; (3) brief personal résumés for the individuals to be appointed as representatives and staff members; and (4) a notarized authorization for each person appointed to the representative office.[15]

With respect to the first item noted above, the home country business licence of the applicant, most companies registered to date have submitted the company's certificate of incorporation, business registration certificate or certificate of good standing, as applicable, to fulfill this requirement. As a matter of practice, Chinese registration authorities will require that the copy of the document submitted be certified by an official of the foreign issuing authority as being true and correct.

The second requirement noted above is a letter from the applicant's bank attesting to the company's creditworthiness. Such a letter need not disclose any financial information about the company which is not already publicly available. A brief statement from the bank as to its relationship with the company and as to the company's record of meeting its financial obligations, together with the annual report of the company, have been sufficient to satisfy this requirement.

The résumés required for each of the representatives and staff members may be very short and, in practice, need only contain dates of birth, nationality and a brief statement of the person's educational and professional qualifications. As to the certificate of authorization for each person appointed to the representative office, notarized letters of appointment from the company's chairman or president are now required.

Once a formal approval document is obtained, the foreign company has 30 days from the date of issue of the approval document to complete the registration procedures with the local branch of the SAIC.[16] The SAIC, which prior to 1983 was known as the General Administration of Industry and Commerce, not only acts as China's companies' registry but among other responsibilities is also charged with enforcement of the various restrictions relating to the foreign commercial presence in China. Under the Registration Regulations foreign companies were required to effect registration with the SAIC's headquarters in Beijing.[17] However, the more recent Circular and SAIC Measures both specifically authorize SAIC local branches to register a representative office of a foreign enterprise located in their jurisdiction.[18]

The final step in the registration process itself is the submission of the approval document within 30 days of its issue together with the registration fee of RMB 600 to the local SAIC branch and the completion of the formal application for registration in triplicate, which forms are tendered at this stage of the process by the local SAIC branch. If the application is not filed within 30 days of the issue of the approval document, it may be considered null and void and must be physically returned to the issuing unit.[19]

The application is a standardized form entitled 'Foreign Business Agencies in China: Application for Registration'. The principal information required by this form is the representative office's name, address, number and names of representatives and foreign staff, scope of business and duration of stay.

For the most part, the application is self-explanatory and straightforward, calling for responses that are short and to the point. This applies particularly to the section requiring a description of the representative office's scope of business. As will be discussed in Part III of this chapter, the SAIC Measures restrict the scope of a foreign representative office's activities to those which are 'not direct business operations'. Therefore, care should be exercised in determining and describing the activities of such an office. To avoid any possible implication that the company might be engaged in 'direct business operations', almost every representative office registered to date has used the characterization 'liaison' to describe its business scope.

'Duration of stay', as it appears on the application, may range from one year to indefinite and is usually coterminous with the validity of the approval document. The SAIC Measures now require annual renewals, but this procedure is merely routine.[20] Of more concern are notices first issued by the Beijing Municipal Bureau of Industry and Commerce in late 1983 (hereafter cited as the Extension Notice) requiring an 'extension' application every three years.

Although not an issue for most foreign companies, the number of representatives and foreign staff members permitted for each representative office has aroused heated debate, particularly with regard to some of the Japanese trading companies which maintain a large staff in China. The problem arose because, until early 1983, Chinese practice was to grant long-term multiple-entry visas only to the resident representatives of a given office, which were limited in all but a few exceptional cases to two or three persons. Foreign staff members, on the other hand, were only eligible in practice for visas good for stays of up to three months. This restriction, naturally, imposed hardships on foreign personnel resident in China and created staffing problems for foreign companies requiring expatriate staff.

As a result of a crescendo of complaints from affected Japanese companies, MOFERT's Bureau of Foreign Trade Administration reached an agreement with the Japanese, which was announced in early February 1983 by Shen Jueren, Director of the Bureau.[21] The new policy, which reportedly applies not simply to the Japanese but to all foreign firms in China, entitles approved foreign staff members of representative offices to 'the same privileges as the official resident representatives with regard to their visas and other matters'.[22] Therefore, it would appear that a representative office may now obtain for its foreign staff members as many long-term visas as it can reasonably demonstrate it needs.

The local SAIC branch will, upon receipt, review all documentation submitted. Once they are satisfied that the application and supporting materials fulfill the statutory requirements, they will issue a registration certificate sealed with the stamp of the SAIC authority. Although the length of time needed by the SAIC to complete its review varies from locality to locality and from case to case, waiting periods of two or three weeks are normal in Beijing.

III. Control Aspects of Registration

Chinese law provides for a high degree of continuing control over the activities of resident representative offices and their employees after registration has been completed. This control is exercised in a variety of ways, the most important of which are examined below.

A. Supplementary Registrations

Immediately after a representative office has received its registration certificate, the office and its personnel must comply with several additional registration formalities. First, the representative and his family members must register with the Public Security Bureau and obtain a foreigner's residence certificate (*waiguoren juliuzheng*) and a commercial domicile registration booklet (*hukou dengjibu*).[23] The Public Security Bureau will require that the representative present his resident representative identification card as well as his office approval certificate as conditions precedent to the issue of these documents. The foreigner's residence certificate, which contains a picture of the representative, the name of his company, and the length of his permitted stay in China, must be carried by the representative at all times.

Secondly, the registered office and the resident representative are also required to register with the local tax authorities for the payment of enterprise income taxes and individual income taxes, respectively.[24] Both registrations are accomplished by filling in simple forms. To date, no representative offices have paid foreign enterprise income taxes as such; being engaged exclusively in liaison and other non-profit-making activities they are not deemed by the tax authorities to be 'doing business' and thus have no taxable income.[25] Nonetheless, tax registration is still required and is strictly enforced. A supplementary regulation issued by the Ministry of Finance requires that tax registration be accomplished within 30 days of the date of 'commencement of operations'.[26] Failure to register in a timely fashion exposes the company to a penalty of up to RMB 5,000.[27]

A final supplementary requirement of the Registration Regulations is that the representative office shall open a foreign exchange account in its name with the Bank of China.[28]

B. Registration Renewal, Updating and Extension

Another method of control can be found in the registration renewal, updating and extension requirements contained in the SAIC Measures and the Extension Notice. Foreign representative offices must renew their registrations annually by submitting an application for extension on a standard form together with a report of the preceding year's business activities and an extension fee of RMB 300.[29] Additionally, the approval document from the Chinese sponsoring unit normally has a limited term of effectiveness and must also be extended, usually annually. Changes to the representative office's name, number and names of resident personnel, business scope, or address, from those stipulated in the original registration application require the filing of a standard form of registration modification together with RMB 100.[30] Changes in personnel also require the submission of new résumés as well as letters of appointment.

The extension procedure described in the Extension Notice at present only applies in Beijing but is likely to be followed elsewhere. It appears to be tantamount to a three-year re-registration requirement at which interval, apparently, the Chinese sponsor organization and the SAIC will reassess the 'genuine need' for the continuing presence of the particular resident representative office. An extension requires first that an extension approval certificate be procured from the applicant's Chinese sponsor unit. This certificate then must be presented to the relevant SAIC bureau together with a completed standard extension application form, a report on the preceding year's business activities, including details of contracts signed and their respective values, and copies of materials submitted to the Chinese sponsor unit to obtain the extension approval certificate.

C. Restrictions on the Scope of the Activity

One of the most important of the controls imposed on foreign enterprises in China relates to the statutory restriction on the permissible scope of activity of the representative office. As noted earlier, under the SAIC Measures representative offices are prohibited from engaging in 'direct business operations' *(zhijie jingying huodong)*. Violations of this provision may be punished by fines of not more than RMB 20,000 and termination of business operations.

At present, the precise dimensions of the concept 'direct business operations' remain clouded. The SAIC Measures themselves contain no definition of the concept, and Chinese officials have done little to elucidate the limits of permissible activity. According to conversations with SAIC representatives, production and sales activities will be seen to constitute 'direct business operations' while liaison activities will not. Obviously, in the absence of a more specific categorization of the activities in which a representative office might engage, companies have little guidance as to the legality of their activities in China and their potential liabilities. From the perspective of the Chinese authorities, however, lack of clarity is viewed as an advantage as it broadens their scope of discretion and thus serves to facilitate supervision and control.

D. Customs Controls

Control over representative offices and their personnel is also exercised by the Chinese Customs authorities. Under Article 10 of the Registration Regulations, representative offices and registered representatives are required to file a declaration with Customs with respect to those items for office or personal use that they wish to import from abroad. In practice, this provision has been implemented by requiring the representative to submit to Customs two lists — one for personal goods, and one for office items — setting forth all the items the office and the representative intend to import. Once the lists are approved by Customs, personal goods on the list may be imported without payment of customs duties or related taxes in any number of shipments within the six-month period dating from the approval of the list. Office items appearing on the list may be imported at any time after payment of customs duties and related taxes. In the event a representative wishes to amend the personal or office list by adding additional items, he must go through separate application and approval procedures for such items. Supplementary imports of personal items, however, are not eligible for tax-free treatment.

Finally, it should be noted that goods imported by representative offices and their registered personnel may not, as a general rule, be privately sold or transferred in China.[31] The expectation is that imported office items will remain with the office and be removed from China at such time as the office terminates operations, and that personal items will be taken out with the representative when he is reassigned. In special cases, however, transfers will be permitted upon prior approval by the Customs authorities. Direct sales may only be made to designated Chinese units such as the Friendship Stores for resale to foreign residents.

E. Employment of Staff

One of the most controversial of the control mechanisms instituted by the Chinese relates to the severe restrictions imposed on the freedom of representative offices to choose and employ staff. Under Article 11 of the Registration Regulations, a resident representative office is required to entrust 'local service units for foreigners or other units designated by the Chinese Government' when hiring work personnel. For registered offices in Beijing, what this provision means is that all secretaries, drivers and other office personnel, as well as household help employed by resident representatives, must be hired from what was formerly called the Friendship Commercial Services Corporation, renamed in August 1983 the Foreign Enterprises Services Corporation (FESCO).

Because of the wide variance in quality and high cost of many FESCO staff, a large number of representative offices in Beijing and elsewhere in China have preferred to hire local expatriates such as foreign students and spouses of diplomatic personnel to provide office assistance. In August 1983, the Beijing office of the SAIC moved to enforce the provisions mandating the use of FESCO staff, and issued a notice requiring all registered offices to submit to the SAIC a list of their personnel for approval.[32] Once approved, such personnel were issued employee identification cards. According to announcements by the relevant municipal governments, no person is permitted to work in a representative office without having first obtained an employee identification card.[33]

According to Chinese sources, there exist a number of 'internal' (*neibu*) regulations supporting the SAIC's move to require all foreign representative offices to employ staff exclusively from the FESCO. One such regulation reportedly requires that only foreigners that come from the home country of the registered foreign enterprise be permitted to work in its representative office in China, except for foreigners who were previously employed by the company outside China. Another regulation, reportedly issued by the Ministry of Foreign Affairs, prohibits family members of diplomatic personnel from working in the representative offices of foreign enterprises. Finally, Chinese officials have indicated that there exists an internal directive issued by the Ministry of Education prohibiting foreign students from working in China. To date, none of these regulations have been published and they have been enforced only haphazardly. Nonetheless, most observers expect that they will be applied more uniformly and strictly in the future.

F. Supervision and Sanctions

Article 14 of the Registration Regulations requires representative offices and their registered personnel to abide by all relevant Chinese laws, regulations and decrees. In addition to the Public Security Bureau and, in extreme cases, the newly constituted State Security Bureau, the SAIC exercises supervision over the activities of representative offices and may penalize such offices and their personnel in the event of breaches of Chinese law or regulations. As noted earlier, for example, foreign enterprises that violate the prohibition on engaging in 'direct business operations' may be fined up to RMB 20,000. The same Article provides for a fine of up to RMB 5,000 for failure to effect changes to the office's registration certificate when such are required by changes in personnel, office location or other reasons.[34] Foreign businessmen should also be aware that China's Criminal Code, in effect since 1980, specifically applies to foreigners and contains prohibitions against dealing in state secrets. The concept of 'state secret' is extremely broad. Normal commercial intelligence may constitute state secrets, thereby exposing businessmen to grave criminal liability.

IV. Variations from the National Registration Regime: Guangdong Province and Foreign Financial Institutions

The Registration Regulations and SAIC Measures together provide the framework for the national registration regime applicable to foreign resident representative offices in China. Variations from this regime exist, however, in at least two special cases. The first relates to representative offices established in Guangdong Province and the second concerns representative offices of foreign financial institutions.

A. The Guangdong Rules

A little over six months after the promulgation of the national Registration Regulations, Guangdong Province issued its own registration rules in a document consisting of 18 articles and entitled Provisional Measures of the People's Government of Guangdong Province for the Registration and Control of Resident Representative Offices of Foreign Enterprises and Overseas Chinese, Hong Kong and Macao Enterprises in Guangdong Province (hereafter cited as the Guangdong Rules).[35] The Guangdong Rules, by their terms, are 'based on the spirit' of the Registration Regulations but take into consideration the 'specific conditions' in Guangdong Province.[36] Therefore, in content the rules parallel in most respects the provisions of the national registration regime but vest greater control in the provincial authorities.

One of the major differences between the Guangdong Rules and the Registration Regulations relates to the scope of the approval power of local authorities. The Guangdong Rules provide that Guangdong Province may approve applications for registration of representative offices by foreign enterprises without reference to the central authorities.[37] The provincial approval-granting authority under the Guangdong Rules is the Foreign Economic Affairs Committee of Guangdong Province.[38] In practice, however, airlines, shipping and banking businesses must still be registered centrally.

In several key aspects the Guangdong Rules[39] anticipated developments in the national registration regime which were subsequently incorporated in the SAIC Measures. For example, the Guangdong Rules contain a clear prohibition against the commencement of business prior to the completion of registration formalities and limit the validity of the registration certificate to one year.[40] These provisions were not formally adopted nationwide until the promulgation of the SAIC Measures two years later. In another example, Article 3 of the Guangdong Rules requires applicants to submit copies of their 'economic and trade agreements' to the approval-granting authority together with their other application documents. No similar requirement existed until the recent Extension Notice required that such information be included with an application for extension after an initial period of three years.

In general, it appears that the Guangdong Rules have been enforced with greater rigour than the Registration Regulations were prior to the promulgation of the SAIC Measures. In 1982 alone, nine cases of non-registration were prosecuted administratively by the Guangdong provincial branch of the SAIC.[41] Most of the defendants were either Hong Kong or Macao compatriots, all of whom were reported to have ignored repeated warnings. Penalties in these cases ranged from RMB 300 to RMB 3,000, coupled with publication of the offenders' names and an account of their misdeeds.

B. Foreign Financial Institutions

Foreign banks and insurance companies are subject to the national registration regime established by the Registration Regulations and the SAIC Measures. However, supplementing this regime is a separate set of regulations issued on 1 February 1983 by the People's Bank of China which, as China's central bank, is, through its Foreign Affairs Department, responsible for the activities of foreign financial institutions in China. These regulations are the Provisional Regulations for the Establishment of Representative Offices in China by Overseas Chinese and Foreign Financial Institutions (hereafter cited as the Financial Institution Regulations).[42]

The basic purpose of the Financial Institution Regulations, as stated in Article 1, is to exercise 'more effective control' over the activities of representative offices of foreign banks and insurance companies. Therefore, the Financial Institution Regulations follow closely the general scheme established under the Registration Regulations and the SAIC Measures but impose additional obligations on banks and insurance companies and spell out more clearly the various limitations imposed on representative offices.

The Financial Institution Regulations permit foreign banks and insurance companies to establish representative offices in Beijing and in the Special Economic Zones; institutions with Beijing offices may establish 'subordinate' representative offices in 'other designated cities'.[43] Bank representative offices must bear names with the description 'representative office' or 'sub-representative office', and representative offices of insurance companies are required to include the designation 'liaison office' in their names.[44]

Registration application procedures are in most respects identical to those required by the Registration Regulations. One significant difference, however, is found in the requirement that an 'authenticated power of attorney' be provided by the chairman or chief executive of the applicant in favour of the appointed representative.[45] Under the Registration Regulations, only a notarized letter of authority is required.

In contrast to the Registration Regulations and the SAIC Measures, the Financial Institution Regulations provide a clear statement of the authorized scope of activity of registered representative offices. Article 8 provides that representative offices of banks and insurance companies must limit the scope of their activities to 'non-profit activities such as carrying on business negotiations, acting as liaison, providing consultancy and other services. They shall not engage in any direct profit-making business activities.'

The Financial Institution Regulations permit an approval term of three years rather than one, anticipating the effect of the Extension Notice.[46] Also, SAIC registration must still be renewed annually. The maximum number of representatives is fixed at four for a representative office in Beijing, three in the Special Economic Zones and two in other 'designated cities'.[47] However, the law specifically provides that there is no limit on the number of Chinese that may be employed from the FESCO or equivalent organizations.[48]

Finally, it should be noted that the Financial Institution Regulations provide the People's Bank of China with extensive powers to supervise the activities of representative offices of foreign banks and insurance companies, and authorize the bank to penalize such offices and their personnel in the event of breaches of the regulations.[49] Supervision is carried out by periodic unannounced visits and through various reporting requirements. In addition to the requirement that reports be made to the People's Bank of China when the office changes its address or any other item appearing on its original application for registration,[50] the representative office must provide an annual report to the People's Bank on or before 15 January giving a 'faithful account' of the office's work during the previous year.[51] Article 12 of the Financial Institution Regulations also imposes a reporting requirement when the registered representative plans to be absent from China for a period longer than one month.[52] In such cases, the representative is required to designate another individual to assume his duties in his absence and to provide a written notice of such designation to the People's Bank of China.[53]

V. Conclusion

When China first initiated its open-door policy in the late 1970s, foreign companies wishing to establish a 'presence' in the People's Republic needed to do little more than rent a hotel room and place a sign on the door. Today, this situation has changed dramatically. As the number of foreign companies resident in China has increased, the authorities have felt the need to impose restrictions on their entry and controls on their activities. With history as a guide, it would seem fair to assume that the future trend will be toward a continuation of these restrictions and controls as China's economic contacts with the outside world grow more numerous and more complex.

Notes

1. See *A Directory of Resident Offices of Foreign, Overseas Chinese, Hong Kong and Macao Enterprises* (Beijing, Commercial Management Press, 1983).

2. Approved by the State Council and promulgated on 30 October 1980. An English translation of the Registration Regulations appears in F. Chu, M. Moser and O. Nee (eds.), *Commercial, Business and Trade Laws: People's Republic of China* (Dobbs Ferry, Oceana Publications, Inc., 1982), Pt. 8, p.3.

3. For an English translation of the Circular, see *Laws and Regulations of the People's Republic of China* (Hong Kong, Kingsway International Publications, 1982), Vol. 1, p. 158.

4. An English translation appears in *East Asian Executive Reports*, May 1983, p. 24.

5. These regulations are discussed in Part IV of this chapter.

6. Registration Regulations, Art. 2, note 2 above.

7. See *China Economic News*, 10 November 1980, p.2.

8. See *China Economic News*, 1 June 1981, p. 2.

9. SAIC Measures, Art. 16, note 4 above.

10. 'Resident Office of China-Swiss Group Company Banned', *China Daily*, 1 April 1983, p. 1.

11. Beijing was the first municipality to establish this requirement by an Announcement of the Beijing Municipal People's Government published in the *Beijing Daily*, 12 August 1983. By December 1983, Shanghai and Guangzhou also had such requirements.

12. Registration Regulations, Art. 4, note 2 above; and SAIC Measures, Art. 7(1), note 4 above.

13. See Registration Regulations, Art. 2, note 2 above.

14. Registration Regulations, Art. 2, note 2 above.

15. Registration Regulations, Art. 3, note 2 above.

16. Registration Regulations, Art. 5, note 2 above.

17. Registration Regulations, Art. 5, note 2 above.

18. Circular, Section 1, note 3 above; and SAIC Measures, Arts. 4 and 6, note 4 above.

19. Registration Regulations, Art. 5, note 2 above.

20. SAIC Measures, Art. 11, note 4 above.

21. See 'Japanese Firms' Beijing Offices Increase Personnel', *China Economic News*, 7 February 1983, p. 7.

22. *China Economic News*, 7 February 1983, p. 7.

23. Registration Regulations, Art. 6, note 2 above.

24. Registration Regulations, Art. 9, note 2 above.

25. For a detailed discussion of this issue, see Chapter 2 of this volume.

26. See Article 1 of the Provisional Regulations of the General Taxation Bureau of the Ministry of Finance of the People's Republic of China Concerning Tax Registration by Foreign Enterprises for the Commencement and Termination of Operations (hereafter cited as the Provisional Tax Registration Regulations) promulgated by the General Taxation Bureau of the Ministry of Finance on 5 April 1982.

27. Provisional Tax Registration Regulations, Art. 8, note 26 above.

28. Registration Regulations, Art. 8, note 2 above.

29. SAIC Measures, Art. 11, note 4 above; and Circular, Section 5, note 3 above.

30. SAIC Measures, Art. 12, note 4 above; and Circular, Section 5, note 3 above.

31. Registration Regulations, Art. 10, note 2 above.

32. Notice of the Beijing Administration for Industry and Commerce (83), Industry and Commerce Reference No. 232, 11 August 1983. The Notice was distributed in Chinese to all registered representative offices of foreign companies in Beijing during the middle of August 1983.

33. See note 11 above.

34. SAIC Measures, Art. 15, note 4 above.

35. Approved by the People's Government of Guangdong Province, promulgated

and effective on and as of 11 May 1981. An English translation of the Guangdong Rules appears in Chu, Moser and Nee, Pt. 6, p. 11, note 2 above.

36. Guangdong Rules, Art. 1, note 35 above.
37. Guangdong Rules, Art. 2, note 35 above.
38. Guangdong Rules, Art. 2, note 35 above.
39. Guangdong Rules, Art. 2, note 35 above.
40. Guangdong Rules, Art. 13, note 35 above.
41. Interview of the author with the Guangdong SAIC.
42. An English translation of the Financial Institution Regulations appears in *East Asian Executive Reports*, May 1983, p. 26.
43. Financial Institution Regulations, Art. 2, note 42 above.
44. Financial Institution Regulations, Art. 3, note 42 above.
45. Financial Institution Regulations, Art. 4 (4), note 42 above.
46. Financial Institution Regulations, Art. 7, note 42 above.
47. Financial Institution Regulations, Art. 9, note 42 above.
48. Financial Institution Regulations, Art. 10, note 42 above.
49. Financial Institution Regulations, Arts. 14 and 17, note 42 above.
50. Financial Institution Regulations, Art. 11, note 42 above.
51. Financial Institution Regulations, Art. 15, note 42 above.
52. Financial Institution Regulations, Art. 12, note 42 above.
53. Financial Institution Regulations, Art. 12, note 42 above.

11. The Role of Arbitration in Economic Co-operation with China

JEROME ALAN COHEN

I. Introduction

China's policy of seeking to attract foreign investment and other forms of long-term economic co-operation with the international business community is still very new. For three decades after its founding in 1949, the People's Republic of China (PRC) engaged in the ordinary export and import of goods and conventional shipping activities. Only in 1979 did it begin to emphasize joint ventures, compensation trade arrangements of various types, assembly, processing, co-production, production sharing and bank loans. These new forms of co-operation involve more intensive, extensive and enduring collaboration with foreign business entities than China has previously experienced. They also require more detailed, complicated contracts than Chinese negotiators have been accustomed to, and the complexity of recording mutual understanding is enhanced by the need to agree upon both Chinese and foreign-language texts for each investment contract and associated legal documents as well as certain other types of contracts.

China's economic development and foreign trade policies are still in the process of evolution. So too is its legal system, which has only recently begun to develop the legislative and institutional infrastructure necessary to facilitate co-operation with private foreign commercial entities. Moreover, the world business environment will continue to be volatile and can be expected to have an increasing impact upon China, itself becoming ever more involved in the world economy. Even if foreign firms can convince Chinese negotiators that their contracts should seek to anticipate all foreseeable problems — an idea that is often resisted — many unanticipated contingencies are likely to occur.

Thus, even in the best of circumstances, disputes will inevitably arise in the interpretation and implementation of the new business contracts that China is concluding with foreign firms. How will these disputes be settled? If they can be disposed of fairly, promptly and inexpensively, foreign confidence in China as a place to do business will grow, co-operation will expand, and this will have a correspondingly positive effect on China's modernization. If disputes cannot be handled in a mutually satisfactory manner, foreign interest in economic co-operation with China will diminish. China's reputation for settling disputes, like its reputation for paying its debts, will be a fundamental element of its standing in the international marketplace.

II. Background

Unfortunately, although the Bank of China has an excellent record in paying its debts, China's record in settling trade and investment disputes is uneven. Since 1949 there have been a great many instances in which contract disputes with Chinese companies have been resolved in a friendly, equitable and efficient manner generally consistent with the principle of 'equality and mutual benefit' that the Chinese never tire of invoking. Yet there have also been enough cases to the contrary to raise questions about the reliability of China's commitment to standard international dispute resolution processes. In 1958, when China broke off all trade relations with Japan as a result of a political dispute, Japanese firms thought it fruitless to pursue the arbitration remedies prescribed by their contracts with Chinese corporations. They decided instead to swallow their losses and await the opportunities for new profits that would come with the restoration of trade, which occurred in the early 1960s.[1]

During the worst days of the Great Proletarian Cultural Revolution in the late 1960s, when politics again interfered with trade, a number of foreign firms did seek to invoke the arbitration remedies provided by their contracts, but to no avail. In the best-known case, the Red Guards had prevented the Anglo-German firm, the Vickers-Zimmer Company, from completing the construction of a petrochemical plant in north-west China. When the foreign company then requested arbitration in Stockholm in accordance with the contract, China's response was twofold. It ignored the arbitration request and arrested two of the firm's employees as spies, sentencing one to deportation and the other to three years in prison.[2] It also announced that the Intermediate Court for Beijing had decided the civil dispute — without Vickers-Zimmer's participation — holding the foreign company liable for failure to fulfill its obligation under the contract and requiring it to pay precisely the amount of damages it claimed to have suffered, £650,000.[3]

The Vickers-Zimmer case was the worst blow that the Cultural Revolution inflicted on China's reputation for settling disputes. Yet even during the early 1970s European commercial attachés in Beijing regaled visitors with stories of how Chinese trade partners used one flimsy excuse after another to reject requested arbitration of disputes. Letters would go unanswered. Personal visits would be deflected with promises to 'study the matter' or with entreaties to try a little harder to settle the problem by negotiation. Occasionally Chinese officials would bluntly state that 'a request for arbitration is an unfriendly act', making it plain that foreigners who wanted to continue to do business with China should resolve their problems informally, as other foreigners did.

Of course, during this era a great many disputes were settled to the satisfaction of both parties, through informal means, as are most disputes in the commerce of other countries. Businessmen and bureaucrats generally prefer to settle disputes through negotiation between the parties or third-party conciliation rather than through arbitration or court decision. This is as true in the China trade as in any other. Furthermore, if it is necessary to resort to some formal means of third-party decision-making to settle an international commercial dispute, Chinese representatives have so far shown a strong preference for arbitration rather than court adjudication. But what has been unique in the China trade has been the extreme reluctance of Chinese entities to seek or to countenance arbitration in the minority of cases in which more informal means of settlement fail to produce, within a reasonable period of time, an outcome acceptable to both parties.

This is not to say that China has lacked institutions for international commercial arbitration. In 1954 the Chinese government established, under the aegis of the China Council for the Promotion of International Trade (CCPIT), a 'non-governmental' organization that is actually part of the state apparatus and is modelled on the Soviet All-Union Chamber of Commerce, the Foreign Trade Arbitration Commission (FTAC).[4] In 1958 the government established a Maritime Arbitration Commission (MAC) under the CCPIT to handle the increasing number of maritime disputes that confronted China.[5] Although both of these institutions have been active, there has been little public evidence of their activity: they have disposed of most of the disputes brought to them without issuing an arbitration award, and, until recently, the awards made have not usually been publicized. Scholars have written learned discourses analysing the many decisions of the Soviet Union's international arbitration tribunals, but no similar materials allow comparable analysis of the work of their Chinese counterparts.[6]

However, the available information indicates that China's reluctance to arbitrate has not been limited to situations involving contracts that call for third-country arbitration or arbitration in the country of the defendant. This reluctance to arbitrate has also extended to contracts that provide for arbitration in China before the FTAC or the MAC. Very few of the cases handled by the two commissions during the late 1970s (approximately 50 per year) were disposed of by actually proceeding to an arbitration award; all the others were settled through conciliation.[7]

Occasionally China has sought to publicize the unique emphasis that its arbitration organs have placed upon conciliation. In October 1963, for example, the Chinese magazine, *Foreign Trade*, carried a lengthy description by the MAC of its successful role as conciliator in a dispute over the proper fee to be charged for Chinese salvage services for a Norwegian vessel that had run aground in Shanghai Harbour. That article took pains to point out the superiority of conciliation over arbitration in arriving at a mutually advantageous solution.[8]

Reference to the role of the judiciary may be useful as a final piece of background information on arbitration. Until very recently China's courts played virtually no part in the settlement of foreign trade disputes. The previously mentioned Vickers-Zimmer case was unusual in this respect as well as in others. Prior to the onset of the Cultural Revolution in 1966, the courts generally were not available to handle such disputes. After 1966 the judiciary was decimated by political turmoil and often served as the tool of 'ultra-leftist' forces hostile to foreign co-operation, as the Vickers-Zimmer judgment and other xenophobic judicial decisions demonstrated. The Chinese courts, which had never inspired foreign confidence, were not restored until the arrest of the ultra-leftist 'Gang of Four' following Chairman Mao's death in the autumn of 1976. And only since 1979, after promulgation of an amended version of the law for the organization of people's courts, have the courts developed special economic tribunals that are available to decide disputes between Chinese and foreign parties as well as purely domestic matters. The Civil Procedure Code that was enacted on a provisional basis in 1982 has confirmed that Chinese courts are generally to be open to foreign nationals, enterprises and organizations, although it prevents parties from instituting a suit if they have a written agreement to submit any disputes to a Chinese arbitration organization or if their dispute has already been arbitrated by such an organization.[9]

III. Arbitration

A. The Need to Reconcile International Agreements, Laws and Regulations

China's new policy of welcoming a broad range of foreign economic co-operation has brought to the fore the entire question of dispute resolution, and of arbitration in particular. Foreign governments concerned with providing adequate dispute resolution facilities for their nationals engaged in the China trade have sought to negotiate assurances with China. The most elaborate provision thus far concluded is Article VIII of the Sino-American trade agreement of 7 July 1979, which states:

1. The Contracting Parties encourage the prompt and equitable settlement of any disputes arising from or in relation to contracts between their respective firms, companies and corporations, and trading organizations, through friendly consultations, conciliation or other mutually acceptable means.
2. If such disputes cannot be settled promptly by any one of the above-mentioned means, the parties to the dispute may have recourse to arbitration for settlement in accordance with provisions specified in their contracts or other agreements to submit to arbitration. Such arbitration may be conducted by an arbitration institution in the People's Republic of China, the United States of America, or a third

country. The arbitration rules of procedure of the relevant arbitration institution are applicable and the arbitration rules of the United Nations Commission on International Trade Law recommended by the United Nations, or other international arbitration rules, may also be used where acceptable to the parties to the dispute and to the arbitration institution.

3. Each Contracting Party shall seek to ensure that arbitration awards are recognized and enforced by their competent authorities where enforcement is sought, in accordance with applicable laws and regulations.[10]

This leaves it to the parties to each contract to decide how to deal with arbitration. In agreements with certain other governments China has been more specific, stipulating that in commercial disputes between entities of the two countries any necessary arbitration shall take place in the country of the defendant.[11] China is seeking to reach such an arrangement with several European countries and has even discussed the idea with the United States.

On the question of dispute resolution, the Law of the People's Republic of China on Joint Ventures Using Chinese and Foreign Investment (hereafter cited as the Joint Venture Law), promulgated on 8 July 1979, is more succinct than the Sino-American trade agreement but similar in certain respects. Article 14 states:

Disputes arising between the parties to a joint venture that the board of directors cannot settle through consultation may be settled through conciliation or arbitration by a Chinese arbitration agency or through arbitration by another arbitration agency agreed upon by the parties to the venture.[12]

Again, it is up to the parties to the transaction to decide, if consultation (that is, direct negotiation) fails, whether to resort to conciliation prior to arbitration; they may also decide whether arbitration is to take place in China or abroad. The 1982 Regulations of the People's Republic of China on the Exploitation of Offshore Petroleum Resources in Co-operation with Foreign Enterprises (hereafter cited as the Offshore Petroleum Regulations) contain an almost identical provision.[13]

The most striking aspect of these provisions is that they refer only to arbitration tribunals and not to courts. The courts, of course, may become involved in the recognition and enforcement of arbitration awards, but Chinese arbitration specialists have long taken the position that China's courts do not entertain cases of foreign trade and maritime disputes when an arbitration agreement is in force. As we have seen, their position has been supported by the new Civil Procedure Code, at least in cases where there is a written agreement to submit any dispute to a Chinese arbitration organization or where the dispute has already been arbitrated under the auspices of such an organization.

The language of the Code suggests, however, that the existence of a written agreement to submit disputes to a tribunal other than one convened by 'a foreign arbitration organization of the PRC', or actual arbitration by a non-Chinese tribunal, may not prevent the parties from filing suit in a Chinese court.[14] Perhaps the draftsmen of the Code did not intend their language to give rise to this inference, but their choice of words does not appear to be inadvertent.

If this inference is correct, the many foreign companies that have signed contracts containing a carefully negotiated clause that calls for arbitration outside China may, much to their surprise and dismay, be exposed to the risk that, despite such a clause, their Chinese partner will have the option to bring suit against them in a Chinese court. This, after all, is what happened in the Vickers-Zimmer case, when a foreign request for arbitration in Stockholm under the contract stimulated the Chinese party to sue Vickers-Zimmer in a Beijing court. Presumably this could happen even if an arbitration award had been rendered abroad.

Yet Chinese judicial and trade officials do not seem to believe that Chinese courts will interpret the Code in a literal fashion with respect to this question, precisely because to do so would yield an outrageous result that would strike a blow against China's foreign trade and investment contracts. Until the Code is tested in this respect, however, one cannot be certain of the outcome. Nevertheless, the 1983 Act for the Implementation of the Joint Venture Law provides support for the view of these Chinese officials, precluding the parties to a joint venture contract from bringing suit in China if they have entered into a written arbitration agreement without specifying that the agreement must call for arbitration by a Chinese organization.[15]

The provisions of the Code give rise to further questions. What is a 'foreign arbitration organization of the PRC'? For example, if the foreign and Chinese parties to a contract agree to arbitrate any disputes in China under the Arbitration Rules of the United Nations Commission on International Trade Law (UNCITRAL), will that arrangement meet the statutory standard?

Moreover, what does Article 193 mean by providing that 'When a case has been arbitrated by a foreign affairs arbitration organization of the PRC, the parties shall not be permitted to file a lawsuit in the people's courts'? When has a case 'been arbitrated' — at the moment when the dispute was submitted to the tribunal or only after an award has been rendered? This, too, is a practical problem of some significance. For example, if in the course of an arbitration hearing one party is dissatisfied with the proceedings and brings a lawsuit over the dispute, will a Chinese court refuse to entertain the suit because of Article 193 on the ground that the case 'has been arbitrated'?

If one reads merely the Civil Procedure Code, one gains the impression that, when writing their contract's dispute resolution clause, the parties are always free to choose a judicial solution rather than arbitration. Yet foreign businessmen must take account of applicable international agreements and special Chinese legislation, which sometimes complicate the situation.

There should be no problem under the Sino-American trade agreement, which authorizes the parties to settle their dispute 'through friendly consultations, conciliation or *other mutually acceptable means*' (my italics). Yet the Joint Venture Law and the Offshore Petroleum Regulations offer no such explicit flexibility. They imply that litigation is not an option. Moreover, in

China's first highly publicized manufacturing joint venture, the Schindler elevator transaction, which was approved in 1980, the contract originally provided for the settlement of disputes before the ordinary courts of the domicile of the defendant, but, upon review by the Foreign Investment Commission (now merged into the Ministry of Foreign Economic Relations and Trade), this provision was dropped. With respect to joint ventures, the 1983 Act for the Implementation of the Joint Venture Law makes it clear, however, that 'the parties may resolve their dispute through arbitration *or judicial means*' (my italics).[16] There has not yet been a clarification concerning the Offshore Petroleum Regulations.

Of course, if the parties conclude an oil contract with a clause that calls for a judicial solution, China's Ministry of Foreign Economic Relations and Trade (MOFERT), which is now charged with the responsibility of reviewing such investments, probably has the power to approve the clause as a matter of statutory interpretation. However, one wonders whether MOFERT would approve such a contract in the absence of legislative clarification, since many judicial and trade officials still believe that the new economic tribunals of the courts should play a secondary role, enforcing arbitration awards but not displacing arbitration.

Still another formal dispute resolution option is found in some other Chinese legislation affecting foreigners — that of bringing a lawsuit if there is dissatisfaction with the result of arbitration. The Regulations on Labour Management in Joint Ventures Using Chinese and Foreign Investment (hereafter cited as the Labour Regulations) provide that, if consultation between the parties fails to settle a joint venture labour dispute, any party to the venture may request arbitration by the provincial-level labour management department with jurisdiction over the venture, but, 'if one party does not accept the arbitration award, it may file a suit in the people's courts.'[17] Similarly, the 1981 Economic Contract Law gives the parties to a dispute the option of immediately initiating a lawsuit if consultation fails, instead of seeking mediation or arbitration by state contract administration authorities, but, if arbitration is selected and any party is not satisfied with the award, that party may file a lawsuit within 15 days of receipt of the award. Although the Economic Contract Law was designed to govern relations between domestic entities, prior to the enactment of contract regulations especially applicable to foreigners it may also govern transactions between a Chinese-foreign joint venture and Chinese enterprises, and possibly even transactions between a foreign enterprise and a Chinese enterprise. Neither the Labour Regulations nor the Economic Contract Law make clear the nature of the lawsuit that may be brought by a party dissatisfied with an arbitration award. Whether the court is to conduct a *de novo* hearing or a more limited review of the merits of the case is not stated.

As China concludes new international agreements and promulgates special legislation regarding compensation trade, co-operative production, leasing, bank loans and other forms of foreign economic co-operation, it will be necessary to take careful note of the extent to which these norms differ from the general framework established by the Civil Procedure Code.

B. Recent Developments Concerning Conciliation

Before discussing arbitration problems *per se*, we should touch upon some interesting developments with respect to conciliation, particularly the advent of joint conciliation of international economic disputes and the articulation in the Civil Procedure Code of what appears to be almost a compulsory conciliation procedure for litigated disputes.

Although China has necessarily begun to pay more attention to both arbitration and litigation than in the past, it continues to emphasize the desirability of settling disputes through conciliation. In recent years Chinese arbitration tribunals have continued their previous practice of making an award only when the dispute cannot be settled through conciliation. If either party insists on avoiding conciliation and going directly to arbitration, although this is not recommended, it is permissible unless it would violate a compulsory conciliation clause in the contract. Yet Chinese arbitration specialists make it plain that, ideally, consultation, conciliation and arbitration are three successive stages, and their hope is that disputes can be settled at the first or second stage.

Similarly, the Civil Procedure Code provides that 'If a civil case that has been accepted by a people's court can be conciliated, the court should . . . conduct conciliation and urge the parties to understand each other's positions and reach an agreement.'[18] Although the Code further provides that 'If no agreement can be reached through conciliation, . . . the people's court should conduct a trial and not prolong conciliation without resolving the issue',[19] so strong is the preference for informal settlement that the Code even authorizes further conciliation at the conclusion of the trial following the final arguments of the parties and prior to judgment,[20] and allows for conciliation during any appeal against the judgment.[21]

If read literally, the Joint Venture Law and the Offshore Petroleum Regulations suggest that, while arbitration of disputes may be conducted in China or abroad, conciliation may only be conducted by a Chinese arbitration institution. But in fact, as Chinese specialists have explained, conciliation under these laws may take place in any location and be conducted by non-Chinese as well as Chinese.

Moreover, in order to meet the concern for equality and mutual benefit, the CCPIT and the American Arbitration Association (AAA) began to experiment several years ago with joint conciliation for resolving disputes in Sino-American trade. Under this arrangement each organization appoints a conciliator, and the two co-operate in helping the parties to find a solution. Joint conciliation has already been successful in the trade area, and can be expected to operate in joint ventures and other forms of co-operation as well.

The CCPIT has now decided to use joint conciliation to resolve problems arising under all Chinese commercial contracts, not merely those with American firms. It contemplates referring a dispute to a commission of two to six persons, composed of equal numbers from the CCPIT and an approved sponsoring organization from the country of the other party.[22] Alternatively, joint conciliation can simply be the very informal, *ad hoc* co-operation of two or more persons representing the respective parties.

Thus far, very few contracts have specifically referred to joint conciliation. The failure of contracts to provide for this new technique is not remarkable, however, in view of the fact that many contracts make no reference to conciliation in any form, despite its prominence in the China trade. Rather, they often give the impression that the parties will or should proceed directly from consultation between themselves to arbitration, contrary to the customary practice. Nevertheless, an increasing number of investment contracts contain a conciliation clause. Some recent joint venture contracts, for example, simply provide for the CCPIT's Foreign Economic and Trade Arbitration Commission (FETAC) — the former FTAC — to conciliate any dispute that the Board of Directors cannot settle. Another such contract authorizes conciliation by either the FETAC or an *ad hoc* panel composed of one conciliator appointed by each of the two parties and a third appointed by the first two conciliators. These contracts make it clear that arbitration is to occur only if conciliation fails.

It is highly unlikely that a foreign investor or trader would object to conciliation as a matter of principle. The experience of many countries demonstrates that conciliation can settle a large number of disputes and possesses distinct virtues. No one is eager to submit to arbitration or litigation. Yet, as the Civil Procedure Code recognizes,[23] an objection arises if conciliation drags on to the point of denying one or both of the parties a desired opportunity to conclude the dispute through a determination on the merits of the case. This is why some foreign firms have persuaded their Chinese counterparts to insert time limits into the dispute resolution clauses of their contracts, prescribing, for example, that if the conciliation process proves ineffective ninety days after it has been invoked, either party may initiate arbitration proceedings. Some parties favour a clause that simply permits either party to resort to arbitration at any time during conciliation.

C. The Place of Arbitration and the Designated Institution

As we have seen, both China's domestic legislation and its international agreements authorize Chinese commercial entities to conclude contracts that call for the arbitration of disputes abroad as well as at home. Yet negotiations in many contexts have made it clear that China continues to prefer that arbitration take place in China rather than abroad. Foreign investors, however, have generally maintained the same attitudes as foreign firms that have exported major capital goods or have licensed technology to China — they tend to find arbitration in China an unacceptable option in the present circumstances. Although they prefer arbitration in their own country, they realize that this is likely to be unacceptable to the Chinese. Some investors put forth such a suggestion in their earliest draft contract, retreating to third-country arbitration as a second line of defence. Others simply start by proposing third-country arbitration.

When confronted with a foreign party's request for third-country arbitration, the Chinese side frequently responds with one of two alternative proposals. According to one alternative, the Chinese party suggests arbitration in the country where the defendant is domiciled. As previously mentioned, this principle appears in some of China's inter-governmental agreements, and has long been used in certain trade contracts. In providing for arbitration or litigation of disputes arising under insurance contracts for ocean marine or overland transportation, the People's Insurance Company prescribes that each shall take place where the defendant is domiciled. And in the newly created policy that insures foreign investors against political risks, the People's Insurance Company also provides for arbitration in the defendant's domicile. A second Chinese alternative is to suggest that the contract provide for arbitration in China unless the parties, at the time a dispute occurs, agree upon arbitration elsewhere. For example, China's Model Contract for offshore petroleum co-operation with foreign companies refers disputes to an arbitration body of China or to another arbitration body agreed upon by the parties.

Potential foreign investors tend to reject both of these alternatives as too similar in effect to a provision that calls for arbitration in China. They believe that in most circumstances that concern them China would be the defendant, and thus in their view the formula that prescribes arbitration in the defendant's domicile is tantamount to prescribing arbitration in China. Moreover, they know from experience in other jurisdictions that such a formula leads the parties to a dispute to manipulate their relationship in an effort to emerge as the defendant. The second alternative is equally unacceptable for it simply offers a pious hope that, if a dispute occurs, China might agree to substitute third-country arbitration for submission in China even though it refuses to do so at the time the contract is negotiated, when relations are still unmarred by a dispute.

By and large, the result of this bargaining has thus far been that China accepts third-country arbitration in investment and loan contracts as well as in contracts for the purchase of capital goods and for technology transfer. In approving investment contracts, MOFERT seems to prefer Stockholm arbitration under the auspices of the Arbitration Institute of the Stockholm Chamber of Commerce to London, Geneva or other possibilities. This has been true of some early hotel joint ventures and also the Schindler elevator transaction. The Schindler agreement originally provided that any party could invoke London arbitration if it did not wish to have the dispute decided in the ordinary courts of the defendant's domicile. After review by the Foreign

Investment Commission, however, that provision was replaced by one that simply calls for Stockholm arbitration. Some loan agreements provide for Stockholm arbitration, but others do not. For example, there have been some semi-syndicated and bilateral foreign loan agreements in which the Bank of China has accepted the London Court of Arbitration for non-British loans, and the Zurich Chamber of Commerce for arbitration of certain non-Swiss loans. Investment contracts that do not require approval of the national government also constitute an occasional exception. For example, in at least one equity joint venture approved by Guangdong Province, disputes are supposed to be arbitrated in London by three arbitrators pursuant to the UNCITRAL Rules.

What future policy will be is uncertain. If at the outset of every negotiation China is prepared to accept Stockholm or other third-country arbitration, the parties will be able to save a good deal of time and devote their energies to other questions. This does occur in some instances, and CCPIT arbitration specialists have stated that China generally agrees to Stockholm arbitration in foreign trade contracts. Yet one still encounters the odd negotiation in the provinces when Chinese representatives adamantly assert that China never accepts any third-country arbitration.

MOFERT has before it a number of as yet unapproved joint venture contracts providing for a variety of arbitration sites. In view of the current close contacts between the CCPIT and the American Arbitration Association (AAA), it will be especially interesting to see whether MOFERT will accept arbitration in the United States under AAA auspices in a situation where one of the venturers is a Chinese entity and the foreign party is not American. China has already approved resort to the Court of Arbitration of the Zurich Chamber of Commerce in a contract that calls for an investment in China by a Swedish group.

The continuing negotiations concerning China's offshore oil co-operation with foreign companies have begun to yield some interesting provisions regarding arbitration, although there is an inevitable time-lag, due to confidentiality restrictions, before such information becomes public. At least one early contract provides that, if the parties fail to resolve any dispute through friendly negotiations within ninety days of its occurrence, they may agree upon arbitration in China before the FETAC, but, if they do not agree upon the FETAC, then within thirty days of the expiration of the ninety-day period they may agree either to submit the matter to an international arbitration agency for resolution under its rules or to submit it for resolution by an *ad hoc* tribunal to be organized under a given set of international arbitration rules. If they fail to reach agreement on this choice, the Chinese party is required, within fifteen days of the end of the thirty-day period, to select an international arbitration organization from a list composed of the Arbitration Institute of the Stockholm Chamber of Commerce (for arbitration in Stockholm); the International Center for the Settlement of Investment Disputes (ICSID) with headquarters in Washington; and any other arbitration institution that the parties may agree to add to the list. Or, if the Chinese party prefers, it may decide not to choose any of the listed agencies and instead agree to arbitration under the UNCITRAL Arbitration Rules.

Perhaps the most interesting aspect of this imaginative and flexible compromise is China's willingness to list the ICSID as a potential agency for arbitration. The ICSID, which is part of the World Bank system, has been eager to have China adhere to the ICSID arrangements ever since China joined the World Bank. Although China has not yet decided to participate in the ICSID, the contractual provision described above is the most tangible evidence thus far available of its interest.

Nevertheless, at least some of the subsequent offshore oil contracts with foreign companies do not mention the ICSID and set forth a simpler formula than the earlier one. It provides that, if the parties fail to agree on FETAC arbitration, they shall form an *ad hoc* tribunal under the UNCITRAL Arbitration Rules, with each side selecting one member of the tribunal and the two thus selected in turn choosing the third member from the nationals of a country that maintains diplomatic relations with both China and the countries of the foreign oil companies involved.

Certainly there may be advantages to China in selecting a single foreign jurisdiction and arbitration institution for the settlement of most disputes outside China, especially at a time when China is still new to the actualities of international commercial arbitration. It must be difficult for the Chinese to become familiar with the variety of places and foreign arbitration organizations as well as the relevant legal environment in each jurisdiction. Concentrating on one place and one organization should simplify matters. China's general preference for Stockholm and the Arbitration Institute of the Stockholm Chamber of Commerce appears to be grounded in careful analysis based on continuing close contacts with officials of the Institute.

Yet other places, some of them much less distant from China than Stockholm and therefore less expensive and more convenient as a forum, are beginning to vie for selection as a suitable site. Tokyo seems to be gaining favour in some quarters in China, not only because of geographic propinquity but also because of the belief that Japanese arbitrators might be more capable of understanding China's circumstances and attitudes toward law and contracts than would Europeans.

Hong Kong has lately established itself as an arbitration centre for the Asian region and hopes to create conditions that will make it an attractive site for the settlement of China-related disputes. At the same time, China is establishing new arbitration organizations in the Special Economic Zones that it has set up in areas of Guangdong Province near Hong Kong, in order to facilitate on-the-spot resolution of disputes that arise from activities related to the zones. One suspects that competitive considerations might lead Chinese arbitration experts to prefer to promote their own organizations rather than those of Hong Kong as forums for arbitration. Moreover, because Hong Kong is a British colony on what will soon become Chinese soil, Hong Kong would seem to stand little chance of winning official Chinese co-operation in this endeavour. It is likely that China will not want to encourage the belief that the colony is neutral, rather than Chinese soil, by accepting Hong Kong as the site of third-country arbitration. Nevertheless, Hong Kong is geographically contiguous to China and relations between it and China are increasingly cordial. Hong Kong has strong linguistic, cultural and economic bonds with China, and China has a great many government offices and companies operating there. Thus, considerations of convenience would appear to favour Hong Kong arbitration. Whether China will allow these considerations to outweigh competitive and political factors remains to be seen.

D. Rules of Procedure

Under Chinese practice, the parties to a contract are free to choose the rules of procedure applicable to arbitration as well as the place of arbitration. More often than not, when a given institution is authorized to facilitate arbitration, Chinese contracts provide for the rules of procedure of that institution to apply. Although contracts that provide for arbitration in China generally state that it shall be conducted under the provisional rules of procedure of the relevant Chinese institution, in the Chinese view such a statement is not necessary. Chinese contract references to arbitration in the defendant's domicile do not usually mention anything about rules of procedure. Contract references to third-country arbitration frequently specify the rules to be used, normally those of the named organization. For example, one joint venture contract provides that:

> In the event such conciliation cannot resolve the dispute, the matter shall be brought before the arbitration panel of the Stockholm Chamber of Commerce, Sweden, for arbitration, and shall proceed according to the arbitration regulations and procedure of that arbitration organization. The decision of the arbitration shall be final and will be binding on both parties.

Sometimes, however, the contract merely authorizes arbitration in Stockholm, adding only that the arbitration decision shall be final and binding on both parties.

Even while prescribing that the rules of a designated third-country institution shall be applied, Chinese contracts sometimes single out certain of those rules for emphasis or stipulate details that the rules contemplate will be agreed to by the parties or that modify the rules in some respects. For example, several Chinese foreign loan agreements that authorize London arbitration, after stating that the rules of the London Court of Arbitration shall apply, go on to provide that the tribunal shall consist of three arbitrators, one selected by each of the two parties and the third by the London Court of Arbitration, and that the tribunal shall state in writing the reasons for its decision. Some such agreements spell out that the language of the proceedings shall be English. And it is not uncommon, as some of these loan agreements illustrate, for contracts to state that the rules to be applied are those of the relevant institution that are in effect on the date the contract is signed. This is usually inserted at the request of foreign parties who are concerned that the rules might subsequently be altered in unacceptable ways.

Consistent with its belief that the parties are free to choose the applicable rules of procedure, China is also willing, as the Sino-American trade agreement indicates, to substitute other international arbitration rules for those of the designated institution, if this is acceptable to the other parties and the designated institution. For example, China is happy to use the UNCITRAL Arbitration Rules under the administration of the Stockholm Arbitration Institute, and, as the offshore oil contracts illustrate, some contracts call for an *ad hoc* tribunal to be constituted under the UNCITRAL Rules, sometimes designating the place of arbitration and at other times omitting any reference to the place.

Only the rules of the International Chamber of Commerce (ICC) remain unacceptable to Beijing. This is not because the ICC is *persona non grata* in Chinese eyes or because of any dissatisfaction with the rules themselves or the high costs of ICC arbitration, but because of Taiwan's continuing participation in the ICC. When this political question is resolved, the ICC rules should enjoy the same respect in Beijing's eyes as the UNCITRAL Rules and others. Both the Chinese and the foreign parties to the Schindler elevator joint venture contract were apparently unaware of this obstacle, for the contract originally provided, as an alternative to litigation in the defendant's domicile, for London arbitration in accordance with ICC rules. As should have been expected, upon review of the contract the Foreign Investment Commission disapproved this clause, and the parties had to remove not only the litigation option but also the reference to the ICC: they substituted arbitration under the Stockholm Institute.

For several years China has been considering whether to revise the rules of procedure of its own arbitration institutions. The State Council did approve a change of name for the Foreign Trade Arbitration Commission, which is now known as the Foreign Economic and Trade Arbitration Commission (FETAC). The new name is meant to symbolize the anticipated expansion of the Commission's work as it prepares to 'take cognizance of the disputes arising from the implementation of agreements and contracts in utilizing foreign funds, joint ventures, foreign technology, co-production by Chinese and foreign firms and compensation trade.'[24]

Although the language of the FETAC's rules, like its original name, is broad enough to encompass these transactions, some Chinese experts think it may be appropriate to change the rules to take account specifically of China's recent participation in such transactions. It is also reported that the Commission 'will be enlarged in proportion to the expansion of its business scope'.[25]

Whether significant changes will actually be made in the Commission's rules and practice remains unclear. One change that Chinese officials have considered would be to permit non-Chinese to serve as members of the arbitration tribunal to be constituted under the auspices of the FETAC.

Because the rules have thus far required all arbitrators to be chosen from among the members of the Commission, who are all Chinese, many foreign firms have preferred third-country arbitration in order to reduce the risk of confronting a potentially biased panel. Although both the FETAC and the Maritime Arbitration Commission are said to be opposed to 'national egoism in making use of arbitration to favour the party of their own nationality,'[26] foreigners would have more confidence in arbitration in China if membership in the tribunal were more broadly based.

Even if the rules of these institutions are not changed to allow foreign arbitrators, the contracting parties could provide for foreign representation on an arbitration tribunal, with the arbitration still conducted in China, by inserting into their contract a clause that calls for UNCITRAL arbitration to take place in China.

E. The Enforcement of Awards

China has concluded a number of bilateral trade agreements and navigation treaties that, like the Sino-American trade agreement, obligate the participating governments to strive to ensure that arbitration awards are recognized and enforced by their competent authorities in accordance with applicable laws and regulations. Yet such provisions are general expressions that lack specific assurances and procedures. China has not yet joined in international conventions for the enforcement of foreign arbitral awards but has long been studying the implications of participating in such conventions. The 1982 enactment of China's first Civil Procedure Code was said by some Chinese officials to have been a necessary prerequisite to adherence to these multilateral conventions.

Although Chinese contracts usually state that the arbitration award shall be final and binding upon the parties, they often make no provision for enforcement. Some contracts, however, including some recent ones for joint ventures and loans, stipulate that the award may be enforced through any competent court. Foreign investors occasionally seek to add to contracts a sentence to the effect that the award shall be entitled to the benefits of the United Nations Convention on the Recognition and Enforcement of Foreign Arbitral Awards of 1958, but these efforts are usually rejected.

There has been little actual experience with arbitration awards in the China trade, and even less with respect to the enforcement of such awards. Knowledgeable Chinese officials have asserted that, since the founding of the People's Republic, there has not been a single case in which China's courts have decreed enforcement of an award involving foreign interests. This is said to be because Chinese foreign trade and maritime entities are state-owned enterprises that recognize that a Chinese arbitration award has the force of law and must be executed by the parties within the time prescribed. Thus, there has been no need to seek court enforcement. Even before promulgation of the Civil Procedure Code, Chinese officials claimed that, should a Chinese enterprise fail to respect a Chinese award, the people's courts would accept a petition from the other party for enforcement.[27] Indeed, the governmental decisions establishing China's two principal arbitration commissions state that their awards are to be final, that 'neither party shall bring an appeal for revision before a court of law or any other organization', and that Chinese courts shall, upon the request of a party, enforce the award of these commissions in accordance with the law.[28]

Article 195 of the new Code confirms this arrangement. It provides that:

When one of the parties concerned fails to comply with an award made by a foreign arbitration organization of the PRC, the other party may request that the award be enforced in accordance with the provisions of this Code by the intermediate people's court in the place where the arbitration organization is located or where the property is located.

How the courts will carry out this mandate — for example, what the scope of their review of Chinese awards will be in an enforcement proceeding — is a matter of considerable interest to foreign companies.

Because the new forms of economic co-operation between China and the industrialized nations generally provide for arbitration outside China, the enforceability of foreign awards in China is a topic of even greater concern to foreigners. Responsible Chinese officials have long offered assurances that 'Chinese corporations and enterprises will, in fact, execute foreign arbitral awards so long as they are fair and not in violation of the Chinese laws and policies.'[29] In the event of non-execution of awards, foreigners have been advised by CCPIT officials not only to petition the Chinese government department concerned but also to request the assistance of the CCPIT in persuading the Chinese party to carry out the award, or to seek enforcement through the people's courts.

In what circumstances can foreigners successfully seek enforcement of foreign awards through the Chinese courts? Even if the contract in question provides for enforcement of a foreign award by any court of 'competent jurisdiction' or 'in an ordinary court of law', such phrases do not make clear the prerequisites to judicial enforcement, and in any event cannot control the standards prescribed in the Civil Procedure Code for enforcement by Chinese courts. The Code appears to preclude direct judicial enforcement of a foreign award. Article 195, as mentioned above, only authorizes direct enforcement of an award made by 'a foreign arbitration organization of the PRC'. Article 195 is part of Chapter 20, entitled 'Arbitration', which is exclusively concerned with arbitration in China.

The possibility of enforcing a foreign arbitral award must be considered in connection with Chapter 22, entitled 'Judicial Assistance'. This chapter is exclusively concerned with legal actions that Chinese courts and foreign courts may entrust each other to take on behalf of the other. Article 202, after establishing the general principle of mutual entrustment, authorizes a Chinese court to reject a case entrusted to the court 'if it violates the sovereignty and security of the PRC'. Article 204 provides that:

In dealing with a judgment or award that has already been confirmed and that a foreign court has entrusted a people's court of the PRC to enforce, the people's court shall examine the judgment or award on the basis of an international treaty concluded or participated in by the PRC or in accordance with the principles of comity, and shall determine to recognize the legal effect of such judgment or award and enforce the same according to procedures prescribed by this Code if the court believes that such a judgment or award does not violate the basic principles of the laws of the PRC or the interests of our country's state and society. Otherwise the matter shall be returned to the foreign court.

It thus appears that a foreign award can be recognized and enforced only after being confirmed by an appropriate foreign court, which must then request enforcement by a Chinese court. In some jurisdictions this requirement will pose a barrier to enforcement. Moreover, what kinds of awards will be deemed to violate the basic principles of Chinese law or the interests of the Chinese state and society is not known, but plainly these criteria give great latitude to the courts. The courts, however, may interpret these standards along the lines of the narrow 'public policy' exception applied by other countries in order to assure maximum international judicial co-operation.

If seeking initial confirmation by a foreign court seems too burdensome or if a foreign court will not request enforcement, perhaps the only alternative open to the party seeking satisfaction of the award would be to initiate a regular civil suit in China and to rely on the award as evidence in support of its claim.

Chapter 22 also authorizes Chinese courts to request the co-operation of foreign courts in enforcing Chinese arbitration awards and judgments. Article 203 provides:

If an applicant requests compulsory enforcement of any legally effective PRC judgment issued by a people's court or award rendered by an arbitration organization and if the person against whom the application has been filed or his property is not within the territory of our country, the people's court may entrust a foreign court to assist in the enforcement on the basis of an international treaty concluded or participated in by China or in accordance with the principles of comity.

Although the language of this provision is not identical with that of Chapter 20 in referring to the type of arbitration award with which it is concerned, it seems clear that Article 203 covers only awards of Chinese arbitration tribunals. Again, as in the case of Chapter 20, it is uncertain whether, for example, a UNCITRAL arbitration held in China would be regarded as a Chinese arbitration tribunal.

F. Applicable Law

What law should the arbitrators apply to a contract dispute? This may be the most delicate legal question that arises in commerce with China. So long as transactions involve ordinary trade or even the sale of complex capital goods to China, the failure to specify the applicability of Chinese law does not seem to trouble Chinese negotiators, who are generally content if the contract is silent about the governing law. This is especially true if the contract calls for arbitration in China, for Chinese arbitration commissions apparently apply Chinese law and policies to the contracts, even though they also take account of what they term 'those reasonable international practices which are . . . favourable to the development of international trade and marine transport'.[30]

Bank loans can be seen as analogous to the importation of capital goods. It is probably for this reason that, even when loan agreements prescribe arbitration outside China, many such agreements, with the Bank of China or with other Chinese borrowers, are either silent about the governing law or contain a provision explicitly recognizing the right of the arbitration tribunal to decide upon the applicable law. One loan agreement, for example, stated that the tribunal would make its decisions 'entirely on the basis of substantive law to be determined by the arbitrators'. Yet in a subsequent, similar loan negotiation, the Bank of China rejected a clause that would have authorized the tribunal to interpret the agreement 'in accordance with its terms and the appropriate law as determined by the arbitrators in accordance with principles of private international law applicable at the place of arbitration'. In that situation, the Bank preferred to avoid the problem through silence.

On some occasions Chinese borrowers have agreed to foreign governing law. Japanese, New York, Hong Kong and Swiss law have all been accepted on occasion. In those still rare instances when Chinese entities accept the jurisdiction of a foreign court, they tend also to agree to foreign governing law, and there have been some instances when foreign law has been prescribed in conjunction with a foreign arbitration clause.

It has been more difficult for Chinese officials to do without a Chinese governing law clause when negotiating with foreigners to build an office building, hotel or manufacturing plant on Chinese soil, whether by means of an equity joint venture, a contractual joint venture, compensation trade or some other investment-type arrangement. Given the history of foreign extraterritorial jurisdiction in China during the century that began with the Opium War of 1839–42, it is understandably important to the People's Republic, which came to power with a deep commitment to vindicating Chinese nationalism, that Chinese law apply to activities conducted in China.

From the perspective of the foreign investor, the problem is one not of principle but of practicality. At the moment there is relatively little Chinese law that can govern the interpretation of contract disputes with foreigners. The Joint Venture Law, even as supplemented by its 1983 implementing regulations, is not very detailed, and the Economic Contract Law may not apply to investment contracts between Chinese and foreign entities, even during the period preceding promulgation of the long-awaited foreign economic contract law. A corporation law, a civil code and other economic legislation are now being drafted by China, but it will be several years before a basic business law structure is completed. Moreover, China does not systematically publish its judicial decisions, and in any event it will take decades before the courts have authoritatively interpreted the many important provisions of the evolving legislative framework.

In these circumstances, the foreigner is understandably concerned that, after he signs a contract with a Chinese company, China might promulgate legislation that, on its face or as officially construed, will adversely affect his interests. Or, if a dispute arises in the absence of legislation, China, through expert witnesses and other means, might inform the arbitrators that Chinese law, although as yet unpublished, actually prescribes a result adverse to the foreign investor. Before investing tens or even hundreds of millions of dollars the foreigner would like to know the rules of the game.

In the absence (or even the presence) of relevant Chinese law, foreign investors would, of course, prefer to invoke the law of their own jurisdiction or of some third country that has developed accessible and fair legal norms. This is unacceptable to the Chinese for contracts involving investments in China. Thus some form of compromise has been required.

What has happened in practice is that no mention of the applicable law has been made in many of the investment contracts that have been approved. Of course, when the contracts are silent, if a dispute does arise, the third-country arbitration tribunal, by using standard private international choice of law principles, may decide to invoke Chinese law. Many foreigners seem prepared to take their chances on this, trusting that no dispute will occur or that, if it does, it may be resolved without arbitration, or that China may by that time have enacted applicable law of general acceptability, or that the arbitrators may interpret Chinese law in a creative manner designed to reach a fair result. The Foreign Investment Commission and its successor, MOFERT, have sometimes been willing to accept silence as a compromise even in circumstances where the arbitrators might decide to apply foreign law. Thus the Schindler elevator joint venture contract reportedly fails to specify the governing law despite the existence of certain facts, such as negotiation and signature of the final contract outside China, that lead the Chinese to acknowledge a risk that their own law might not be chosen by an arbitration tribunal.

The 1983 Act for the Implementation of the Joint Venture Law, however, rules out the possibility of future compromises, with respect to equity joint ventures, for it flatly prescribes that Chinese law is to govern such contracts.[31] At the time of writing it is unclear whether this provision of the Act will be applied to existing contracts, thereby undoing the compromises already worked out. Presumably a similar provision will become part of forthcoming legislation regulating contractual joint ventures, wholly-owned foreign enterprises and other foreign investments in China.

Although China has pressed foreign negotiators on the governing law question when contracts for the exploitation of mineral resources are involved, thus far it has been willing to compromise. While the Model Contract for offshore oil co-operation prepared by the Chinese contains a simple provision requiring that Chinese law govern any contract disputes, the foreign oil companies have succeeded, at least in some cases, in modifying this clause to allow reference by some means or other to international standards. At least one early Sino-foreign oil contract, for example, states that the decision of any arbitration tribunal shall principally take into account the provisions of the contract and shall refer to relevant international custom. It goes on to state, however, that when the issues in dispute require an interpretation of the law the arbitrators shall inform themselves of the interpretation given by Chinese — not foreign — experts on Chinese law. Very recent negotiations during the first round of offshore bidding have produced a slightly less satisfactory compromise from the foreign viewpoint, providing that, in the absence of relevant Chinese law, 'the principles of the applicable laws widely used in petroleum resources countries acceptable to CNOOC (the China National Offshore Oil Corporation) and the Contractor shall be applicable.' Obviously, it would prove to be a challenge to implement so vague a formula.

What should arbitrators do if no choice of law is made in the contract? It appears to be the opinion of at least certain specialists in the Chinese government that, instead of applying traditional private international law rules, the tribunal should look to the law of China, the law of the foreign investor's country, international practice and basic principles of fairness, and come up with the wisest decision that it can. Occasionally Chinese officials put this formula more inscrutably, stating that on the question of applicable law they take into account three principles: independence and initiative; equality and mutual benefit; and international practice.[32]

IV. Conclusion

In China, as in other socialist states based on Marxism-Leninism, international commercial arbitration is the creature of a government bureaucracy and the servant of a planned economy. Nevertheless, as part of its new policy of welcoming foreign investment, loans and other forms of co-operation with business firms that generally are privately owned, the People's Republic has recently taken several steps to improve facilities for resolving the disputes that will inevitably arise in the course of these developing relationships.

Consistent with its traditional preference for conciliation rather than arbitration in those cases where the parties cannot resolve a dispute by themselves, China has adopted the innovation of joint conciliation as a means of expanding conciliation's acceptability and efficacy. And in line with its long-standing preference for arbitration rather than litigation in those cases where conciliation is unsuccessful, China, in order to make arbitration more attractive to foreign businessmen, has usually agreed to arbitrate in third countries under the procedural rules of the designated foreign institutions, even though China would prefer that arbitration take place in China or in the country of the defendant. Moreover, at least until China enacts a full set of commercial laws, it does not always insist that its contracts with foreign business partners prescribe Chinese law as the governing law but is often willing, except in the case of equity joint ventures and natural resources contracts, to leave the problem of applicable law to the arbitrators of any dispute. Finally, within certain limits, Chinese courts are now available to enforce arbitral awards, directly in the case of Chinese awards and indirectly in the case of foreign awards.

Such a reasonable and flexible system for dispute settlement can be expected to stimulate the economic transactions that China desires with the capitalist world. The challenge ahead will be to implement this system to the satisfaction of all concerned, while China's economic policy and legal system continue to evolve in ways that are sure to have an impact upon dispute resolution.

Notes

1. See Jerome Alan Cohen and Hungdah Chiu, *People's China and International Law* (Princeton, Princeton University Press, 1974), pp. 1088–94 and 1448.

2. Cohen and Chiu, pp. 656–68, note 1 above.

3. Cohen and Chiu, pp. 705–7, note 1 above.

4. English translations of the Decision of the Government Administration Council of the Central People's Government Concerning the Establishment of a Foreign Trade Arbitration Commission within the CCPIT (hereafter cited as the Decision Concerning FTAC) and the Provisional Rules of Procedure of the Foreign Trade Arbitration Commission of the CCPIT may be found in Hsiao, *The Foreign Trade of China* (California, University of California Press, 1977), pp. 245 and 247, respectively.

5. English translations of the Decision of the State Council of the PRC Concerning the Establishment of a Maritime Arbitration Commission Within the CCPIT (hereafter cited as the Decision Concerning MAC) and the Provisional Rules of Procedure of the Maritime Arbitration Commission of the CCPIT may be found in Hsiao, pp. 252 and 254, respectively, note 4 above.

6. In recent years Chinese arbitration experts have begun to disseminate substantial information about the actual handling of concrete arbitrations. See, for example, Tang Houzhi, 'Foreign Trade and Economic Arbitration in China', undated. Four cases discussed by Mr Tang, Deputy Chief, Division of Foreign Economic and Trade Arbitration, Legal Affairs Department of the CCPIT, are reproduced in Walter Sterling Surrey and Stephen M. Soble, 'Recent Developments in Dispute Resolution in the People's Republic of China', in Jerome A. Cohen (ed.), *Legal Aspects of Doing Business in China* (New York, Practising Law Institute, 1983), pp. 402–9.

7. Holtzmann, 'Dispute Resolution Procedures in East-West Trade', *International Lawyer*, No. 13, 1979, p. 249.

8. 'How the Case of the M/S *Varild* was Settled', in *Foreign Trade of the People's*

Republic of China (Beijing), October 1963, p. 4; reproduced in Cohen and Chiu, pp. 1453–4, note 1 above.

9. See Arts. 186, 192 and 193 of the Civil Procedure Code. Note that Article 187 restricts foreign access to Chinese courts to the same extent as the foreigner's country restricts the access of Chinese persons or institutions to the courts of that country.

10. The English and Chinese texts of what is formally known as The Agreement on Trade Relations Between the United States of America and the People's Republic of China, dated 7 July 1979 and effective as of 1 January 1980, may be found, respectively, in Treaties and Other International Acts Series (T.I.A.S.), No. 9630, reproduced in *International Legal Materials*, No. 18, 1979, p. 1041, and *Chinese Yearbook of International Law* (1982), pp. 428–32.

11. See, for example, 'The Protocol on the General Conditions for the Delivery of Goods Between the Foreign Trade Organizations of the People's Republic of China and the Union of Soviet Socialist Republics of 1950; and The Protocol on the General Conditions for the Delivery of Goods Between the Foreign Trade Organizations of the People's Republic of China and the People's Republic of Romania of 1961, English translations of which can be found in *Chinese Law and Government*, Vol. 5, 1972–3, pp. 14 and 109, respectively, as well as the Trade Agreement with Finland of 5 June 1953, and the Trade Agreement with the French Trade Delegation of 5 June 1953.

12. For an English translation of the Joint Venture Law, see *China's Foreign Economic Legislation* (Beijing, Foreign Languages Press, 1982), Vol. 1, pp. 1–7.

13. See Art. 27 of the Regulations, which were promulgated by the State Council on 30 January 1982.

14. Art. 192, para. 1, of the Code provides that: 'In disputes arising out of foreign economic relations, trade, transportation or maritime affairs, if the parties have a written agreement to submit [such a dispute] to a foreign arbitration organization of the People's Republic of China for arbitration, then they may not institute proceedings in the people's courts; absent such written agreement, proceedings may be instituted in the people's courts.'

15. Art. 111 of the Act, which was promulgated by the State Council on 20 September 1983.

16. Art. 109 of the Act.

17. See Art. 14 of the Regulations, which were promulgated by the State Council on 26 July 1980.

18. Art. 97 of the Code.

19. Art. 102 of the Code.

20. Art. 111 of the Code.

21. Art. 153 of the Code.

22. Ren Jianxin, 'Some Legal Aspects of our Import of Technology and Utilization of Foreign Investment' (speech delivered in Hong Kong on 29 September 1980), translated and reprinted in *China Law Reporter*, Vol. 1, Fall 1980, pp. 85 and 99–100.

23. Art. 102.

24. From the State Council's Notice Concerning the Conversion of the Foreign Trade Arbitration Commission into the Foreign Economic and Trade Arbitration Commission, Beijing, 26 February 1980.

25. See note 24 above.

26. Ren Jianxin and Liu Shaoshan, 'Arbitration in China', translated and reprinted in *Doing Business With China: Legal, Financial and Negotiating Aspects* (New York, Harcourt, Brace and Jovanovich, 1979), pp. 222.

27. Ren Jianxin, 'The Establishment and Development of Foreign Trade, Economic and Marine Arbitration in China', speech reprinted in English, p. 7.

28. See Decision Concerning FTAC, Arts. 10 and 11, note 4 above, and Decision Concerning MAC, Arts. 10 and 11, note 5 above.

29. Ren and Liu, p. 228, note 26 above.

30. Ren, p. 2, note 22 above.

31. Art. 15 of the Act.

32. Speech by Ren Jianxin, Head of the PRC Delegation to the Third Session of UNCITRAL's Working Group on International Contract Practices, February 1982.

12. China's New Patent Law

MICHAEL J. MOSER

ON 12 March 1984 the Patent Law of the People's Republic of China was passed by the Standing Committee of the National People's Congress.[1] Consisting of 69 articles in 8 chapters, the law is due to come into effect on 1 April 1985. More than five years in the making and reportedly the product of in excess of twenty different drafts,[2] the law provides the first significant statutory protection for inventions by foreigners since the founding of the People's Republic in 1949.[3] As such, it has been anxiously awaited by foreign businessmen involved in technology licensing and manufacturing in China. This chapter provides a description and preliminary analysis of the new Patent Law with special attention to its relevance to foreign businesses operating in China.

I. The Scope of the Law

The law provides for three types of patentable subject matter: inventions, utility models and designs.[4]

Inventions and utility models are required to meet three criteria before patent rights may be granted. These criteria are: (1) novelty, (2) creativity, and (3) practicability.[5] 'Novelty' is defined by the law to mean that before the date of the patent application no similar invention or utility model has appeared in any publication inside or outside China, or has been publicly used or made known to the general public either inside or outside China, and no application for a similar invention or utility model has been submitted by any other party to the Patent Bureau and been recorded in a patent application made public after the date of the application.[6] Under the law, novelty will not be lost where within six months prior to the submission of the application any of the following has occurred: (1) the invention or utility model has been exhibited for the first time in an international exhibition under the sponsorship of, or recognized by, the Chinese government; (2) the invention or utility model has been published for the first time at a specified academic conference or technical meeting; or (3) the contents of the invention or utility model have been revealed by third parties without the consent of the applicant.[7]

'Creativity' is defined by the law to mean, with respect to inventions, that the invention possesses 'outstanding substantive characteristics' and 'represents obvious progress' and, with respect to utility models, that the utility model merely possesses 'substantive characteristics' and 'represents progress', in both cases as compared with technology already in existence before the date of the patent application.[8] 'Practicability' is defined to mean that the relevant invention or utility model can be used or manufactured and is capable of producing 'positive effects'.[9]

The Patent Law requires that designs for which patent rights are applied for should not be identical, nor bear a close resemblance, to designs that have already appeared in publications inside or outside China, or that have already been publicly used inside China before the date of the application.[10]

The law further specifies a number of items with respect to which patent rights may not be granted. These include scientific discoveries; rules and methods of intellectual activity; methods of diagnosing and treating diseases; and substances obtained from atomic nucleus alternation methods.[11] In addition, patent rights may not be obtained for foods, beverages and seasonings; pharmaceuticals and other substances obtained through chemical processes; and varieties of animals and plants.[12] In these cases, however, the production methods relating to the products, if not the products themselves, are patentable.[13]

In addition to the specific exclusions from patentable subject matter noted in the above paragraph, the Patent Law prohibits the granting of patent rights to inventions and other creations that are illegal, or that violate social ethics or are injurious to the public interest.[14] Moreover, inventions and other creations that involve state security or the 'major interests of the state' and that need to be kept confidential are apparently outside the scope of the Patent Law.[15] Under the law, applications for patents with respect to such items are to be handled according to unspecified 'relevant stipulations'.[16]

II. Procedures for Obtaining Patents

The Patent Law permits foreign individuals, enterprises and other organizations outside China to apply for patents in China in accordance with bilateral agreements signed between China and the applicant's home country, international agreements to which both China and the applicant's home country are signatories, or the principle of reciprocity.[17] Under the law, foreign applicants are not permitted to submit applications directly to the Patent Bureau but must entrust the agency designated by the State Council to handle applications and related matters on their behalf.[18] According to Chinese sources, this agency will be the Patent Office of the China Council for the Promotion of International Trade.[19] A patent agency office has also been established in Hong Kong with authority to handle foreign applications.[20]

The Patent Law mandates a three-step procedure for obtaining patents. First, a formal application must be submitted to the Patent Bureau. The second step involves examination of the application by the Patent Bureau and the issue of a decision either to reject or approve the application. The final step is the formal issue of letters patent with respect to the invention, utility model or design for which patents are applied for.

A. Application Procedures

Applicants for patents on inventions and utility models are required to submit to the Patent Bureau three documents: (1) a 'letter of request' *(qingqiu shu)* setting forth the name of the invention or utility model, the name of the inventor or designer, the name and address of the applicant and other information; (2) a 'manual' *(shuoming shu)* consisting of an explanation of the invention or utility model together with an 'abstract' *(che yao)* of the main technical points; and (3) a 'letter asking for rights' *(quanli yaoqiu shu)* which is based on the manual and explains the scope within which patent protection is being requested.[21] Applications for patents on designs must include a letter of request together with a photograph or other representation of the design in question and must clearly state the product using the design and the classification to which it belongs.[22] According to the Patent Bureau, standard forms for the above-mentioned documents, as well as a classification schedule similar to that used for trade marks, are now being developed for use by applicants.

Under the Patent Law, applicants generally are required to submit a separate application for each distinct invention or utility model.[23] However, an exception to this rule exists in cases where one or more inventions or utility models are part of a single 'overall concept of invention'.[24] In such cases, a single application covering multiple inventions or utility models is permitted. Similarly, a separate application rule is also applied to designs for 'outward appearances', except that a single application may be submitted to cover multiple designs used for products of the same classification that are sold or used as one set.[25]

As a general rule, where two or more applicants file for patents on the same or similar inventions, utility models or designs, the Patent Bureau is required to grant the patent right to the first applicant.[26] As a consequence of this 'race' provision in the Patent Law, the date of the application is of paramount importance. The rule of thumb established by the law is that the date on which the Patent Bureau receives the application documents is deemed to be the date of application.[27] However, exceptions to the basic rule are also provided for. For example, where application documents are sent by post, the date of the postmark is taken as the date of application.[28] Moreover, a special priority right is granted in certain circumstances to foreign applicants. Where a foreign party submits an application in China for an invention or utility model within twelve months, or for an 'outward appearance' design within six months, of the date of the first application abroad for a patent with respect to the same invention, utility model or design, the Patent Bureau may take the date of the applicant's foreign application to be the date of application in China.[29] The priority right is not automatic but must be requested by the applicant at the time of submission of the Chinese application documents.[30] When requesting the priority right, the applicant is required to submit a written declaration to the Patent Office containing relevant information pertaining to the foreign patent application.[31] Within three months of the date of the Chinese application, the applicant must also provide a certified copy of the foreign application documents to the Patent Office.[32] Failure to provide such materials constitutes sufficient grounds for denial of the priority right.[33]

B. Examination and Approval Procedures

The Patent Law prescribes different procedures for the examination and approval of patent applications for utility models and designs on the one hand, and patent applications for inventions on the other.

With respect to applications for patents on utility models and designs, the law requires the Patent Bureau to conduct a preliminary examination of the application.[34] Presumably, the contents of this examination are limited to a review of the application document to determine whether the application is prima facie in conformity with the requirements of the Patent Law. If the Patent Bureau considers that the requirements have been met, it is required to announce the application and notify the applicants immediately.[35] No further substantive examination of the application is required.

Applications for patents on inventions are also subject to preliminary examination by the Patent Bureau. Applications considered to be in conformity with the requirements of the Patent Law must be publicly announced within eighteen months of the date of the application.[36] Not later than three years from the date of the application, the applicant may request the Patent Bureau to conduct a substantive examination of the application.[37] If the applicant fails 'without legitimate reason' to request such an examination within the stipulated period, the application will be regarded as having been withdrawn, although the Patent Bureau may conduct a substantive examination of its own accord when it deems such to be necessary.[38]

When requesting substantive examination of a patent application, the applicant is required to submit reference materials relating to the invention.[39] If an application for a patent on the same invention has already been submitted abroad, the applicant must provide copies of the materials inspected by the foreign patent authorities, as well as any materials relating to the results of the examination.[40] Failure to provide such materials will be deemed to constitute a withdrawal of the application.[41]

Upon completion of a substantive examination, the Patent Bureau is required either to approve and announce publicly the application or to notify the applicant that the application does not conform to the requirements set forth in the Patent Law.[42] In the latter event, the Patent Bureau may request that the applicant submit its opinion regarding issues in connection with the application, or amend the application within a specified period of time.[43] If the applicant fails to make a timely response, or if the response fails to satisfy the Patent Bureau, the application will be rejected.[44]

After a patent application has been publicly announced, any person may file an objection to the application with the Patent Bureau.[45] Objections must be filed within three months of the date of the announcement and copies of the objection must be sent to the applicant.[46] The applicant is required to respond in writing to the objection within three months of the date of receipt of the objection.[47] Upon review of the objection and response, the Patent Bureau will then decide either to reject or to concur with the objection. If the objection is upheld, the application will be rejected and the parties will be notified accordingly.[48]

The law requires that the Patent Bureau establish a Patent Re-examination Committee to handle appeals in connection with patent applications.[49] The applicant may appeal against a decision of the Patent Bureau to reject an application before the Patent Re-examination Committee within three months of the date of notification of rejection.[50] In the event of disagreement over a decision of the Patent Re-examination Committee, applicants for patents on inventions are permitted to bring a suit before the people's courts within three months of the date of notification of the Committee's decision.[51] Committee decisions regarding requests for the re-examination of applications for patents on utility models and designs are final and may not be appealed against in the courts.[52]

C. The Granting of Patent Rights

Once a patent application has been approved and publicly announced and any relevant objections and appeals have been disposed of, the Patent Bureau is required to grant patent rights to the applicant by issuing letters patent and registering the patent in China.[53] Following registration, the patent holder has the right to use the patent and to mark patented products and the packaging of such products with their patent sign and number.[54] From the year the patent rights are granted, the patent holder will be obliged to pay annual fees to the Patent Bureau for the duration of the patent.[55] At the time of writing, the scale of fees to be applied by the Patent Bureau has not yet been announced.

The term for patent rights issued with respect to inventions is fifteen years; for patents on utility models and designs the term is five years.[56] In both cases, the term is calculated from the date of the patent application. Extensions of three years may be applied for by the patent holder prior to the expiry date.[57] The Patent Law provides for several circumstances under which patent rights may be terminated or revoked prior to the expiry of the scheduled term. Termination may occur where the patent holder has failed to pay annual patent fees or where the patent right has been renounced by the holder in a written declaration.[58] Revocation may also occur where the Patent Re-examination Committee determines that a patent has been granted in error.[59] Under the law, any unit or individual has the right to seek a declaration of the patent's invalidity from the Patent Re-examination Committee if it believes that the granting of the patent was not in conformity with the Patent Law.[60] Decisions of the Patent Re-examination Committee regarding the revocation of patents on inventions may be appealed against in the people's courts.[61] However, decisions of the Committee regarding patents on utility models and designs are final.[62] Patent rights determined to be invalid are void *ab initio*.[63]

III. The Assignment and Licensing of Patents

Under the Patent Law, both rights to apply for patents and patent rights themselves may be assigned to third parties.[64] In the event of an assignment, the assignor and assignee are required to conclude a contract in writing which is effective upon registration and announcement by the Patent Bureau.[65]

The Patent Law also provides for the licensing of patents. The law requires that before any party other than the patent holder may be permitted to 'use' a patent, that is, to manufacture patented products or utilize patented processes, it must conclude a written licensing agreement with the patent holder and pay 'patent-use fees'.[66] One exception to this rule pertains to patents held by Chinese state-owned enterprises. Under the law, Chinese government authorities have the right to designate other units to use certain patents in their production activities in accordance with the state economic plan.[67] In such cases, patent-use fees are required to be paid to the patent-holding unit 'in accordance with state stipulations'.[68]

The second, and for foreign patent holders, far more important exception to the voluntary licensing rule lies in the provisions contained in the Patent Law regarding compulsory licensing. The law requires patent holders to use their patents in China or to license others to do so.[69] In cases where holders of patents on inventions and utility models have failed 'without legitimate reason' to use their patents by the end of the three-year period commencing from the date of the granting of the patents, the Patent Bureau may grant compulsory licences to use the patents to units possessing the capability to do so.[70] Compulsory licensing may also occur where the use of a new patent which is technologically advanced is dependent on access to less sophisticated or older patented technology or inventions owned by another party. In such a case, the holder of the new patent may apply for the granting of a compulsory licence to use the older patent, and the holder of the older patent may request compulsory licensing of the new patent to it.[71] When applying to the Patent Bureau for a compulsory licence to use a patent, the applicant is required to provide evidence that it was unable to conclude a voluntary licensing contract 'on reasonable terms' with the patent holder.[72] If a compulsory licence is granted, the licensee does not enjoy an exclusive right to use the patent but shares the right with the original patent holder.[73] Moreover, the licensee is required to pay patent-use fees to the patent holder, the amount of which is to be agreed by the parties or, failing agreement, is to be determined by the Patent Bureau.[74] Decisions of the Patent Bureau regarding the granting of compulsory licences and patent-use fees may be appealed against in the people's courts.[75]

IV. The Protection of Patent Rights

The Patent Law grants patent holders exclusive rights to use their patents. Under the law, no unit or individual may, without the permission of the patent holder, manufacture, use or sell for production or business purposes patented products or processes.[76] Conduct in violation of these provisions may constitute infringement of the patent holder's rights.

The standard to be applied in determining whether an infringement has occurred is whether the alleged infringing conduct has invaded the scope of protection of the patent right. In the case of patents on inventions and utility models, the scope of protection is the scope specified in the 'request for rights' submitted by the patent holder at the time of application.[77] The scope of protection for patents on designs is the patented product of the 'outward appearance' design patent as shown in pictures or photographs.[78]

In the event of an alleged infringement of patent rights, the patent holder or other interested party may either submit the case to the designated patent control organs or bring a suit before the people's courts.[79] Such proceedings must be initiated within two years of the date on which the patent holder or interested party learns of, or should have learned of, the alleged infringing conduct.[80] Where the case is submitted to the patent control organs, they may order infringers to desist from any further infringing conduct and compensate the patent holder for losses incurred due to the infringement.[81] Such orders may be appealed against by the alleged infringer in the people's courts within three months of the date of the order.[82]

The Patent Law specifies five kinds of conduct which shall not be deemed to constitute infringement of patent rights.[83] The first pertains to cases where, after a patented product manufactured by or with the permission of the patent holder has been sold, the product is then used by or sold to a third party. The second relates to cases where a patented product is used or sold by a party who did not know that the product was manufactured or sold without the permission of the patent holder. The third exception applies to cases where products or processes of the same type as those which have been patented by another party had already been manufactured or used before the date of the patent application and where such manufacture or use is contained within the scope existing prior to the patent application. The fourth exclusion set out in the law pertains to the use of patents in facilities and equipment of foreign aeroplanes and vessels that pass temporarily through China, provided that similar treatment is granted to Chinese means of transport in accordance with international treaties or the principle of reciprocity. Finally, the fifth exclusion relates to patents used specially for scientific research and experiments.

The Patent Law provides for enforcement of decisions regarding infringement in accordance with the compulsory execution provisions contained in the Law on Civil Procedure.[84] In addition, criminal penalties may be applied in serious cases of infringement. For example, conduct involving the 'false passing off of others' patents' may be punishable in accordance with Article 127 of the Criminal Code which provides for penalties of up to three years' imprisonment, detention, or a fine.[85]

V. Comment

China's new Patent Law contains little that will come as a surprise to foreign businessmen. The main features of the law closely follow published reports on the draft legislation described by Patent Office officials.[86] Moreover, the law conforms in most respects with internationally accepted patent practices and was clearly drafted with the Paris Convention for the Protection of Industrial Property in mind.[87] Although China was not a signatory to the Convention at the time the Patent Law was passed, Chinese officials involved with patent matters have indicated that it is China's intention to join in the near future.

Although there are few substantial surprises in the law, the legislation gives rise to a number of questions which will require clarification. For example, while the law defines patentable subject matter to include 'inventions', 'utility models' and 'designs', it does not define further the three types of patentable items. Uncertainty also exists with respect to the provisions regarding infringement. Little is known, for instance, of the 'patent control organs' which are designated to handle infringement cases outside the courts and how these organs will make decisions regarding infringement, compensation and related matters. Of special concern are the law's provisions regarding foreigners. Under Article 19 of the law, foreign applicants who have 'no residence or place of business in China' are directed to apply for patents in accordance with bilateral treaties, international conventions or the principle of reciprocity. As 'regular residence' and 'place of business' are not defined, the meaning and proper interpretation of this provision is unclear. If such concepts were extended to representative offices of foreign companies in China, however, they could subject such companies to the law's provisions relating to Chinese organizations.[88] As noted previously, such provisions include those permitting the state to order the transfer of patent rights to other Chinese units in accordance with the requirements of the state economic plan.[89]

As was expected, the Chinese have chosen to exclude a number of items from patentability, including pharmaceutical and food products. In so doing, China has apparently decided to follow the lead of a growing number of developing countries which have denied patent protection to such products in order to encourage and protect local industrial capability in these areas. This view seems to be supported by the statement of Mr Huang Kunyi, Director of the Patent Bureau, who has written that the major justification for disallowing protection for the products themselves is that 'China's industrial and scientific level is comparatively backward' and that the restriction may be reconsidered 'in view of actual conditions' at a later date.[90]

Although food and pharmaceutical products and other items mentioned in the law may not themselves be granted patent protection, the law does provide for patentability of the production processes relating to such products. Although intended to alleviate the disappointment of foreign companies who had hoped to obtain full product patent protection under the new law, the extent to which the production process patent provisions will provide meaningful protection to patent holders is unclear. The law provides no obvious obstacle, for example, to the manufacture and sale by a Chinese unit of a pharmaceutical product similar to one marketed by a foreign producer whose production process is patented in China. So long as the Chinese producer's manufacturing process is apparently only slightly different from the patented process employed by the foreign manufacturer, it seems that no infringement will be deemed to have occurred.

The question of the patentability of computer programmes is not addressed directly in the law. However, Chinese sources indicate that software will be treated as 'rules and methods of intellectual activity' and as such will not be eligible for the granting of patent rights.[91] In adopting this approach, China has followed the lead of a number of countries, including the United Kingdom.

A point of special significance to foreign businessmen raised by the new law is how China's patent system will apply to existing inventions. Under the 'novelty' requirement imposed by the law, previous publication or use of an invention outside China will in most instances disqualify such inventions from patentability in China. Therefore, unless a foreign applicant is able to come within the scope of the 'priority right' provisions or otherwise avoid disqualification under the law, attempts to register patents in China that have already been applied for or registered elsewhere will be unsuccessful. As a result, the main significance of China's Patent Law will be found in the protection afforded to future inventions and creations, rather than existing ones.

VI. Conclusion

China's new Patent Law is a major contribution to the development of the nation's legal system. However, the law itself is only the first step in the establishment of a system of protection for industrial property rights. According to Chinese sources, work is now under way on detailed implementing rules which are expected to clarify many of the uncertainties in the law.[92] Moreover, other preparatory work — such as the organization of procedures for the review of patent applications, the training of patent examiners and the establishment of a patent publication and registration system — is now being undertaken.[93] Once China's new patent system is in place, it can be expected to provide significantly greater protection to foreign inventors and, as such, an additional incentive to investment and technology transfer in China.

Notes

1. The Patent Law of the People's Republic of China, passed on 12 March 1984 by the Fourth Meeting of the Standing Committee of the Sixth National People's Congress (hereafter cited as the Patent Law). All references to the Patent Law in this chapter are to an English translation on file with the author.
2. See O. Sin, 'Office to Handle China Patent Queries', *South China Morning Post Business News*, 28 February 1984, p. 1.
3. China provided limited protection to Chinese and foreign patents pursuant to the 1950 Provisional Regulations on the Protection of Inventions and Patent Rights, but this law was rescinded in 1963 and replaced by the Regulations on Rewards for Inventions, passed in the same year. The 1963 statute was repealed in 1978 and superseded by the Regulations of the People's Republic of China on Awards for Inventions, issued on 28 December 1978. Both the 1963 statute and the 1978 regulations rewarded inventors for their creations but vested ownership of all such inventions in the state.
4. Patent Law, Art. 2, note 1 above.
5. Patent Law, Art. 22, note 1 above.
6. Patent Law, Art. 22, note 1 above.
7. Patent Law, Art. 24, note 1 above.
8. Patent Law, Art. 22, note 1 above.
9. Patent Law, Art. 22, note 1 above.
10. Patent Law, Art. 23, note 1 above.
11. Patent Law, Art. 25, note 1 above.
12. Patent Law, Art. 25, note 1 above.
13. Patent Law, Art. 25, note 1 above.
14. Patent Law, Art. 5, note 1 above.
15. Patent Law, Art. 4, note 1 above.

16. Patent Law, Art. 4, note 1 above.

17. Patent Law, Art. 18, note 1 above.

18. Patent Law, Art. 19, note 1 above. The legal basis for patent applications in China by American companies and individuals is supplied by the Sino-American Trade Agreement, signed on 7 July 1979 and effective from 2 February 1980. Article VI of the Trade Agreement provides that each contracting party shall ensure to nationals of the other party 'protection of patents . . . equivalent to the patent . . . protection correspondingly granted by the other [party]'.

19. Conversation with officials of the China Council for the Promotion of International Trade (CCPIT). The CCPIT also acts as the agent for foreigners with respect to applications and other matters related to trade marks. See Chapter 9 in this volume.

20. See Sin, note 2 above.

21. Patent Law, Art. 26, note 1 above.

22. Patent Law, Art. 27, note 1 above.

23. Patent Law, Art. 31, note 1 above.

24. Patent Law, Art. 31, note 1 above.

25. Patent Law, Art. 31, note 1 above.

26. Patent Law, Art. 9, note 1 above.

27. Patent Law, Art. 28, note 1 above.

28. Patent Law, Art. 28, note 1 above.

29. Patent Law, Art. 29, note 1 above.

30. The priority right is available in accordance with the terms of bilateral agreements signed between China and the country of the applicant, investment treaties to which both China and the applicant's country are parties, or the principle of 'mutual recognition of priority rights'. Patent Law, Art. 29, note 1 above.

31. Patent Law, Art. 30, note 1 above.

32. Patent Law, Art. 30, note 1 above.

33. Patent Law, Art. 30, note 1 above.

34. Patent Law, Art. 40, note 1 above.

35. Patent Law, Art. 40, note 1 above.

36. Patent Law, Art. 34, note 1 above.

37. Patent Law, Art. 35, note 1 above.

38. Patent Law, Art. 35, note 1 above.

39. Patent Law, Art. 36, note 1 above.

40. Patent Law, Art. 36, note 1 above.

41. Patent Law, Art. 36, note 1 above.

42. Patent Law, Arts. 37 and 39, note 1 above.

43. Patent Law, Art. 37, note 1 above.

44. Patent Law, Art. 38, note 1 above.

45. Patent Law, Art. 41, note 1 above.

46. Patent Law, Art. 41, note 1 above.

47. Patent Law, Art. 41, note 1 above.

48. Patent Law, Art. 42, note 1 above.

49. Patent Law, Art. 43, note 1 above.

50. Patent Law, Art. 43, note 1 above.

51. Patent Law, Art. 43, note 1 above.

52. Patent Law, Art. 43, note 1 above.

53. Patent Law, Art. 44, note 1 above.

54. Patent Law, Arts. 11 and 15, note 1 above.
55. Patent Law, Art. 46, note 1 above.
56. Patent Law, Art. 45, note 1 above.
57. Patent Law, Art. 45, note 1 above.
58. Patent Law, Art. 47, note 1 above.
59. Patent Law, Arts. 48 and 49, note 1 above.
60. Patent Law, Arts. 48 and 49, note 1 above.
61. Patent Law, Art. 49, note 1 above.
62. Patent Law, Art. 49, note 1 above.
63. Patent Law, Art. 49, note 1 above.
64. Patent Law, Art. 10, note 1 above.
65. Patent Law, Art. 10, note 1 above.
66. Patent Law, Art. 12, note 1 above.
67. Patent Law, Art. 14, note 1 above.
68. Patent Law, Art. 14, note 1 above.
69. Patent Law, Art. 51, note 1 above.
70. Patent Law, Art. 52, note 1 above.
71. Patent Law, Art. 53, note 1 above.
72. Patent Law, Art. 54, note 1 above.
73. Patent Law, Art. 56, note 1 above.
74. Patent Law, Art. 57, note 1 above.
75. Patent Law, Art. 58, note 1 above.
76. Patent Law, Art. 11, note 1 above.
77. Patent Law, Art. 59, note 1 above.
78. Patent Law, Art. 59, note 1 above.
79. Patent Law, Art. 60, note 1 above.
80. Patent Law, Art. 61, note 1 above.
81. Patent Law, Art. 60, note 1 above.
82. Patent Law, Art. 60, note 1 above.
83. Patent Law, Art. 62, note 1 above.
84. See the Law on Civil Procedure of the People's Republic of China, promulgated for trial implementation on 8 March 1982, Arts. 171–84.
85. The Criminal Law of the People's Republic of China, promulgated on 1 July 1979.
86. See E. Theroux and T. Peele, 'China's Coming Patent Law', *East Asian Executive Reports*, April 1983, pp. 7–10; and C. Berney, 'China's Draft Patent Law', *China Business Review*, May–June 1981, p. 39.
87. See T. Gelatt and R. Sweetman, 'China's New Patent Law Needs Clarification', *Asian Wall Street Journal*, 2 April 1984.
88. See Gelatt and Sweetman, note 87 above.
89. See notes 67 and 68 above and accompanying text.
90. See K.Y. Huang, 'China's Patent System Is Actively Being Established', *Guoji Maoyi (International Trade)*, February 1984, p. 4.
91. See Gelatt and Sweetman, note 87 above.
92. The implementing rules are to be formulated by the Patent Bureau and approved by the State Council. See Patent Law, Art. 68, note 1 above.
93. See G.F. Chen, 'Economic Growth Necessitates First Patent Law', *China Daily*, 28 March 1984, p. 2.

Appendix: Table of Legislation

The salient laws and regulations of the People's Republic of China governing foreign trade, investment and other economic affairs which have been discussed in this book are listed below.

The Law on Civil Procedure of the People's Republic of China, 中华人民共和国民事诉讼法(试行), promulgated for trial implementation on 8 March 1982.

Economic Contracts Law of the People's Republic of China, 中华人民共和国经济合同法, promulgated on 13 December 1981 and effective from 1 July 1982.

Provisional Regulations of the People's Republic of China on Notarization, 中华人民共和国公证暂行条例, promulgated on 13 April 1982.

Provisional Customs Law of the People's Republic of China, 中华人民共和国暂行海关法, promulgated on 18 April 1951.

Procedures of the People's Republic of China Concerning the Levy of Import Duty on Articles in Passengers' Baggage and Personal Postal Articles, 中华人民共和国关于入境旅客行李物品和个人邮递物品征收进口税办法, approved on 16 June 1978 and effective from 1 August 1978.

Provisional Implementing Regulations of the Customs of the People's Republic of China Concerning Import and Export Duties, 中华人民共和国海关进出口税则暂行实施条例, approved on 4 May 1951.

Provisional Rules of the Customs of the People's Republic of China for the Supervision and Control of Articles in Baggage of Incoming and Outgoing Overseas Chinese and Other Passengers, 海关对进出国境华侨等旅客的行李物品监管暂行规定, promulgated on 5 April 1978.

Provisional Procedures of the Customs of the People's Republic of China for Levying Tonnage Dues on Vessels, 中华人民共和国海关船舶吨税暂行办法, issued on 19 September 1952.

Provisions of the Ministry of Finance Concerning the Levy of and Exemption from Industrial and Commercial Tax for Import and Export Commodities, 财政部关于进出口货物征免工商统一税的规定, approved on 30 December 1980 and effective from 1 January 1981.

Rules for the Levy and Exemption of Customs Duties and the Consolidated Industrial and Commercial Tax on Imports and Exports in Connection with the Chinese-Foreign Co-operative Exploration of Offshore Petroleum, 关于中外合作开采海洋石油进出口货物征免关税和工商统一税的规定, promulgated on 1 April 1982.

Regulations Regarding the Supervision and Control of and Levy and Exemption of Tax on Goods Imported and Exported by Chinese-Foreign Co-operative Ventures, 关于中外合作经营企业进出口货物的监管和征免

税规定, promulgated on 31 January 1984 and effective from 1 February 1984.

Procedures of the Customs of the People's Republic of China for the Supervision and Control of International Civil Aircraft, 中华人民共和国海关对国际民航机监管的办法, issued on 1 October 1974.

Provisional Procedures of the Customs of the People's Republic of China for the Supervision and Control of Bonded Cargo and Bonded Warehouses, 海关对保税货物和保税仓库监管暂行办法, issued on 10 February 1981 and effective from 1 March 1981.

Procedures of the Customs of the People's Republic of China for the Supervision and Control of Goods Imported for Exhibition, 中华人民共和国海关对进口展览品监管办法, promulgated on 3 November 1975.

The Law of the People's Republic of China on Joint Ventures Using Chinese and Foreign Investment, 中华人民共和国合资经营企业法, promulgated on 8 July 1979.

The Implementing Act for the Law of the People's Republic of China on Joint Ventures Using Chinese and Foreign Investment, 中华人民共和国中外合资经营企业法实施条例, promulgated on 20 September 1983.

Regulations on Labour Management in Joint Ventures Using Chinese and Foreign Investment, 中外合资经营企业劳动管理规定, promulgated on 26 July 1980.

Provisional Measures for Providing Loans to Joint Ventures Using Chinese and Foreign Investment by the Bank of China, 中国银行办理中外合资经营企业贷款暂行办法, promulgated on 13 March 1981.

Measures for the Registration of Joint Ventures Using Chinese and Foreign Investment, 中外合资经营企业登记管理办法, promulgated on 26 July 1980.

Provisional Regulations on Standards for the Payment of Registration Fees by Joint Ventures Using Chinese and Foreign Investment, 中外合资经营企业登记费标准暂行规定, issued in March 1982.

The Income Tax Law of the People's Republic of China Concerning Joint Ventures Using Chinese and Foreign Investment, 中华人民共和国中外合资经营企业所得税法, promulgated on 10 September 1980.

Detailed Rules and Regulations for the Implementation of the Income Tax Law of the People's Republic of China Concerning Joint Ventures Using Chinese and Foreign Investment, 中华人民共和国中外合资经营企业所得税法实行细则, promulgated on 14 December 1980 and effective from 10 September 1980.

Consolidated Industrial and Commercial Tax Regulations of the People's Republic of China (Draft), 中华人民共和国工商统一税条例(草案), promulgated on 13 September 1958.

Detailed Rules and Regulations for the Implementation of the Consolidated Industrial and Commercial Tax Regulations of the People's Republic of China, 中华人民共和国工商统一税条例实行细则(草案), promulgated on 13 September 1958.

The Income Tax Law of the People's Republic of China Concerning Foreign Enterprises, 中华人民共和国外国企业所得税法, promulgated on 13 December 1981 and effective from 1 January 1982.

Detailed Rules and Regulations for the Implementation of the Income Tax Law of the People's Republic of China Concerning Foreign Enterprises, 中华人民共和国外国企业所得税法实行细则, promulgated on 21 February 1982 and effective from 1 January 1982.

Provisional Regulations of the Ministry of Finance of the People's Republic of China Regarding the Reduction and Exemption of Income Tax Relating to Interest Earned by Foreign Business from China, 中华人民共和国财政部关于外商从我国所得的利息有关减免所得税的暂行规定, issued on 7 January 1983 and effective from 1 January 1983.

Provisional Regulations of the Ministry of Finance of the People's Republic of China Regarding the Reduction and Exemption of Income Tax on Fees for the Use of Proprietary Technology, 中华人民共和国财政部关于对专有技术使用费减征、免征所得税的暂行规定, issued on 13 December 1982 and effective from 1 January 1983.

Provisional Regulations of the General Taxation Bureau of the Ministry of Finance of the People's Republic of China Concerning Tax Registration by Foreign Enterprises for the Commencement and Termination of Operations, 中华人民共和国财政部税务总局关于外国企业开业、停业税务登记暂行规定, promulgated on 5 April 1982.

The Individual Income Tax Law of the People's Republic of China, 中华人民共和国个人所得税法, promulgated on 10 September 1980.

Detailed Rules and Regulations for the Implementation of the Individual Income Tax Law of the People's Republic of China, 中华人民共和国个人所得税法实行条例, promulgated on 14 December 1980 and effective from 10 September 1980.

Provisional Urban Real Estate Tax Act, 城市房地产税暂行条例, promulgated on 8 August 1981.

Provisional Regulations of the People's Republic of China Governing Foreign Exchange Control, 中华人民共和国外汇管理暂行条例, promulgated on 18 December 1980 and effective from 1 March 1981.

Detailed Rules for Foreign Exchange Control for Enterprises with Overseas Chinese Capital, Enterprises with Foreign Capital and Chinese-Foreign Joint Venture Enterprises, 对侨资企业、外资企业、中外合资经营企业外汇管理施行细则, adopted on 19 July 1983 and effective from 1 August 1983.

Regulations on Special Economic Zones in Guangdong Province, 广东省经济特区条例, adopted on 26 August 1980.

Provisional Regulations of the Special Economic Zones of Guangdong Province Governing the Registration of Business Enterprises, 广东省经济特区企业登记管理暂行规定, adopted on 17 November 1981 and effective from 1 January 1982.

Provisional Regulations of the Special Economic Zones of Guangdong Province

Governing Labour and Wages for Business Enterprises, 广东省经济特区企业劳动工资管理暂行规定, promulgated on 17 November 1981 and effective from 1 January 1982.

Provisional Regulations of the Special Economic Zones of Guangdong Province Governing the Entry and Exit of Personnel, 广东省经济特区入境出境人员管理暂行规定, promulgated on 17 November 1981 and effective from 1 January 1982.

Provisional Regulations Governing Land in the Shenzhen Special Economic Zone, 深圳经济特区土地管理暂行规定, promulgated on 17 November 1981 and effective from 1 January 1982.

Provisional Measures of Shenzhen Municipality Governing Urban Construction, 深圳市城市建设管理暂行办法, issued on 1 July 1982.

Regulations of the Shenzhen Special Economic Zone on the Control of Commercial Real Estate, 深圳经济特区商品房产管理规定, promulgated on 15 November 1983.

Provisional Regulations of the Shenzhen Special Economic Zone on the Introduction of Technology, 深圳经济特区技术引进暂行规定, promulgated on 8 February 1984.

Regulations of the Shenzhen Special Economic Zone on Foreign Economic Contracts, 深圳经济特区涉外经济合同规定, promulgated on 7 February 1984.

Provisional Regulations of the State Council of the People's Republic of China Concerning the Control of Resident Representative Offices of Foreign Enterprises, 中华人民共和国国务院关于管理外国企业常驻代表机构的暂行规定, promulgated on 30 October 1980.

Measures of the State Administration for Industry and Commerce of the People's Republic of China Regarding the Control of Registration of Long-Term Representative Offices of Foreign Enterprises, 中华人民共和国国家工商行政管理局关于外国企业常驻代表机构的登记管理办法, issued on 15 March 1983.

Provisional Measures of the People's Government of Guangdong Province for the Registration and Control of Resident Representative Offices of Foreign Enterprises and Overseas Chinese, Hong Kong and Macau Enterprises in Guangdong Province, 广东省人民政府关于外国企业及华侨、港澳企业在广东省设立常驻代表机构登记管理暂行办法, promulgated on 11 May 1981.

Provisional Regulations of the Bank of China for the Establishment of Representative Offices in China by Overseas Chinese and Foreign Financial Institutions, 中国人民银行关于侨资外资金融机构在中国设立常驻代表机构的管理办法, issued on 1 February 1983.

Notice of the State Administration for Industry and Commerce of the People's Republic of China Concerning the Registration of Foreign Companies that Come to China to Engage in Co-operative Development and Contract Projects, 国家工商行政管理局关于来我国合作开发和承包工程的外

国公司注册登记问题的通知, issued on 12 March 1983 and effective from 1 April 1983.

Explanations Regarding the Notice of the State Administration for Industry and Commerce of the People's Republic of China Concerning the Registration of Foreign Companies that Come to China to Engage in Co-operative Development and Contract Projects, 关于来我国合作开发和承包工程的外国公司注册登记问题的通知的说明, issued on 4 May 1983.

Regulations of the People's Republic of China on the Exploitation of Offshore Petroleum Resources in Co-operation with Foreign Enterprises, 中华人民共和国对外合作开采海洋石油资源条例, promulgated on 30 January 1982.

The Environmental Protection Law of the People's Republic of China, 中华人民共和国环境保护法, promulgated on 13 September 1979.

The Marine Environmental Protection Law of the People's Republic of China, 中华人民共和国海洋环境保护法 , adopted on 23 August 1982 and effective from 1 March 1983.

Control Act of the People's Republic of China on Environmental Protection in the Exploration for and Development of Offshore Petroleum, 中华人民共和国海洋石油勘探开发环境保护管理条例, promulgated on 29 December 1983.

Food Hygiene Law of the People's Republic of China (For Trial Implementation), 中华人民共和国食品卫生法(试行), approved on 19 November 1982 and effective from 1 July 1983.

Regulations of the People's Republic of China on the Quarantine of Animal and Plant Imports and Exports, 中华人民共和国进出口动植物检疫条例, promulgated on 4 June 1982.

Interim Procedures of the State Import-Export Commission and the Ministry of Foreign Trade of the People's Republic of China Concerning the System of Export Licensing, 进出口管理委员会、对外贸易部关于出口许可制度的暂行办法, promulgated on 3 June 1980.

Provisional Act of the People's Republic of China on the System of Import Licensing for Imported Goods, 中华人民共和国进口货物许可制度暂行条例, promulgated on 10 January 1984.

The Trade-mark Law of the People's Republic of China, 中华人民共和国商标法, promulgated on 23 August 1982 and effective from 1 March 1983.

Detailed Implementing Rules for the Trade-mark Law of the People's Republic of China, 中华人民共和国商标法实施细则, promulgated on 10 March 1983.

The Patent Law of the People's Republic of China, 中华人民共和国专利法, adopted on 12 March 1984 and effective from 1 April 1985.

Contributors

JESSE T.H. CHANG is a graduate in law of the Australian National University. He is a solicitor with an international law firm, dividing his time between Hong Kong and Beijing.

FRANKLIN D. CHU was born in China and studied law at Yale University. He has practised law in Hong Kong and the United States and now advises clients doing business in China as a member of a New York City law firm.

JEROME ALAN COHEN, formerly Professor of Law and Director of East Asian Legal Studies at the Harvard Law School, is the author and editor of many books and articles on China and Chinese legal topics. He is currently a member of a New York law firm, resident in Hong Kong.

CHARLES J. CONROY, a graduate of Yale University and the Columbia University School of Law, specializes in advising foreign clients doing business in China. He is a partner in an international law firm and divides his time between Hong Kong and Beijing.

TIMOTHY A. GELATT has written a number of articles relating to Chinese taxation and other legal topics. He is a graduate of the Harvard Law School and currently practises law in New York City.

JAMIE P. HORSLEY is a graduate of the Harvard Law School and has spent over two years in Beijing advising foreign companies doing business in China. She is now practising law with a major firm in New York City.

STANLEY B. LUBMAN, a graduate of the Columbia University School of Law, is a frequent writer on Chinese legal topics. He has taught Chinese law at Columbia, Yale, the University of California (Berkeley), and Harvard, and now practises law with a San Francisco firm.

MICHAEL J. MOSER, who holds a Ph. D. degree from Columbia University and a JD degree from the Harvard Law School, is the author of numerous books and articles on Chinese law. A practising attorney with an international law firm, he resides in Beijing.

RICHARD D. POMP received his undergraduate training at the University of Michigan and studied law at Harvard University. He currently teaches law at the University of Connecticut.

CLARK T. RANDT, JR., a graduate of Yale University, is Commercial Attaché and First Secretary to the United States Embassy in Beijing. Before assuming his current post, Mr Randt practised law in New York and Hong Kong.

PRESTON M. TORBERT holds a doctorate in Chinese history from the University of Chicago and a JD degree from the Harvard Law School. Now a practising attorney with an international law firm, he is a frequent visitor to China.

Index

Administrative Committee for the Special Economic Zones of Guangdong Province (ADCOM), 148–9, 150, 152–3
Agricultural Bank of China, 231–2
Allocable profit oil, 189
American Arbitration Association (AAA), 303
Arbitration, 97–8, 120, 166, 186, 192, 218–20, 296–318
Asian Development Bank, 243
Assembly projects, 25–6, 56–7, 109

Bank of China, activities in Hong Kong, 238–9; joint ventures, 122–3, 129; legal status, 233–4; lending activities, 235–7; organization, 233; Special Economic Zones, 156; trade financing, 247–53; trust and consultancy services, 237–8
Banking, Chinese banks, 230–43; foreign banks, 243–7, 292–3
Beijing Economic Development Corporation, 242

China Council for the Promotion of International Trade (CCPIT), 12–13, 97, 271–2, 298, 303, 306, 311, 320
China International Trust and Investment Corporation (CITIC), 240–1
China Merchants' Steam Navigation Company Ltd. (CMSN), 165
China Nanhai Oil Joint Services Corporation (CNOJSC), 183
China National Offshore Oil Corporation (CNOOC), formation, 180; functions, 182–5; legal status, 182; local subsidiaries, 182
China National Oil and Gas Exploration and Development Corporation (CNOGEDC), 179
China National Technical Import Corporation (Techimport), 87, 89–91, 93–5, 215, 223
C.I.F., 248, 250
Civil Procedure Law, 219, 299–301, 303–4, 310–11
Commodity inspection, 18–20
Compensation trade, defined, 109–10; statistics, 109; taxation of, 25–6, 53–5
Consolidated industrial and commercial tax, application, 52–8; exemptions, 25–6; joint ventures, 114, 132–3; legislation, 41–2; offshore oil exploration, 201–2; Special Economic Zones, 151–2
Construction projects, 56–7, 145–6, 160–3
Contracts, approval of, 106–8; authority of contracting party, 216–18; enforcement, 218–20; governing law and interpretation, 222–5; joint ventures, 119–20; offshore oil exploration, 186–94; standard forms, 214–16; subsequent legislation, 220–2
Contractual joint ventures, capital contributions, 112–13; defined, 111; foreign exchange controls, 114; forms of, 111–12; management and operation, 113–14; profit distributions, 113; registration of, 114–15; taxation of, 55–6, 114
Co-operative investment arrangements, 110–15
Co-operative ventures, *see* Contractual joint ventures
Cost recovery oil, 188
Customs, duty, 23–5; exemptions, 25–6; formalities, 21–3; General Administration of Customs, 20; joint ventures, 114, 132–3; legislation, 21; offshore oil exploration, 26, 205–6; resident representative offices, 288–9; Special Economic Zones, 151–2, 155
Customs Law, 21

Decentralization policy, 6–9, 87–8

Deemed profits tax, 201
Dispute settlement, 96, 97–8, 120, 166, 185–6, 218–20, 275, 296–316, 323
Dividends, 48, 134

ECONOMIC CONTRACTS LAW, 113
Environmental law, 206, 215
Equity joint ventures, accounting rules, 133–4; approval procedures 123–4; capitalization, 120–2; defined, 117; documentation, 119–20; domestic market sales, 130–1; foreign exchange controls, 131–2; labour 126–8; land use, 128–9; legal status, 117; loans to, 122–3; management, 124–6; marketing 130–1; registration, 124; statistics on, 115–16; taxation, 42–5, 57–8, 132–3; technology transfer to, 131; term and termination of, 134–5
Exhibitions, 21
Export credits, 251–3
Export licensing, 14–16

F.O.B., 250
Force majeure, 221
Foreign Economic and Trade Arbitration Commission (FETAC), 13, 97, 219, 304, 306–7, 309–10
Foreign enterprise income tax, applications, 50–7, 98–100, 195–201; legislation, 45–50
Foreign Enterprises Services Corporation (FESCO), 289
Foreign exchange, 229
Foreign exchange controls, contractual joint ventures, 114; equity joint ventures, 131–2; legislation 253–60; lending transactions, 256; offshore oil exploration, 193; Special Economic Zones, 168, 259–60; trading, 255–6
Foreign investment, approval procedures, 106–8; statistics, 106, 109, 110, 115
Foreign Trade Arbitration Commission (FTAC), 298, 304
Foreign trade bureaux, 11
Foreign trade corporations (FTCs), 10–11, 13–18
Fujian Province, 9, 169n

GENERAL ADMINISTRATION OF CUSTOMS, 20
General Agreement on Tariffs and Trade (GATT), 6
Gold reserves, 229
Governing law, *see* Contracts
Guangdong Province, 9, 145
Guangzhou Export Commodities Fair, 13

HONG KONG, 145–7, 155, 183, 307

IMPORT LICENSING, 16–18
Individual income tax, legislation, 37; rates, 41; source rules, 39–40; Special Economic Zones, 163; taxpayers, 37–9
Installation projects, 56–7
Insurance, 129, 150, 231, 248–9
International Center for the Settlement of Investment Disputes (ICSID), 306–7
International Chamber of Commerce (ICC), 309
International Fund for Agricultural Development, 242
International Monetary Fund (IMF), 242
Investment Bank of China, 240
Investment recovery oil, 189

JOINT DEVELOPMENT, 110–11
Joint management committee, 189–91
Joint ventures, *see* Contractual joint ventures and Equity joint ventures
Joint venture income tax, foreign dividends, 44, 132–3; legislation, 43, 132; rates, 44–5, 132; Special Economic Zones, 152–3, 163; tax holidays, 44–5, 57–8; taxable income, 43–4

LABOUR UNIONS, 127–8
Leasing, 49, 199, 241
Legislation, types of, 2
Letter of credit, 247–53
Licensing, acceptance tests, 92–3; confidentiality provisions, 94–7; coverage, 89–90; duration, 91–2; equity joint ventures, 131; guarantees, 93–4; policies, 84–7; price and payment conditions, 90–1; royalties, 90; Special Economic Zones, 164–5; taxation, 49–50, 98–100
Loans, Bank of China, 232–5; equity

joint ventures, 122–3; foreign banks, 245–7; foreign exchange loans, 236–7; renminbi loans, 236–7; syndicated loans, 235
London Court of Arbitration, 308

MARINE ENVIRONMENTAL PROTECTION LAW (MEPL), 206
Maritime Arbitration Commission, 298
Ministry of Finance, 44, 53, 98, 99, 198, 244
Ministry of Foreign Economic Relations and Trade (MOFERT), 9–10, 12–21, 107–8, 118, 123–4, 302, 305–6
Ministry of Petroleum Industry, 182–3, 186–7
Model contract, 184–94

NATIONAL COUNCIL FOR US–CHINA TRADE, 218
Norway, 183, 186
Notary Law, 218

OFFSHORE OIL, environmental protection and, 206; legal aspects, 179–207; reserves, 179; tax aspects, 194–203
Offshore Oil Tax Bureau (OOTB), 202–3
On-lending 241

PATENT BUREAU, 320
Patents, legislation, 319–20; licensing of, 324–5; protection of, 325–6; registration, 321–4
Payment trade, 13
People's Bank of China, 230–1
People's Construction Bank of China, 232
People's Insurance Company of China, 231
Profit oil, 189
Proprietary technology, 49–50, 98–100, 200
Public Security Bureau, 286

REAL ESTATE, 58, 146, 160–3
Registered capital, 120–2
Registration, contractual joint ventures, 114–15; equity joint ventures, 124; offshore oil contractors, 203–5; representative offices, 281–93; Special Economic Zones, 155–6
'Renegotiation clauses', 118
Representative offices, customs rules relating to, 288–9; foreign banks, 243–5, 292–3; legislation, 281–2; local rules, 290–1; registration procedures, 283–6; registration requirements, 282–3; restrictions on, 288; taxation, 51–2
Royalties, 49–50, 90, 200–1

SERVICE CENTRES, 52–3
Shanghai, 9, 220, 247
Shanghai Trust and Investment Corporation (SITCO), 242
Shantou, 146
Share oil, 189
Shekou Industrial Zone, 145, 165–8
Shenzhen, 145–7, 160–3, 164–5
Special Economic Zones (SEZs), administration, 148–9; approval of investment projects, 148–9; background, 143–7; business registration, 148, 155–6; customs rules, 151–2, 155; entry and exit rules, 154–5; foreign exchange, 150–1, 259–60; forms of investment, 149–50; investment patterns, 146–7; labour management, 153, 157–9; land use 153, 160–3; legislation, 147, 154–65; marketing, 151; taxation, 152–3, 163; urban construction, 161–3
State Administration for Industry and Commerce of the People's Republic of China (SAIC), 114–15, 124, 203–5
State Administration of Import and Export Commodity Inspection (SACI), 18–20
State General Administration for Exchange Control (SGAEC), 193, 253–9
Stockholm Chamber of Commerce, 219, 306
Subcontractors, 184, 194, 201, 204–5

TIANJIN INTERNATIONAL TRUST AND INVESTMENT CORPORATION, 242
Technology transfer, *see* Licensing
Tonnage dues, 24–5
Trade commissioners, 8–9
Trade financing, 247–53

Trade marks, infringement of, 276–7; legislation, 267–9; licensing of, 274–5; registration, 269–76; sanctions, 275–6
Trade statistics, 229

UNIFORM CUSTOMS AND PRACTICE FOR DOCUMENTARY CREDITS, 247
United Nations Commission on International Trade Law (UNCITRAL), 219, 301
United Nations Convention on the Recognition and Enforcement of Foreign Arbitral Awards, 310
United Nations Development Programme, 242

VICKERS-ZIMMER CASE, 297, 299

WHOLLY-OWNED FOREIGN INVESTMENTS, 135–6, 150
World Bank, 242–3
World Intellectual Property Organization (WIPO), 100

XIAMEN, 168–9n
'X factor', 189

ZHUHAI, 146